THE COMMON POT

Indigenous Americas

Robert Warrior and Jace Weaver, Series Editors

THE
COMMON POT

The Recovery of Native Space in the Northeast

Lisa Brooks

Indigenous Americas Series

University of Minnesota Press

Minneapolis • London

The University of Minnesota Press gratefully acknowledges the generosity of the Tenure-Track Publication Fund of the Faculty of Arts and Sciences, Harvard University, which contributed to this book.

Royalties from the sale of this book will be donated by the author to Chief Leonard Lampman Scholarship Fund, Swanton, Vermont.

A previous version of chapter 3 appeared as "Two Paths to Peace: Competing Visions of the Common Pot in the Ohio Valley," in *The Boundaries between Us: Natives, Newcomers, and the Struggle for the Old Northwest, 1740–1840*, ed. Daniel P. Barr (Kent, Ohio: Kent State University Press, 2005). Reprinted with permission of the Kent State University Press.

Excerpt from "Beth Brant, 1982: Letter & Post Card" by Maurice Kenny originally appeared in *Tekonwatonti/Molly Brant*. Copyright 1992, 1993, 2002 by Maurice Kenny. Reprinted with permission of White Pine Press, www.whitepine.org.

Excerpt from "The Paperbark Tree," by Joseph Bruchac originally appeared in *No Borders* (Duluth, Minn.: Holy Cow! Press, 1999), 57–58. Reprinted with permission of Holy Cow! Press.

The University of Minnesota Press is grateful for permission to reprint excerpts from the following material. Quotations from the Samson Occom Journal, Eleazar Wheelock Papers, Special Collections, are reprinted courtesy of the Dartmouth College Library. Quotations from "William Johnson to Correspondents of the Society for Promoting Christian Knowledge, Dec. 9, 1761," French and Indian War Collection, and from "Observations on the Western Territory and the Indian War," Thomas Wallcut Papers, are reprinted courtesy of the American Antiquarian Society. Quotations from "Indian Petition to the General Assembly, 1747 Apr. 1"; "Petition of Mahomet to the King, 1736, in Land Disputes between the Colony of Connecticut and the Mohegan Indians, 1736–1739"; "Address of Ben Uncas, 1739, in Land Disputes between the Colony of Connecticut and the Mohegan Indians, 1736–1739"; "Owaneco, Complaint and Prayer of Owaneco and Ben Uncas, 1700"; "Zachary Johnson, Letter to Richard Law, 1781 May 30"; and "John Norton, Letterbook, John Norton Papers, 1804–1816," all from the Edward E. Ayer Manuscript Collection, are reprinted courtesy of the Newberry Library, Chicago. Quotations from the Samson Occom Papers and from the William Samuel Johnson Papers are reprinted courtesy of the Connecticut Historical Society Museum. Quotations from the Indian Papers, Connecticut State Library, are reprinted courtesy of the Connecticut State Library.

Published by the University of Minnesota Press
111 Third Avenue South, Suite 290
Minneapolis, MN 55401-2520
http://www.upress.umn.edu

Printed in the United States of America on acid-free paper

Library of Congress Cataloging-in-Publication Data

Brooks, Lisa Tanya.
 The common pot : the recovery of native space in the Northeast / Lisa Brooks.
    p.   cm. — (Indigenous Americas series ; 7)
 Includes bibliographical references and index.
 ISBN 978-0-8166-4783-5 (alk. paper)   ISBN 978-0-8166-4784-2 (pbk.: alk. paper)
    1. Indians of North America — Psychology.   2. Indian philosophy.   3. Sacred space — North America.   4. Geographical perception — North America.   I. Title.
 E98. P95B66 2008
 970.004'97 — dc22
                                                                           2008009635

The University of Minnesota is an equal-opportunity educator and employer.

15 14 13 12 11 10 09 08   10 9 8 7 6 5 4 3 2 1

This work is dedicated to
Alyssa Brooks, Jolie Mellor, and Kathryn Bednarsky,
who hold the future of this land we all share
in their small but capable hands

Tar Baby talks Rabbit into a boiling pot by telling him
a story. Now, you might ask, given our story inside a
story, or stories inside stories, who is the inventor, and
who is the invented? You might even wonder which parts
I made up and which actually happened. I didn't know
the answer. I only knew at that point that I wanted out of
the kettle, especially if someone else was going to be
throwing logs on the fire. The way out wasn't by leaning
over the side and spitting on the flames. I'd have to
climb out, up over the words, and into a new story.
I was still here, Jimmy was still in Weleetka, and
Creek land was still waiting for us to take it back.

—CRAIG WOMACK, *Drowning in Fire*

Contents

Acknowledgments

Like most of the writings in this book, this project emerged from ongoing conversations and a network of collaborative thinking. Without the support of the many people who have entered my life, this book simply would not exist. I know I will not remember to thank everyone, so to anyone I have left out, my apologies. Any misunderstandings, misinterpretations, mistranslations, or other mishaps in the text are entirely my own.

To Boston College, Cornell University, Harvard University, and the Ford Foundation, I offer my great thankfulness for financial support. Without these sources, the level of dedication and direction I was able to give to this work would not have been possible.

Beginning with Boston College, to Alan Crowley, Alan Richardson, Amy Boesky, and Kathy Beres, for support and encouragement in the early stages of this project, thank you. At Cornell, to all the grad students of the Cornell Council of American Indian Graduate and Professional Students, for ongoing conversations, debates, and subversive humor, and especially to Kevin Connelly, Michael McDaniel, Alyssa Mt. Pleasant, Vera Palmer, and Alice TePunga Somerville: interacting and wrestling with your extraordinary minds was my privilege. To Brian Baker, who might have been a great intellectual inspiration if he had not always been trying to make me laugh. To David Moore and my companions in his "Native and Nation" class, for the most enriching course I have ever taken. To both David and Kate Shanley, for an extraordinary first year, for your caring and thoughtful ways, and for making me believe in the power of my own thought. To Dan Usner, for being a continual source of intellectual and personal support, for giving me the best research advice I ever received, and for vital lessons in diplomacy. To Mary Beth Norton, for teaching me a great deal about writing and researching history and for indispensable support of work on women's leadership. To Bob Venables, for a great course in Iroquois history. To Joel Porte, for valuable lessons in teaching, fruitful conversations about New England, and continual support. To Shelley Wong, for taking me on and keeping me, for asking good strong questions, and for providing continual support. To Darlene Flint, for treating me like family. To Jenka Fyfe, for making my work away from Ithaca so much easier than it could have been. To Sandy Cook, for always being there to help not only me but every Native student who crossed her path. To Jane Mt. Pleasant, for being a solid support and foundation for the American Indian Program during much of my time at Cornell. To Zahid Chaudhury, for challenging my mind, sharing space, and being a constant source of sustenance. To Kellie Dawson, for unconditional friendship and moral support. Thank you all.

At Harvard I was privileged to have the mentorship and support of many colleagues while I was revising this manuscript, including Amy Besaw, Stephen Biel, James Engell, Jill Lepore, Carmen Lopez, Malinda Maynor Lowery, Jackie Old Coyote, Kay Kaufman Shelemay, Werner Sollors, and John Stauffer. Thank you. I am also grateful for support from the Clark Fund for enabling the production of the maps. For this I am especially grateful to Jenny Davis, who worked tirelessly as my research assistant and co-creator. Also, to Elizabeth Goodwin, for research support in the final stage of this project, and to my Narrations of Nationhood classes, for critical dialogue with many of the texts and ideas that appear in this book, thank you.

To the Newberry Library, for the funding and research support that launched this project, I am grateful. I am especially thankful for the opportunity to converse with Lavonne Ruoff and Bernd Peyer, whose scholarship on early Native writing inspired my own and whose knowledge and advice helped me to shape my conceptualization of this book. I can only hope that it will be a contribution as valuable as those you have made to the field. Thank you.

To the American Antiquarian Society, for an enriching fellowship experience and especially for the opportunity to delve into the John Milton Earle Papers, which provide an invaluable view of Native New England in the nineteenth century, thank you. Special thanks to Joanne Chaison for guiding me through the "gov docs" that led to my third chapter, to Dennis Laurie for quickly locating congressional sources that would have taken me weeks to find, and to Caroline Sloat for making a research institution feel like an ongoing intellectual gathering and a welcoming home. Also, to Holly Izard for encouragement and research suggestions, to Ollie for conversations on the two brothers and the woods, and to my housemates for providing inspirational conversation and companionship, thank you.

To the John Carter Brown Library, for fellowship support and for providing the research materials that unexpectedly transformed the shape of this dissertation, I am grateful. To Richard Ring, for immediately making me feel welcome and for leading me directly to the treaty literature. To Norman Fiering, for creating an atmosphere of intellectual elegance. And finally, to my colleagues, who provided good company and tremendous emotional support when my life took an unexpected turn. Thank you all.

To Colin Calloway, for deeply valued encouragement and a careful reading of this manuscript, as well as for the work that stimulated and guided so much of the history that lies herein, thank you. To Barry O'Connell, for graciously meeting with and encouraging me when I was in the midst of Apess's writings and for scholarship that inspired me early on. To Melissa Tantaquidgeon Zobel and Faith Davison, for valuable feedback on the manuscript, and to Melissa and Randy for hosting our trip to Mohegan. To the many other readers from Native New England who took the time to read this manuscript, including Ramona Peters, who shared with me the significant influence of Apess's writings and the Mashpee petitions on her own life and that of her community. Thank you all.

I am tremendously grateful to Robert Warrior and Jace Weaver for bringing this manuscript to the University of Minnesota Press and to Robert for providing support for this project since its inception and vital critiques and advice throughout its production. To Michael Eliot, for valuable advice on revision in the early stages, and to Daniel Justice, for crucial suggestions in the final stages, thank you. Finally, I give special thanks to Jason Weidemann and the production team at the Press for ushering this project through the publication process with careful and considerate hands.

Back home in northern New England, the list gets longer. In many ways this project began with the question that plagued my mind one night over a decade ago, when I could not sleep for the resulting conflict and chaos and spent hours driving along the Missisquoi River and around Lake Champlain. Looking back now, I believe I may have spent the past decade seeking an answer to that question. I hope this book does it justice. To Homer St. Francis, for teaching me hands-on lessons in sovereignty, for being brave enough to speak loudly that which was not supposed to be spoken, and for always offering a seat at his table, thank you. Thanks as well to Patsy St. Francis, who demonstrates a strength that all have admired. To John Lawyer and Mike and Ina Delaney, for putting me up (and putting up with me), for our conversations over poker and skip-bo, and for always pulling together in the heat of battle. To John Moody, for being an excellent teacher and for your tireless participation in reconstructing communal history. To Donna Roberts Moody, for support and encouragement. Thank you. To Dorcus Churchill, for drawing me in and for your deep care for all your relations: I hope I did not disappoint you in my youthful ambitions. To Doris Minckler, for teaching me about stillness and compassion and for quietly directing the course I would take, thank you. To Nanatassis, for giving me what I needed to stay at a critical time. To Robert Wells, for sharing your vision of unity and your knowledge of plants, your words have always stuck in my mind. Thank you. To Joe Bruchac, for saying just the right words years ago to make me want to keep writing, even when I would not let anyone else read my words. To Marge Bruchac, for our conversations, for your dedication to recovering our history, and for sharing the fate of being a fellow *nerdnôbaskwa*. To Judy Dow, for being a model of bravery and compassion in reconstructing the pieces of the puzzle. To Natalie Michell and Anna and Sage Rapp, for taking the journey with me and providing food and inspiration. To Siobhan Senier, for strong support, for your good work, and for reading and promoting this manuscript early on. To Gordon Russell, for our many shared journeys, for deep encouragement, and for careful reading. Thank you all. To Cheryl Savageau: your mentorship and friendship have been invaluable; for being the best of teachers and readers, I am deeply grateful. To Louise Lampman Larivee, one of the toughest, deepest women I have ever had the privilege to know, thank you for letting me help and for giving me what I came home for. To Lenny Lampman, the most educated man I have known despite his few years of schooling, for amazing late-night conversations over coffee and for recognizing my face. My deepest thanks to all of you.

I am grateful for the support of my own extensive family; although big families are always full of drama and dissension, mine has also been a source of strength. This work would be pointless without them. They have taught me more about the responsibilities of kinship than they will ever know. To my mother, Christine Karoliszyn Brooks, for always celebrating my achievements, no matter how small, and for instilling pride and resolve. To the Karoliszyn family, for your dogged determination and capacity to endure. Thank you. Without you, I would not be here. And especially to my Uncle Stash and Aunt Judy, who were there for me when I needed them most and whose profound strength and care I deeply admire. To the Brooks family, for unending laughter and unconditional love, and especially to Aunt Kathy, Aunt Joy, and my cousin Donna, for being women I admired for their courage, strength, and concern before they knew I was watching. Thank you. To Kathryn, an extraordinary young woman whom I already admire: we're counting on you to take the reins! To Babcia and Grandpa Babe: it was listening to your stories that made me want to write. So much of this is from, and for, you. To my brother Jaimie and to Amy, for always having a place for me by the fire and for starting the next generation off with a bang. To my nieces Alyssa and Jolie, for being an inspiration, for being amazingly quiet while I was working, and for helping to plant new ideas and carry the stories on. To my sister Andrea, for always being there to look after my house while I was doing research and for being the special young woman that you have become. To my sister Charissa, for being an invaluable first reader and for always feeding me, offering love and nourishment. To my sister Cassandra, an incredibly sharp thinker and a continual source of inspiration who has increasingly become the best "friend to my mind" (to quote Toni Morrison). To my father, Brian Brooks, for my education, for always challenging me, and for your constant encourage- ment. To my husband, Rick Pouliot, for feeding me in more ways than I can count and for your boundless patience and understanding. Thank you all.

So many of the names I recall here as I write belong to those who have already traveled on, including my father. I am deeply grateful that I had the honor to know them while they were still on this side of the world. *Ktsi wliwni, nidôbak. Wli bamkanni.*

A Note on the Maps

The maps that follow are designed as interactive guides. Some, like Maps 9 and 14, note the locations of places and place-names mentioned in a chapter. Others, like Maps 4, 10, and 11, convey particular conceptualizations of Native space. Small-scale maps are included within the body of each chapter; however, readers are encouraged to refer to the large-scale versions to locate themselves within the geographic and social terrain. Full-scale color versions of the maps are available on the author's Web site at http://www.fas.harvard.edu/~lbrooks.

Concentric circles have been used to denote village locations in order to convey a sense of the village territory spreading outward from a center rather than existing as a single point on a map. Please note that these maps are designed not to delineate fixed territories but to convey conceptualizations of space.

Rivers, lakes, and topographic features are designated with italics.

The maps were created by Jenny Davis and Lisa Brooks using ArcGIS 9.2, courtesy of Harvard University, with a grant from the Clark Fund. Special thanks to Guoping Huang, Wendy Guan, and Jeff Blossom of the Center for Geographic Analysis for the creation of the base map and for critical technical assistance.

In addition to those cited in the chapters, the following sources were consulted: Helen Hornbeck Tanner, *Atlas of Great Lakes Indian History* (Norman: University of Oklahoma Press, 1987); Map Tech, "Historical Maps," USGS topographic maps, http://historical.maptech.com; and Pocumtuck Valley Memorial Association, "Raid on Deerfield: The Many Stories of 1704," http://1704.deerfield.history.museum/.

The Key to Map Symbols *is on page xvii, following the maps.*

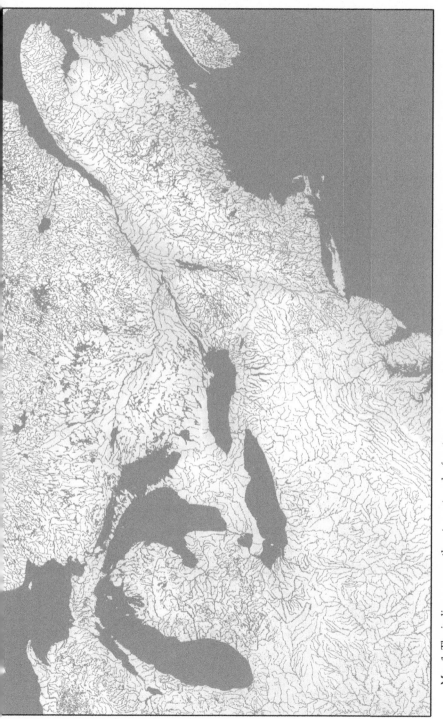

Map 1. The indigenous northeast: a network of waterways.

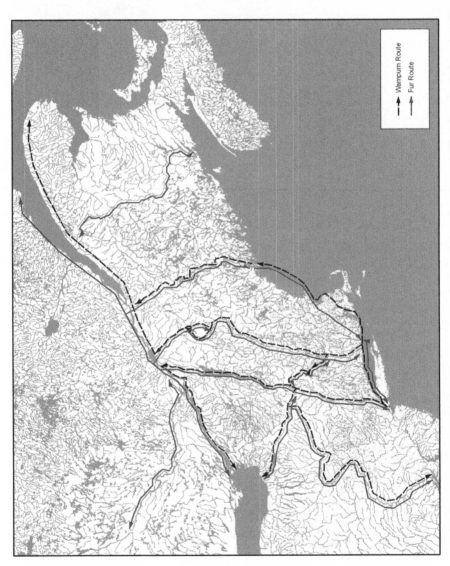

Map 2. Major routes of the wampum and fur trade, from the southeast coast to Ktsitekw, the St. Lawrence River.

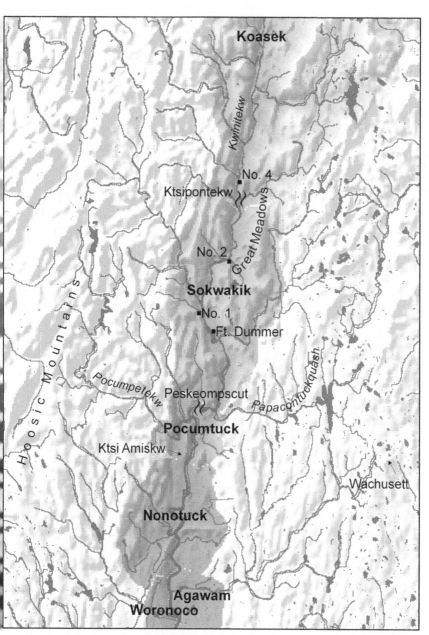

Map 3. The river Kwinitekw from Ktsipôntekw to Peskeompscut, with Native
wôlhanak highlighted.

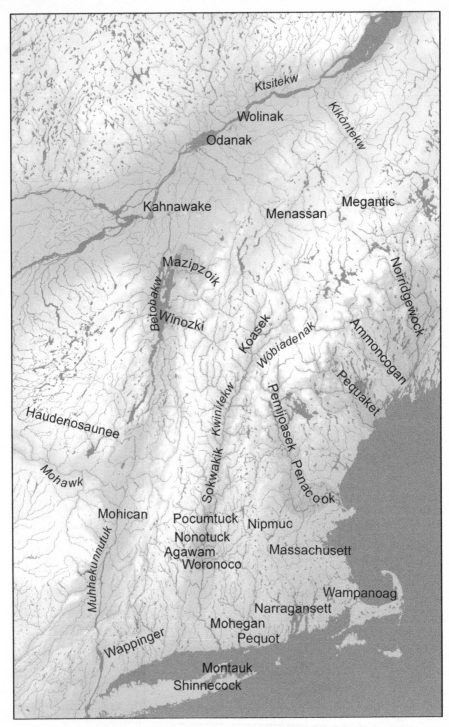

Map 4. The environs of Kwinitekw, showing Wabanaki *wôlhanak*, mission villages, and neighboring Native territories from Sobakw, the sea, to Ktsitekw, the St. Lawrence River.

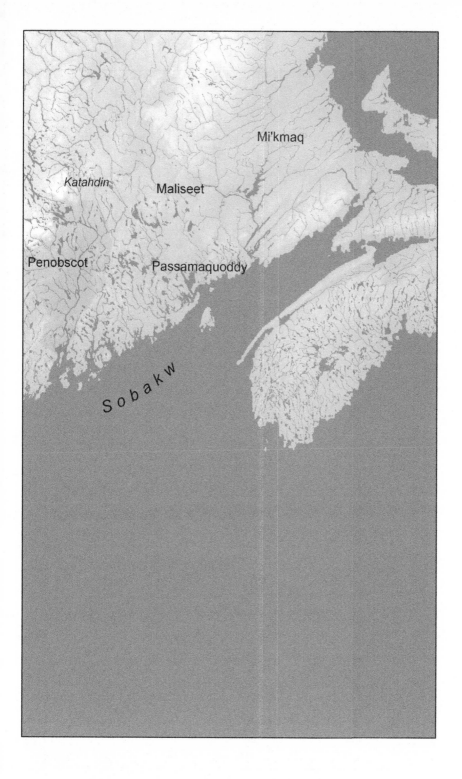

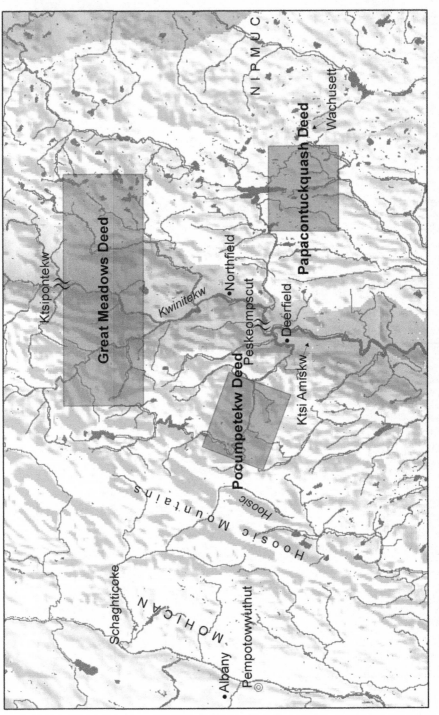

Map 5. Deerfield Conference deeds: Kwinitekw from Ktsipôntekw to Peskeompscut, with the boundaries of the three deeds outlined.

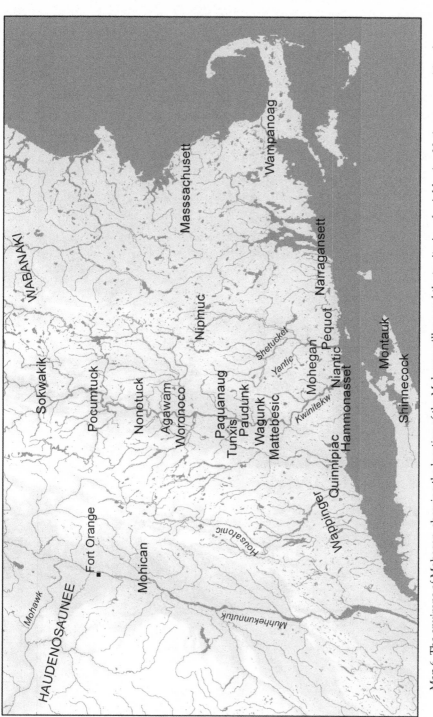

Map 6. The environs of Mohegan, showing the location of the Mohegan village and the territories of neighboring Native communities, from the "wampum-makers" on the coast to the inland Wabanaki and Haudenosaunee.

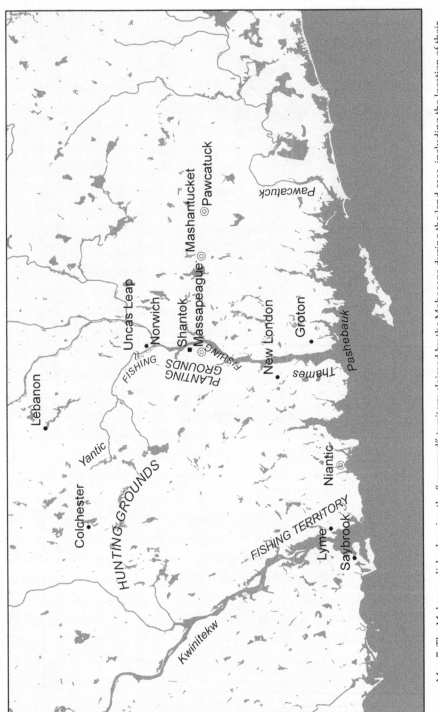

Map 7. The Mohegan dish, showing the "reserved" territory claimed by the Mohegans during the land case, including the location of their planting, hunting, and fishing grounds.

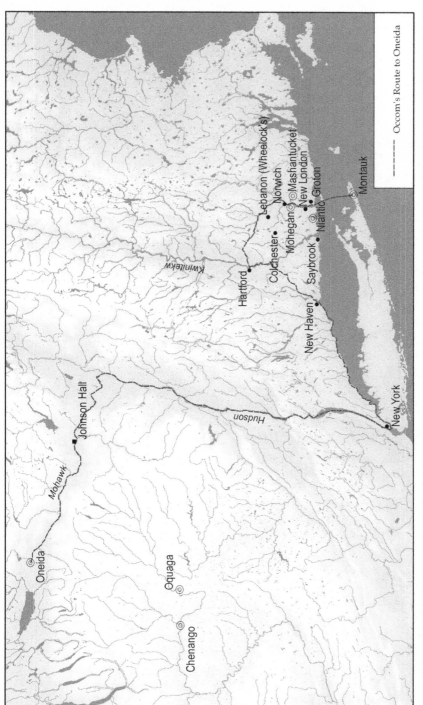

Map 8. Samson Occom and Samuel Ashpo's travels, showing Native villages and colonial towns, with Occom's route to Oneida indicated.

------ Occom's Route to Oneida

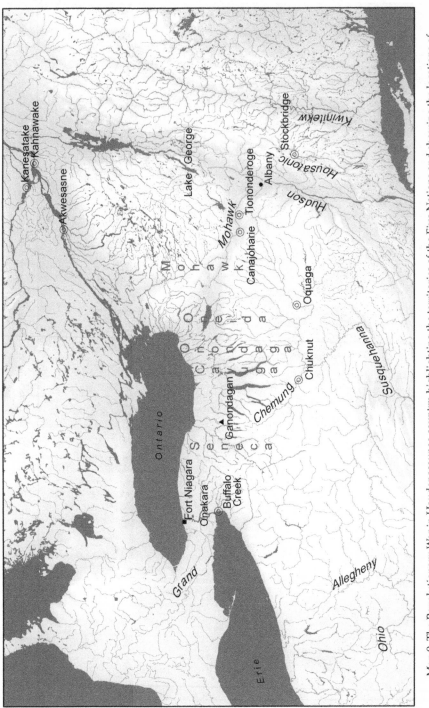

Map 9. The Revolutionary War in Haudenosaunee country, highlighting the territories of the Five Nations and showing the locations of Native villages, colonial towns, and other places mentioned in the text.

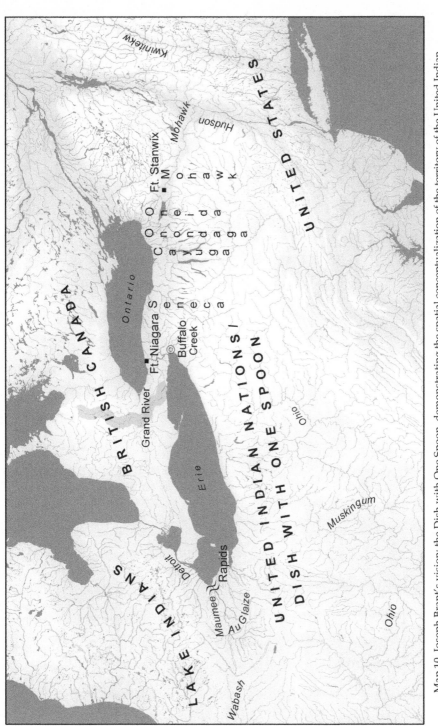

Map 10. Joseph Brant's vision: the Dish with One Spoon, demonstrating the spatial conceptualization of the territory of the United Indian Nations.

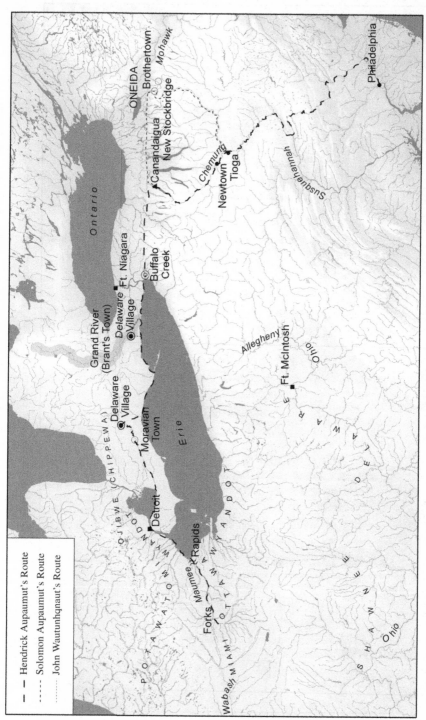

Map 11. Hendrick Aupaumut's vision: renewing the "Path of My Ancestors," demonstrating the spatial conceptualization of the same territory within a Mohican framework.

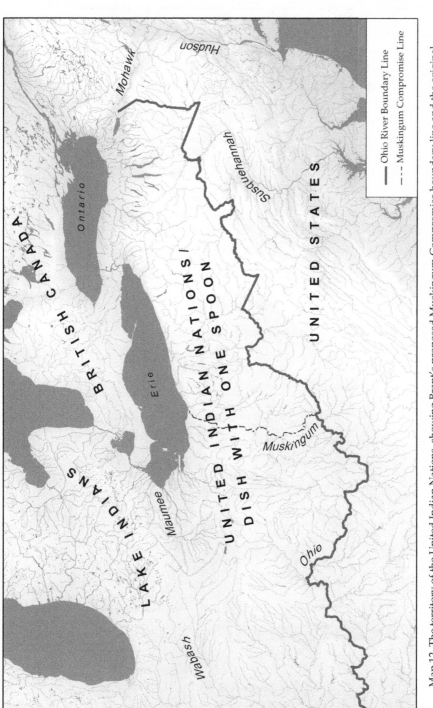

Map 12. The territory of the United Indian Nations, showing Brant's proposed Muskingum Compromise boundary line and the original Ohio River boundary line established by the Fort Stanwix Treaty of 1768.

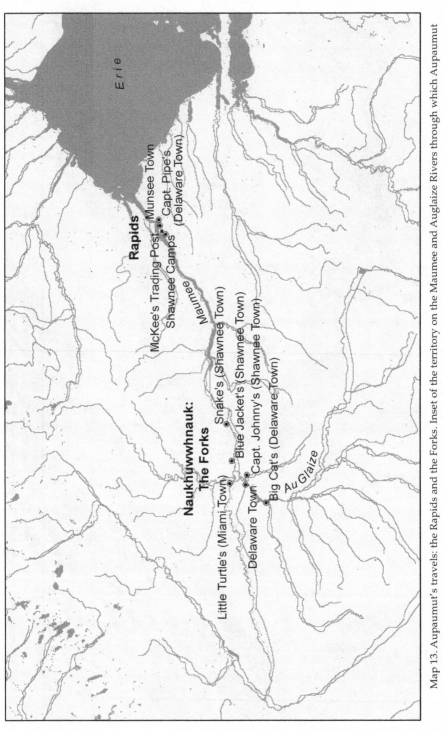

Map 13. Aupaumut's travels: the Rapids and the Forks. Inset of the territory on the Maumee and Auglaize Rivers through which Aupaumut traveled, showing the locations of Algonquian villages where he visited, camped, and participated in council.

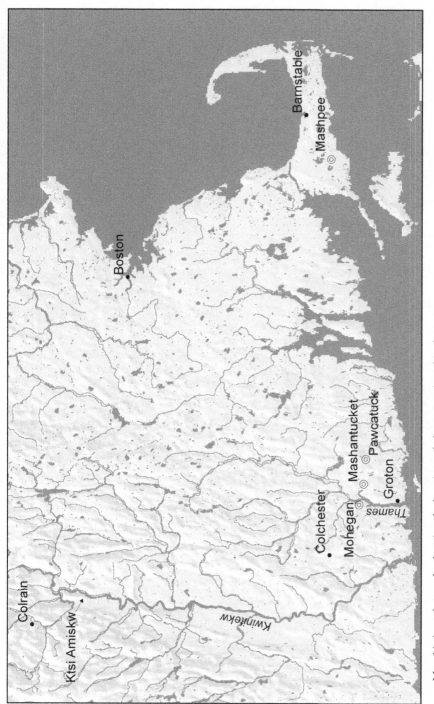

Map 14. Apess's travels, showing the locations of places mentioned in the text.

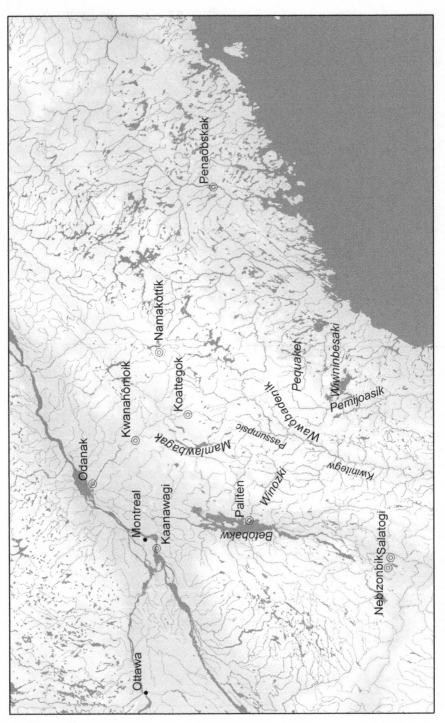

Map 15. Laurent's map, demonstrating a conceptual map of Wabanaki space, showing the locations of the places mentioned by Laurent.

Key to Map Symbols

◎ Native Village/Territory/Homeland

• English/French/U.S. Town

○ Mission Village or Indian Town

⊙ Native Village/Town within a Territory

▲ Peace Town

■ Fort or Trading Post

≈ Rapids or Waterfall

Introduction:
A Map to the Common Pot

We are sitting on the grass, stretching our legs, beside this old river-side trail, which I know her ancestors walked, and probably mine, too. You go back far enough, and we are all related somewhere. The black-top has been hard, and on this stretch it has been difficult to find a spot to rest that is not someone else's land, even though this area is, without a doubt, her family's home. The man who owns this place comes out to inquire, suspicious of these strangers parked on his lawn. We explain, and since things have changed some in the past century, he acquiesces to our presence, somewhat embarrassed. But, then again, we are only two women and two children. My husband is running ahead.

I have my laptop open. I brought it thinking, mistakenly, that I might have some time to work on this book during our several days' journey. Natalie's come over and sat down beside me to interrupt...no, to continue...my thinking. "You working on that book?" she says, inviting conversation. "Yeah," I say, then begin to explain the words that are forming the introduction — about birchbark writing and Mayan codices, about the intertwining of writing and the oral tradition. She nods her head, understanding. I don't need to explain much. We are on old trails, stretching our legs, grateful for the sun.

Yesterday, as we were walking through a high-traffic town that came up on the river sometime over the past couple of hundred years, her daughter had brought up the old Mayan codices, the way they reckoned time, the way they prophesied the world, even the one we inhabit now. She had seen a program about them on TV. We talked about the burning of those libraries, the destruction of their systems of learning, the knowledge lost. We deliberated about the meaning of those cycles of history and considered what they might mean for us here, now. We talked about how those codices need to come home. As we crossed over the river, we noticed a corn plant that had taken root in the interstices of the green metal bridge that made our passage possible. We had noticed squash growing in the gravelly sand on the side of the road earlier that day, after we had left the island where Natalie grew up. We laughed out loud at the wonder of it – the resilience of these plants, the unpredictable places they show up, their ability to adapt to the strangest and most hostile of circumstances. Their stubbornness. Their capacity for regeneration. We talked about how far corn had traveled from the Mayan country to make its way up here. Some stories that the land tells are more obvious than others.

We are sitting on the grass, stretching our legs, talking about birchbark scrolls, Mayan codices, and the intertwining of writing and the oral tradition. "I always knew," Natalie says, "that there were things that were taken from us, kept from us . . . knowledge that was hidden. Deep inside of me, I always knew." That is why I don't have to explain; you see, she already understands. But we think of those libraries, burned by Spanish priests. And we think of the birchbark that we gathered yesterday to start our cookfire, the birchbark that can be used to make canoes, baskets, homes . . . and books. We think of how it is the best thing to use to start a fire. We think of those scrolls . . . we think of the priests. We think of how easy it would have been. . . .

This book is only an attempt . . . to weave together fragments found, fragments of words written down, recorded by our ancestors. Most of all, it is an opportunity to hear their voices, however mediated by the particularities of their place and time, as well as our own. It is an attempt to recover some of that which has been taken, hidden, or lost, with the hope that this writing, too, can play a role in regeneration, to be the beans to that corn and squash, and to walk, for a while, along these old trails, along the riverways that have always been our home.

The Map and the Book Are the Same Thing

In her recent journey journal, *Books and Islands in Ojibwe Country*, Louise Erdrich tells us that in the Ojibwe language the words for *book* and *rock painting* are almost identical, and the root of both these words, *mazina*, is "the root for dozens of words all concerned with made images and with the substances upon which the images are put," including those of photographs, movie screens, and television sets. Erdrich observes, "The Ojibwe people were great writers from way back and synthesized the oral and written tradition by keeping mnemonic scrolls of inscribed birchbark. The first paper, the first books." She writes, "I figure books have been written around here ever since someone had the idea of . . . writing on birchbark with a sharpened stick. Books are nothing all that new."[1]

Leslie Marmon Silko, in discussing the Mayan codices on which her novel *Almanac of the Dead* is based, has remarked on their "rich visual languages," noting that just because European tradition has separated image from word does not mean that this is a universal practice. "The Mixtec and Maya," Silko writes, "combined painting and writing, two activities that European culture considers distinct."[2] The word for the artisans who created the codices meant both "painter" and "scribe."

The same is true in the Abenaki language, which is kin to Ojibwe. The root word *awigha-* denotes "to draw," "to write," "to map." The word *awikhigan*, which originally described birchbark messages, maps, and scrolls, came to encompass books and letters.[3] An Ojibwe scroll is an *awikhigan*. The road map that Natalie and I used to navigate our trip is an *awikhigan*. Erdrich's account of her travels among the islands of Ojibwe country is an *awikhigan*. *Almanac of the Dead* and the codices on which it is modeled are all *awikhiganak*. You are reading one now. For Abenakis, as well as for Mayans, Mixtecs, and Ojibwes, writing and drawing are both forms of image making, and they are not always easily read.

Just as Native writers spin the binary between word and image into a relational framework, they also challenge us to avoid the "oppositional thinking that separates orality and literacy wherein the oral constitutes authentic culture and the written contaminated culture," as Muskogee author Craig Womack argues in *Red on Red*. He suggests that such notions may actually hinder our understanding of a "vast, and vastly understudied, written tradition" in Native America. Like Silko, Womack raises the example of the codices, "written in Mayan pictoglyphic symbols before contact, and in Mayan in the Latin alphabet afterward," as "a fascinating study in these regards." As he rightly points out: "These books were used as a *complement* of oral tradition rather than a *replacement*. The books were recited and even read in precontact schools to educate the young in the oral tradition. The idea, then, of books as a valid means of passing on vital cultural information is an ancient one, consistent with the oral tradition itself."[4]

Similarly, Silko speaks strongly about the interdependence of oral and written traditions and points to the adoption of alphabetic writing as a form of adaptation. In an interview, she relates that the original Mayan codices had complementary texts that were composed after the arrival of the Europeans. She explains that they were written in Spanish and Latin "by the first generation [of Mayan children] that the priests put in schools. And they could read and write. When they went home, the elders saw that the oral tradition could not be maintained, where you have genocide on this scale.... The old folks thought about it, had people explain to them what writing was. It dawned on them; it's a tool. It's a tool."[5]

Again, the same is true in Abenaki. The other root of the word for "book," *-igan,* denotes an instrument. *Awikhigan* is a tool for image making, for writing, for transmitting an image or idea from one mind to another, over waterways, over time.

Womack also emphasizes the "pragmatic" and "utilitarian" instrumentality of the oral and written word, noting, "Native artistry is not pure aesthetics, or art for art's sake: as often as not Indian writers are trying to *invoke* as much as *evoke.*"[6] Literature, he tells us, like "ceremonial chant," has the potential to "actually cause a change in the physical universe." However, as Womack emphasizes, he is speaking not just of mystical "invocation" but of the power of words to bring about practical and political change. This idea brings to mind another critical concept in the Abenaki language: *awikhigawôgan,* the activity of writing. Like many indigenous languages, Abenaki revolves around activities, energy in motion; until an *awikhigan* has taken shape as an instrument, the process of *awikhigawôgan* is ongoing.[7] Even when it is complete, that instrument can cause a whole new wave of activity to occur. I am absorbed in this process now, perhaps you are, too, as you write notes to me, or to yourself, in the margins of this book or in your own *awikhigan,* a spiral notebook or a laptop computer. *Awikhigawôgan* is an activity in which we are all engaged.

This book, then, is at once an activity in which we participate, an instrument, and a map. It is a map of a network of writers and texts, as well as a process of mapping the historical space they inhabit. It is a mapping of how Native people in the northeast used writing as an instrument to reclaim lands and reconstruct communities, but also a mapping of the *instrumental* activity of writing, its role in the rememberment of a fragmented world.

Mapping Place-worlds

As is clear from the story with which I opened this Introduction, *awikhigawôgan* operates within particular, tangible spaces. This is necessarily a book that is rooted in place. Each of the following chapters begins with an *awikhigan*, then expands out into the "place-world" from which it emerged. As anthropologist Keith Basso defines the term, "Essentially... instances of place-making consist in an adventitious fleshing out of historical material that culminates in a posited state of affairs, a particular universe of objects and events — in short, a *place-world* — wherein portions of the past are brought into being."[8] *Awikhiganak* not only emerge from particular place-worlds but engage them as active participants within them and, potentially, within other place-worlds at distant spaces and times.

Furthermore, the practice of "place-making," as Basso defines it, is also a form of narrative art; it functions as literature as well as history. For me, the line between what is literary and what is historical, particularly in Native American writing, may be as problematic as the divide between imagery, orality, and the written word.[9] Just as it may be difficult to maintain a firm boundary between what constitutes a historical document and a literary text, my own narrative art may resist placement in either the literary or historical camp. What will be clear, I hope, is that my own writing is as much an instrument that operates in particular place-worlds as are the texts it ponders. This *awikhigan* is about a literary and historical tradition, but it is also a participant in that tradition.

Accordingly, in concert with Basso's description of place-making, this book puts as much emphasis on "*where* events occurred as on the nature and consequence of the events themselves."[10] A key influence is the work of Dakota scholar Vine Deloria Jr. In discussing Native oral traditions, religions, and histories in his landmark *God Is Red*, Deloria argued that creation stories are actually much more concerned with geography and spatiality, "what happened here," than with chronological origins and temporality, "what happened then." These stories, he maintains, function practically and artistically as narrative maps of "an ecosystem present in a definable place." Within their extensive oral traditions, which are always linked to particular places, he writes, "Indian tribes combine history and geography so that they have a 'sacred geography,' that is to say, every location within their original homeland has a multitude of stories that recount the migrations, revelations, and particularly historical incidents that cumulatively produced the tribe in its current condition.... The most notable characteristic of the tribal traditions is the precision and specificity of the traditions when linked to the landscape." As Dakota historian Waziyatawin Angela Wilson explains, following Deloria, "An Indigenous perspective may differ from a Western historian's in the emphasis each places on time and place and its role in history. While many historical stories from Indigenous oral traditions do not contain information on when a particular event occurred (especially according to a Julian or Gregorian calendar), the stories often contain detailed information about where specific events took place."[11] While emphasizing the importance of place-based history, I have tried to be mindful of noting time frames to locate readers who rely on chronological markers. Still, my hope is that this book will make clear that the interpretation of early Native texts simply cannot take place without widespread understanding of the extensive place-worlds they inhabit.

This approach is not merely an academic exercise but a methodology rooted in my own land-based experiences. I have spent a good deal of time on the ground and on the waterways, walking, canoeing, and driving in the places that I write about, usually with friends and relations, often exchanging histories of the places to which we belong. I also spend a lot of time tracking the forested marshes and uplands where I live, in the country of my Abenaki ancestors, and my writing reflects this familiarity. To be clear, what I am talking about here is not an abstraction, a theorizing about a conceptual category called "land" or "nature," but a physical, actual, material relationship to "an ecosystem present in a definable place" that has been cultivated throughout my short life, and for much longer by those relations who came before me, which, for better or for worse, deeply informs this work. As Wilson quotes Winona Wheeler: "The land is mnemonic, it has its own set of memories, and when the old people go out on the land it nudges or reminds them, and their memories are rekindled." If documents, oral stories, and place-names are among the "'tracks' that have survived into the present," I have tried my best to flesh out a story that makes sense of the tracks, not just by quantitative measurement of individual prints but by viewing them within the context of their whole environment. This has entailed an evolving process of mapping the relationships between people, places, rivers, words, and the plethora of beings who inhabit any place-world.[12]

In many ways, the writing that follows reflects Basso's description of indigenous history:

> It is pointedly local and unfailingly episodic. It is also extremely personal, consistently subjective, and therefore highly variable among those who work to produce it. For these and other reasons, it is history without authorities — all narrated place-worlds, provided they seem plausible, are considered equally valid. . . . Its principal themes are the endless quest for survival, the crucial importance of community and kin, and the beneficial consequences, practical and otherwise, of adhering to moral norms. Accordingly, one of its basic aims

is to instill empathy and admiration for the ancestors themselves . . .
and to hold them up to all as worthy of emulation, except, of course,
when they fail to do what is right and threaten by their actions the
welfare of the group.[13]

If ever readers find themselves frustrated by the lack of a singular argument, steady chronology, distanced objectivity, or other familiar markers
of academic writing, I hope they will remember these words. I think they
best describe the project I have attempted here. To echo Basso's descriptive
words, more than anything else I have tried to "fashion possible worlds,
give them expressive shape, and present them for contemplation as images
of the past that can deepen and enlarge awareness of the present."

An Interactive Text-Map

Because *awikhigawôgan,* like storytelling, is an interactive process, I invite
the reader of this text-map to play a participatory role. Rather than tracing a single argument and forming agreement or argument, I hope you
will feel free to interact, deliberate, and grapple with the images and ideas
raised herein, stopping at the ends of quotations, sections, and chapters
to contemplate the connections between them. My greatest aspiration is
that readers will feel themselves entering a place-world and will be
compelled to use their minds interactively to try to comprehend it. The
Dena'ina Athabaskan author and storyteller Peter Kalifornsky described
this process as a crucial part of interactive "language work." In his way of
thinking, storytellers craft words that "move into a cavity" of your mind,
allowing you to "complete your complex thought." As Wilson writes in
a similar vein, "Within Dakota culture, history is an interpretation of
the past that becomes active only when a relationship has been developed between a storyteller and a listener." And, as Miwok/Pomo literary scholar Greg Sarris writes of Pomo storyteller Mabel McKay, "If
Mabel's talk initiates . . . a kind of internal dialogue . . . that dialogue can
be carried over to an ever-widening context of talk in stories and conversations, such that the inner dialogue can inform and be informed by new
stories and conversations."[14] In this way, this *awikhigan* may operate as an
instrument, in the Abenaki sense, which, now in your hands and working in your mind, may foster thoughts and activities that I could not
have imagined.

I hope this book has the potential to work like Mabel McKay's
talk, embedding you, the reader, in the text to foster a participatory conversation between us and this world we share. In his latest work, *The*

People and the Word, Osage scholar Robert Warrior discusses reading as a "process that highlights the production of meaning through the *critical interaction* that occurs between a text as a writer has written it and a text as readers read it." This idea follows on Sarris's work with Native oral traditions and reader response theory, but also builds on indigenous understandings of participatory communication. It coincides with the "language work" of Kalifornsky and Basso, suggesting that writing, like interactive storytelling, is a tool and an activity that produces "gaps" in the mind of the listener/reader that must be "worked." As Benson Lewis, an Apache elder from Cibecue, told Keith Basso, "Stories go to work on you like arrows. Stories make you live right. Stories make you replace yourself."[15]

Mapping Influences and Audiences

This book seeks to speak with multiple audiences at once without necessarily striving to communicate to everyone all the time. As with many stories, there are multiple layers of potential meaning herein. While I was writing and revising, my own mind was engaged in conversation with a network of texts that informed the work. Some were foundational as I embarked on the project, while others showed me the gaps that needed filling, and still others seemed to strengthen its relevance. My aspiration is that this book can enter those conversations and provide a site of engagement for scholars in multiple fields and members of multiple communities. It follows that different readers might be drawn to some aspects of the book and inclined to skip others. The following is an acknowledgment of key influences and audiences, followed by a basic map that can guide readers to particular places.

Native American Studies, Indigenous Studies, and Native Literary Criticism

When I was a graduate student, Linda Tuhiwai Smith's *Decolonizing Methodologies,* which I first encountered in Robert Warrior's seminar at Cornell, crystallized my thinking. The words of this Maori (Ngati Awa and Ngati Porou) scholar worked their way into the cavities of my mind, providing an important motivation for "rewriting" history:

> A critical aspect of the struggle for self-determination has involved questions relating to our history as indigenous peoples and a critique of how we, as the Other, have been represented or excluded from

various accounts. Every issue has been approached by indigenous peoples with a view to *re*writing and *re*righting our position in history. Indigenous peoples want to tell our own stories, write our own versions, in our own ways, for our own purposes. It is not simply about giving an oral account or a genealogical naming of the land and the events which raged over it, but a very powerful need to give testimony to and restore a spirit, to bring back into existence a world fragmented and dying.[16]

In concert with Tuhiwai Smith, Acoma author Simon Ortiz insists that literature has always been vital to these activities of testimony and restoration. In his seminal essay "Towards a National Indian Literature," Ortiz eloquently described the celebration of saints' days at Acqu, elucidating the creative adaptation of a Catholic ritual by Acquumeh people to serve their own culturally specific needs, as, like Native peoples throughout the hemisphere, they made "use of foreign ritual, ideas, and material in their own — Indian — terms." He maintained that "today's writing by Indian authors is a continuation of that fundamental impulse."[17] Perhaps Ortiz's most salient point is that Native people have adopted and adapted European languages creatively, for their own purposes:

> Along with their native languages, Indian women and men have carried on their lives and their expression through the use of the newer languages, particularly Spanish, French, and English, and they have used these languages on their own terms. This is the crucial item that has to be understood, that it is entirely possible for a people to retain and maintain their lives through the use of any language. There is not a question of authenticity here; rather it is the way that Indian people have creatively responded to forced colonization. And this response has been one of resistance; there is no clearer word for it than resistance.[18]

Thus, the idea that writing has been an instrumental tool for the reconstruction of "Native space" and for resistance to colonization is not a new one but has been contemplated by indigenous authors for some time. Therefore, scholars are increasingly calling attention to the need to recover and recognize (as Daniel Justice describes this process, "to know again") the work of early Native writers, which shows this process of adaptation in action.[19] In *Tribal Secrets*, Warrior called on Native scholars to reexamine the "intellectual history" in the writings of the "Native writers and scholars" who preceded us. He asserted:

When we take that tradition seriously...we empower our work. First, we see that, far from engaging in some new and novel practice that belongs necessarily to the process of assimilating and enculturating non-Native values, we are doing something that Natives have done for hundreds of years — something that can be and has been an important part of resistance to assimilation and survival. Such a generational view...provides a new historical and critical site that invites us to see contemporary work as belonging to a process centuries long, rather than decades long, of engaging the future contours of Indian America. Second, we stand on firmer ground in our interlocutorial role with Eurocentric scholarly theories and categories.... Third, critically reading our own tradition allows us to see some of the mistakes of the past as we analyze the problems of the present.[20]

Building on Warrior's work as well as a wide array of scholarship in Native American studies and postcolonial theory, Cherokee scholar Jace Weaver introduced the idea of "communitism" as a theoretical framework, arguing in *That the People Might Live* that much of Native literary production has reflected the authors' "proactive commitment to Native community, including the wider community" of "non-human relations." He emphasized the combination of "activism" and "community" in Native American writing and reminded scholars that "the linkage of land and people *within* the concept of community, reflecting the spatial orientation of Native peoples, is crucial." Both Weaver and Warrior stressed that this concept of community was neither static nor nostalgic but constantly changing.[21] Like Silko and Ortiz, Warrior and Weaver accentuated the role of writing as an adaptive tool and a map that guides communal activity in a changing landscape.

Following Ortiz, Warrior, and Weaver and in concert with Tuhiwai Smith, there is a growing trend toward scholarship that focuses on tribal and regional literatures, with an emphasis on the specificities of indigenous political and cultural history. My own focus on the place-worlds of a particular region, as well as my methodological approach, was bolstered by the emergence of this scholarship. For me, Craig Womack's *Red on Red* marked a watershed moment, breaking the barriers of what defined literary scholarship and asking questions that worked furiously in the cavities of my mind. Here I would like to summarize a few influential points. Womack sought to "open up a dialogue ... regarding what constitutes meaningful literary efforts," asking us to think deeply about how writing can be, and has been, a tool for creativity and construction as well as disempowerment and destruction. He asked us to consider the vast literature produced by "past generations of Native writers and thinkers" and the possibilities for scholarship that focused on the particular places and literary traditions with which we were most intimate, the outpouring of our own nations. He called for more work on early Native literature, "a vast, and vastly understudied, written tradition," and accentuated the need for the "reconstruction" (versus the "deconstruction") of history from Native perspectives. Womack, like many Native scholars, consistently emphasizes the plurality of indigenous "perspectives," lest anyone misunderstand him as endorsing anything that resembles a monolithic "Indian point-of-view." Rather, just as I emphasize the plurality of Native voices in my own reconstruction of particular place-worlds in the northeast, he insists on honoring diverse perspectives, as articulated by individuals, leaders, scholars, and speakers from multiple nations, places, and experiences. With this in mind, Womack began his own work within the geographic and political space of the Muskogee Creek nation. In *Red on Red* he traced the kinship relations and literary influences in a body of Creek texts, from the creation stories of the oral tradition through nineteenth- and twentieth-century political writings to the contemporary poetry of Louis Oliver and Joy Harjo. He provided a map to the landscape of Creek literature that I have found invaluable in reading and teaching an extensive body of southeastern texts.[22]

Moving from within the same region, Cherokee scholar Daniel Justice has continued this effort in *Our Fire Survives the Storm: A Cherokee Literary History*. Justice uses frameworks drawn from Cherokee political culture to provide a complex and compassionate reading of Cherokee writers, breaking down the binaries that would divide them into traditionalists and assimilationists, pursuing either resistance *or* acquiescence. He gives us a layered, intricate reading of a multifaceted literary landscape and, like Womack, provides us with a strong model and a clear lens through which to view our own literary traditions as indigenous scholars. As he writes, "Nationhood is woven in large part from the lives, dreams, and challenges of the people who compose the body politic; as such, examining the interplay of broader social issues with lived human realities can immeasurably strengthen our understandings of the complicated discourses of community. To write about family and history is to try to give voice to silenced ghosts as much as to give strength to the living." I hope that my own work can help to bring the often marginalized voices and "lived human realities" of Native people in the northeast into the center of conversations in Native literature and Native studies, for the sake of what we might learn from those who came before us and to foster deeper understanding and strengthen relationships among all of us who are here today.[23]

Other scholars have adopted and adapted this approach, and they are demonstrating that although we benefit greatly from having scholars from particular nations or regions write about their communities' literary traditions, tribally specific scholarship is not by any means confined to those who are indigenous to the place and people about which they write. Indeed, we can learn a great deal from reading the work of a Seneca scholar who has immersed herself in Dakota texts, Penelope Kelsey's *Tribal Theory in Native American Literature: Dakota and Haudenosaunee Writing and Indigenous Worldviews*. Siobhan Senier, a non-Native scholar who works in Abenaki country and has made strong efforts to form relationships of collaboration with Native people in New England, provides important culturally and historically specific insights into the work of authors like Abenaki poet Cheryl Savageau, in part because of her own interaction in the network of relations and her "pro-active commitment to community." Although I have chosen to stay close to home, I am energized by the work that is emerging, from multiple perspectives and diverse places, which is highly cognizant of "what constitutes meaningful literary efforts" in Native studies, and in Native space.[24]

Early Native American Writing

The call for greater attention to the writings of those who came before has arisen not only from Native studies circles but from scholars of early American literature and history. Attention to early Native authors, including Samson Occom and William Apess, has increased in the critical literature, and a number of volumes focus exclusively on Native writing of the eighteenth and nineteenth centuries. Lavonne Ruoff's wide-ranging scholarship has been instrumental in bringing these literatures to both American and Native American literary circles. Bernd Peyer's *The Tutor'd Mind* serves as an invaluable guide to the ethnohistorical and biographical territory of individual Native writers while providing critical frameworks for understanding these texts within postcolonial power dynamics. Several volumes of collected works have also emerged, beginning with Barry O'Connell's publication of William Apess's writings, including an extensive introduction that placed his work firmly within the context of

Native continuance in New England. Laura J. Murray subsequently produced a collection of the writings of Joseph Johnson, a young Mohegan leader, with a richly researched contextual history, and Joanna Brooks has lately published a long-awaited volume of the works of Samson Occom, fleshing out the multifaceted and politically complex world of the Mohegan minister. Other important works include a critical anthology of articles, *Early Native American Writing*, edited by Helen Jaskoski, and *Writing Indians*, Hillary Wyss's insightful exploration of the relationship between Christianity, literacy, and community among Indian converts in New England, as well as numerous articles and essays concerned with the conflicts and cultural challenges of literacy.[25]

Most recently, Maureen Konkle, building on scholarship in Native American studies, has shifted the paradigm through which we view early Native writing. In *Writing Indian Nations*, Konkle argues that little attention has been paid to "the political autonomy of Native peoples" in "the scholarship on the representation of Native peoples and on Native writing." Instead, she claims, such scholarship has been "largely driven by a fixation on determining, describing, and analyzing the cultural difference of Native peoples and Native writing." She observes, "Although scholarship on early Native writing has recognized Native criticism of white violence and oppression, it has for the most part largely attended to the problem of explaining how an Indian who is a Christian and writes in English could still be an Indian."[26]

This focus on questions of authenticity, and the maintenance of binaries that assume that the adoption of Christianity or literacy is concomitant with a complete loss of Native identity, has obscured the complex ways in which Native communities have adopted and adapted foreign ideas and instruments in particular places. In contrast to such writers as Ortiz, some literary scholars have assumed, and argued, that the only "authentic" Native literature is oral and that when Native people adopt writing, they are moving away from a "pure" Native culture.[27] As Konkle rightly argues, these arguments are based on a temporal model of culture in which the most "authentic" is that which exists only in the precontact past; this culture cannot change but can only be "preserved" in the present. As I have heard the Salish writer Lee Maracle wittily remark, you can preserve peaches, but you'd have a tough time getting a dance or a song into a mason jar. Culture, like anything that is alive and "engaged," must grow and change, must take its own course. In the anthropological framework of preservation, it would seem that the only "real Indian" is a "dead

Indian." We can observe the artifacts and documents from without, through the glass of the mason jar, but we cannot get inside; we cannot interact. As Konkle asserts, such frameworks not only create a false picture of Native culture but deny Native people the right and the ability to survive, adapt, and change — as communities, as families composed of living beings, over time. And, as writers from Silko to Maracle and Womack have emphatically insisted, that which does not change dies. Womack summarizes the point succinctly when he writes, "Indian cultures are the only cultures where it is assumed that if they change they are no longer a culture. In most other cultures, change is viewed as a sign that the culture is vibrant and alive, capable of surviving."[28]

Furthermore, the idea of "pure," "authentic," and static Native culture also ignores centuries, indeed millennia, of cultural change and exchange in Native space. In truth, this activity — of adapting to change; of adopting new ideas, practices, and technologies; of engaging in cultural exchange — is long-standing on this continent. As Bernd Peyer, among others, has written, "Highly sophisticated communication networks existed among native societies in the Americas long before the advent of Europeans." He adds, "Social change is not a postcontact phenomenon in North America, as can be readily deduced from oral history and archaeological finds. What is new is not so much the act of accommodation itself but the purpose and degree of transformation that occurs in a colonial situation." The important difference, which we *all* must confront, lies in the power dynamics of colonialism and in the weight of devastation wrought by dispossession and forced assimilation. The challenge, as Kanienkehake scholar Taiaiake Alfred sees it, is that "survival is bending and swaying but not breaking, adapting and accommodating without compromising what is core to one's being." For some, including myself, that "core" lies not in the preservation of obvious markers of Indian identity but in the ongoing relationship and responsibility to land and kin. Not that this process of adaptation and survival is easy. In fact, this is exactly the challenge that the Native writers and leaders who came before us struggled with during their own time. We may learn a great deal by paying close attention to their examples, their successes, and their mistakes.[29]

Thus, I offer this book as a tool that can operate in Native communities today, an instrument that might encourage contemplation, deliberation, and imagination. For, as Womack writes, "To exist as a nation, the community needs a perception of nationhood, that is, stories . . . that help them imagine who they are as a people, how they came to be." These early writings help us to see how Native nations continued to imagine themselves into being even as they grappled with forces that threatened to annihilate them. Moreover, these stories help us to imagine ourselves here, in relation to those that preceded us, with the benefit of the wisdom of their experience. How did Native people adopt and adapt new technologies, new social frameworks, new epistemologies? What traditions did they draw on in responding to, incorporating, or rejecting new instruments and ideas? How were new people incorporated into extant political networks? What tools and tales were used to adapt to the new conditions brought on by colonization?[30]

The more the early writings come to the surface, the more we can see the deep waters of this long-standing and intellectually potent tradition. In his recent work Warrior has focused on the centrality of nonfiction in Native American literature, remarking that "though contemporary fiction and poetry receive the lion's share of scholarly attention in studies of Native literature, the historical centrality of nonfiction in Native writing in English since the late eighteenth century is inarguable." As he points out, if we accept the novel "as the high-water mark or gold standard of literary achievement," then "Native literature" appears to be a "latecomer to the feast of modern literacy and literature." However, if we conceive of "literature" differently, the "historical arc of Native writing" is lengthened considerably and a vibrant intellectual and political conversation comes to the fore.[31]

Native History in New England

This growing body of important work on early Native American writing has coincided with equally significant work on Native history in this region. The series Native Americans of the Northeast, edited by Colin Calloway and Barry O'Connell, has been instrumental. This series has included Peyer and Wyss's work, as well as anthologies and monographs that have thoroughly demonstrated Native continuance in New England. In *After King Philip's War*, for instance, multiple contributors elucidate the complex stories of Indian survival long after that conflict, which was supposed to eliminate Indian resistance and existence. Concurrently, Jean O'Brien's *Dispossession by Degrees* and Daniel Mandell's *Behind the Frontier* have shown how Indians in eighteenth-century Massachusetts reconfigured their communities in the wake of increasing colonial control

over their lands and bodies. In *Captors and Captives,* Evan Haefeli and
Kevin Sweeney have illuminated the complex tapestry of interaction between multiple Native nations and European colonies, focusing on the
varying motivations of Abenaki, Huron, Mohawk, English, and French
participants in the 1704 Deerfield raid. Most recently, Amy Den Ouden's
Beyond Conquest has made an important contribution to our understanding of the politics of land and law, as well as the rhetoric of authenticity
in the struggles of Native nations with the Colony of Connecticut. This
scholarship has overturned the myth of the "vanishing" New England
Indians and has established the persistence of indigenous communities
in their social and political struggle with the colonial apparatus that
orchestrated their "disappearance."[32]

At the same time, regional battles over land claims, aboriginal
rights, and federal recognition have brought Native communities to the
forefront of public and political space and have contributed to the local
recovery of Native histories. Tribal historians such as Melissa Tantaquidgeon Zobel (Mohegan) and community-authored anthologies such as
Rooted Like Ash Trees have made crucial contributions to communal understandings of Native history and contemporary realities in the region.
Creative writers such as Joseph Bruchac (Abenaki) and Cheryl Savageau
(Abenaki) have also begun to reframe the historical landscape while working creatively to bring contemporary Native experience to the fore. Ongoing work in both archival research and oral history by Native historians
such as Marge Bruchac (Abenaki), Thomas Doughton (Nipmuc), James
Francis (Penobscot), Daniel Paul (Mi'kmaq), Trudie Lamb Richmond
(Schagticoke), Ella Sekatau (Narragansett), and Donald Soctomah (Passamaquoddy) have been a critical center to the project of historical recovery. As I have often heard Abenaki basketmaker and ethnobotanist Judy
Dow say, we all have pieces of the puzzle, and it is only by coming together that we can hope to reconstruct the full picture. And the daily
work of community members in the process of rememberment, of which
many academics remain unaware, has been absolutely vital.[33]

This book could not have been written without the work that
came before it, those *awighiganak* that have sat on my shelves, with their
pages worn, and the stories that have become embedded in my mind. At
the same time, this book would not have been written had I not been embroiled in the legal defense of aboriginal rights and land cases in my
own youth. I realized the power of writing early on, so when I started
the research for this project I was not surprised to find that the bulk of

early Native writings was focused on the politics of land. When I first began, I was told that looking for writing by Indians would be like looking for needles in a haystack. But I figured if you know the names of the needles and the places they are from, it might be easier to find them. There were more writings than could fill this book, and I have tried my best to bring the Native voices they express to the forefront. However those voices may be mediated, through the recording and interpretation of their time and through the lens of our own, I have tried to cultivate a space of interaction between their world and ours.

For this reason, I invite readers to pay particular attention to the block quotes in the chapters that follow. Although our eyes often skim over such passages, these have been included at length to highlight the voices of these writers. I hope that readers will benefit from interaction with their words as much as from my analysis of them.

Most important, I have tried my best to write a book that Native people, especially in New England, might want to read. Much of this book has been written with my own family and community in mind, because I believe strongly that we must engage deeply with our own histories in order to comprehend the complex world we inhabit, our place within that world, and our responsibilities to those who will follow the paths we lay down now.

American Studies/Postcolonial Studies

This approach of "prioritizing Native voices" may also have important implications for American studies.[34] Although I am not advocating this method for all scholars, I hope this work poses questions that can contribute to a shift in perspective. What happens to our view of American history when Native narratives are not just *included* but *privileged*? What happens to our conception of literature when we momentarily set aside the literary frameworks of Europe and consider what constitutes Native American writing? What happens when we put Native space at the center of America rather than merely striving for inclusion of minority viewpoints or viewing Native Americans as a *part* of or on the *periphery* of America? What does the historical landscape look like when viewed through the networks of waterways and kinship in the northeast, with Europe and its colonies on the periphery? What happens when the texts of Anglo-American history and literature are participants in Native space rather than the center of the story? What kind of map emerges?

Such questions may enable us to reverse past trends in academic writing that have elided the perspectives of Native people. As Linda Tuhiwai-Smith observes:

> The negation of indigenous views of history was a critical part of asserting colonial ideology, partly because such views were regarded as clearly "primitive" and "incorrect" and mostly because they challenged and resisted the mission of colonization. Indigenous peoples have also mounted a critique of the way history is told from the perspective of the colonizers. At the same time, however, indigenous groups have argued that history is important for understanding the present and that reclaiming history is a critical and essential aspect of decolonization.[35]

In a similar vein, building links between cultural and political theorists, anthropologist Jonathan Boyarin reflects:

> The past is not unproblematically "known" for [Walter] Benjamin, and as long as it remains the stakes of contention in the present, it is not dead. [Frantz] Fanon, complementing and extending the reach of Benjamin's purview, suggested that a people's past may be colonized as well. In a sense, [Michel] Foucault's call for a spatialized sense of struggle and Benjamin's articulation of the past as a political field complement each other. Foucault reminds us of those living with us on the planet; that they are "distant" from us does not make them "fixed, dead, and immobile," as the lingering discourses of primitivism, racism, and Orientalism would have us believe. Benjamin reminds us of the demands of our ancestors who died unjustly; their death is, in a powerful sense, not "past," but subject to the meaning it is given through action in the present.[36]

Drawing a relationship between memory and imagination, Boyarin argues for the "potential for creative collaboration between present consciousness and the experience or expression of the past." Through fostering such a process, this book also seeks to influence the landscape of the future.

Today, Native America continues to be located on the periphery of America in the minds of most Americans, despite the fact that this country continues to be home to over five hundred indigenous nations. Many American children are still taught that Indians are "fixed" in the landscape of the past. And although there has been a growing effort to include Native texts both in the canon of American literature and in the conversations of critics, Native studies remains on the periphery of American studies. I remember being disturbed to open up a fairly recent volume titled *The Futures of American Studies* to find that not one indigenous scholar had been included in the collection of essays and that "Native Americans" were treated only momentarily and largely as subjects of study, not as intellectuals who might have something to say about the future of the field. Native American studies was framed as one of many marginalized and somewhat passé "discourses," lumped in with "African American studies, Asian American studies, Chicano/a studies ... women's studies, [and] queer studies," all of which, according to the authors, "display a tendency towards a monocausal essentialism or identity politics in terms of race, ethnicity, gender, sex, or territory," in comparison to "border discourses," which "deconstruct" this tendency through a focus on "complex interactive dynamics" and "multiple interactions." The authors seemed oblivious that the "multiple interactions" of Native America might be central to the study of America and unaware that Native American studies represents a diversified and interactive interdisciplinary field and methodological framework with which they might directly engage. This oversight was particularly striking in relationship to "territory" as a category. This seemed to be one more example of the displacement of Native people (and Native territorial claims) from the territory of America onto the fringes and frontiers of American space and, once more, into the past.[37]

As Konkle views this predicament, it is not simply an error of omission but lies at the heart of the underlying political psychology of the American nation. She writes, "Native peoples' connection to land is not just cultural, as it is usually, and often sentimentally, understood; it is also political — about governments, boundaries, authority over people and territory." And the emphasis on Native peoples' "chronological precedence" (they *were* the ones who *were* here *before*) rather than "a claim to geography" (this *is* Abenaki, Wampanoag, or Mohawk land; these *are* Nipmuc, Narragansett, and Pequot people; this *is* the Mohegan, Penobscot, or Seneca nation) is a rhetorical construction that has political power. It is one way that Americans have historically resolved the problem of "what to do about these 'indigenous residents' ... who, inconveniently, didn't just disappear" — place them in the territory of the past. After all, if there are no "real" Indians left, there are no "real" Indian land claims.[38]

Those of us in American studies have a responsibility to think carefully through the problematic relationship between Native nations and the United States, as well as our own embeddedness in this fraught political territory. As Konkle discusses recent trends in American literary studies, she notes that "Native American literature has been incorporated into a narrative of the multi-cultural coherence of the United States, where Native peoples constitute one of many ethnic groups to be recognized and appreciated through their literary works." However, as Konkle argues, within much of this scholarship "Native political struggles" are nearly absent, and, in particular, the ongoing colonial status of the United States and Native nations' continuing battles, in public, in private, and in print, are elided. The irony of this predicament, as will be apparent in the chapters that follow, is that so much Native writing is focused on the very subjects that are often absent from the contemporary scholarship. In concert with Konkle, literary scholar Chad Allen notes in his discussion of indigenous literature and postcolonialism that "the United States has been included in studies of 'settler colonies' only rarely, with little attention paid to American Indians or their textual production. Although various multiculturalist projects have brought a greater number of American Indian texts into the American literary canon, they have often done so by leveling distinctions between peoples indigenous to what is now the United States and other nondominant U.S. 'minorities.'" Whether through the incorporation of Native people into a multicultural melting pot or the displacement of Native people in time, these frameworks serve to erase the "distinction between America as geographic space, and the United States as a political entity that is common in Native discourse." That is, in the words of Konkle, "Native peoples' connection to land precedes and persists through European colonization and the formation of the United States to the present day."[39]

Finally, as Bill Ashcroft argues in *On Post-Colonial Futures*, even the ways by which we determine what constitutes "literature" are lodged in colonial frameworks. He writes, "When we examine the surprisingly recent development of the field called English literature we discover how firmly it is rooted in the cultural relationships established by British imperialism. The discipline of English was conceived, initiated, and implemented as a programme of cultural study. Virtually from its inception, it existed as a promotion of English national culture under the guise of the advancement of civilization." And he further argues: "One can either accept the orthodoxy of English literature with its huge edifice of disciplinary and cultural assumptions (as is often still the case in post-colonial societies), one can reject it and leave it altogether, or one can interpolate a local view of cultural textuality." The latter, I believe, is what I am trying to achieve herein. The writings that follow, like much "postcolonial writing," are "conceived in a dynamic of political and cultural engagement at both the discursive and institutional level, [and therefore are] peculiarly placed to initiate cultural transformation. Political and social change only occur because they occur in the minds of those who imagine a different kind of world."[40] Together, these texts represent an alternative framework for conceiving literature, drawn from a culturally specific view of textuality, which may have applications and implications far beyond the region and time from which they first emerged. In this sense, writing is a tool both in the time and place in which it is used and for the education of future generations.

I sincerely hope that the field is ripe for such imaginative transformation and that some of the important works that we have seen emerge in recent years represent a new development in regard to the place of Native space in the field of American studies. The recovery of indigenous voices and indigenous knowledge is instrumental not only to the adaptation and survival of Native nations but to a deeper and more complex engagement with the past, present, and future landscape of America, however we might define it.

A Map to the Chapters

Because this book seeks to speak to multiple audiences, different people may be drawn to different aspects of the book. The richness of historical detail may appeal to historians interested in the Native northeast and Native people about whose communities I am writing. At times, these are the morsels I most crave. Other readers may find the details tedious and will be inclined to browse through those sections; literary readers in particular may be more interested in the textual analysis, the interpretation of text-maps through the frameworks of indigenous language. Others might be drawn to a particular place on which a chapter is focused, whether for their own research or because of a relationship to that place. Thus, I'm including a brief map to the chapters to guide readers to the places that they might be most inclined to visit.

The first five chapters form the body of the book, and as I have noted, each chapter begins with an *awikhigan*, then expands into the place-world from which it emerges and in which it operates. While the fifth chapter functions as a culmination, the final two chapters serve as a denouement, concluding thought pieces that operate in a reflective mode, building on the previous chapters to generate insight into this literary tradition while circling back to key themes raised in this Introduction.

There is a stylistic progression of chapters, from an emphasis on comprehending the historical context through which we read these texts to a display of the depth of literary analysis that can emerge once the reader is grounded in the historical, cultural, and political geography of Native space. The first four chapters are more historical; each is a mapping of a place-world that revolves around a network of Native texts. The last three chapters have a more literary slant; they include a close reading of an increasingly popular Native text within an Algonquian linguistic framework, a summary analysis of the preceding chapters that delineates the genres of indigenous writing, and a conclusion on the intertwining of orality and literacy in this spatial writing tradition.

There is also a progression of textual production. This is meant to represent not a progression in time, a chronological development of Native writing, but a progression, in the space of the text, from a single petition to a group of interlocking petitions that are part of a written communal history, to treaties and journey journals, to a multivoiced published narrative that contains both petitions and communal history, and finally to a culmination in William Apess's *Eulogy on King Philip*, a text that perhaps contains all forms.

Chapter 1, "*Alnôbawôgan, Wlôgan, Awikhigan:* Entering Native Space," is the proper introduction to the book, drawing readers into Native space and laying out the meanings of key terms. I admit that I mean to plunk readers right in the middle of the territory and provide a map to enable navigation. (If you feel a bit disoriented, that's okay. You'll find your way. Use the maps.)

This chapter continues by introducing a single petition, posted on an English fort in the Connecticut River valley by four Native men in Abenaki territory. We begin in the interior, in a center of trade and exchange, and in the north. The history of the beaver wars, the French and Indian wars, and the Anglo-Abenaki wars opens up from here as we track the petition through an extensive network of waterways and relations and come to understand its meaning through the lens of traditional stories. Here we also see the processes through which the "common pot" is transformed, physically and conceptually, from an abundant bowl that feeds the whole to an inescapable dish enmeshed in conflict, to a clearing in which its participants strive to create a kettle of peace, and finally to a dish reclaimed in an attempt to protect its inhabitants from the sources of its destruction. This chapter serves as a model for reading indigenous texts within the network of rivers and relations, and it illuminates the understanding that can emerge when we view them through a culturally and historically specific lens. Finally, it explores the multiple routes through which writing entered this particular Native space.

Whereas the first chapter looks at the common pot as a vast web of familial, political, and geographic relationships, the second focuses on the common pot as the village and is concerned with its reconstruction. In chapter 2, "Restoring a Dish Turned Upside Down: Samson Occom, the Mohegan Land Case, and the Writing of Communal Remembrance," we take a journey deep into the politics of the Mohegan land case, a legal battle that spanned nearly a century, in which writing played an instrumental role. For this chapter we move downriver, to the mouth of the Connecticut River and the southern coast, where wampum emerged. The history of the wampum wars, the split between the Pequots and the Mohegans, and the subsequent division and reconstruction of the Mohegan communal body are explored through a series of Mohegan-authored texts, with a lens drawn from oral literature. As the relationship between wampum and the written word becomes apparent, we will also encounter two more categories of writing: communal histories and the formalized agreements between nations.

This chapter also emphasizes the need to read individual authors such as Samson Occom within a network of relations, and it examines how our view of Occom changes when we consider his role in the Mohegan land case. Most of the scholarship on Occom centers his life and writings around his relationship with Eleazar Wheelock and the Indian Charity School at Lebanon (later Dartmouth College). By foregrounding his role as a leader at Mohegan, a very different picture emerges. The emphasis on Wheelock (as if this was Occom's primary relationship) and the Indian school (as if Lebanon was his "home and center") has skewed our perceptions of the role of this colonial institution in Occom's life and in Native New England. By centering his life and writings around other spaces and allowing Wheelock to remain in the background, we can see that Wheelock's home was only one site within Occom's extensive network and that the school was operating not only as a colonial project but as a location within Native space.

In chapter 3, the need to maintain relationships in the regional network of the "dish with one spoon" and the need to look after the needs of the local community "kettle" come into relational opposition. This chapter, "Two Paths to Peace: Competing Visions of the Common Pot," opens with Mahican leader Hendrick Aupaumut's account of his confrontation with Mohawk leader Joseph Brant at Niagara in the wake of the American Revolution. We track the conflict between the two men back to the Connecticut River valley through the American Revolution, then travel west with them, through the network of rivers and relations, to the Ohio Valley, where each attempted to mediate a peace between the newly formed United States and the "United Indian Nations."

The persistence of indigenous political systems, relationships, and epistemologies even as the United States materialized as a political body is evident in the journey and treaty journals of Brant and Aupaumut. These texts, which form the foundation of this chapter, present a very different vision of the historical landscape during the period that is most often referred to as that of the early republic. Further, this chapter demonstrates the importance of understanding intellectuals such as Brant and Aupaumut in relation to and in conflict with each other, as leaders in dialectical critique and within the context of their particular positions in Native space.

Chapter 4 returns to the village dish and its regeneration. Focusing on Pequot author William Apess's account of the Mashpee Woodland Revolt, *Indian Nullification of the Unconstitutional Laws of Massachusetts Relative to the Mashpee Tribe*, we move southeast from Apess's birthplace in the Connecticut River valley, following his return to Pequot and then his journey, farther east, to join the Wampanoags at Mashpee. This chapter, "Regenerating the Village Dish: William Apess and the Mashpee Woodland Revolt," tells a story of Native resilience, long after the United States had taken hold, in the "commonwealth" that laid the greatest claim to its birth. This chapter shows how Native people used not only writing but the political rhetoric of American independence to reassert their indigenous claims to land, as well as the right to maintain their own resources. This chapter builds on the exploration of treaties and communal histories to analyze Apess's *Indian Nullification*, and it delves into the continuing use of writing as a powerful instrument of change.

Chapter 5 extends from the previous chapters, revisiting the idea of the common pot as an expansive network of relations while remaining focused on the writing of William Apess. This chapter, "Envisioning New England as Native Space: William Apess's *Eulogy on King Philip*," positions Apess's final work as an apex of Native northeastern writing in this period. In the *Eulogy*, Apess reclaims the historical landscape and envisions an alternate future, presenting a model for us to consider carefully today. In many ways, all of the themes and forms of the previous chapters are tied to this one. Here the place-world is all of New England, a multilayered landscape of diverse and often conflicting inhabitants that continues to be Native space. The theme of writing as an instrument of transformation comes to the fore in Apess's work, and thus this chapter also marks a turn to the literary with a close reading of Apess's provocative text through a framework drawn from Algonquian linguistics.

Chapter 6, "*Awikhigawôgan*: Mapping the Genres of Indigenous Writing in the Network of Relations," is mainly for those interested in the literary implications of this tradition of indigenous writing. This chapter, while telling some interesting stories about students who escape from mission schools and speakers who contradict English versions of treaties, lays out a map of the genres of indigenous writing. This map traces the relationships between earlier indigenous forms, such as birchbark *awikhiganak* and wampum, and the modes of writing that Native people most frequently employed during the eighteenth and nineteenth centuries, including petitions, letters, journey journals, treaties, and communal histories. Some scholars, both academic and community-oriented, may find the discussion of treaty literature and communal histories particularly interesting. This chapter reflects on the form and function of the writings discussed in previous chapters and returns to a discussion of the implications of writing as both activity and instrument in the common pot.

Chapter 7, "Concluding Thoughts from Wabanaki Space: Literacy and the Oral Tradition," returns to the interior of the north, reflecting briefly on the representations of writing Indians by James Fenimore Cooper and Henry David Thoreau, then moving into an exploration of the text-maps published by several Wabanaki writers in the late nineteenth and early twentieth centuries. These *awikhiganak* were used in their own time as tools to instruct Abenaki and Penobscot people in English, but they are being used today in the retention and recovery of indigenous languages and oral traditions. They contain critical knowledge about particular places, as well as the words, concepts, and stories that are the maps, the language, of the land. These writings are crucial examples of the role that books can play as vehicles for the storage of knowledge and instruments for regeneration. At the same time, they also reflect the idea, raised in this Introduction, that in practice writing and the oral tradition have often been traveling companions, at least in the Native space of the northeast.

The Writing, the Walking, and the Reading Are the Same Thing

In *Decolonizing Methodologies*, Linda Tuhiwai Smith writes:

> Coming to know the past has been part of the critical pedagogy of decolonization. To hold alternative histories is to hold alternative knowledges. The pedagogical implication of this access to alternative knowledges is that they can form the basis of alternative ways of doing things. Transforming our colonized views of our own history (as written by the West), however, requires us to revisit, site by site, our history under Western eyes. This in turn requires a theory or approach which helps us to engage with, understand and then act upon history.[41]

Similarly, in *Justice, Nature, and the Geography of Difference* David Harvey suggests, "The reconstruction of places can reveal hidden memories that hold out the prospects for different futures."[42] For me, the researching and writing of this book has been such a process, with the result that one of its overall goals is not so much to convince the rest of the world to turn their eyes and ears to a "truer" history but to enable a process of reclaiming and reknowing that historical landscape for ourselves in the hope that it will lay out possible paths to "different futures." In this respect, this project has always been a shared endeavor, and as I have returned to it over the course of the past year, this work has been further shaped through my interactions with the people and places with whom this history is shared.

You might say that my own training began on the ground, in the Abenaki network of relations to which I belong. My father was a highly intelligent man who, to my knowledge, never read any of the books on Abenaki or Northeastern Native history (although he did give me both my first book of Native literature and my first copy of Colin Calloway's *The Western Abenaki of Vermont*) but was incredibly knowledgeable about the landscape of our history and was one of my most important teachers. With him, learning the land was learning its stories, and vice versa. There

were lessons I learned on the ground as a child and those that were recalled, many years later, as we walked the mountains or fished the streams.
My father read every paper and story that I gave him, and the questions
he posed to me in the margins were far-reaching and profound. When I
gave him my first essay on the beaver wars, he wrote on the cover page:

> What is sharing?
>
> How do you avoid power?
>
> Is competition evil?
>
> How does jealousy fit in?
>
> Beavers . . . they do affect those downstream and upstream — what
> do they create or destroy?
>
> Were Europeans sent here to disrupt, but then restore balance?
> The future will tell.
>
> Power is based on many virtues, principles, values, etc. . . . It is not
> bad except when it is misused.
>
> Have you ever wondered that humans were introduced to give
> animals an existence or did they have one without?

Many questions to work in my mind as I continued to think, research,
and write.

Long before I ever thought of writing such a book, I learned a
great deal from working in the tribal office of the Abenaki Nation at Missisquoi. Although it is just one of many Abenaki communities that has
adapted and survived in old places, it was certainly the most active during my youth, when I was seeking to understand my own family's history and my place in the network of relations. Returning to these old
grounds up north was probably the most important decision I made as a
young person. In the tribal office, we were embroiled every day in legal
cases involving issues ranging from fishing rights to tribal license plates
to the protection of burials and family hunting lands. I learned as much
from conversations over late-night coffee as I did in the courts, not to
mention what I learned while slogging through the marshes looking for
the tracks that would stop development from eradicating subsistence
grounds and sacred sites. That was also when I first fully grasped the
power of words. While writing this book, I have often thought of Lenny
Lampman, who could travel through marshes like no one else I know
and who helped me understand not only my place but the full picture.
When I think of indigenous knowledge, I think of him. I hope his extensive family will consider this a gift in return.

Finally, my travels in Wabanaki over the years have grounded my writing, and I am grateful for those friends and relations who have invited me into their home territories and have tracked with me through our shared histories. This book is also theirs. Ultimately, my greatest hope is that the words contained herein can in some way contribute to the continuance of our land and to the ongoing regeneration in which every indigenous inhabitant of the North Country now seems to be engaged.

1

Alnôbawôgan, Wlôgan, Awikhigan

Entering Native Space

The Gaspesians do not know how to read nor how to write.
They have, nevertheless, enough understanding and memory
to learn how to do both if only they were willing to give the
necessary application. But aside from the fickleness and
instability of their minds, which they are willing to apply
only in so far as it pleases them, they all have the false and
ridiculous belief that they would not live long if they were
as learned as the French.... Some of these Indians, however,
for whose instruction some trouble has been taken, have in
a short time become philosophers and even pretty good
theologians. But after all, they have ever remained savages.... They have rendered themselves wholly unworthy
by leaving their studies in order to dwell with their fellow-
countrymen in the woods, where they have lived like very
bad philosophers, preferring, on the basis of a foolish
reasoning, the savage to the French life.

—CHRESTIEN LeCLERCQ, *New Relation of Gaspesia*, Kespek, 1691

Alnôbawôgan: Defining Native Space

Buried within the vocabulary at the back of an obscure nineteenth-
century "teaching" book is a word that defines an Algonquian conception

1

of nativity. According to Abenaki author Peter Paul Wzokhilain, *alnôba-wôgan* means both "human nature" and "birth." It is translated literally as the activity of "being (or becoming) human." So it would seem that, in Wabanaki philosophy, the very nature of being human is rooted not in the consciousness of our mortality but in our natality. The missionary Chrestien LeClercq observed that the Mi'kmaq "rejoice all in common on the birth of their children, even to making feasts, public speeches, and all kinds of rejoicings." As part of this celebration, LeClercq observed, the "Indians wash their children in the river as soon as they are born." When Algonquian or Haudenosaunee children were born, they entered into a network of relations: the marriages and kin relationships that connected people and the places they inhabited. These places were connected not only by relationships but by a network of waterways, which people traveled by canoe and footpath from the southeast coast to the northwest lakes (see Map 1.).[1]

In the traditional Haudenosaunee (Iroquois) creation story of Sky Woman, only a mass of water exists beneath the sky, and the water animals are its only inhabitants. When they see a woman falling from a hole in the Sky World, the animals gather in "council together...to devise a way to provide for her." Each animal dives to the bottom of the sea, grasping for mud. Each returns, gasping for air, empty-handed. Finally, muskrat, it is said, dives deep down into the water until he can go no farther, grasps a handful of earth in his paw, and rises to the surface. He gives up his life, but in his last breath, he releases the mud onto turtle's back. Geese fly up to catch Sky Woman in their wings, and, as they lay her on turtle's back, the woman releases a seed she had carried from the Sky World, and the earth is born.[2]

The story of Sky Woman emphasizes the primacy of water in the northeastern landscape. Sky Woman enters a world of water and water beings from within which the land emerges. The story suggests that the earth is neither solid nor constant, but exists only through the interrelated activity of its inhabitants. Moreover, the creation of the earth requires thought. The story emphasizes the resourceful intelligence of the water animals and of Sky Woman herself. The thinking that results in creation is cooperative, drawing on the insights and abilities of all members of the group to solve the problem at hand. As the newest arrival, Sky Woman becomes a participant rather than being portrayed as an outsider. Before falling though a hole in the Sky World, she reaches out to grab a seed from a tree, with the thought of earth in mind. When she arrives in the water world, she plants the seed, making her own contribution, as the

Map 1. The indigenous northeast: a network of waterways.

grandmother of all humans, to creation. Rather than being planted in a void by a divine male creator, the earth requires the conduit of a woman's body and mind.

Both the Abenaki word *alnôbawôgan* and the Haudenosaunee story of Sky Woman connect nativity to human emergence and the active state of transformation that birth implies. This framework provides a striking contrast to conventional constructions of Native "tradition" as static and inherently mortal while confirming the idea of tradition as an ongoing process, both cyclical and transformative. When Europeans arrived on the Algonquian coast, they entered into this Native space: a network of relations and waterways containing many different groups of people as well as animal, plant, and rock beings that was sustained through the constant transformative "being" of its inhabitants.

Wlôgan: Defining the Common Pot

The conceptualization of a cooperative, interdependent Native environment emerges from within Native space as a prominent trope in the speeches and writings of the eighteenth and nineteenth centuries, reflected in the metaphor of the "common pot." Although the concept was rooted in earlier traditions, Native writers evoked it more frequently as colonial control over Native lands increased.[3] The common pot is that which feeds and nourishes. It is the wigwam that feeds the family, the village that feeds the community, the networks that sustain the village. Women are the creators of these vessels; all people come from them, and with their hands and minds they transform the bodies of their animal and plant relatives into nourishment for their families. The pot is made from the flesh of birch trees or the clay of the earth. It can carry or hold; it can be carried or reconstructed; it can withstand fire and water, and, in fact, it uses these elements to transform that which it contains. The pot is Sky Woman's body, the network of relations that must nourish and reproduce itself.

In the Abenaki language, the word for "dish" is *wlôgan*.[4] This word has a direct linguistic relationship to the word for the river intervales where Abenaki families flourished: *wôlhanak*. These "hollowed-out places" were not empty spaces to be filled but deeply situated social and ecological environments. There is a certain poetic resonance between these words and the phrase that invokes "thanks to all our relations," *wlidô-gawôgan*. In the coincidental formation of letters, "all our relations" can be contained within the "dish."[5] The land, *aki*, is a self-sustaining vessel, but it requires participation from all its interwoven inhabitants. When humans deliberate on their relationships to the other beings in their *wôl-hana*, their thoughts lead to more conscientious action within that environment. Every human community in the northeast has a way of thinking through their relationships to others, of forming and renewing relations through ceremonial councils, and of acknowledging their dependence on nonhuman inhabitants through rituals of thanksgiving.

For example, as Seneca scholar Arthur Parker explained, whenever the Haudenosaunee hold a Confederacy council, they open with the Thanksgiving Address, offering

> thanks to the earth where men dwell, to the streams of water, the pools, the springs and the lakes, to the maize and the fruits, to the medicinal herbs and trees, to the forest trees for their usefulness, to the animals that serve as food and give their pelts for clothing, to the great winds and the lesser winds, to the Thunderers, to the Sun, the mighty warrior, to the moon, to the messengers of the Creator who reveal his wishes and to the Great Creator who dwells in the heavens above, who gives all the things useful to men, and who is the source and the ruler of health and life.[6]

The address calls the community to deliberate on the dish that sustains it. This opening encourages people to acknowledge that they draw their

life from these many beings and are indebted to them for their continuance. The ceremony invokes shared space, making the longhouse a microcosm of the world and reminding humans of their place in it.

Roger Williams observed the other side of the cyclical dish as it
manifested itself among the Narragansetts in the seventeenth century:
"Whoever commeth in when they are eating, they offer them to eat of
that which they have, though but little enough prepared for themselves.
If any provision of fish or flesh come in, they make their neighbors par-
takers with them."[7] Inherent in the concept of the common pot is the
idea that whatever was given from the larger network of inhabitants had
to be shared within the human community. This ethic was not an altruis-
tic ideal but a practice that was necessary to human survival. Sharing
space meant sharing resources, and Algonquian and Haudenosaunee
communities relied on equal distribution to ensure social stability and
physical health. All inhabitants of the pot were fed from the pot and
were part of the pot. Every part affected the whole. If one person went
hungry, if certain individuals were excluded from the bounty of the dish,
the whole would face physical and/or psychological repercussions from
this rupture in the network of relations.

The common pot was invoked in daily life and in ceremony, as
the missionary John Sergeant observed at a Mohican gathering in the
eighteenth century:

> After we had been there for some time, two Men, appointed for the
> Service, took a Deer down that hung up in the wigwam, which was
> to be offer'd, and laid the four quarters upon a bark in the Middle
> of the House, (the Rest sitting round very serious;) the Skin was
> taken off with the entire Head and Neck to the Shoulders; the four
> Quarters were laid one upon another, and the Skin, doubled length
> wise, was laid upon them, so as to make it look as much like a whole
> Deer as might be. When this was done, an elderly Man, appointed
> for that Purpose, stood up over it; and, with a pretty loud Voice,
> spake to the following purpose. "O great God pity us, grant us
> Food to eat, afford us good and comfortable sleep, preserve us from
> being devoured by the Fowls that fly in the Air. This Deer is given
> in Token that we acknowledge thee the Giver of all Things." . . .
> After these Ceremonies were ended, the two Men before mentioned,
> cut the Deer in Pieces and boil'd it; and when it was made ready, a
> piece was given to every one, of which they all eat, except he that
> offer'd it, (for he eats none of it) which is to signify it is a Gift, and
> therefore free, and he desires none of it back again. While they were

eating, one of the Waiters gave the Skin with the Feet, and some of the Inwards, to an old Widow Woman, which is a Deed of Charity they always practice upon such Occasions.[8]

This Mohican ceremony enacted distribution of resources, equality between community members, and the interdependency inherent in the network of relations, but it also emphasized the role of human action in rebalancing a loss in the network. People had the right and the responsibility to give part of their share to another person, especially to one who had suffered a loss or was in need, but they did not have the right to take more for themselves than they required for subsistence. Leaders often established their status by giving away what they had acquired to other community members. The consequences of disrupting the distributive flow of energy could be dire. Numerous Abenaki stories tell of the disastrous effects of hoarding resources and acting on selfish impulse, while the Haudenosaunee creation story emphasizes the critical difference between participatory thinking and impulsive action. Any act, whether destructive or creative, reverberates in the network of relations. When the network falls out of balance, everything else must shift into action to create a new equilibrium. Here lay the central problem with European newcomers. As soon as Europeans settled on the coast, they became inhabitants in Native space. In the common pot, shared space means shared consequences and shared pain. The actions of the newcomers would affect the whole.[9]

The Jesuit priest Pierre Biard recorded one of the earliest criticisms of European behavior among the Mi'kmaq of the northeast coast. According to the missionary, "They consider themselves better than the French traders and fishermen; 'For,' they say, 'you never cease fighting and quarreling amongst yourselves; as for ourselves, we live in peace; you are envious of each other, and usually disparage each other; you are thieves and liars; you are covetous, without generosity and mercy; as for us, if we have a piece of bread, we divide it amongst ourselves.'"[10] Although Biard himself dismissed this statement as "self-deception," such quotes are emblematic of the common trope of the "noble savage" in French and English texts, which were often used to critique European culture. Yet the statement also has specific meaning within an Algonquian context. The Mi'kmaq were not merely asserting moral superiority but were expressing profound concern for the consequences of acquisitiveness. They were speaking largely of the fishermen and traders on their coasts, who demonstrated, on a daily basis, a desire for resources that seemed unquenchable. The maintenance of the common pot relied on awareness of the delicate balance of give and take, and Europeans appeared to have little understanding of this system or of their role in it.

Many northeastern people recognized that Europeans had already suffered repercussions in their own land. Roger Williams related that the Narragansetts believed that the English had traveled across the sea because they had burned up all their wood. "Have you no trees?" the Narragansetts asked their new neighbors.[11] The Mi'kmaq had similar suspicions about the French. In ironic contrast to Biard, some apparently believed that it was the Jesuits and traders who "deceive[d]" themselves. According to Chrestien LeClercq, a Mi'kmaq leader asked the fishermen and traders at Kespek:

> If France, as thou sayest, is a little terrestrial paradise, art though sensible to leave it? And why abandon wives, children, relatives, and friends? Why risk thy life and property every year... to the storms and tempests of the sea in order to come to a strange and barbarous country which thou considerest the poorest and least fortunate of the world? Besides, since we are wholly convinced of the contrary, we scarcely take the trouble to go to France... seeing, in our own experience, that those who are natives thereof leave it every year in order to enrich themselves on our shores.... Learn now, my brother, once for all, because I must open to thee my heart: there is no Indian who does not consider himself infinitely more happy and more powerful than the French.[12]

Europeans were in the common pot, whether they knew it or not, and they had brought with them ideas, behaviors, and materials that could potentially disrupt or even destroy it. A central question that arose in Native communities throughout the northeast had to do with how to incorporate the "beings" from Europe into Native space and how to maintain the network of relations in the wake of the consequences — including disease and resource depletion — that Europeans brought to Algonquian shores. This question would play an important role in the conversation among Native leaders in the northeast for four centuries, and that conversation would become manifest through one of the most powerful "beings" brought over from Europe: the written word.

Williams claimed that when the Narragansetts encountered English writing, they said, "Manittowoc," which Williams translated as, "They are Gods."[13] However, a more accurate translation suggests that the Narragansetts believed writing "held *Manitou*," the power of transformation. As Karim Tiro has insightfully observed,

> It is unlikely that the Indians Williams met mistook the English for gods; rather, they acknowledged that the "Bookes and Letters" themselves manifested an abundance of *Manitou,* the spiritual power that suffused things in varying degrees.... However, Native recognition of *Manitou* was not necessarily a mark of approbation, because *Manitou* was ambivalent power. It could be creative, but it could be destructive as well. Their assessment proved to be close to the mark.[14]

Mi'kmaqs held a similar belief about books and letters. LeClercq observed, "They suppose that there is some enchantment or jugglery in them," he wrote, "or that this letter has a mind, because, say they, it has the virtue of telling to him who receives it everything which is said and everything which is done, even the most hidden and most secret."[15] It was among these Mi'kmaq that writing began to transform in Native space.

Awikhigan: Writing in the Network of Relations (Kespek, 1677)

In a village at Kespek, "the last land," on the extreme northeast coast of Wabanaki, children circle around a "black robe," reciting a prayer. A couple of the children pick up birchbark fragments that their mothers have discarded from the baskets they are making, along with some charcoal from the fire used to cook their morning's meal. As the priest speaks, the children scrape charcoal on birch. It takes a while for the missionary to catch on, but when he does, he is utterly astonished that, all on their own, the children have developed a system for writing and remembering the Lord's Prayer. Each phrase is represented by a figure, and each child uses his or her own set of "characters." The priest decides to institute their technique. He makes the characters uniform and has each child copy them onto birchbark with charcoal. Parents begin to follow their children's lead. When the missionary leaves for six months and then returns, he finds that the birchbark scrolls have traveled along the rivers and spread throughout the interior villages. He observes that even relations "who had come from a long distance... could already decipher the characters with as much ease as if they had always lived among us."[16]

In this way, these birchbark writings traveled rapidly over rivers through the network of relations. LeClercq noted, "The principal advantage and usefulness which results from this new method is this, that the

Indians instruct one another in whatsoever place they may happen to be. Thus the son teaches his father, the mother her children, the wife her husband, and the children the old men." In this way, communities adapted an old technology within an extant system of communication to pass new knowledge through Native space.[17]

This process of transmission was not an entirely new phenomenon; the children's impulse arose from a familiar practice. The Jesuit Gabriel Druillettes, who lived among the Norridgewocks on the Kennebec River, farther down the Wabanaki coast, had observed the same kind of writing some twenty-five years before LeClercq's arrival in "Gaspesia": "Some would write their lessons after a fashion of their own, using a bit of charcoal for a pen, and a piece of bark instead of paper.... They used certain signs corresponding to their ideas; as it were, a local reminder, for recalling points and articles and maxims which they had retained. They carried away these papers with them, to study their lessons in the quiet of the night."[18] LeClercq himself observed: "They have much ingenuity in drawing upon bark a kind of map which marks exactly all the rivers and streams of a country of which they wish to make a representation. They mark all the places thereon exactly and so well that they make use of them successfully, and an Indian who possesses one makes long voyages without going astray."[19]

Indeed, the *Jesuit Relations* are full of references to *awikhiganak*, writings on birchbark (see Figures 1 and 2). They were used for making messages, remembering songs, and recording stories and communal history. Hunters would commonly post pictographic "message maps" on trees to inform each other of the location of game and the routes they would travel. As LeClercq noted, rivers and streams appeared prominently on indigenous maps, and it was along these waterways that messages were carried from village to village. *Awikhiganak* conveyed knowledge from one person or place to another across the system of waterways that connected them.[20]

Wampum, another form of indigenous "writing," moved along these same rivers. All wampum originated in coastal villages between the Muhhekunnutuk (Hudson) River and Narragansett Bay, traveling upriver to inland sites of exchange, then on to Wabanaki and Haudenosaunee territory to the north and west (see Map 2.).

Women wove wampum beads into strings and belts that represented the binds between nations, recorded communal narratives and commitments, and enacted renewal and change (see Figure 3). According

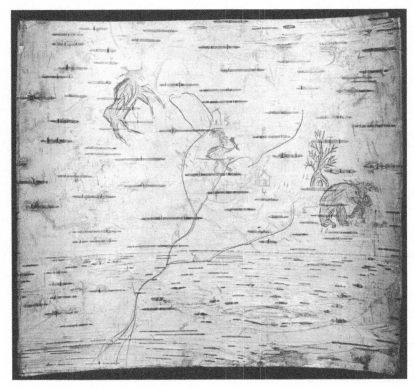

Figure 1. Passamaquoddy birchbark scroll, ca. 1877. Department of
Anthropology, Smithsonian Institution, cat. no. 393432.

to Arthur Parker, the Haudenosaunee used wampum as a mnemonic de-
vice to "call to mind" the "laws" that held the Confederacy together, to
"record matters of national or international importance," to symbolize
political relationships, to condole those in grief, and to secure a "pledge
of truth." The Jesuit Jerome Lalemant, who was familiar with both Haudenosaunee and Algonquian customs, wrote of wampum, "Presents
among these peoples dispatch all the affairs of the country. They dry up
tears; they appease anger; they open the doors of foreign countries; they
deliver prisoners; they revive the dead: one hardly ever speaks or answers except by presents. That is why, in the harangues, a present passes
for a word." While *awikhiganak* were often temporary, characterized by
their "portability," wampum symbolized permanence. When an agreement, an alliance, or an event was put in wampum, a transformation in
Native space was solidified.[21]

Figure 2. Montagnais birchbark scroll with writing in French. Copyright
2007 Harvard University, Peabody Museum, 94-38-10/52507 N35423.

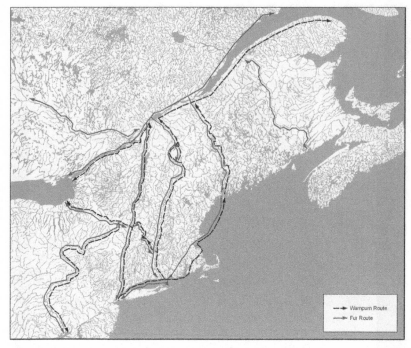

Map 2. Major routes of the wampum and fur trade, from the southeast
coast to Ktsitekw, the St. Lawrence River.

Both *awikhiganak* and wampum exemplify a spatialized writing
tradition. Geographer G. Malcolm Lewis has written extensively on Native mapmaking during the "encounter," noting that although "writing"
as Europeans knew it "did not exist among Native North Americans,"
Native people quickly began using maps "to communicate to whites," a
phenomenon that occurred "much less frequently" in the reverse. According to Lewis, "A shared nonlinguistic mode for communicating spatial
information emerged quickly and spontaneously," and Native people
"were almost certainly drawing on an indigenous pictographic method
for leaving messages and recording cultural traditions." *Awikhiganak* and
wampum were facets of an indigenous writing system that was based on
"cartographic principles." The graphic symbols used in both forms represented the relationships between people, between places, between humans
and nonhumans, between the waterways that joined them. The communal stories recorded on birchbark and in wampum would even connect
people with their relations across time, bringing the past, present, and
future into the same space.[22]

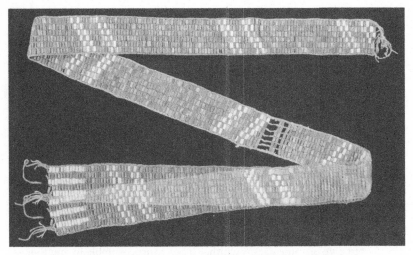

Figure 3. Wampum belt. Copyright 2007 Harvard University, Peabody Museum, 03-9-10/62375 N28261. Lake Constance, Ontario, ca. 1600.

In the chapters that follow I explore the ways in which the writing that came from Europe was incorporated into this spatialized system. It is no coincidence that the word *awikhigan* came to encompass letters and books or that wampum and writing were used concurrently to bind words to deeds. Transformations occurred when the European system entered Native space. Birchbark messages became letters and petitions, wampum records became treaties, and journey pictographs became written "journals" that contained similar geographic and relational markers, while histories recorded on birchbark and wampum became written communal narratives. All of these forms were prolific in the northeast long before Indian people began writing poetry and fiction. These texts, which emerged from within Native space, represent an indigenous American literary tradition.[23]

Awikhiganak in the Great Beaver's Bowl: Pinewans's Network of Relations (Kwinitekw, 1747)

In the spring of 1747, an Abenaki raiding party posted an *awikhigan* outside an English fort on the "long river," Kwinitekw. It read:

> Gentlemen. Whereas there have been very grievous complaints in the province of —— with respect to ye support and maintenance of your frontiers in a time of war, we . . . have undertaken to free

you from such an extraordinary charge by killing & taking captive the people & driving them off & firing their fortifications. And so successful have we been in this affair that we have broke up almost all the new settlements in your western frontiers: so that you need not be at one half the charge you were in the year past in maintaining a war in those parts: for now there are but little else besides the old towns, and if they will not fortifie and defend themselves; we think they ought to be left to our mercy. And for this good service that we have done the province, we humbly ask a suitable reward; but if your honours see fit we will wait till a peace is concluded and then receive it in presents. But in the mean time if some small matter of encouragement be given us we will go on to bring your frontiers to a narrower compass still & make your charges still smaller; but if your honours approve of this our design we humbly request of you to give us information whither it be more acceptable to you that we man your defeated garrisons our selves and eat up the provisions which your poor distressed neighbours leave in ym when they flee in their hurry & confusion or whither we burn up the forts with the provisions; for we assure you we find much more in them than we want for our own support whilst carrying on this business. Gentlemen however some may look upon us now yet we can assure you we are your very humble, obsequious servants.[24]

The "petition" was signed by "Old Town, Chee Hoose, Pene wonse, and Prik Fore English, in the name of & on behalf of others."[25] The men gave their location as "Number 2 on Connecticut River," identifying for their English readers a recently constructed settlement in Abenaki space. Although the document, even at first reading, seems a radical text, the full meaning of this *awikhigan* cannot be comprehended unless we enter the network of relations through which the petition's authors traveled and the places to which they belonged. By opening the world of just one of the authors, Pene wonse (often spelled *Pinewans*), and his relationship to the site where he left his message, we can learn volumes about the implications of the text.

Origin Stories: Ktsi Amiskw, the Great Beaver

Ordinarily, Pinewans and his relations might have been coming to this place to fish. Every spring, as the icy floods receded from the banks of the river Kwinitekw, Sokokis (or Sokwakiak), who inhabited the south-

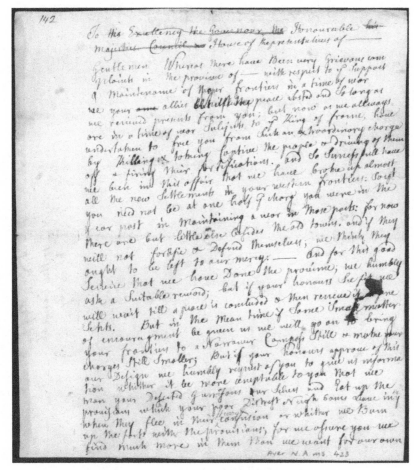

Figure 4. Indian petition to the General Assembly, 1747. Courtesy
Edward E. Ayer Collection, Newberry Library, Chicago.

ernmost stretch of Abenaki country, descended from the uplands just in
time for the arrival at Ktsipôntekw, the "great falls," of the spawning
salmon and shad, which provided needed sustenance after a harsh northeastern winter. Pinewans and his relations were part of an extensive ecological system that reached from Ktsipôntekw to Peskeompscut, the
Pocumtuck "great falls" to the south, where many of the fish stopped before climbing its rocky steps to swim upriver toward Abenaki country.
Kwinitekw's annual flooding provided fertile ground for the women who
planted in the intervale. The "great meadows" where Pinewans posted
his *awikhigan* hosted "some of the best farmlands in the whole valley."

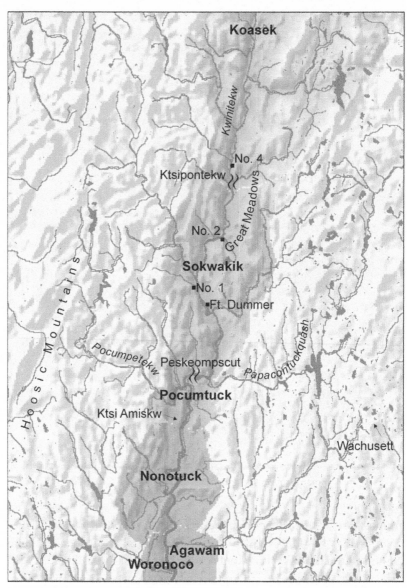

Map 3. The river Kwinitekw from Ktsipôntekw to Peskeompscut, with Native *wôlhanak* highlighted. Note the mountains (Hoosic range and Mount Wachusett) that form geographic and political boundaries between territories and the location of colonial fort settlements within Native space.

The annual planting of corn, beans, and squash stabilized the riverbanks, added nutrients to the soil, and, when abandoned for a new field, created a meadow habitat where waterfowl, game animals, and edible plants abounded. This relationship between the river, fishing, and planting had been ongoing for centuries, perhaps millennia.[26]

Downriver, just below Peskeompscut, lay Ktsi Amiskw, the Great Beaver, looming above the "ancient crossroads" of Pocumtuck. During the great floods, this area had been his pond, and when the waters receded they left behind a long, deep impression in the land that fostered abundant growth. In vital contours of the valley, major centers of inhabitation formed, from the northern "place of pines," Koasek, to the southern place of Sokwakik, and farther downriver to Pocumtuck, Nonotuck, Agawam, and Woronoco. These *wôlhanak* were fertile bowls between mountain ranges that were capable of sustaining the many families who gathered there, forming permanent communities and hosting trading parties who came through with news and goods from far away.[27]

Well-traveled canoe routes and trails spread out from below Ktsi Amiskw, connecting Native homelands. Riverways led northwest to the Winozki and Mazipskoik *wôlhanak* on the eastern shore of Betobakw, the western emergence place of Wabanaki, and "the lake between" Abenaki and Haudenosaunee country. To the northeast were the Penacook *wôlhanak* on the river Molôdemak, leading upriver to the Pemijoasek *wôlhana*, the western intervale of Wôbiadenak, the White Mountains, the central emergence place of Wabanaki. Paths led through the mountains to the eastern *wôlhana* of Pequaket on the Saco River, farther east to the Ammoncogan *wôlhana* on the Androscoggin, and on to the *wôlhana* of Norridgewock on the Kennebec, with riverside trails moving through indigenous settlements to Ktsitekw, the "great river" in the north, and to Sobakw, the sea. From Mount Katahdin, the eastern emergence place of Wabanaki, riverways led to the easternmost *wôlhanak* of the Penobscot, Passamaquoddy, Maliseet, and Mi'kmaq, reaching northeast toward the daily emergence place of the sun. Back at Ktsi Amiskw, trails extended to the east along the river Papacontuckquash to Wachusett Mountain in Nipmuc country and west along the river Pocumpetekw to Mohican territory on the Housatonic and Muhhekunnutuk. Near the central village of Pempotowwuthut, the Muhhekunnutuk travel corridor connected with the Mohawk River and its western routes into Haudenosaunee country. Here the Mohawks maintained the eastern door of the Haudenosaunee Confederacy, which included their relations, the Oneidas, Onondagas,

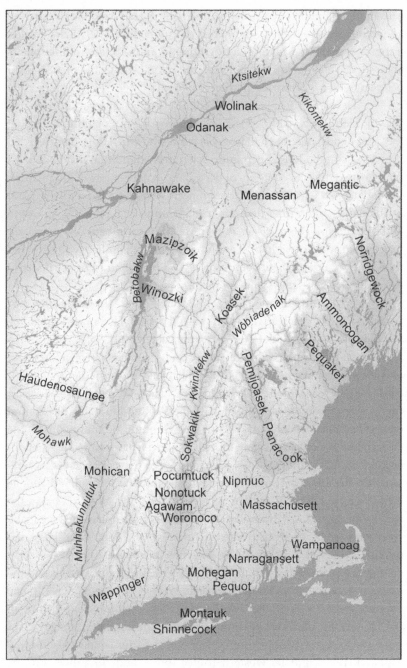

Map 4. The environs of Kwinitekw, showing Wabanaki *wôlhanak*, mission villages, and neighboring Native territories from Sobakw, the sea, to Ktsitekw, the St. Lawrence River.

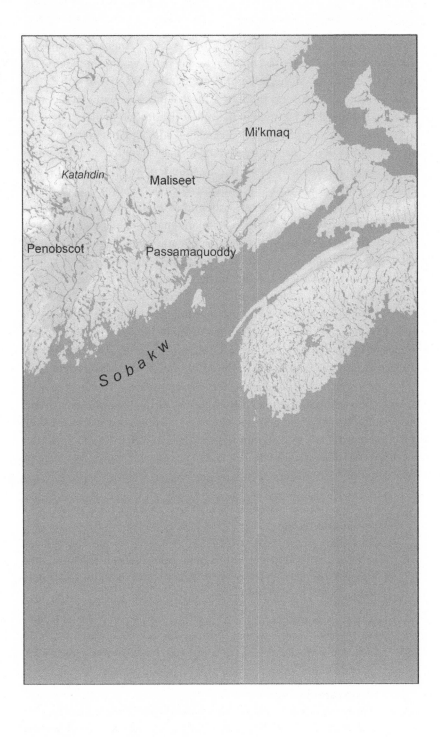

Cayugas, and Senecas. To the south, beyond Ktsi Amiskw, Kwinitekw traveled to the southern coast of Sobakw, where the wampum-making nations of the Niantic, Mohegan, and Pequot gathered by its mouth.[28]

The families who inhabited the Kwinitekw watershed contributed to the shape and growth of the valley. In addition to planting on the riverbanks, women cultivated medicinal and edible plants in the marshes and meadows, while men cultivated the forests through controlled burns and harvests of firewood, ensuring an abundant supply of berries and other low bush growth to support a healthy population of game. Ktsi Amiskw's children, the beavers, abounded in this environment and played a similarly critical role in its maintenance. Their dams created many of the marshes that provided people and animals alike with a diversity of plant foods, as well as habitat for the water animals whose furs and flesh sustained families through long winters. When beavers abandoned a pond to move to another part of the watershed, the marshes transformed into meadows, creating a rich habitat for large animals like deer and bear, as well as the fields of berries that provided so much sweet taste in summer stews. In this way, beavers participated productively, along with humans, in the continuation of this abundant dish.

However, Ktsi Amiskw's story has another side, a tale that arose during the wars that dominated Kwinitekw during the seventeenth and eighteenth centuries and resurfaced in the twentieth century along with the beavers that once more fill the valley. Abenaki writer Cheryl Savageau captured the story in a poem:

At Sugarloaf, 1996
... for Marge Bruchac

i. Ktsi Amiskw
In the big pond, Ktsi Amiskw, the Beaver, is swimming. He has built a dam. The water in his pond grows deeper. He patrols the edges, chasing everyone away. This is all mine, he says. The people and animals grow thirsty.

Cut it out, Creator says. And turns Ktsi Amiskw to stone. The pond is drained. There is water and food for everyone. See those hills, Ktsi Amiskw's head, body, and tail? He's lying there still, this valley his empty pond.

ii. Ktsi Amiskw Dreams
For living out of balance, Ktsi Amiskw lies still, while for centuries, his descendants are trapped in every stream, caught in every river,

killed by the millions for fur-lust from across the sea. Their pelts buy blankets, cloth, weapons, knives.

In this world out of balance, Ktsi Amiskw dreams a hard dream: a world without beavers. Then, far away, like the promise of a winter dawn, he dreams the rivers back, young mothers building, secure in their skins, and a pond full of the slapping tails of children.[29]

Ktsi Amiskw sat above the *wôlhana*, watching as women planted and men fished below. When Europeans entered the Kwinitekw Valley, they brought a desire for beaver pelts and plenty of rum, as well as more useful goods, for trade. Ktsi Amiskw watched as John Pynchon built a trading post downstream, at Agawam, where men traveled with canoes full of skins, returning with iron pots for their wives, guns for themselves, and bellies full of rum. Ktsi Amiskw watched as unfamiliar sicknesses spread through family networks and tore them apart. Pynchon's rum seemed to ameliorate the pain of loss, but also increased the desire for furs and fostered the anger and competition that could lead to violence. Ktsi Amiskw's children became vehicles for the reconstruction of human networks disrupted by disease and warfare. Their pelts were traded for wampum, and people used both as conduits for condolence and reparation. Yet, ironically, competition over the materials required for the ceremonies of rebalancing could lead to further cycles of war. Ktsi Amiskw sat there, watching these transformations in the valley, the whole time.

To the west of Ktsi Amiskw, families on Muhhekunnutuk found themselves in an ideal position for trade with Dutch newcomers on the coast. The Mohicans had been active in indigenous trade networks as far north as Ktsitekw, and they took up this distributive role with European goods as well. Until the Dutch moved upriver and established Fort Orange (later Albany), the Mohawks could acquire European goods only through trade with the Mohicans or people on Ktsitekw, and the Mohicans took advantage of their geographic position by charging the Mohawks tribute. When trade did not work, the Mohawks tried raiding, which led to full-scale war between the two nations for the beaver grounds of the Muhhekunnutuk Valley and to the reversal of the tributary relationship when the Mohawks unleashed the full power of the increasingly forceful Haudenosaunee Confederacy on the Mohicans.[30]

Mohicans had frequently hunted the mountains to the west of Kwinitekw, but as the demand for beavers increased, they appeared more often in the Kwinitekw intervales, seeking to expand their hunting territory through intermarriage and, at times, through war. Some Mohicans sought refuge from Mohawk raids in the villages of their eastern relations. This movement directed Mohawk attention to the marshes of Kwinitekw. Haudenosaunee land, in historian George Hunt's words, was not a "productive beaver ground," and overhunting soon depleted the beaver population in the Muhhekunnutuk and Mohawk Valleys. The connections Mohicans made within the Kwinitekw family network only added justification to Mohawk raiding of the fertile bowl. Ktsi Amiskw watched as the bodies piled up on the banks of the river: beaver skins on Pynchon's table, human flesh in the forests and fields.[31]

This violent redistribution of resources sent the valley through cycles of dissolution and reconstruction. During one winter, a huge number of people gathered to weave themselves together in Ktsi Amiskw's bowl. Sokokis, Pocumtucks, Penacooks, and Mohicans met for three months, cementing relationships through marriage, trade, and ceremony to strengthen the defense of their contiguous lands against Haudenosaunee raids. With this new energy in manifestation, warfare intensified, transforming the landscape of the valley. The people gathered their families on a secluded forest hill northwest of the river, where they built a large fortification. In the winter of 1663, after the completion of harvest, Haudenosaunee warriors attacked the hill settlement, with "heavy losses on both sides." Relations came from the north, south, and east to assist the people on the hill in the defense of their "fort," and they provided refuge in their own villages for the families to recover. Some of the people fled all the way north to the French settlements on Ktsitekw, where several mission villages emerged, including the "town" of Odanak (or St. Francis). In the wake of this shared loss, the Pocumtucks tried to forge a path to peace between the Mohawks and the Sokokis, but the councils were disrupted when a Mohawk chief and his party were killed on their way to Pocumtuck, and then a whole new course of warfare spilled into the Kwinitekw Valley. The raiding was so intense that men were forced to temporarily abandon their fishing sites and women their planting grounds, often subsisting on what could be acquired on the run or through trade.[32]

After the Algonquians of the valley joined together to raid the Mohawks in their own country, the Mohawks launched an overwhelming counterattack on Ktsi Amiskw's home, laying siege to the Pocumtuck *wôlhana* and claiming the whole of the Great Beaver for themselves. The

survivors scattered, leaving their destroyed fields to seek refuge with relations to the north and south. A year later, Englishmen from Massachusetts Bay targeted the seemingly "empty" site for a new settlement. They
would come to call it Deerfield. These settlers would hear the story of the
Great Beaver from the people who returned to their *wôlhana* in the years
to come, and it would become a part of their oral tradition as well.[33]

In the midst of these transformations in Native space, the English desire for land steadily replaced their desire for furs. Stories came
upriver from the sea, traveling along Molôdemak and Kwinitekw, that
the Penacooks and coastal peoples were experiencing land loss and violence as the English craving for space and resources grew. Algonquians
could no longer rely on fur pelts for trade, and traders stacked up their
debts. Meanwhile, beavers were hiding out in enclaves, their abandoned
ponds turning to fields.[34]

Just as harvest was set to begin in 1672, an "old woman" named
Mashalisk, who had likely lost the majority of her family to disease and
warfare and had witnessed the valley's brutal transformation, made a
dramatic move to rebalance a world that had spun out of control. Mashalisk granted a "tract of land" on "Quinetticot River" which was bounded
by "ye lower point of ye Hill called Wequomps" to the trader John Pynchon "for & in consideration of a debt of ten large Bevers & other debts
of Wuttawolunksin her sons."[35] According to Abenaki historian Marge
Bruchac, "Wequomps" refers to "the hill at the end of the Pocumtuck
Range," the formation known to Natives and colonists alike as the Great
Beaver.[36] When Mashalisk sold this land, she transferred the burden of
Ktsi Amiskw's legacy from her own sons to Pynchon and all "his heirs &
assignes forever." And when she received "sixty fada of wampum" from
the trader, he accepted the responsibility. Pynchon thought he was getting the better deal. In return for ten pelts and some strings of shell
beads, he was gaining access to the Great Beaver itself. But Mashalisk
had him fooled.

At the heart of Ktsi Amiskw's story is the danger of acquisitiveness in the common pot. The Great Beaver gets greedy and uses his tal-
ent for building dams to hoard water, and everyone in the bowl suffers
the consequences of his desire. Through the beaver trade, the individual-
istic values for which the Mi'kmaq had expressed such disdain made
their way into the kinship networks that had sustained Algonquian families for millennia. As historian Kenneth Morrison has explained, "The

fur trade challenged the redistributive imperative and made the ideal more difficult to achieve."[37] The result was rupture in the networks that constituted the common pot, violence that spread like rapids through a river, and a shared grief that could not be contained. Still, Ktsi Amiskw's story also contained the seeds of rebalance, planted by one woman who transformed the soil of Kwinitekw, as every woman before her had done in the spring when the waters receded from the shore. She took Ktsi Amiskw's bowl in her hands, full with the season's harvest, and handed over to the trader the legacy of his own greed.

Creating a Kettle of Peace (Deerfield/Pocumtuck, 1735)

In the Petition "at [Fort or Town] No. 2," Pinewans and his relations referred to the "new settlements in your western frontiers," the "old towns," and the "defeated garrisons" and "forts" that English settlers had fled in haste. At the time, these "western frontiers" were merely the southern stretches of Kwinitekw and Molôdemak. Rather than conceding to a constantly expanding "frontier," the "petitioners" referred to multiple "frontiers" in flux, movements up riverways that could be reversed. The petition described a bounded English space that might be brought "to a Narrower compass still." Neither the movement of colonization nor its repulse was naturalized; each was the result of human agency. From the perspective of its authors at the time when the petition was written, the "frontiers" of English expansion were shrinking back toward the coast, where the "old settlements" remained vulnerable. "New settlements" and "forts" constituted not permanent fixtures, evidence of conquest accomplished, but rather temporary, "abandoned" sites within Native space.

To comprehend the petition, we need to understand how these "new settlements" came about, how "frontiers" could fluctuate, and why the petition's authors would have pursued the containment of settler space. The Deerfield Conference of 1735, in which Pinewans and his relations were key participants, provides a gateway to comprehension. This attempt to create a "kettle of peace" took place in the shadow of Ktsi Amiskw and included Abenakis, Mohawks, Mohicans, and English, each with different stakes. Two critical documents emerged: the minutes of the conference and a group of three deeds signed by Pinewans and his relations. Both concerned the land between the two "great falls" of Kwinitekw and the agreements that would allow for shared inhabitation. Before exploring these texts, it is necessary to frame the deeds, the conference, and the subsequent petition within a geographically and historically specific landscape and to map the various routes that participants took to Deerfield.[38]

New Towns, Old Towns

Over the course of several decades and in the wake of war, English settlers moved up Kwinitekw, settling on its banks and acquiring deeds for the new towns of Deerfield and Northfield, located within the Pocumtuck and Sokwakik *wôlhanak*. These deeds often recognized the subsistence rights of Native families who continued to return to the intervales, and conflict over their exact meaning was a factor contributing to the heavy raiding of those settlements in the years that followed. By the time of the Petition at No. 2, Deerfield and Northfield were referred to as "old towns." The new group of deeds that emerged during the Deerfield Conference in 1735 allowed colonial settlement to push farther north into the valley, extending west along the river Pocumpetekw to the mountains that separated the Kwinitekw and Muhhekunnutuk watersheds and east across the river Papacontuckquash to Nipmuc territory at Wachusett Mountain. Pinewans and his brothers signed a deed for the eastern portion and witnessed the deeds for the western and northern sections along with Keewauhoose, or "Chee Hoose," one of the signers of the Petition at No. 2. The deeds they witnessed included all the land below Ktsipôntekw, including the women's fertile fields at Great Meadows.[39] (See Map 5.)

Women's names appeared frequently in deeds concerning Kwinitekw lands, largely because they held the strongest claim to the fields they planted. Mashalisk's deed for Ktsi Amiskw was not an anomaly. When Pinewans and his brothers authorized a deed for their ancestral lands, they signed on behalf of their "deceased" mother, Woolauootaumesqua, along with the son of her sister Nepuscauteusqua, their brother Francis.[40] Their signatures demonstrate the descent of land rights through the female line, but also signify a change in the gender dynamics of land tenure and the strong preference of colonial officials for dealing with male representatives.

Pinewans, his brothers, his cousin, and Keewauhoose signed the deeds with a group of fifteen men and women, all of whom were related through their connection to the "new refugee village" of Schaghticoke, at

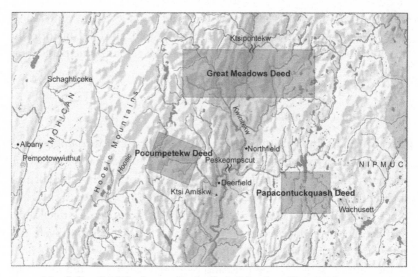

Map 5. Deerfield Conference deeds: Kwinitekw from Ktsipôntekw
to Peskeompscut, with the boundaries of the three deeds outlined.
Note the locations of colonial towns and the new refugee village of
Schaghticoke.

the junction of the Hoosic and Muhhekunnutuk Rivers. This "new town"
emerged when numerous Kwinitekw families fled to their Mohican relations during the colonial conflict known as King Philip's War, which
erupted only a few years after Mashalisk's transfer of Ktsi Amiskw and
sparked what historians Evan Haefeli and Kevin Sweeney call the "Anglo–
Abenaki Wars." As violence spread northwest from the resistance on the
Algonquian coast, thousands of Wampanoags, Narragansetts, and Nip-
mucs joined families from Kwinitekw at a sheltered Sokwakik gathering
place. There, the captive Mary Rowlandson observed, they "asked one
another questions, and laughed, and rejoiced over their gains and victo-
ries." As families took refuge for the winter, they met in council to make
plans for a spring offensive on the English settlements within their
homeland. During the previous fall, the men had repulsed the towns of
Deerfield and Northfield, and in the spring the women once more descended from the uplands to replant their fields on the riverbanks. While
families were gathered at Peskeompscut for the salmon and shad runs,
the English attacked, launching the northernmost raid of the war. This
massacre of hundreds was especially disturbing because Peskeompscut
was recognized as common space. In response to the assault, Kwinitekw's
inhabitants turned to their Mohican neighbors for assistance and were

given a place of asylum beyond the mountains, on another waterway, far from the New England settlements.[41]

Although the "Schaghticokes" came to be identified with the village that the Mohicans and the Albany English created for them, their personal names spoke to the close relationship they maintained with their original homeland. For instance, the name of Pinewans's brother, Wallenas, meant "valley person," while Keewauhoose was likely named for Koasek, the *wôlhana* on the northern stretch of Kwinitekw. The families who sought refuge at Schaghticoke continued to return to Kwinitekw for subsistence and trade (as well as raids) and continued to interconnect with Abenaki relations to the north and east. The Earl of Bellomont expressed concern that the "Eastern Indians" and the Schaghticokes "still retain their friendship and intermarry with each other," while an embittered John Pynchon complained that the Schaghticokes could not be contained despite their status as "protected" Indians, saying, "Sometimes they live at Skachkook, sometimes to the eastward, intermingling with the Eastern Indians, sometimes in Canada." He told the Albany English that they had "nourished vipers" by giving the Kwinitekw natives a refuge. The Albany settlers remarked that the "Eastern Indians" regarded the Schaghticokes as "a part of themselves."[42]

This "intermingling" had become a prominent feature of Native space. Marriage was one of the best ways to make family out of "strangers" or to resolve tensions between groups, and it was instrumental to maintaining ties across geographic distance. During the beaver wars, intermarriage became a common strategy for sharing space, especially as communities took in refugees from families disrupted by disease and warfare. Mohawks, in particular, sought to replace lost family members through the tradition of captive adoption, ironically forging kinship alliances through war. These relationships produced a network of multifaceted family links in the northeast. In the corridors and crossroads of Kwinitekw, people often encountered relatives as they traveled through with hunting, trading, or raiding parties, even if the groups had originated from communities that were a great geographical distance apart. The valley had been transformed not only by warfare but by the marriages that served to defuse it.[43]

These alliances provided strengthened trade relations, places to stay if conflicts arose at home, resources for assistance if food or supplies were short, and coalitions against "a common threat." Thus, Sokokis knew they could seek refuge with the Mohicans and their Abenaki relations to the north when the English struck their home. This dispersal provided for stronger ties and further intermarriage with northern Abenakis, as well as Mohicans and Mohawks who frequented the trading posts at Albany. Meanwhile, on Ktsitekw, the "great river" to the north, a shared religion, ties to the French, and geographical proximity had brought the Abenakis at Odanak and the Mohawks at Kahnawake into closer alliance, while both maintained their affiliations with their relations to the south. Furthermore, both Schaghticokes and northern Abenakis sustained relationships with their eastern cousins from Penacook to Pequaket and even to villages near the coast. All of these groups continued to frequent the Kwinitekw Valley for subsistence, trade, and councils. From within this space, as Haefeli and Sweeney have observed, "Deerfield" emerged as "the center of a web of political, commercial, and familial interests that stretched from Mohawk country in the west to the Canadian mission villages to the north, and to Penacook-Pigwacket country in the east." "Much to the colonists' consternation," they write, "Deerfield remained a vital crossroads for Natives."[44]

Routes to the Deerfield Conference, Relational and Historical

The people who gathered at Deerfield in 1735 represented this reconfigured Native space. Here nations who had learned from the beaver wars that "disputes and quarrels" over resources would "bring on their destruction" arrived at the tail of the beaver to engage in a process that was quite familiar in Native space: they would "eat together" and attempt to create a "kettle of peace."[45] The largest number came from the "Schaghticoke" nation, many of whom were living upriver in their ancestral *wôlhana*. These included Pinewans and his brothers. A number of Mohicans arrived with the Schaghticokes, likely traveling from their village on the Muhhekunnutuk to the Hoosic, then crossing over the mountains and following the course of Pocumpetekw to Kwinitekw. Mohicans from the Housatonic came upriver to join them, while Abenakis from Odanak and Mohawks from Kahnawake traveled from the north together, following Kwinitekw downriver until Ktsi Amiskw came into view.[46]

The *wôlhana* of Pocumtuck had long been an important meetingplace for Native nations, but increasingly it was becoming a space shared by Natives and colonists. The network of relations exemplified by the Deerfield Conference included English people as well. While the governor of Massachusetts, representatives from the King's council, and legislators from the House of Representatives had come to the meeting from colonial centers, at least two of the most prominent figures had entered Kwinitekw's network through captivity. This is an important aspect of the Petition at No. 2 as well. When Pinewans and his relations referred to "taking captive the people," they referred to a practice that was both familiar and terrifying to their English readers.

Two major participants in the conference, Stephen Williams and Joseph Kellogg, had been taken captive as children in the famous 1704 raid on Deerfield by a coalition of Abenakis, Mohawks, French, and Wyandots during the third "Anglo-Abenaki War" (also known as Queen Anne's War). The young Williams spent the winter and spring of 1704 traveling through Abenaki country with the Penacook leader Wattanummon and his relations, living upriver at Koasek, traveling to Winoskik when warfare disrupted subsistence, and finally trekking to the refugee village of Odanak, where he was eventually "redeemed" and returned to his family. In 1735, in the same town from which he had been captured, Stephen Williams attended the conference in the hope of encouraging the Mohicans on the Housatonic to establish a mission at their village of Wnahtukook. He had brought wampum to them the year before to introduce the idea, and some had been receptive. Captives, including several of the Williams clan, often became part of the network of relations, keeping in touch with their "families" long after their release. Colonial and indigenous decisions were often affected by the presence of family members within adopted communities. Stephen's father, John Williams, wrote one of the most famous captivity narratives of his day, but he maintained contact with his "relations" from Odanak, noting friendly visits from his former captors in his journals. Later generations of Abenakis, recalling their relationship to this place and this family, referred to Deerfield as "Williamsecook." Stephen's sister, Eunice, was taken captive as a child to Kahnawake, where she was adopted into a Mohawk family and chose to remain as a Mohawk wife and mother. As an adult, Eunice renewed her kinship ties to her birth family, even visiting her English relations at Deerfield. Despite the Williamses' endless efforts to persuade her to return to her "native home," Eunice was steadfast in her desire to remain at Kahnawake.[47]

While Abenakis sought land reclamation through the Deerfield raid, one of the Mohawks' main motivations was the acquisition of captives. Eunice was taken to replace a mother's only child, and eventually she produced children of her own. The Mohawks took home children from the neighboring Kellogg family as well. Joseph Kellogg, whose grandfather had participated in the attack on Peskeompscut, was carried to Kahnawake along with his brother and two sisters. Both of his sisters remained at the Mohawk village until they were grown women. Joseph was able to take home the youngest, Rebecca, more than twenty years later under the condition that she could bring the "Indian man and boy with whom she lived." His sister Joanna, like Eunice Williams, remained at Kahnawake and married a Mohawk man, returning to visit her brothers later in life as a Mohawk mother. Joseph spent a year living as part of that community himself before being taken in by the French. At the Deerfield Conference, he served as an interpreter and was offered as a fair trader for the new fort that the English had established in the Sok-wakik *wôlhana*.[48]

Fort Dummer, where Kellogg served as truckmaster, was located upriver from Deerfield on a site between the two "great falls," near a marsh where Kwinitekw's inhabitants hunted waterfowl and gathered wild rice. The English established this northernmost post in 1724 during Greylock's War, or the "Fourth Anglo-Abenaki War," a resistance against English expansion led by a Kwinitekw refugee. "Greylock," or Wawanole-wat, had drawn many other Kwinitekw men to his adopted *wôlhana* of Mazipskoik, including Schaghticokes. From the deep wetlands of the river Mazipskoik, Abenaki raiding parties repeatedly traveled south by canoe routes and footpaths, striking English settlements and then swiftly withdrawing into the forested mountains that they knew so well. Wawa-nolewat's "strategy of draining the colonists' resources by small-scale guerilla attack and the threat of lightning-fast raids," like Mashalisk's deed, worked to reverse the dynamic of the beaver wars. The colonists were behaving like the Great Beaver, hoarding the pond's resources for themselves, and Wawanolewat disrupted that pattern, draining the pond piece by small piece, poking holes in the dams of colonization, and reclaim-ing his Native space for all its inhabitants.[49]

During Greylock's War, Joseph Kellogg was commissioned to lead scouting expeditions in the Kwinitekw Valley and the surrounding mountains from a base at Deerfield. His job was to protect the towns of Deerfield and Northfield; having been built within the Pocumtuck and Sokwakik *wôlhanak*, they were particularly vulnerable targets. Inundated by Wawanolewat's raiding parties, Massachusetts Lieutenant Governor William Dummer assigned Colonel John Stoddard, an influential land speculator, to supervise the construction of a fort above Northfield. Stoddard recruited Kellogg's lieutenant, Timothy Dwight, to command the fort and procured some of Kellogg's soldiers to man it. Dummer and Stoddard planned to use the fort as a base camp for scouting parties that would intercept Wawanolewat's raiding parties before they reached the colonial settlements. They hoped to recruit "Western Indians" to lead the expeditions, but when Kellogg traveled to Albany to enlist Mohawks, few were receptive.[50]

The Mohawks as a nation refused to fight with the English in this war, reversing the path taken by their ancestors, who had played a critical role for the English in King Philip's War and engaged in their own campaigns to acquire access to Algonquian space. Family ties and political empathy likely held back many Mohawks from opposing Wawanolewat's resistance. However, the Mohawk sachem Theyanoguin, or Hendrick, was much more receptive to Kellogg's invitation. He had worked previously with Joseph's brother Martin, serving as a guide on an expedition to Montreal to redeem captives from the Deerfield raid, and these connections in the Mohawk network of relations worked to the advantage of the fort's designers. Hendrick took a position at Fort Dummer and, along with the Mohican sachem Aupaumut, recruited warriors to scout with them. Hendrick and Aupaumut spent several years working with Dwight and Kellogg, scouting Kwinitekw from the fort to Ktsipôntekw, often climbing the mountains overlooking the falls to search for the campfires of Wawanolewat's war parties.[51]

Hendrick's family ties and familiarity with the territory made him an ideal scout. The man who rose to become the famous "King Hendrick" had been born near Agawam, not far from Wawanolewat's native Woronoco, to a Mohican father and a Mohawk mother united in a marriage that strengthened a precarious alliance between the two nations. Wawanolewat and Hendrick were both sons of the beaver wars, born just south of Ktsi Amiskw, near Pynchon's trading post, in the midst of violence and exchange. Through the transformations of the beaver wars, Mohawks and Mohicans became invested in Kwinitekw's resources; through trade, marriage, birth, and death, their lives became embedded in the valley.[52]

Although Mohawks had an interest in the abundant resources of this dish, they were also invested in the maintenance of its social networks. Thus, even as they tried to sustain a neutral position, Mohawk councilors retained a respect for Abenaki sovereignty and attempted to mediate a peace between Abenaki and English. They met with colonial representatives at Deerfield and also sent three messages to the east with wampum. Delivering the Abenaki response along with their own estimation to John Stoddard and Joseph Kellogg, they remarked, "The Eastward Indians . . . said that in order to Peace with Boston Government they did desire two things viz the Return of the Land, and secondly the return of the Hostages." The Haudenosaunee speaker added, "From that we think the matter respecting Peace seemed to lye with you."[53]

At the Beaver's Tail

The English "lit a council fire at Deerfield" during Greylock's War to meet with the Mohawks and request their intervention, then rekindled that fire to institute a reconciliation. When the nations gathered at Deerfield in 1735, it was, according to Haefeli and Sweeney, to "reaffirm the peace secured in 1727 at the end of the Fourth Anglo-Abenaki War." After Wawanolewat's resistance stayed English expansion into the northern intervales, there remained the question of how to share the space of Ktsi Amiskw's bowl, in which Schaghticokes and their Abenaki relations, as well as Mohawks, Mohicans, and English, all had interests. A lesson learned well during the beaver wars was that the best way to create a "kettle of peace" was through interdependent exchange. As one Haudenosaunee leader put it, "The trade and the peace we take to be one thing." While trade goods offered a practical way to share materials, the symbolic exchange of wampum and pelts in council made manifest the activity of sharing space.[54]

Algonquians and Haudenosaunee alike enacted such exchanges regularly during the beaver wars, as "overlapping utilization of resources" created tensions that could be resolved only by formal agreement on the terms of distribution and by rebalancing through condolence. When nations agreed to share space, they often referred to the land as a bowl with a beaver tail from which they all might eat. One nation might invite another to hunt or even relocate in their territory, or agreements might be formed that would enable peace in an area on which multiple groups drew. However, the bowl of beaver tail could not contain a knife, which represented the potential for violence. Nations that pledged to share space were also committing to enact peace. Therefore, it is significant that the Native participants in the Deerfield Conference insisted on meeting at

Deerfield, at the foot of the beaver's tail. In council at Deerfield, Englishmen engaged in these indigenous protocols, and through their participation they were making clear commitments in the common pot.[55]

Under a wide tent on the Pocumtuck *wôlhana*, beneath the great
beaver and before more than one hundred Native ambassadors, the new
governor of Massachusetts, Jonathan Belcher, opened the conference
with the familiar Haudenosaunee ceremony of condolence, expressing a
desire to maintain a peaceful relationship and trade with the colony's
Indian neighbors, in contrast with the aggressive ambitions of his prede-
cessor.[56] He engaged in wiping away the blood of war and making a clear
space for open minds and hearts, offering wampum to seal his words.
The Mohawks, along with their Abenaki neighbors (some of whom had
strong roots in the valley), returned the gesture, telling Belcher, "The
Way is now clear... for Freedom of Speech."[57] Here both the colony and
the Native nations made a commitment to create a space where the grief
and bitterness of war could be diminished, where they could speak
freely, and where minds could open to the activity of making peace.

Emphasizing a change in colonial policy, Belcher spoke to the
Mohawks and Abenakis about Fort Dummer, where "some of your people... resort," as a trading post, and pledged that Kellogg, a man who
already belonged to the network of relations, would serve as a fair truckmaster. The governor wanted them to confirm that if war broke out between England and France, "your Justice and Faith, as well as your Interest will hold you to Peace with us," and he assured them, "You will be
always honestly dealt with by Capt Kellogg at the Truck House." The
statement revealed British concern over the ties Abenakis and Mohawks
had to the French in Quebec, but also demonstrated Belcher's understanding of the relationship between maintaining the trade and maintaining
the peace.[58]

Sharing space was at the forefront of the colony's negotiations
with the Mohicans from the Housatonic, who had come to Deerfield to
discuss the establishment of a mission at Wnahtukook, their own "great
meadow." The governor promised protection for their persons and lands
and encouraged them to settle in a manner more "compact" so that they
might be better served by the colony and their new minister. This meeting
paved the way for the town of Stockbridge, an experiment in cooperative
living between Natives and colonists that began with the mission. While
Stephen Williams was reading a translation of the Housatonic sachem
Konkapot's speech, a message came from the Hudson River sachem,

Aupaumut, saying he was ill but had sent his son to stand in his place. Aupaumut had multiple stakes in the conference, because many of his relations would be participating in the mission experiment and because the fort he had helped establish was undergoing a major transformation.[59]

In addressing the Schaghticokes, Belcher expressed his desire to fully convert Fort Dummer into a space for exchange. He related that he had "set up a Trading House under Captain Kellogg's care, that you may be continually supplied in the best manner, and not cheated in your Trade," offering wampum to seal his words. The speakers, Massoqunt and Naunautookoah, responded by thanking the governor for his words, laying "down three Beaver skins in token thereof." They gave him another three pelts to thank him for keeping the path "very plain and clear," a recognition and expectation of commitment to the open space of peace, trade, and communication. Giving them a belt of wampum, the governor expressed his happiness that they were living near the fort, his invitation to communicate with him through Kellogg, and his assurance that they would "have land to live on."[60]

Belcher's language clearly implied that the large number of Schaghticoke men and women who gathered at the conference were inhabiting the Kwinitekw intervale and using Fort Dummer as their primary location for trade. During the years of relative peace that followed, the sachems Massoqunt and Naunautookoah took the place of Hendrick and Aupaumut at Fort Dummer. Rather than serving as scouts, their main task was to facilitate the trade and the peace. They were in attendance from 1734 through 1742, arriving every year in the spring and leaving in early winter. Their seasonal occupation of the fort, in combination with other evidence, suggests that a sizable group of Schaghticokes were living in the intervale from the spring fish runs through harvest, then returning to their refuge near Albany (or the surrounding mountains) for winter hunting and the guarantee of food that their "protection" from the Albany English provided, following a pattern similar to that of the traditional Sokwakiak seasonal use of their *wôlhana*.[61]

The names of both Massoqunt and Naunautookoah appeared on all three of the deeds signed at the Deerfield Conference to indicate that they were witnesses. Massoqunt's wife, Nechehoosqua, was the primary signer on the deed for the Great Meadows, a right passed to her through her own mother, Conkesemah. Massoqunt "and Aumesaucooanch and Tecaumis[,] children of the said Massoqunt and Nechehoosqua," consented to the deed as her heirs, while the rest of the Schaghticokes,

including Pinewans and Keewauhoose, confirmed it. The Great Meadows agreement was made at Fort Dummer just before Massoqunt and
Naunnautookoah left for the conference. However, Pinewans and his
brothers signed their deed for the eastern Papacontuckquash lands only
after the council was concluded.[62]

Because the governor's own words demonstrated that the
Schaghticokes were living in the Kwinitekw Valley and that the English
were aware of their presence, the release of lands implied by the three
deeds makes little sense. However, if we consider what the deeds may
have meant in the context of the conference, a different picture comes to
light. Traditionally, Algonquian land transactions were essentially diplomatic agreements concerning land use. Negotiations involved delineating territorial boundaries or common hunting areas with the goal of balanced accommodation of the needs of both groups. The bowl of beaver
tail is only one example of the ways in which nations conceptualized cooperative negotiation of space and resources. Even as the European customs of land alienation and written deeds entered Native space, words
on paper held less weight for Native people than oral communication
and material exchange in council. Furthermore, because Algonquians
did not immediately adopt the European concept of land as commercial
property, many leaders continued to believe they were negotiating usufruct
rights. They often resettled or resold land occupied and then abandoned
by colonials, and in many cases Native leaders perceived that they were
granting settlers the right to occupy land in common, or to settle a town
within the *wôlhana*, rather than relinquishing their own right to inhabit it.
In the context of the discussions over shared space and the symbolic
meaning of trade at the Deerfield Conference, for Pinewans, Keewauhoose,
and Massoqunt the "deeds" likely represented their acknowledgment
of the English presence in Ktsi Amiskw's bowl and their commitment to
co-inhabit this space in peace.[63]

In fact, the combined conference and deeds clearly delineated
the relationships between people and places in the region. The Schaghticokes were confirmed as the primary Native inhabitants of their ancestral territory, while both northern Abenakis and Mohawks were recognized
as having the right to trade, camp, and (probably) hunt there, based on
the kinship and political ties between them. The Mohawks were honored as the closest allies of the English, and both the Schaghticokes and
the Mohicans were acknowledged as people under English protection.
The Mohicans' right to their own territory on the Housatonic was also

confirmed, and they were encouraged to associate and trade with the English closest to them, at Northampton, and with those settlers who would join them at Wnahtukook. The English towns on Kwinitekw (including Deerfield and Northfield) were likewise recognized, and the English trading post at Fort Dummer was confirmed as a shared space and meeting-place in whose use the Schaghticokes, Abenakis, and Mohawks would all partake. For Mohawks and northern Abenakis, the location of the fort would provide easier access to English goods and a central place to trade and council with the Abenakis' southern relations and with the English from Massachusetts. For the Massachusetts colony, the conference forged an agreement that might draw these nations away, both politically and economically, from the rival French and would also draw the Indian trade away from Albany and closer to Boston. At the same time, the conference and trade ensured the security of their settlements in the aftermath of Greylock's War. For the Schaghticokes, the conference was vital because it ensured that their habitations on Kwinitekw would be protected from violence through political relationships, family ties, and the interdependence of trade; it held out the promise that their abundant *wôlhana*, which had been ravaged by war, might be transformed into a kettle of peace.

In the years that followed, the agreements made during the Deerfield Conference were enacted in the valley. Soon after the council, Kahnawake Mohawks were employed at Fort Dummer to work with Kellogg, Massoqunt, and Naunautookoah. The process of trade was facilitated by the presence of leaders who were connected to the local community as well as to the larger network of Mohawks and Abenakis who came to the post, who spoke Haudenosaunee and Algonquian languages, and who were keenly familiar with diplomacy. Fort Dummer became a center of interaction between Mohawks, Abenakis, Schaghticokes, and English, people tied to each other through marriage, captivity, trade, and the common experience of both peace and war. In 1737, Stoddard and Kellogg participated in a renewal of the "Covenant of Peace and Unity" that had been rekindled "two years past at Deerfield." The conference took place at Fort Dummer, and a Mohawk speaker spoke "for our Three Tribes." Laying down wampum, he said, "We now return in answer for our three Tribes, that our desire is that it might remain firm and unshaken, and do from our heart promise that the Covenant shall not be broken on our parts, but if ever there shall be any breach, it shall begin on yours." Stoddard and his compatriots promised that they would continue "to cultivate the friendship" they had "contracted with your tribes" made "two years ago at Deerfield," and laid down wampum to confirm it.[64]

Yet even as they pledged to share space peacefully, the English had other plans in the works. A few years after the construction of Fort Dummer, as Greylock's War was coming to a close, the Massachusetts colony had devised a strategy for the construction of "Defense Towns" above Northfield (see Map 3). These plans were not altered when peace entered the valley. The winter before the Deerfield Conference, the Massachusetts General Assembly had authorized John Stoddard and Israel Williams to acquire deeds for these lands from the Indians who held claim to them and ordered a survey of the lands all the way to "the Great Falls." Both Stoddard and Williams had large land investments on Kwinitekw and played commanding roles in colonial defense. They were implicated in the Stockbridge project and were the primary organizers of the Schaghticoke deeds. Both men were present at the conferences at Deerfield and Fort Dummer, participating in the commitments to share space. Kellogg, too, played an important role, serving as an interpreter at the conferences and for the drawing up of the deeds. In 1736, only shortly after the Deerfield Conference, the committee was ready to put the plan into action, recommending that "a line of towns" be laid out along the river all the way to "the Great Falls," designed "for further defense and protection" of the colony. Even as the English engaged in councils that set up structures for sharing the valley, they were seeking to transform it into colonial space, perhaps using the conference as a way of ameliorating suspicions as they acquired a route upriver into coveted Abenaki lands.[65]

Reclaiming the Great Beaver's Bowl (Western Wabanaki, 1744–1754)

Susannah Johnson, an Englishwoman captured along with her husband from the uppermost "new town" on Kwinitekw in August 1754, gave birth on the path to Odanak. Her Abenaki captors provided her with a captured horse, built a shelter for her to use while she was in labor, and made a litter, then a pack saddle, so that her husband could carry her on the long trek north. On the western shore of Betobakw, her husband, James, watched as his captors swept up those relations who remained at Schaghticoke and carried them across the lake on a French boat to Mazipskoik, then upriver to Odanak, where they "were by them received as part of their nation." At Odanak, Susannah observed her "family" in the wigwam as they sat on the ground to eat: "A spacious bowl of wood, well filled, was placed in a central spot, and each one drew near with a wooden spoon." Both James and Susannah witnessed the common pot in action. According to James, the Abenakis had just returned from raiding the Kwinitekw settlements, and they told him they had struck his town, Charlestown, at Fort No. 4, in particular "because the English had set down upon lands there which they had not purchased." They said "that they intended next spring to drive the English on Connecticut River so far as Deerfield." By the time Susannah was captured, Pinewans and his relations were fully engaged in an effort to reclaim their relatives as well as their homelands, delineating and defending the bounds of their dish and seeking to push the English back to the "old towns."[66]

In her own account, Susannah Johnson described the atmosphere in which she had lived as a child at Fort No. 4 during the decade before she had been carried away in captivity: "At this time Charlestown contained nine or ten families, who lived in huts not far distant from each other. The Indians were numerous, and associated in a friendly manner with the whites. It was the most northerly settlement on the Connecticut River, and the adjacent country was terribly wild."[67]

Charlestown was one of the "defense towns" on Kwinitekw, the outermost "new settlement" on the "western frontiers" to which Pinewans's petition referred. Susannah Johnson had grown up living alongside Pinewans's family, and in taking her as a captive (for whom they would seek ransom), they treated her as if she already belonged to them, a sign of kinship and of reclamation of those "lands" the English "had not purchased." Pinewans's family was also well acquainted with the commander of Fort No. 4, Phineas Stevens. Stevens had been captured by Wawanolewat as a boy, and after his return had become a military captain and trader. Like many, he often traveled to visit his Indian "family," and he kept up a fairly healthy relationship with his Native neighbors on Kwinitekw. Pinewans frequented Stevens's trading post, and the two knew each other well. During the years of their acquaintance, Ktsi Amiskw's bowl was undergoing yet another transformation as settlers moved into the area and built forts, mills, and homes. The movement from the ideal of shared space in the Deerfield Conference to the delineation of separate spaces in the Petition at No. 2 can be understood only in the context of the changes that took place in the intervening years, particularly in the space between Northfield and Fort No. 4, between Peskeompscut and Ktsipôntekw.

Only five years after the Deerfield Conference, Joseph Kellogg gave up the command of Fort Dummer to become the Massachusetts Bay Colony's official "Interpreter in the Indian Language and for Indian Affairs." Captain Josiah Willard, whose grandfather was a notorious trader and land speculator in Penacook country, took Kellogg's place. He proceeded to outfit the fort for defense, including the construction of a stockade and the addition of "swivel guns," and encouraged settlement in the town of "No. 1," in which he held substantial financial interest. By 1742, both Massoqunt and Naunautookoah had left their positions at Fort Dummer. By 1744, the English had constructed multiple forts on Kwinitekw, including Fort No. 4 and another, Fort No. 2, right on the Great Meadows.[68]

At the same time, transformations were taking place in both European space and the Native network of relations. While the Deerfield Conference may have allowed an opening for behind-the-scenes claiming of space by the English, it also offered an opportunity for communication and alliance-building between Native nations. Mohawks, Abenakis, and Mohicans had become all too aware of the impacts of war and had begun to resist the pull of French and English allies. As tensions brewed overseas in Europe, the Mohawks sent messages and wampum through the networks of the northeast. In 1739, Abenaki communities in the north and east received messages from their Mohican and Schaghticoke relations confirming the alliance between them and requesting that they join with them and the Mohawks in maintaining a neutral stance if war broke out between France and England. With wampum belts they emphasized, "We only destroy ourselves by meddling with their Wars."[69]

However, as the English intent to push farther into Abenaki country became increasingly clear, relationships within Native space began to realign. In the spring of 1744, shortly after the construction of Fort No. 2, Schaghticoke leaders traveled north to visit the old war leader Wawanolewat, to renew their alliance with their Abenaki relations, and to "keep open the road" between them. Inevitably, they must have discussed the impending war between France and England, as well as the increasing English infiltration of the valley, and the Schaghticokes likely sought advice from the man who had once led the movement to reclaim it. With conflicts brewing on Kwinitekw, many of the Schaghticokes remained up north, settling with families at Mazipskoik, Winooskik, and Odanak. Only a few months after this meeting, the Mohawk chief Hendrick threatened some "Eastern Indians" on the streets of Boston, declaring that the Mohawks would "cut [them] off from the earth" if they went to war against the English. And at Deerfield, as Ktsi Amiskw watched, Eunice Williams visited her English relations on the fortieth anniversary of the famous raid.[70]

By the following year, Abenakis and their allies began raiding the valley settlements, both in coalition with the French forces and in independent guerilla campaigns that followed Wawanolewat's paths. One of the first targets was Great Meadows, where Abenakis captured a settler named Nehemiah Howe. As they traveled upriver from Great Meadows, Howe related, his captors had him leave an *awikhigan* for the English who might follow on their tracks. He wrote, "On the fourth day morning, the Indians held a piece of bark, and bid me write my name, and how many days we had traveled; 'for,' said they 'may be Englishmen will come here.'" The Abenakis' continued inhabitation of the area is especially evident in Howe's account. He noted a place where they had a "hunting house," complete with a kettle and caches of food, and another where they kept canoes for crossing the large lake Betobakw, along with a supply of corn, pork, and tobacco. After crossing the lake, the Abenakis stopped at the French fort at Crown Point, where Howe encountered "Amrusus, husband to her who was Eunice Williams. . . . He was glad to see me, and I to see him. He asked me about his wife's relations, and showed a great deal of respect to me."[71]

We know that Pinewans was participating in these raids in the Kwinitekw Valley because of the appearance of his name on the Petition at No. 2. However, he may have also appeared in another captivity account, that of Mary Woodwell Fowler, who was captured from the Hopkinton fort above the river Bagôntekw, not far from Kwinitekw. Fowler's narrative related that when one Indian man "presented a musket to Mary's breast, intending to blow her through . . . a chief by the name of Pennos, who had previously received numerous kindnesses from her father's family, instantly interfered, and kept him from his cruel design, taking her for his own captive." This man was likely Pinewans, and the account demonstrates one of many moments when the relationships that were formed in Native space between settlers and Abenakis prevented violence, even in the midst of war.[72]

As Abenakis began raiding settlements, the Albany English increased their pressure on Hendrick and his relations to "take up the hatchet" against the "Eastern Indians." However, the Mohawks had doubts about their English "brothers." They even sent a message to the Mohicans at Stockbridge that they were considering war against the English and traveled to the Housatonic with some Schaghticokes in the spring of 1745 to council with them. The English occupation of Kwinitekw was clearly an issue for all three groups. At the Albany conference that followed in the fall, Hendrick told John Stoddard, "We the Mohawks are apprehensive we shall be served at last as our brethren the River Indians, they [the English] get all their lands and we shall soon become as poor as they. You in the Broad Way (addressing himself to Colonel Stoddard) have got our lands and driven us away from Westfield, [where] my father lived formerly."[73]

The English, however, were more concerned with securing the Mohawks' assistance in defending the valley against Abenaki raids. They called on the Mohawks' own promises "to strike" the "hatchet... against the French and their Indians in case of any infraction made by them of the neutrality" and told the Mohawk leadership that they were bound by treaty and by wampum to honor that pledge. The English even appealed to Mohawk bravado, reminding Hendrick that his Eastern relations had ignored his words at Boston and had "little regard" for his power. Governor George Clinton of New York emphasized that the Abenakis had broken the agreements to share space, saying, "Belts of Wampum will not bind them to the performance of their promises." They called on the Mohawks to defend the commitments made at Deerfield, complaining that the Abenakis had already killed "two Englishmen near Connecticut River" and were "enemies to... all their fellow Creatures, who dwell round them."[74]

The Mohawks were not so easily swayed. They were suspicious of rumors that "the people of this Province had a design to destroy them" and continued to raise "the old cause that we have been cheated out of our lands." These immediate concerns, combined with the news that came from Abenaki country, made them reluctant to join the English despite heavy pressure from their Albany neighbors, on whom they depended for trade and alliance against the French. Thus, as a last resort, the English raised the issue of the French threat in council the following year. The Haudenosaunee had promised to try to persuade the Abenakis to "make satisfaction" for English deaths, but they had disregarded English requests to strike. The English reminded them of the past insults and injuries of the French, related dramatic accounts of recent French attacks, and continually associated Abenaki action with French motivation. Finally, the Mohawks agreed to "take up the hatchet," but they seemed much more inclined to strike the French towns in Quebec rather than the Abenaki *wôlhanak*. In fact, Governor Clinton expressed concern that if the English pushed the Haudenosaunee too hard on this point, they might lose "their assistance" altogether. Given their degree of "discontent," they might "join with the French instead of assisting the English."[75]

Abenakis and Mohawks alike traveled to Fort Dummer and Albany to trade; such meetingplaces increased the opportunity for social ties and exchange of news. The neutrality pact demonstrated the Mohawks' awareness of the shared space of colonization, and the Albany meetings revealed the precariousness of their relationship to the English. It would not take much for a Mohawk to join his relations in resistance to English expansion. At least one Mohawk man seems to have made this move, uniting with Abenakis in their reclamation of Kwinitekw and signing his name to the Petition at No. 2.

The Mohawk called "Old Town" was most likely in attendance, along with Pinewans and Keewauhoose, at the great council at Montreal in the spring of 1747, during which Abenakis and their northern allies gathered to declare war against the English *and* the Mohawks. They made plans to raid settlements in the Kwinitekw Valley and in New York. Old Town and Pinewans soon returned to the Sokwakik intervale, where they set fire to the first house built in the upper valley, camped overnight in Great Meadows, and joined a large group of their relations who had traveled south with a French company to launch a three-day siege of Fort No. 4, battling with their old friend, Phineas Stevens. But before leaving Great Meadows, Old Town and Pinewans left an *awikhigan* for the English at Fort No. 2.[76]

There is a story that comes from the east, where during these same wars Abenakis struggled to oppose the dams that prevented the passage of salmon up the river Presumpscot, named for its "swarming fish." It is the Penobscot story of the "Great Bull Frog," who dammed the flow of the river and hoarded all the water for himself. It is said that Gluskap, the great transformer, saw that the people downriver were dying of thirst and sought to rebalance the water supply himself. On arriving at the pond's edge, Gluskap saw a huge monster in human form — a bloated giant with green skin and "great yellow eyes that stuck out like pine-knots." Standing strong, Gluskap exclaimed,

"Give me water to drink, and the best, at once, you Thing of Mud!" But the [monster] said, "Get out of here. Go find water where you can." Then, Gluskap thrust a spear into his belly, and lo! there gushed forth a mighty river; even all the water which should have run before, for he had put it into himself. And Gluskap, rising high as a giant pine, caught the chief in his hand and crumpled his back with a mighty grip. And it was Bull Frog. So he threw him with contempt into the stream, to follow the current.[77]

The Petition at No. 2 contains all the elements of this traditional story: the teasing, sarcastic humor; the reclamation and redistribution of hoarded resources; the transformation of a being who acts powerful into something very small. The petition's satiric style evokes the "trickster" stories of Matigwes (the rabbit) and Azeban (the raccoon) and even anticipates the ironic voice of nineteenth-century Pequot writer William Apess.[78] While demonstrating familiarity with the submissive form demanded of colonial instructors, Pinewans and his relations mastered that rhetoric only to subvert it. These men laid bare the colonists' weakness by satirizing their obsessions, addressing the issue of greed that was so profoundly present in Mashalisk's deed with heavy irony, and contrasting the stereotypical English hunger for money and land with their own "wealth." One of the worst effects of war in Indian country was starvation, but Pinewans and his companions insisted that they had more than enough provisions in their own villages and that they were well aware that this was not the case in the English settlements.[79] As a historical and literary document, the petition poses a challenge to narratives of progressive colonial expansion, revealing the constantly shifting power dynamics of the northeast and the impacts of Abenaki resistance. Most important, this "text" demonstrates that writing was operating as a tool of communication and delineation in Native space, independent of colonial institutions and even in direct opposition to the colonial project. It may be the first piece of American Indian protest literature.

Pinewans and his relations put the English in the role of Ktsi Amiskw and the Great Bull Frog, writing a story in which they were the transformers, the ones who would break up the dam and let loose the flow of the river. No colonial history from the eighteenth or nineteenth century mentions this petition or even a raid on No. 2 at the time. There were no English inhabitants around to record it. Rather, the petition reveals a moment when Native people chose to record a place in their own history, when they reclaimed their *wôlhanak* on Kwinitekw and reversed the tide of English acquisition. As Colin Calloway, the first historian to recover the petition, has written, by 1749 "every English settler was driven out of [the territory that would become] Vermont. Only Fort Dummer and Fort Number Four remained as English toeholds on the upper Connecticut."[80]

After the war, Pinewans returned to Kwinitekw and renewed his relationship with Phineas Stevens, despite their opposition during the conflict. In fact, the former captive wrote, "if not for the French, it would be easy to live at peace with the Indians." Stevens met up with his old friend at the Albany truckhouse in the late winter of 1752, and Pinewans told him he would be back at Kwinitekw in the spring, when he would pick up the traps he had left at the fort before the war. Pinewans was hunting Amiskw still.[81]

That spring, while Pinewans and Stevens were reuniting on Kwinitekw, Old Town participated in a meeting at Stockbridge, along with Hendrick's brother Abraham and a representative from the Massachusetts colony. Colonial leaders wanted to know "what measures" could be taken by the English "to promote and effect the reunion of the Six Nations." They were concerned about the Senecas and Onondogas, who seemed to be moving closer to the French. Rather than answering the question directly, the Mohawk men told Joseph Dwight, "I will tell you what has happened in former times," and then related a long narrative of dispossession and deceit. They talked primarily of the history between the Seneca, the French, and the western country, but concluded with a veiled challenge to the English: "The Governor of Canada has frequent communication with the Nations and tells them the English will undoe them. The time will come when they will build a house at the upper end of the Mohawk Land and then a second and third and then descend upon it. This the Governor of Canada says to the Mohawks." This was the story of Kwinitekw, a narrative that was becoming all too familiar in Native space. Old Town and Abraham challenged their "brethren" to reverse their course, relating how the French "by cunning fair Speeches and great presents has gained possession of the Senecas' country" and saying that the Senecas had told the Mohawks that "they can't move one foot but that the English take Possession of the Ground." Relating their message without the offense of direct accusation, Old Town and Abraham warned that if the same story manifested itself in Mohawk space, the English might lose their most valuable ally. Old Town may have fought for the reclamation of Kwinitekw, but he would not be forced to fight the same battle for the Mohawk Valley.[82]

Later that summer, in council at Montreal, Pinewans' relations asked their "brother," Phineas Stevens, to relate a stronger message to "your Governor of Boston." They made clear that any settlement above Fort No. 4 threatened their existence at Koasek and would be interpreted as an offensive act of war. They stated:

> We hear on all sides that this Governor and the Bostonians say that the Abenakis are bad people. 'Tis in vain that we are taxed with having a bad heart. It is you, brother, that always attack us; your mouth is of sugar but your heart of gall. In truth, the moment you begin we are on our guard. Brothers, we tell you that we seek not war, we ask nothing better than to be quiet, and it depends, brothers, only on you English, to have peace with us. We have not yet sold the lands we inhabit, we wish to keep the possession of them. . . . We will not cede one single inch of the lands we inhabit beyond what has been decided formerly by our fathers.[83]

Faced with a recurring English failure to share space, Abenakis finally chose to exclude them from the common pot, drawing a clear boundary between their land and the English settlements on the coast. As the Abenaki orator Jerome Atecouando told them,

> You have the sea for your share from the place where you reside; you can trade there. But we expressly forbid you to kill a single beaver, or to take a single stick of timber on the lands we inhabit. . . . We acknowledge no other boundaries of yours than your settlements whereon you have built, and we will not, under any pretext whatsoever, that you pass beyond them. The lands we possess have been given to us by the Master of Life. We acknowledge to hold only from him.[84]

Atecouando emphasized Abenaki indigeneity, insisting, as many Native leaders would after him, that possession of their homelands rested on a relationship that had more power than English paper. These Native rights were inherent, bolstered by generations of inhabitation, and gave Abenakis the power to proclaim that the "boundaries" that the English asserted on paper were null and void. They would delineate the bounds and determine the uses of their land. In the Petition at No. 2, Pinewans and his relations told the English that they were bringing colonial space to a "narrower compass," pushing back the "frontiers" that the English sought to transcend and reasserting Abenaki sovereignty over the land. Likewise, in reclaiming their Native lands, Atecouando and the Abenakis forbade the English to draw from the Great Beaver's bowl and especially prohibited them from taking those resources for which the English had shown an uncontrollable greed. They were to leave the forests and Ktsi Amiskw's ponds alone.

Awikhigawôgan in the Great Beaver's Bowl

Although Calloway, in recovering the Petition at No. 2, assumed that it was "dictated" by Pinewans and his relations, it is likely that they were the true composers of the petition. There are several routes through which writing may have entered the Kwinitekw Valley. As early as the seventeenth century, Penacooks and their relations were learning to write from the English missionary John Eliot and his students. A man named Samuel Numphow, a grandson of the Pawtucket sachem George Numphow and the Penacook sachem Passaconaway's daughter, was a teacher at Wamesit, just downriver from the Penacook wôlhanak on Molôdemak. There were strong ties between these communities, and many refugees from Wamesit were taken in by the Penacooks in the wake of King Philip's War. These included Simon Betokom, the Native scribe who composed letters for Nipmuc sachems during King Philip's War and for Passaconaway's grandson Kancamagus in 1685. Penacooks also took in refugees from the Sokwakik wôlhanak, while others sought refuge at Schaghticoke, and there was much travel and interchange among these families and places as they regrouped after the war. Thus, some Schaghticokes may have acquired the tool of writing from within the Abenaki network of relations, which included relatives from Penacook and Wamesit.[85]

Writing also could have entered Pinewans's network through the Mohicans, who recognized the power of paper early on. Shortly before leaving for Fort Dummer, Aupaumut made a speech in Albany on behalf of the Mohicans and Schaghticokes that revealed his awareness that their inability to read made them targets for deceit and dispossession: "We have no more Land — the Christians when they buy a small spot of Land of us, ask us if we have no more Land & when we say yes they enquire the name of the Land & take in a greater Bounds that was intended to be sold them & the Indians not understanding what is writ in the Deed or Bill of Sale sign it and are so deprived of Part of their Lands."[86]

Not surprisingly, Aupaumut's grandson would grow up to be one of the most literate Indians of his generation. Hendrick Aupaumut, whose story will unfold in chapter 3, was born just a few years after his grandfather led a group of families from Muhhekunnutuk to join their relations at Stockbridge, where for some twenty years the missionary John Sergeant taught the Mohican children to read and write.[87] In 1747, at the same time Abenakis were preparing for a spring offensive on the Kwinitekw settlements, Sergeant wrote to a colleague:

> Their Language is extremely hard to learn, and perhaps I shall never be a thro' Master of it: there never having been any European that ever was, except one or two, and they learn'd it when they were Children. But the young People among them learn English well; most of them at this place understand a great deal of it, and some speak it freely & correctly. There are many that can read English well; and some are able to write.[88]

Jonathan Edwards, Sergeant's successor, related, "If any one among them is able to read and write, it is looked upon as a great attainment."[89] The skill of literacy was sought by Native people because they recognized the rising impact of writing in Native space. At the Deerfield Conference, the Mohican sachem Konkapot requested that the governor put the treaty in writing, and Jonathan Belcher agreed, saying, "All I have said to you from Our first meeting here shall be printed, and then be sent to you, that you may as often as you please refresh your Memories with it." Writing was taking on a function similar to that of wampum in preserving the memory of councils and enabling the community to collectively recall them on a regular basis. Konkapot also requested that laws "may be given us in Writing" to protect "our Children [from being] taken away from us for Debt." Here, writing was being called upon to operate like wampum, sealing the promises of the governor, but Konkapot's request also demonstrated the Mohicans' recognition of the binding power of written law on Massachusetts' colonists.[90]

At Deerfield, Belcher also offered literacy to the Schaghticokes and their relations, proposing to send a minister to Fort Dummer to educate their children. Writing, it seems, was something to be presented for exchange. It is possible, then, that Pinewans or Keewauhoose penned the petition. They might have learned to write from Penacook and Mohican relations or received lessons at Fort Dummer. However, the most likely candidate for authorship of the petition was the first signer, Old Town.[91]

In April 1737, a missionary arrived in the Mohawk Valley, home
to Hendrick, Abraham, and Old Town. Charles Barclay had grown up in
Albany, been educated at Yale, and then been hired by the Society for the
Propagation of the Gospel to serve as a minister and teacher to the Mohawks. Early in his stay, he wrote to John Sergeant, "I am almost amazed
at the Progress the Youth make in Reading and Writing their own Language." He related, "All the young Men, from 20 to 30 Years, constantly
attend school when at home, and will leave a Frolick rather than miss.
Sundry of them write as good a Hand as myself." Barclay remained in
the Mohawk Valley for nearly ten years, and Old Town was probably a
student, for he was part of a group of Mohawks who relocated to Stockbridge in the 1750s after Barclay's successor failed to provide an ade-
quate education for his Mohawk pupils.[92]

In the summer of 1751, Hendrick joined his old acquaintance
Aupaumut at Stockbridge, where he and other sachems participated in a
council with Joseph Dwight, Joseph Kellogg, Jonathan Edwards, and
"Colonel Pynchon." After much deliberation, the Mohawks, according to
Edwards, "signified their compliance with the proposal that had been
made, of sending their children here to be instructed, and coming, a number of them, to live here, and gave a belt of wampum in consideration of
it." The Mohawk families who traveled to Stockbridge were strong supporters of education and were presumably among those most respon-
sive to Barclay's teachings. Because Old Town was a primary leader of
this group, it is likely that he had acquired the valuable skill of writing.[93]

Further evidence of Mohawk literacy, in English as well as "their
own language," lies in a strategically eloquent "Petition" to Governor
Clinton, in which "the Mohawk Warriors" protested Barclay's abandon-
ment of his post "for the love of money" and argued against his claim to
land that they had reserved for a teacher "as his particular property." In
the petition they also addressed the problem of false deeds, complaining
that some of the local colonists had obtained a patent for lands that had
"never been bought from them or payd for, notwithstanding some Indian
hands may be produced."[94] Ten Mohawks signed the petition "in behalf
of the Conojohary Castle," including Hendrick's brother Abraham and a
man named Odyoughwanoron, perhaps the original Mohawk version of
a name that the English would pronounce as "Old Town," and perhaps
the man who wrote the *awikhigan* at Fort No. 2. Native writers would
raise the issue raised in the petition for centuries to follow, in speeches

and petitions that would echo the rhetoric, strategy, and style of Abraham and Odyoughwanoron.

Of course, there was another route through which writing entered Pinewans's network of relations. The forest that Pinewans, as a hunter, inhabited was full of marks and signs. The otter, fox, and bear who lived in the valley left signs on the marsh's edge, on trees, on stumps, and on trail crossings, giving messages to each other about the space they inhabited. Some messages were designed to prevent conflict over resources, while others might draw the opposite sex into union. Messages could be aggressive, informative, or deeply expressive of desire. Humans, although less capable of leaving appropriate messages in scent, are quite skilled at communication through signs. Thus, hunters left family blaze marks on trees to avoid competition within a watershed and left *awikhiganak* to inform other family members where the good hunting was or what space they might cover in their journey.

The *awikhiganak* left near Fort No. 2 served similar purposes as declarations of spatial relationships. The men who left the petition were marking and reclaiming their family territory against an aggressive competitor, while the birchbark message that Howe recorded gave information to the English who might follow in their tracks. Finally, Abenakis sent a message with clear spatial markers to the English through Stevens in formal writing. The message reverberated so strongly that the powerful Massachusetts authorities directed New Hampshire's Governor Benning Wentworth to abandon his plans to claim the northern country of Koasek.[95]

Even as Abenakis vehemently opposed the occupation of Koasek and the Massachusetts authorities made their own opposition clear, Wentworth sent Robert Rogers to blaze a trail through the northern forests to the upper Kwinitekw. As Rogers went through with his men, he left blaze marks on the trees, nearly mimicking the markings Native families used in their hunting territories. Yet, as soon as Rogers left, Pinewans's relations went back through the woods and defaced the marks entirely, making their own message clear: Kwinitekw would remain Native space.[96]

Amiskw, of course, left more signs than any other being. Even decades after beavers have left a marsh, the signs of their work are evident. So strong are their marks on the terrain that many generations later, when it was safe again for beavers to return en masse to reclaim the waterways, these descendants of Ktsi Amiskw could locate the places where their ancestors had been. For even in their absence, the land was working as they had designed, making better beaver habitat from the resources of the forest.[97] Ktsi Amiskw, the Great Beaver, sits on Kwinitekw still; you can see him as you come off I-91 and turn south on Route 116. He looms above the industrial cornfields and the moribund mill towns. Ktsi Amiskw is the beaver; Ktsi Amiskw is the Abenaki and the Mohawk; Ktsi Amiskw is the English; Ktsi Amiskw is a sign of how difficult *alnôbawôgan* can be in Native space.

2

Restoring a Dish Turned Upside Down

Samson Occom, the Mohegan Land Case, and the
Writing of Communal Remembrance

Moving from the interior toward the coast, we travel downriver from Ktsi
Amiskw to Pashebauk, "at the mouth of the river," where Kwinitekw
empties into Sobakw, the sea. From the extensive fields beneath Ktsi
Amiskw, the Pocumtuck sent corn to feed starving English settlers in the
fledgling "Connecticut" colony at the mouth of the river, which in turn
fed the colonists' notorious assault on the Pequot village, in which their
relations, the Mohegans, participated. Generations later, the Pequots and
Mohegans would serve as scouts for the former captive Joseph Kellogg
at Deerfield during Greylock's War. Stephen Williams recalled that it was
Mohegan scouts, not English rangers, who were able to track Abenaki
warriors all the way up to Koasek after the Deerfield raid in 1704. Yet,
despite their steadfast alliance with the English, the Mohegans still faced
the impact of colonial dispossession, exemplified by the following petition, composed by two of its prominent leaders.[1]

Dividing the Dish (Mohegan, 1789)

Writing from their village on the Thames River in 1789, "the Mohegans
by the hands of their brothers, Henry Quaquaquid and Robert Ashpo,"
sent the following "memorial" to the Connecticut Assembly:

> We beg leave to lay our concerns and burdens at your excellencies'
> feet. The times are exceedingly altered, yea the times are turned up-
> side down; or rather we have changed the good times, chiefly by
> the help of the white people. For in times past our forefathers lived
> in peace, love and great harmony, and had everything in great plenty.

When they wanted meat, they would just run into the bush a little way, with their weapons, and would soon return, bringing home good venison, raccoon, bear and fowl. If they chose to have fish, they would only go to the river, or along the seashore; and they would presently fill their canoes with variety of fish, both scaled and shell-fish. And they had abundance of nuts, wild fruits, ground nuts and ground beans; and they planted but little corn and beans. They had no contention about their lands, for they lay in common; and they had but one large dish, and could all eat together in peace and love. But alas! it is not so now; all our hunting and fowling and fishing is entirely gone. And we have begun to work our land, keep horses and cattle and hogs; and we build houses and fences in lots. And now we plainly see that one dish and one fire will not do any longer for us. Some few there are that are stronger than others; and they will keep off the poor, weak, the halt and blind, and will take the dish to themselves. Yea, they will rather call the white people and the mulattoes to eat out of our dish; and poor widows and orphans must be pushed aside, and there they must sit, crying and starving, and die. And so we are now come to our good brethren of the Assembly, with hearts full of sorrow and grief, for immediate help. And therefore our most humble and earnest request is, that our dish of suckutash may be equally divided amongst us, so that every one may have his own little dish by himself, that he may eat quietly and do with his dish as he pleases, that every one may have his own fire.[2]

In this petition, Quaquaquid and Ashpo recalled a balanced world and grieved its loss, lamenting the fact that the common pot had been "turned upside down." Where there had been "abundance," "harmony," and land "in common," there was now scarcity, acquisitiveness, and division; misery, starvation, and death. The portrait of "one large dish" from which all could "eat together" may represent a nostalgic ideal, even strategic romanticization, as Mohegan historian Melissa Tantaquidgeon Zobel has suggested, but the image also evokes the genuine experience of an "altered" physical and social environment.[3]

The petition presents the communal remembrance of a world in which balance was the aim, even if it was not always achieved, with systems in place for dealing with scarcity, conflict, and individual desire, in striking contrast with a "time" marked by seemingly insurmountable imbalance. While Quaquaquid and Ashpo suggested that the only solution to this predicament was the division of their "large dish" into smaller, individual ones, they also expressed great regret that they were no longer able to "eat together" from "one dish." In this instance, the "dish" referred specifically to the village. As Mohican leader Hendrick Aupaumut wrote, the village was the "kettle" from which Algonquian families drew "their daily refreshment." Coastal villages like Mohegan contained planting grounds along the river, fishing sites, and inland hunting territories, as well as access to bountiful marine resources. Sachems were responsible for ensuring that access to these resources was allocated equally among families and for regulating distribution through trade in the larger network. The people indigenous to the village held the primary responsibility for maintaining the "kettle's" environment so that it would continue to sustain them. Their sovereignty rested on this responsibility.[4]

During their lifetime, Quaquaquid and Ashpo experienced a decrease in the availability of resources in the village space and an increase in colonial control over their usage and distribution. Colonization created the physical division of land within the territory and the subsequent political division of the Mohegan community into two "parties" that occupied separate "towns." Predictably, the two parties emerged from a conflict between acquiescence with and resistance to the Connecticut colony's authority over Native land. Quaquaquid and Ashpo were born into leadership families from opposing towns, but both men participated in a movement from within to reclaim the ideal of the common pot and operate as "one family" that would act "for the benefit of the whole" in all political and legal matters. Under the conditions of escalating colonization, however, it seemed that the only way these leaders could envision a fair distribution was to equally divide what remained of the dish itself.[5]

Unlike chapter 1, which explored the dynamics of division and reconstruction within the common pot as an extensive network of relations, this chapter focuses on the common pot of the village dish. The bounds of this space and the families within it may alter over time, with gradual changes in geographic and social configurations or with sudden rupture, as exemplified by the events surrounding the Pequot War. The village can be moved or reconstructed from within. This chapter explores the complex dynamic between unity and division, dispossession and reconstruction at Mohegan, from the seventeenth century wampum wars that divided the Mohegans from the Pequots to the division of the body politic during a critical eighteenth-century land case to the Mohegans' attempt to reconstruct their "family" and reclaim the whole of their dish. Most important, this chapter reads these events through a series of petitions like the one of Quaquaquid and Ashpo, authored by Mohegans themselves.

Origin Stories: The Power of Wampum

The Dish "Turned Upside Down" (At the Mouth of the River, 1630–1643)

In order to understand the dynamic between division and unity at Mohegan, we have to look back to the origins of the village, to the Mohegans' split from their Pequot relations during the "time" in which the pot was being turned "upside down." This rift was rooted in the competitive discord that arose in the network of wampum-makers on the coast under the initial onslaught of European colonization.

The Abenaki story "The Origin of Wampum" tells us that wampum came from the mouths of powerful *medeolinowak*. The purple and white beads, hand crafted from quahog shell, held the potential for transforming relationships in Native space (See Figures 5 and 6). As the story relates, "Whenever they want to make a treaty, two nations exchange wampum beads worked into a belt." Such belts made the agreements between nations manifest and bound leaders to the promise that there would be no more "fighting" between them — that they would refrain from "hunting one another forever." Wampum was exchanged to create and maintain relationships as well as to reverse the destructive dynamic of war. It was instrumental to achieving social balance in the network of relations. Yet its power, like that of writing, was ambivalent. For the story also tells us that black wampum, which often symbolized war, had the power to enable one *medeolinu* to take all from the others, even though they may have possessed more than he did at the start. Thus, wampum held the potential for both making peace and making war in Native space, and the key to its power was in the process of exchange and distribution.[6]

All wampum originated in the sea into which Kwinitekw emptied. The wampum-makers who inhabited the region "at the mouth of the river" *(pashebauk)* had an obligation to send the carefully crafted shell-beads upriver in the trade that enabled peace (see Maps 2 and 6). Wampum traveled north along Kwinitekw's extensive route of exchange, passing through the villages of the Mattabesic, Wagunk, Paudunk, Tunxis, and Paquanaug and then through Woronoco, Agawam, and Nonotuck to reach

Figure 5. Quahog shell. Photograph by the author.

Pocumtuck, the land of the Great Beaver, where the trade continued to the north, east, and west. To the west of the mouth of the river were the territories of the Hammonasset and Quinnipiac, which connected Kwinitekw up with Wappinger country to the west, eventually moving through the Housatonic River to the Muhhekunnutuk (Hudson) River and on into the Haudenosaunee Confederacy to the northwest. To the east of the mouth of the river were the Niantics, the Mohegans/Pequots, the Narragansetts, and the Wampanoags on the southeast coast. Directly to the south, on a narrow island across the sound, were the Montauks and Shinnecocks, who were also significant participants in the wampum trade. All of these nations were intimately linked through the kinship and trade networks that connected the interior forests to the coast. However, as these networks were ruptured by disease and warfare, wampum's value as a means of rebalancing grew, fostering an excessive demand for the shell-bead, especially among the Haudenosaunee, who required wampum for ceremonies of condolence and adoption.[7]

While the demand for wampum increased in the interior, European traders and settlers were establishing sites along the coastal waterways. First the Dutch, then the English, began trading at the mouth of the river, acting as middlemen in the wampum–pelt exchange. The English

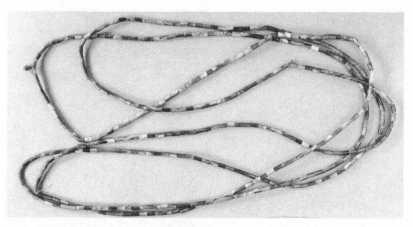

Figure 6. Wampum string. Copyright 2007 Harvard University, Peabody Museum, 99-12-10/53011 N34998.

took the name of the river for their fledgling colony at its mouth. The existence of these newcomers in Native space presented two more reasons for a rise in trade: the need to create and sustain relationships with these "strangers" and the influx of new goods into indigenous networks. The Europeans also brought their own desire for fur, for which wampum was often exchanged, and an economic perspective that applied a very different symbolic value to the shell-bead, a value that may have invoked the potential for its destructive power.[8]

Two indigenous nations assumed an intermediary role in the developing wampum trade on the coast. The Narragansetts, who had acquired prestige in the region for demonstrating resistance to disease and displaying diplomatic skill with neighboring communities and English newcomers alike, "obtained their hegemony" on the eastern part of the coast (according to historian Neal Salisbury), "through persuasion rather than violence."[9] The Pequots, with their Dutch trading partners, monopolized distribution in the trade between the Pawcatuck River and Kwinitekw, transforming their geographic "access" to wampum from a position within a system of reciprocal relations to a situation through which they might acquire power over others. The Pequots took in vast amounts of wampum from the surrounding nations to trade to the Dutch, from whom they received European goods that they distributed to neighboring communities. The Dutch, in turn, carried the wampum west to Fort Orange to trade for the furs brought to them by the Mohicans, then the Mohawks. The Dutch also transformed the function of wampum to that

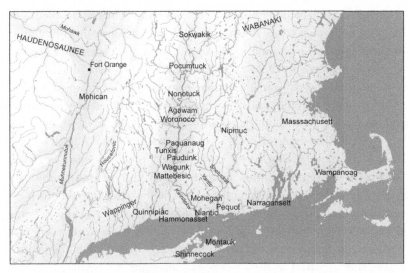

Map 6. The environs of Mohegan, showing the location of the Mohegan village and the territories of neighboring Native communities, from the "wampum-makers" on the coast to the inland Wabanaki and Haudenosaunee.

of currency in colonial trade networks, and they encouraged their Native partners to adopt this practice as well. The wampum trade transformed geographic space as production stations sprang up on the coast and islands, and it transformed political space as the Pequots expanded their control to the islands and the southern stretch of Kwinitekw. The Pequots often used warfare to gain access to territory, drawing power from their control over wampum to gain political and economic preeminence in the region.[10]

Kwinitekw, ideally situated between the wampum coast and the fur-trading regions to the north, quickly became embroiled in competition. The Dutch claimed a settlement site on the river (near the present site of Hartford) through their alliance with the Pequots, obtaining consent from the Narragansetts even as they built trading ties with the local Saukiaug that left Pequot middlemen out of the exchange. Meanwhile, as Pequot-Narragansett competition developed into open warfare, Plymouth colonists belatedly accepted an invitation from the local Paudunk sachems to settle among them as a form of protection against the Pequot. Obtaining the consent of the Narragansetts as well as the local leadership, the English built a fort upriver of the Dutch site (at the present site of Windsor), intercepting the fur trade and directly challenging the

"Dutch-Pequot hegemony." As the European trade entered the mouth of the river, epidemics swept up Kwinitekw's southern stretch, killing hundreds of families, including political and spiritual leaders, and leaving survivors in turmoil. As the "times turned upside down," this swirl of conflict, grief, and upheaval culminated in the violent death of the Pequot's primary surviving sachem, and a struggle ensued over resources and leadership succession that swiftly split the Pequot Nation in two.[11]

The division originated, according to at least one colonial source, when some in the nation "grew so great and proud" that they began to "quarrel" over hunting rights, a conflict that led to warfare within the group and to the strategic strengthening of political ties between the Narragansetts and the estranged ones. The splinter group was led by an ambitious survivor named Uncas, who led his followers to create a separate village in his family territory of Shantok, on the west side of the Pequot River. They referred to themselves as Mohegans, reclaiming an older name that emphasized the nation's original position in the network of relations.[12]

This chaotic explosion of conflict over the wampum trade was a key factor in the infamous "Pequot War." While the English certainly had their own objectives in assaulting the central Pequot village, motivations also arose from within Native space. The Mohegans, in a later petition to the King of England, claimed that they had participated to punish the Pequots "for their greed." As Kevin McBride has observed, "The Pequot War can just as easily be seen as a conflict between Native protagonists as a colonial-Pequot war," which resulted from the Pequots' "aggressive...control of the fur and wampum trade." Yet, as illustrated previously, the Pequots accused the Mohegans of the same violation. In truth, each faction censured the other for the crime of hoarding resources, without fully recognizing its own culpability in this destructive business.[13]

Wampum was valued as a conduit for rebalancing, but, as the Abenaki story suggests, its power was not always invoked in peace. When some held more than others, refusing to distribute their resources fairly, they could be subjected to violent redistribution, just as Gluskap made the Great Bull Frog release the contents of his belly through the force of his hand. And just as the Mohawks attacked the Mohicans for dominating the fur trade, the Narragansetts and Mohegans who participated in the Pequot massacre enacted a similar enforcement of the distribution imperative, claiming the power of wampum for themselves.

However, in contrast to the Mohawk–Mohican situation on the Hudson, the English were already deeply embedded in Native networks on the coast and acted as a direct catalyst for war. As McBride has observed, "Many of the tribes who fought against the Pequots perceived the English as a means of ending Pequot domination." Yet, while the Mohegans and Narragansetts watched the English torch the Pequot village and helped them kill the hundreds of inhabitants who ran from the flames, including the women and children whom the Narragansetts had asked the English to spare, Algonquian people were confronted with the overwhelming destructiveness of English power. Although reportedly amazed at its force, the Narragansetts told an English officer at the scene, "Machit, machit; that is, It is naught, it is naught because it is too furious and slays too many men." The European style of warfare, and the "furiousness" with which the Englishmen participated in it, involved much more than a rebalancing of power. As many Native leaders came to realize, colonial warfare arose from emotions and motivations that presented an immediate danger to the survival of the common pot.[14]

In the wake of the Pequot War, the charismatic Narragansett leader Miantonomo arose to unite Algonquians against the threat of English destructiveness while the Mohegan leader Uncas sought to bolster the power and security of his own village by utilizing the English as allies. The English, in turn, flattered the ambitious Uncas and encouraged him to take charge of the distributive role previously held by his Pequot relations while undermining the Narragansetts' standing in the region. However, as tribal historian Melissa Tantaquidgeon Zobel has pointed out, this relationship went both ways; Uncas was able to successfully draw these allies to him by flattering their own desire for power. Competition over wampum collection and distribution continued to foster tensions in the region, while English misunderstanding and manipulation of the role of wampum complicated the process of rebalancing.[15]

As Salisbury has observed, while the English strove to subordinate Native nations in the region after the Pequot War by "extracting tribute in the form of wampum payments," the Narragansetts continued to perceived such "payments" within the framework of the common pot — as "gifts freely presented to potential allies with the expectation that they would be reciprocated." While both groups perceived wampum exchange as "a symbolic expression of allegiance," English leaders regarded such gifts as deference to their power in a hierarchical system. To the Narragansetts, on the other hand, English failure to reciprocate implied an unwillingness to participate in exchange, which, as historian Daniel Richter has written, "could easily lead to a presumption of hostility." Even the Narragansetts' long-time friendship with Rhode Island leader Roger Williams began to break down in the face of such pressure.[16]

As colonial governors transformed wampum into a vehicle for enforcing their political power, Narragansett leaders turned their attention to Native networks, utilizing wampum to solidify relationships of reciprocity. Narragansetts regularly traded wampum for fur with the Mohawks to cement ties across linguistic and geographic boundaries and to bolster their security by allying themselves with the nation perceived as the most powerful by the English. By this time, the Mohawks had also begun to forge connections with the nations that gathered at John Pynchon's newly established trading post on Kwinitekw, at Agawam. While cultivating alliances in the north, the Narragansett sachem Miantonomo also carried wampum to his relations on the coast. According to Paul Robinson, "Whereas Miantonomo formerly received presents during his visits, he now gave them to his listeners," emphasizing the value of equal distribution.[17]

In his travels, Miantonomo conveyed a vision with the potential to restore balance to networks torn apart by disease, death, and accumulative desire. His vision is exemplified by a speech he delivered to the Montauks in 1642:

> For so are we all Indians as the English are, and say brother to one another; so must we be one as they are, otherwise we shall all be gone shortly, for you know our fathers had plenty of deer and skins, our plains were full of deer, as also our woods, and of turkies, and our coves full of fish and fowl. But these English having gotten our land, they with scythes cut down the grass, and with axes fell the trees; their cows and horses eat the grass, and their hogs spoil our clam banks, and we shall all be starved. Therefore it is best for you to do as we, for we are all the Sachems from east to west, both Moquakues and Mohauks joining with us, and we are all resolved to fall upon them all, at one appointed day.[18]

Miantonomo invoked the ideal of the common pot to summon the communal memory of abundance, entreating his relations to reclaim it for their own survival. Having witnessed the success of the English divide-and-conquer strategy, the Narragansett sachem urged his relations to recognize colonization as the source of social imbalance and resource depletion. Furthermore, he urged his relations to realize that they had the power and the responsibility to reverse the flow of destruction and restore equilibrium. Miantonomo's speech was the first recorded Native articulation of the disparity between the balance of the common pot and the imbalance of the world turned upside down, a trope that, as Salisbury has pointed out, would be echoed in Native writings and speeches for centuries to come.[19]

The call for Indian union to oppose the destructiveness of colonial division emerged from the shores of the Algonquian coast to become one of the resounding themes of the common pot. On the eve of the Pequot War, the Pequot sachems had called for union against the English, saying that these "strangers" had begun "to overspread their country, and would deprive them thereof in time, if they were suffered to grow and increase." However, the Pequots had realized the impacts of colonization too late to save their own village. Miantonomo, more than any other leader, came to understand the significance of the Pequots' last-ditch plea for coalition, realizing its wisdom only after seeing the violence of the alternative. The key to rebalancing, in Miantonomo's vision, was for all Indians, "from east to west," to unite "as one" to counteract the destruction. Lieutenant Lion Gardiner, who recorded the speech, related, "There were divers objections" to the plan because "the English were too strong for them," but Miantonomo responded, "It is true if they did not all join they should be too weak but if all join then they should be strong enough."[20]

According to Gardiner, the greatest obstacle to forming "all the Indians" into "one man" was "howe they might compasse Uncas." The Mohegan sachem had amassed considerable power through his coalition with the English, and through "strategic marriage alliances" and coercion he had incorporated many people into his village dish. Uncas himself married "as many as six or seven wives," including women from key Pequot families, which helped to cement the authority granted to him by the English over Pequot survivors. Most of his wives were "powerful Algonquian women" in their own right, and these alliances bolstered his position within the coastal network while opening multiple routes to Shantok for those who might join him. The Mohegan leader also continued to pursue the raiding tactics employed by the Pequots before the war, gathering followers and goods through the threat of force and taking advantage of the apprehension shared by all coastal communities in the wake of the Pequot War.[21] Uncas constructed a multifaceted, sustainable stronghold protected by a social palisade of marriages, trade, and dependencies and bolstered by a formidable alliance with the English.

While the Narragansetts presented a continual threat to Uncas's base of power, the Mohegan leader fostered divisiveness between the Narragansetts and their English neighbors, and competition erupted into sporadic warfare between the two groups. At one point, some of the Narragansetts' allies reported to Roger Williams that Uncas's followers were planning to intercept Miantonomo's trade and alliance-building: the Mohegans said they would "lay in way and wait to stop Miantunnomues passage to Qunnihticut, and divers of them threatened to boil him in a kettle." Not long afterward, Miantonomo invited Uncas and his counselors to eat from their dish, to share a meal of venison provided by Narragansett hunters, but Uncas declined, perhaps uncertain whether the offer was an extension of peace or a deadly deception.[22]

Even as tensions between the two leaders mounted to a climax, Miantonomo made one more effort to invite Uncas to share the same dish. The deal, however, was offered only under extreme pressure. Following a battle on the "great plains" at Mohegan, Miantonomo took flight, running for a "great waterfall" on the Yantic River known as "Uncas Leap." A Mohegan "swift runner" known as Tantaquidgeon captured Miantonomo, who was hampered by an unwieldy coat of chain mail given to him by a well-meaning Rhode Island settler. At Shantok, Uncas received a present of wampum from the Narragansetts and apparently engaged in long deliberation with their leader. Although Miantonomo refused to plead for his own life, he did appeal to the Mohegan sachem to consider the fate of the common pot that fed them both. He asked him to contemplate the transformations that had taken place since the English arrival and to seriously consider joining the Indian union. Miantonomo offered to marry one of Uncas's daughters to create an alliance, which might heal the ruptures between them and bind them in mutual obligation to each other and would serve as a formal recognition of the broader network of relations to which they both belonged.[23]

As Mohegan leader Samson Occom later wrote of the Montauks, to join in marriage was to eat from the same dish. Uncas used marriage to draw families into the "dish" of Mohegan while also taking from the "dishes" of other villages to distribute those goods among his followers, offering both security and sustenance to those who joined him. Miantonomo, on the other hand, envisioned a larger dish from which all might eat and the reclamation of this common pot from the English. In proposing an alliance, Miantonomo offered Uncas a deal that would encompass both visions. The marriage of Uncas's daughter to Miantonomo would reinforce the power of the Mohegan village within the Native network that Miantonomo sought to reconstruct, and Uncas would then be obligated to demonstrate loyalty to the Narragansetts and the Indian union. Miantonomo asked Uncas to reconsider his alliance with the English and to join those with whom he was united by kinship to sustain the pot from which their ancestors had eaten together.[24]

Uncas apparently deliberated carefully before deciding to reject Miantonomo's offer, instead offering the Narragansett leader to his English partners as a captive. The colonial court, now representing the "United Colonies" of Connecticut, New Haven, Massachusetts Bay, and Plymouth, condemned Miantonomo for his "ambitious designs to make himself universal sagamore or governor of all these parts of the country, [and] his treacherous plots by gifts to engage all the Indians at once to cut off the whole body of the English in these parts." They concluded that "Uncas cannot be safe while Myantenemo lives," ruling that although they did not "have sufficient ground" to execute him, Uncas "justly might put such a false and bloodthirsty enemie to death." They sent a message to Uncas asking him to retrieve the captured Narragansett leader and to "put him to death so soon as he came within his own jurisdiction," thereby putting the knife back into Native hands. Uncas retrieved the captive himself and, upon returning to Shantok, had his own brother kill Miantonomo at the place where he had been captured, on a plain above Uncas Leap where Uncas had himself avoided capture by the Narragansetts in an earlier raid. This was the site of the final contest between the two leaders. By bringing him back to the falls, Uncas demonstrated to Miantonomo that all of his skill and agility did not match that of the Mohegans. Where Miantonomo had been captured, Uncas had escaped. Where Uncas had escaped, Miantonomo would be killed. To Uncas, sustaining the village was the best strategy for survival, while forming a coalition against the English was the means to sure death.[25]

Uncas has often been portrayed as "a self-serving collaborator" and a force of destruction in the common pot. But, as historian Eric S. Johnson has noted, while most Algonquian communities were devastated by their participation in movements to resist colonization, the Mohegans "retained their guns, much of their land, their religion, and their political autonomy" by consistently siding with the English. "To the Mohegans," Johnson relates, "Uncas is a hero" for successfully negotiating colonial politics in order to empower his own community. Indeed, in a 1995 address Mohegan leader Jayne Fawcett remarked: "Every Mohegan here today is a living testimonial to the wisdom of Uncas' strategy of survival through friendship. We are all descendants of that great man."[26] Whether we regard Miantonomo and Uncas as visionaries or collaborators, as prescient leaders or individuals caught in a whirlwind of change, the conflict between them was symptomatic of a broader dilemma. The tension between the desire to protect the village and the need to preserve the larger network of relations, and the question of which would entail the best solution to the problem of colonization, would dominate Native politics for generations to come. Paradoxically, it was the ethics present in Miantonomo's unifying vision that Uncas's descendants called on over a century later to counteract colonial division and protect their village "dish" from English control.

Dismemberment and Re-memberment: Framing the Mohegan Land Case

Miantonomo's call was renewed decades later by a Wampanoag leader known most prominently for the colonial conflict called King Philip's War. Although named for the sachem Metacom, alias Philip, the war is more accurately described as the formation of a multifaceted coalition against English expansion.[27] At the start of the war, when his village of Montaup and his sister-in-law Weetamoo's village of Pocasset were attacked by the English, Metacom traveled north to Nipmuc country, where he broke up and distributed his coat of wampum, demonstrating his willingness to distribute power and share in the leadership of the resistance.[28]

Yet, at the end of the war, many of these same leaders faced a different kind of "breaking up": the dismemberment of nations and families as leaders were assassinated and their families sold into slavery, while survivors were forced to disperse and seek shelter with nations to the north. They also faced the literal dismemberment of bodies. Metacom's corpse was quartered and his head was displayed in Plymouth, while Weetamoo's severed head was displayed in Taunton before her grieving kin as a sign of triumph and a warning to those who remained.[29]

Just as they had served as allies to the English in the Pequot War, the Mohegans served as colonial scouts in this conflict, which they later referred to as "the warres with the Generall Nations of Indians." Four years after the death of Metacom, colonial officials met with Uncas to determine and settle the bounds of their "reserved" territories. This entailed another kind of dismemberment — that of Native lands. While Mohegans continued to conceive of their village territory as a whole, on paper it was divided up into three major parcels: the planting and fishing grounds on the west side of the Thames River, the hunting grounds in the uplands to the north and west, and the fishing grounds at the mouth of Kwinitekw (see Map 7). These lands were meant to "remayn to them and their heirs for ever." While Connecticut officials recorded these meetings as the formalization of colonial policy, Mohegans remembered them as part of the "League of Alliance and Friendship" between Uncas and the English colonists who had settled, by agreement, in their midst. As his descendants later related, however, the majority of colonists did not honor this agreement. Rather, the Mohegans saw their subsistence territory gradually dismembered by colonization, with only a small portion of their village — the planting grounds on the Thames River — allowed to them by the colony.[30]

Time and again, Mohegans reminded the English of their service and sacrifice during the Pequot War and the many wars that followed in resistance to English expansion. As Mohegan councilor Papaquanaitt put it in 1703, "In the Pequot war... they gave their heads to the English; in the Narragansett and Paremtuck [Pocumtuck] war, they gave their heads to the English; and they have lately done the same to the eastward in the war with the Indians and French there; and there is no strange thing with us; if there be any strange it is among themselves."[31] Despite their consistent loyalty, the Mohegans faced a constant struggle against colonial encroachment, which they fought primarily with paper and pen. The Mohegan land case, initiated in 1700 by Uncas's sons Owaneco and Ben, spanned nearly a century and divided the community, even as it embedded the Mohegan presence in Native space. Through the writing of petitions and the recording of communal memory, the Mohegans demanded recognition of their "Native rights" to their entire village territory, utilizing both indigenous tradition and English law to solidify their claim.

The petition quoted at the beginning of this chapter, bemoaning the loss of the village dish, reflects the processes of dismemberment and re-memberment in which the community was embroiled during the land case and beyond. The African writer Ngũgĩ wa Thiong'o has spoken eloquently about the practices and methods of "dismemberment" wrought by the colonial project (in Africa and elsewhere) and those of "re-memberment" acquired in the "quest for wholeness" that is decolonization.[32] His

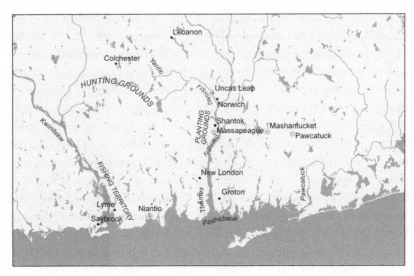

Map 7. The Mohegan dish, showing the "reserved" territory claimed by the Mohegans during the land case, including the location of their planting, hunting, and fishing grounds, as well as the locations of neighboring Native villages, colonial towns, and other places mentioned in the text.

analysis provides an ideal framework for reading the texts of the Mohegan land case.

Just as there are multiple kinds of dismemberment, Ngũgĩ tells us, there are multiple ways to think about re-memberment. There is the idea of "memory," which can take place in the individual or communal body and is stored in the cavity of the mind. In the Abenaki language, the words for memory, *mikwaldamwôgan* and *mikwaldigan*, suggest that, like writing, it can be both an activity and a powerful instrument for finding something stored in one's mind. The processes through which indigenous people retrieve, recall, and reclaim memory represent a collective re-memberment, a process of "bringing pieces together" that have been carefully kept, dispersed, or even buried. Correspondingly, as Ngũgĩ relates, one of the most important vehicles for re-memberment is literature, which is carried on the spoken voice and in the written word. The land case reflects the utilization of both.[33]

The "texts" of the case to be explored begin with Uncas's League of Alliance, followed by Owaneco and Ben Uncas's petition to Queen Anne in 1700, both of which affirmed the Mohegans' "Native rights" to their "reserved lands." Facing increasing encroachment, Uncas's great grandson, Mahomet II, traveled to England in 1736 to present another petition to King George II, reminding him of the "ancient alliance" of their nations and requesting the restoration of the Mohegans' "Native lands." Following the death of Mahomet in England, Mohegan leaders presented several "declarations" written in a communal voice, recalling the history of dispossession, countering colonial misrepresentation, and reasserting their common land rights. All of these petitions were penned with the assistance of English neighbors. However, in the generation that followed, a group of literate Mohegans banded together, using writing to reconstruct their body politic, re-member their collective history, and reclaim their "Native rights." This group included Samson Occom, the famous Mohegan minister, and the authors of the "dish" petition, Henry Quaquaquid and Robert Ashpo. Each generation grounded its claims in the arguments made by their predecessors, passed down through oral tradition and recorded in the written word.[34]

As Ngũgĩ conceptualizes it, the process of re-memberment entails a careful reconstruction of the communal body, a "quest for wholeness" that is essential to the healing of the fragmented political, social, and cultural "base." Through a reconstruction of collective history, based on the voices and writings of the Mohegans themselves, this chapter explores the dismemberment of the Mohegan lands and social body, the adoption and adaptation of writing as a tool of communal remembrance, and the Mohegan "quest for wholeness," the routes through which the Mohegans sought to re-member the village dish.

Dividing the Dish

The Dismemberment of Mohegan Lands and a Developing Narration of Native Rights (Mohegan, 1680–1743)

Having provided a framework for interpreting the texts of the land case, I would also like to provide a historical framework for defining the "Native rights" that these texts repeatedly invoke. William Cronon's landmark *Changes in the Land* offers lucid analysis of the critical differences between the English and Algonquian land tenure systems that were operating in colonial New England, which I attempt to summarize here. The English system rested on a conceptualization of land, especially within the realm of property transactions, as "an abstract area" with "fixed" boundaries, irrespective of usage. The "owner" acquired property through an economic and legal transaction and owned it as an individual against other individuals in the larger territory. Native rights, on the other hand, referred to the "sovereign rights that defined a village's political and ecological territory." These rights included resource usage, the right to manage the distribution of resources within the community and within the larger trade network, the right to regulate spaces of shared usage, and the responsibility to ensure that resources would continue to sustain the village. The village was generally defined by the watershed it inhabited, and its "collective sovereignty" was based on long-standing inhabitation and continuing use, which was recognized by contiguous communities.[35]

While European land tenure, in both conceptualization and practice, involved delineating boundaries between subjects and between subjects and objects, Native understandings of land "rights" were always relational. Native land tenure was rooted in the interdependent relationship between a community and its territory. Families had particular relationships to hunting and planting grounds within the village territory, which facilitated even distribution of space and resources and tempered competition. As Cronon points out, in situations in which resources were plentiful, such as spring fishing and fall hunting, families would come together to fish the spawning falls or to engage in deer drives. However, when conditions were more challenging, such as during winter hunting or small-game trapping, families split up along the watershed. Although such rights were often based on long-standing use by particular families, the community as a whole still retained sovereignty over the territory, and the sachem was responsible for overseeing this distributive system. For instance, when a family planting ground needed to recover, the land would revert back to the general community, and the sachem would assign a new plot to the family that had used it. The successful operation of the land tenure system was therefore dependent on the relationship between a sachem and his village. Cronon has explained that the sachem was invested with a kind of "symbolic possession" that represented "the entire group's collective right." His (or her) authority was dependent on the consent of the whole and his success in maintaining balance within the group. He (or she) also acted as the voice of the whole in negotiating with other communities. The maintenance of these relationships among people, and between people and space, within a village was crucial to its survival.[36]

These relationships also extended outside the village territory. As Cronon has pointed out, "kin networks" could hold land usage rights "both *within* and *across* villages." As on Kwinitekw, multiple nations had relationships to places such as trading and fishing sites, and the marriages and alliances between nations were crucial to maintaining harmony at these places of convergence. Regularly held councils kept relationships intact and ensured that usage rights were clearly defined. These land conferences were more akin to "diplomatic" events than "economic" transactions. Sachems might meet to make agreements over specific rights in a particular area of shared space, or one sachem might grant usage rights within his community's territory to another group in order to create or support a relationship of alliance. Thus, considerable confusion erupted when English deed making began to enter the space of Algonquian councils and the practices of Algonquian sachems began to enter the space of colonial land transactions.[37]

The "League of Alliance and Amity" between Uncas and the English, enacted in 1681, is a clear example of the interaction of these divergent cultural systems. In the most relevant part of the agreement, Uncas stated:

> I do resign up to the Colony of Connecticut all my Lands and Territories, hereby, for myself, my Heirs and Successors, binding myself and them that I will make no other Dispose of them to any person or people whatsoever, without their Grant and Allowance first had and obtained; and that they shall be disposed in Plantations, Villages, or Farms, according as the General Court of Connecticut shall order or determine the same, I always to receive such reasonable Satisfaction for my property in them according as we shall agree.[38]

Although the document's recorders used the language of English law and land alienation, important distinctions reveal the Algonquian context. Apparently, for Uncas the agreement was an activity and instrument that involved "binding myself and them," and a close reading reveals that all references to land grants used the future tense, suggesting that Uncas conceded only the rights of shared inhabitation and preemption. The English were already occupying much of the former Pequot lands at the south end and on the eastern bank of the Thames River. Uncas agreed that if and when he did make grants of his land on the western side, it would be to the English and no other nation. In terms of land tenure, this was an important agreement for the sachem to make. The resources within a given area were limited, so it was important for a sachem to be clear on which nations had the right to use them. For the English, the right of preemption meant that they would have a first crack at Uncas's lands;

however, for Uncas the agreement laid out the terms for sharing the space of the watershed, and writing, like wampum, solidified the "binds" between the two groups and enabled their mutual inhabitation.[39]

Having solidified the "League of Alliance & Friendship with the English," as Uncas's great grandson Mahomet (II) explained several generations later, "from time to time" Uncas, representing the Mohegans, made "gifts and grants for small consideration" of "tracts of their land," always ensuring that the bulk of the village territory was "reserved" to themselves. However, sometime after Uncas's death, "a generation arose in the Colony of Connecticut who knew not Unchas & his successors, but did contrary to the faith of their fathers' leagues, their publick records, & the terms of the Royal Charter, encroach upon the remainder of the Mohegan Lands which your petitioners' ancestors had reserved to themselves and their people for their hunting and planting grounds."[40]

Furthermore, Mahomet asserted, "the Mohegans were threatened to be slain if they came upon those lands." This account reflected communal memory, corresponding to speeches made by Mohegan councilors and recorded during the initial land case proceedings. The complaints addressed two primary assaults on Mohegan territory: the establishment of a new settlement, called Colchester, in the reserved hunting grounds and the expansion of the older settlement of New London into the planting grounds along the Thames.[41] In a speech recorded in 1703, Mahomet II's father, Mahomet I, related that "four of his men [were] taken at Colchester the last winter, and carried to New London, and there threatened to be hanged, when they had done nothing worse than that they went into a cellar and warmed themselves by the fire." He said these actions "seemed strange to him, and he was ashamed."[42] Another Mohegan leader, Ashenunt, protested that "the English had turned them out of their houses in the time of snow" from their planting grounds at Massapeage, "which occasioned their women and children to cry."[43]

Like Mahomet I, Ashenunt expressed bewilderment at the colonists' conduct. The Mohegans had held to their commitment to share space with the English, but the English appeared to be acting more like enemies than allies. Ashenunt further related that since this incident, the Mohegans had been called on as "scouts" for the English, remarking that "as they and the English have been friends and brethren, so they are our brethren still."[44] The English, Ashenunt asserted, demonstrated inconsistent behavior in asking the Mohegans to act as allies in war while failing to respect the rights and responsibilities of "friends and brethren" in shared space.

The Mohegans also accused the English of using their status as "friends" to deceive their leaders and unlawfully claim lands. For example, in 1698 Fitz-John Winthrop, the governor of the Connecticut Colony, and Gordon Saltonstall, the minister of New London, sought a grant for the town of Colchester from the General Court without acquiring those lands from the Mohegans. In order to legitimate the grant under British law, they coerced Uncas's son and successor, Owaneco, to release the hunting grounds to them on paper while he was "intoxicated."[45]

The Mohegans' experience of dispossession was thus complicated by Owaneco's acknowledged weakness for alcohol, enabling colonists to acquire deeds without the community's consent. However, Owaneco took several steps as sachem to protect the Mohegan lands from colonization, as well as from his own fallibility. In 1684, shortly after Uncas's death, Owaneco formally recorded collective Native rights into English law, granting "my right" to the planting grounds "unto the Mohegan Indians for their use to plant" and ensuring that "neither I, nor my son, nor any under him, shall at any time make sale of any part thereof; and that tract of land shall be and remain forever for the use of the Mohegan Indians." As Mahomet II later related from communal memory, "Those lands which your petitioner's ancestors had reserved to themselves & their tribe for their hunting and planting grounds was afterward confirmed by the General Court to Sachem Owaneco the oldest son & heir [of Uncas] and to his son Mahomet your petitioner and their heirs."[46] The rights that had always been confirmed with wampum in council were thus formalized through the writing that confirmed agreements in colonial courts. At the same time, Owaneco entered into a formal trust relationship with the neighboring Mason family in Norwich, who had maintained a firm alliance with Uncas and his descendants since the Pequot War. This relationship was solidified in written law, ensuring that the sachem "might not pass [the Mohegan lands] away to any without the Consent of Captain Samuel Mason."[47] Mason had to be present whenever words were written down, to translate to Owaneco and to ensure that words were recorded accurately. Thus, the Colchester grant was unlawful because it was transacted without Mason's participation, and the expansion of New London into Massapeage was null and void because Owaneco had recorded the Mohegans' perpetual rights to their planting grounds into law.

As the Mohegans' attorney William Bollan later argued, with their land protected by writing, "The Mohegan Indians flattered themselves that their Boundaries and Properties were now sufficiently ascertained and secured, and expected that they should not have been interrupted by the English in the quiet Possession of their entailed or sequestred Lands, and that the same should have remained to them in Perpetuity unalienable."[48] However, as Mahomet II later argued, Governor Fitz-John Winthrop and his compatriots, "contrary to the faith of their fathers' leagues, their publick records, & the terms of the Royal Charter," continued to expand their settlements into the Mohegans' reserved lands, dismembering the Mohegans from the land on which they were dependent for subsistence. Thus, in 1700, the Mohegans appealed to the highest authority over the colonists, using writing to communicate directly to the British Crown.[49]

From their seat at Mohegan, the sachem Owaneco and his brother Ben addressed a formal "complaint and prayer" to Queen Anne, with the assistance of Samuel Mason and New London advocate Nicholas Hallam. Their petition specifically addressed the recent settlement of Colchester in their hunting territory, asserting that "the whole grant of the township is their proper right & therefore ought not to be taken from them." The establishment of this town, they said, "denied their Native rights which hath been of ancient standing." Here, Owaneco and Ben invoked their indigeneity to demonstrate that their "Native rights" held greater weight than the claims of colonial settlers. Like their contemporaries Ashenunt and Mahomet I, Owaneco and Ben emphasized "their assistance afforded to the English in their warres with the Generall Nations of Indians," demonstrating that they had placed higher priority on their friendship with the English than on their relations with neighboring nations. "Yet," they protested, the Mohegans "are injured in their just rights and possessions." Encroachment defied the respect due them by other nations in their territory. The petition did not request land in exchange for "assistance," but rather called the English to task as allies for failing to respect the Mohegans' seemingly obvious right to inhabit their Native land.[50]

The petition persuaded Queen Anne to appoint a commission to review the case in 1705. The commissioners, under the influence of a sovereign who sought more control over her colonies and cognizant of Britain's need to retain their allies in ongoing war with the French and Abenaki, concluded that the Mohegans had "been very unjustly dispossessed" and ordered the colony to restore the lands in question to the

Native inhabitants. The commission confirmed the Mohegans as "constant friends and allies," observing that "in this time of war, [we] are in great danger of deserting their ancient friendship." They affirmed that the Colony had wrongly "granted away considerable tracts of the planting grounds" and that in particular, the Mohegans "have been very unjustly dispossessed and turned out of a tract of planting ground, called Massapeage." They also upheld the Mohegans' rights to their hunting lands, including the town of Colchester. Furthermore, the commission concluded that "the said Moheagan Indians are a considerable tribe of people, consisting of 150 fighting men . . . and cannot subsist without their lands, of which they have been deprived and dispossessed."[51] However, as Mahomet later related in his 1736 petition, the colonists in Connecticut did not "restore" to the Mohegans "any part of their lands of which they had so unjustly deprived them." Contrary to their Queen's decision, they "proceeded further to deprive the Mohegans of the small remainder of their lands."[52]

The colony, rather than fulfilling the commission's directive, developed a solution to the "controversy" that entailed the dismemberment of the Mohegan "sequestered lands" (the planting grounds and central village on the Thames River). In 1717, Governor Gordon Saltonstall and his council passed an act designed to convert the Mohegans from their "pagan manner of living" by creating a "parish at Mohegan Hill" where they might settle "after the English manner." This included the division of their common lands into family lots that would pass through the father's line, the lease of a sizable proportion to settlers, and the appropriation of five hundred acres for the settlement of a minister. Although a committee was formed to "take account" of the Mohegan families and the "quality and quantity of said lands," the program failed to take hold among the Mohegans. In fact, Mohegan leaders continued to make complaints about settler encroachment on all of their lands. Significantly, when one settler in the "sequestered lands" offered money to Owaneco's son Cesar and Ben Uncas "to be quiet and not complain against him," they responded that "the lands were not theirs to dispose of, but it was to descend to their Children." As Amy Den Ouden has observed, even as the colony sought to dismember their territory, the Mohegans continued to assert their "*collective* rights to their existing land base."[53]

In 1721, Connecticut governors further resolved the "controversy respecting the lands" by confirming their own titles and allowing that the Mohegans could keep a portion of their planting grounds for their own maintenance until "the whole Nation or Stock should be extinct." Ironically, it was dispossession that had the potential to produce that result and make the lands "now settled upon the Indians" the property of "the town of New London."[54]

By the time Mahomet II presented his petition in 1736, the impacts of dispossession were dire. He related that the "Colony of Connecticut" had "proceeded to further deprive the Moheagans of the Small Remnant of their Lands, & your petitioner, his tribe are now reduced to less than 2 miles square, out of their large territories for their hunting and planting, and that land so rocky that they are not able to subsist upon it." Yet, rather than surrender to the inevitable "extinction" presumed by colonial leaders, Mahomet followed a course previously pursued by his grand-father Owaneco, traveling with Captain John Mason, along with his kins-man Augh Quant Johnson, across the sea to bring his protest directly to the son of Anne's successor, King George II.[55]

In his petition Mahomet invoked the Mohegans' sovereignty within the land and their dependence on the land in arguing for their Native rights, asserting that the English had a reciprocal obligation, and a legal duty, to respect them. Exactly one hundred years after the Pequot War, Mahomet stood before King George II, recalling the long-standing friendship between them. Mahomet reminded the King that "upon the first arrival of the English in his ancestors' territories...His great-grandfather Unchas...had received and entertained them with the high-est forms of hospitality & friendship, freely affording them large tracts of land for their new settlements." He recalled that the Mohegans and the English had engaged in mutual defense against the Pequots' "greed," then against "the neighboring Indian tribes" who "combined together" to challenge them after the Pequot War, and most recently "against the French and Indians" to the north. Under the "League of Alliance and Friendship," the Mohegans had "reserved" their "Native lands" for them-selves even as they gave "gifts and grants...of their land" to their allies. Mahomet requested only that the English honor "the ancient friendship & alliance between them" and comply with that commitment by ensur-ing that "he & his people may be restored to and protected in the part of their ancestors' lands which they had reserved to themselves & their tribe for their hunting and planting."[56]

Attention to Mahomet's language illuminates the kind of sover-eignty invoked in the Mohegan narration of Native rights. He did not allow the British any rights over the Mohegan lands that were not granted directly by his ancestors. He did not refer to the lands the Mohegans "reserved" as tracts *within* the colony, but rather described lands that encompassed a village territory, including the "hunting and planting grounds" on which the community was dependent for subsistence and over which they maintained the right and responsibility of maintenance. While the colony sought to dismember the land into parcels of property that could be sold and settled, the Mohegans strove to maintain their village space as a political and ecological whole.

Furthermore, Mahomet strategically reminded the English of their own position in Native space. The Mohegans had recently served as scouts, traveling far up Kwinitekw to help protect the English from Greylock's raids, and Mahomet delivered his petition only eight months after the Deerfield Conference of 1735. He asked whether, "having proved themselves for the Space of 100 years faithfull friends & Allies to your Colony of Connecticut & true to your Majestie, & your Royal Predecessors, against all your Enemies, they may not now be forced to fly to some Indian Tribe for Subsistence, who are friends to the French, & Enemies to the English in time of War." Mahomet warned that the Mohegans, deprived of their subsistence grounds, would have to seek shelter with Abenakis or other nations to the north if they could not rely on their English "friends." In future wars, the English might find themselves facing their former allies on the opposing side. Still, Mahomet related, his "sincere prayer" was that the Mohegans would "obtain a redress of their grievances" from the "royal justice" of the King.[57]

Although Mahomet fell ill and died during his diplomatic trip to England, the British King did follow through on his petition, appointing a commission to review the case two years later. This particular commission, after a brief and dubious hearing, supported the position of the Colony, ruling that only the "Mohegan Fields," or the planting grounds along the Thames River, constituted the "reserved lands." The Masons and Mohegans appealed the decision immediately, and a fuller hearing of the case took place before a new commission in 1743.[58]

For this new hearing at the Norwich court, the Masons hired the dynamic attorney William Bollan to represent the Mohegans. Bollan grounded his legal argument in Mohegan communal memory, as recorded in Uncas's league and the petitions that followed. Extending the legal argument for collective sovereignty, he translated the "Native rights" of

Owaneco and Ben's petition into "property rights" under English law. Bollan insisted that "the Mohegan Indians are, and were, when the English began to settle in that Part of America since called the Colony of Connecticut," a "free" and "independent" people who were "immemorially possessed of and intitled to a large Tract of Country." Building directly on Mahomet's petition, Bollan maintained that the Mohegans "received" the English "in a friendly Manner, and permitted them to plant and settle among them." He asserted that it was well known in the colony "that all the Land within the original Boundaries of the Moheagan Country, which had not been granted away by them or their Sachems to the English, still belonged to and was the Property of the Moheagans" as "the original Natives." Bollan thus tied indigeneity directly to English property rights, asserting that Native land tenure was equivalent to the sovereignty of any European nation.[59]

In employing the language of property, Bollan contested the long-standing argument that Native people held only usage rights and that land had to be "improved" in the European manner to be owned. This was the legal foundation the opposition were using to argue that the Mohegans had only the right to inhabit their planting grounds.[60] When the case commenced in 1700, Owaneco and Ben Uncas expressed special concern for the two-hundred-acre "Mohegan hunting land," which was crucial to both subsistence and social balance. Colonial settlement within family hunting territories would foster tensions within the village, while destruction of the forests would lead to hunger, or even starvation, for animals and humans alike. However, the legal status of hunting grounds in the colonial system was a subject of much debate. The majority supported a position articulated early on by John Winthrop, the first governor of Massachusetts Bay Colony and father of the Connecticut governor with whom the Mohegans were contending. He had argued that "the Natives in New England" did not legally possess the land they inhabited because "they inclose noe Land, neither have any settled habytation, nor any tame Cattle to improve Land by, and soe have noe other but a Naturall Right to those Countries." On the other hand, Roger Williams, who had cultivated a greater intimacy with Native people, advocated for the legitimacy of Indian land grants over those acquired from the Crown. Although Williams certainly had his own political motivations for making this argument, the Rhode Island leader seems to have had a deeper understanding of "Native rights" than most of his contemporaries. For example, in

A Key into the Language of America, he related, "They say themselves, that they have sprung and growne up in that very place, like the very trees of the wildernesse," and he argued to his contemporaries that this indigenous status allowed the Natives land rights that the king of England did not have the legal authority to grant away. Furthermore, Williams advocated that Native hunting grounds constituted improved land because of the burning practices the Algonquians performed "twice a year" to facilitate travel through the forest and create a better environment for game.[61]

Pushing Williams's line of reasoning even further, William Bollan argued that "Native rights" held the same legal standing as "property," if not greater, regardless of the question of improvement. Bollan referred to the Mohegans as "the original Owners and Possessors of the Country," and insisted that the entirety of "the Mohegan Country" was the community's "possession" unless they, as the owners, granted it to someone else. The dispossession of the Mohegans, Bollan insisted, was completely illegal and should be reversed, even if English settlers had made improvements on those lands. Thus Bollan argued for the legitimacy of "Native rights," not only in Native space but in the realm of international law.[62]

In the writings that emerged during the land case, the Mohegans and their advocates attempted to articulate a relational system of land tenure. They communicated that the Mohegans had an "ancient" relationship to the land, on which they continued to rely for subsistence. They emphasized that they had a long-standing relationship of alliance with the English *within* their "ancestors' territories." The Mohegans had given the English specific rights and privileges in "friendship," but they had "reserved" their "Native lands" for themselves. The land was shared space to which the Mohegans had the prior claim, and the English were bound by the relationship of reciprocity between allies to respect their "Native rights." In a 1703 council speech, Appagese, a contemporary of Owaneco, succinctly expressed the relationship between his community, their land, and their English "friends," as well as their bewilderment at their allies' behavior: "He saith, from a boy their ground and he grew up together, and they have always been friends to the English, and why our ground and we should be parted now, we know not."[63]

Appagese used a metaphor of being planted in and growing with the land in order to convey his relationship to Mohegan. "Native rights" involved a cultural and corporeal intimacy with an environment in which humans were literally intertwined with the ground that sustained them. As the Mohegans resisted dismemberment by challenging abstract property rights and physical encroachment, a new narration of Native rights grew from the contested ground of Mohegan, a narration on which a new generation of leaders would draw to re-member the village "dish."

Dismemberment of the Communal Body, Writing as Re-membement (Mohegan, 1723–1743)

The dismemberment of the land caused by colonial settlement created both ecological and social changes in the village space. While the clearing of forests altered the physical environment, the politics of the land case caused a rift in the social structure that eventually split the village into two districts, "Ben's Town" and "John's Town," divided by loyalties to competing leaders and divergent courses in regard to their "Native rights." During the land case, the Mohegans faced a different kind of colonial warfare, fought largely with paper, that functioned as an assault on the political body of the dish.

In order to undermine the power of Mohegan petitions and protests, the Connecticut government supported the installment of a sachem who would act as their ally. After Owaneco died, his oldest surviving son, Cesar, succeeded him as sachem. When Cesar died amid the rumblings of war in 1723,[64] Mahomet II, as the heir of Owaneco's eldest son (Mahomet I, who had died before his father), would have assumed the role if deemed a suitable successor by the community. However, Major Ben Uncas, the youngest son of Uncas, apparently "threatened to kill" Mahomet II if the young successor opposed his claim to the sachemship. Ben "obtained" an "order" from Governor Saltonstall supporting his ambitions and thereby "usurped" the role of sachem as well as the right of the Mohegan community to select their primary leader. Ironically, this was the same Ben who had initially protested against colonial encroachment in the petition to Queen Anne.[65] Upon Ben's death shortly thereafter, his son, Ben Uncas II, "by the Contrivance and Assistance of the Colony of Connecticut, seized on the Sachemship against the Will and Inclination of Mahomet and the greater Part of the Moheagan Tribe." The General Assembly had previously acknowledged the young Mahomet as the rightful heir, but in supporting Ben Uncas II, they acquired "a Creature of their own," who "was prevailed upon shamefully to betray to the colony the Rights of the Tribe."[66]

Despite this opposition, the young Mahomet prevailed in his renewal of the land case. But as King George II's commission commenced in the spring of 1738, colonial officials sought to counteract the power of Mahomet's "public instrument" with one of their own. Taking advantage of Mohegan illiteracy, they tricked the majority of the tribe into signing a statement recognizing Ben as the rightful sachem. Then they persuaded Ben to sign a statement that "release[d] and forever quit claim[ed], all the right [and] title" to lands claimed by the colony and confirmed all of the deeds "granted and patented" by the "general court." However, the very next day, a large group of Mohegans signed a "declaration" that not only contradicted these statements but exposed the context under which they were produced. The "Mohegan Indians" asserted that, "through the importunity of some English persons," they

> sign[ed] an instrument...by which they now hear, they did acknowledge Ben Uncas as their Sachem, which then they knew nothing of, but being in a time when we thought ourselves in danger of losing our lives by means of the eastward Indians coming upon us, and his honour the governor writing a letter to us, we thought nothing more thereby only to give his honour an account of the number of our soldiers, and of those that would stand together and fight in time of war.[67]

The Mohegans then counteracted the colony's statements, declaring "that at a general meeting of the Moheagan, Pequot, and Niantick Indians, the whole body of them did renounce Ben Uncas as Sachem, in and by an instrument bearing date some time in September 1736." They insisted that they stood by that decision and "disown[ed] and protest[ed]" the false "recognition." Indeed, after Mahomet's death, they had chosen John Uncas, a "grandson of Uncas," as Mahomet's successor, to whom the majority remained loyal.[68] "And by virtue of these presents," they concluded, "we do disapprove of and make void whatever Ben Uncas has acted or may act in the capacity of Sachem or King over us in the conveyance of any lands, rights, and privileges whatsoever belonging to us."[69] The Mohegans' acknowledgement that they were joined by Pequots and Niantics in their "general meeting" demonstrates the rebuilding of relations that was taking place in the region. As Amy Den Ouden has discerned, "Mahomet's death had not left Mohegan resistors entirely on their own, for they had gained the support of members of neighboring reservation communities — Pequots and Niantics." Their participation in the general meeting represents an "act of cooperative resistance" that suggests that they "acknowledged their common struggle against dispossession and perhaps recognized that Mahomet's complaint to the Crown had created an opportunity for all of them to be heard."[70]

The Mohegans' declaration is also important for what it reveals about the process of communal remembrance. In using the names of the Pequots and Niantics, the Mohegans asserted the continuance of these communities and revealed multiple witnesses to communal memory. Interestingly, while Governor Joseph Talcott struggled to find the paper trail for the land case, the Mohegans consistently related a clear memory of collective history, from the establishment of Uncas's league to the "black dance" at the "general meeting" by which they had formally deposed Ben. Furthermore, they had learned to use writing, like wampum, to present their decisions and their remembrance in material form.

Among the signers of this declaration were John Ashpo, his brother Samuel, and a young Mohegan from Ben's town named Samson Occom. The marks of Occom and others from Ben's town demonstrated that even Ben's supporters objected to the colony's tactics, as well as Ben's complicity in their deceit. They also showed that the Mohegans were able to unite on matters that concerned the whole community. Samuel Ashpo was the only Mohegan who signed in script, indicating that he had begun to acquire literacy, although his signature on the "recognition of Ben Uncas" suggests that his reading skills were not yet well developed. Still, the appearance of a single signature marked the community's consciousness of the potential power of this force in their lives. Although Ben had failed as a sachem to speak the voice of the community, the Mohegans took it upon themselves to speak as "a whole body" through the vehicle of writing, even as the colony sought to use that tool against them.

However, these instruments were not enough to force a full hearing in the colonial court. In 1738, King George II's commission decided that Connecticut officials had produced sufficient evidence to support Ben Uncas's claim, although, ironically, they refused to hear testimony from the people he was supposed to represent. The commission consisted of political representatives from neighboring colonies who were deeply prejudiced in favor of maintaining colonial order in New England. Having fulfilled their obligation to hear the "voice" of the Mohegans through Ben Uncas II, who disavowed the land claim, the commission dismissed the case in favor of the colony. Colonial officials thus manipulated the Algonquian institution of the sachemship in order to bolster their own legal position.[71] In affirming that Ben II was the rightful sachem, they asserted that his word held the authority of the whole.

Samuel Mason traveled to London almost immediately to appeal the decision. The colony responded with another "address" by Ben Uncas II, which essentially presented their entire legal argument in the voice of the purported sachem. Ben's statement conceded that Mohegan existed "in the Colony of Connecticut" and that the "Mohegan Indians" were "subject[s]" of the King. Rather than appealing to alliance, Ben used the language of colonial benevolence to describe their affiliation, saying, "Your majesty's English subjects have always treated the Mohegans with great kindness." Furthermore, he added, "I have in my hand" a gift given "to my grandfather Uncas" by King Charles II. This statement supported Ben's claim to the sachemship but also served to contradict Mahomet's portrayal of the relationship between the Mohegans and the English. Rather than showing Uncas granting land to colonists, Ben depicted the king as the giver of gifts and therefore the holder of sovereignty. Finally, Ben counteracted Mahomet's account of the effects of encroachment by insisting, "We are in the quiet possession of our land which is far more than we can Improve and [are] joined to us by the Laws of the Colony." This statement negated the case's central arguments. If the Mohegans did not require more land for subsistence than that which the colony allowed them, they could not claim usage rights to the whole of their original territory. Furthermore, if that land was theirs by "the Laws of the Colony," they had no claim to "Native rights." Finally, in emphasizing the language of improvement, the statement confirmed that the Mohegans had need of and rights to only their planting grounds on the Thames River, not the hunting territory claimed by Mahomet.[72]

A new hearing began in 1743 with another round of dueling petitions. With a more diverse commission in place, the attorney William Bollan was allowed to present the Mohegans' full case, and the Mohegans were called upon to address the sachemship directly. In addition to testifying in court, a majority of the community members signed two powerful statements that disavowed Ben Uncas and presented their communal remembrance of recent history. They asserted, "The said Ben," both "before and since the time of the decease of our late rightful Sachem Mahomet, has been endeavouring to convey away our rights of lands to the English subjects of Connecticut, and to defeat us in those legal measures we have been and are still taking to recover our rights and possessions, to our great prejudice and dissatisfaction."[73]

The Mohegans reiterated that at their general meeting in 1736 they had unanimously "vote[d]" to "disown" Ben and "did likewise then declare our satisfaction in the proceedings of the rightful Sachem Mahomet, who was then prosecuting our cause in Great Britain." They argued that Ben had made "pretences to the right Sachemship" before the previous commission "and did assume the power and right of acting in behalf of the tribe as such, and of disposing of their lands as he pleased, to the great dissatisfaction and injury of the said tribe of Indians." They related the circumstances under which they had unwittingly signed their acknowledgement of Ben's sachemship in 1738 and reiterated, "We do therefore hereby utterly disown the said Ben to be or ever to have been our rightful Sachem, notwithstanding the aforesaid constrained acknowledgment of him as such, and do disallow of the said Ben's acting as the head or Sachem of our tribe in any respect whatsoever."[74]

The Mohegans further declared that they had reorganized their government; they had recognized John Uncas as having "according to the ancient custom of our tribe, the best right to the Sachemship of any Indian surviving since the decease of our said late Sachem Mahomet" and had "lately" selected twelve men to serve as counselors. Forty-three men signed the first petition in 1742, including Henry Quaquaquid, who was listed as a counselor, as well as Robert and Samuel Ashpo. Eighty men signed the second petition in 1743, including the Ashpos.[75]

To counteract these damaging statements, Ben Uncas produced an "address and declaration" in 1743, signed by the minority of Mohegans who continued to support him. He claimed that it was "evil-minded white people" who sought "to set up one John Uncas to be chief Sachem of the Moheagan Indians" and insisted that "neither I nor any of my people have any dispute or controversy with the king of Great Britain's people of this colony of Connecticut, touching or concerning any ground claimed by me or my people." He reasserted that the Connecticut settlers and government "have at all times behaved in a very friendly manner towards me and my people" and requested that they continue to serve as guardians and protectors. "I have no claims or demands against them or any of them," Ben insisted, "by virtue of the original and Native right of me the said chief Sachem and my Moheagan Natives," and he further declared, "I now hold for myself and people about four thousand acres of good and valuable land, which is more than sufficient for the habitation and improvement of me and my nation, and with which I am fully content." Through this writing, Ben once more denied his own grandfather's claim

to the Mohegans' "Native rights," as well as their claim to land necessary for subsistence. Bollan, speaking for the Mohegans, concluded that
Ben "was prevailed upon shamefully to betray to the colony the Rights
of the Tribe." The document's eleven signers represented Ben's "counselors," including Henry Quaquaquid and the newly appointed Samson
Occom.[76]

Samson Occom, the Land Case, and the Power of Literacy

While the Ashpos lived in the part of the village known as John's Town,
Henry Quaquaquid and Samson Occom lived in Ben's Town.[77] Unfortunately, there are no written records that relate Occom and Quaquaquid's
motivations for supporting Ben's complicity with the colony. It is possible that their families believed they were righteously upholding Uncas's
policy of cooperation with the colonists in the community's best interests.
They may have believed, as Ben Uncas claimed, that their best strategy
for survival was to accept the "protection" of the government against
encroachment by individual settlers. However, Ben's faithfulness to the
colony was greased with financial compensation. As the recognized
sachem, Ben received money for leasing land through the overseers appointed by the colony, and both he and his counselors were entertained
by the colony with gifts and feasts during the land case to ensure their
continuing cooperation. Bollan told the court that "the governor and
company" admitted to having given Ben "valuable consideration" for his
statements. "It is apparent from his conduct" Bollan commented, "that
this pretended Sachem Ben has sold himself to the governor and company and is endeavouring to sell the whole tribe, or, which is the same
thing, their ancient and rightful inheritance as fast as he can."[78]

Bollan also insisted that Ben was "now only the head of a corrupt
party or faction, seduced, deluded, and made by a little money, added to
the great artifice of the English, who have cunningly spread corruption
and caused divisions amongst this tribe." Of the four men (John and
Samuel Ashpo, Henry Quaquaquid, and Samson Occom), only Occom
actually appeared in the Norwich court to hear Bollan's accusations. We
cannot know what his reaction to these statements was, but it is clear
that over the next twenty years, both he and Quaquaquid changed their
positions dramatically, joining with the Ashpos to offset the "corruption"
and "divisions amongst the tribe" and actively pursuing the reclamation
of their Native rights.[79]

Occom may have also been present when Bollan revealed the connection between literacy and dispossession. The attorney stated that "the Moheagans beg leave to observe, that they are a people unskilled in letters" and that the English held the upper hand in "penning" the "treaties" and "transactions" between them, including several dubious documents presented as evidence by the colony. The English, insisted Bollan, "doubtless took care to express favorably for their own interest," leaving the Mohegans disempowered by the very instruments that were supposed to safeguard their rights.[80]

Clearly, the best route to protecting their lands was for the Mohegans to acquire the power of literacy for themselves. Uncas had relied on John Mason to write letters to the Connecticut authorities, while his sons had received help from Samuel Mason and New London attorney Nicholas Hallam in writing their petition to Queen Anne. Similarly, Mahomet II had obtained John Mason's assistance to compose his petition to King George II. The Connecticut Colony had taken advantage of the Mohegans' illiteracy to bolster their own position, and the Mohegans continued to rely on Englishmen for the interpretation and composition of correspondence with colonial officials. However, by 1743 a few of the Mohegans had begun to read and write. Augh Quant Johnson, who had traveled to England with Mahomet in 1736 and served as one of John Uncas's counselors, acquired these skills early on, as evidenced by correspondence with one of the friends he had made in England. His son Joseph inherited his ability and shared it with his family. Samuel Ashpo had begun to learn writing from a missionary at Mohegan. Only ten years after the land case hearing, he would be passing on his knowledge to Pequot students at Mashantucket while Joseph Johnson wrote letters to his wife from the battlefield on Lake George. Finally, just after his appearance in court, Samson Occom left Mohegan for Eleazar Wheelock's house in Lebanon, a town within the original Mohegan village territory, to learn how to teach his kin.[81]

In his autobiographical "Short Narrative of My Life," Occom related that as a child he had run from the grabbing hands of a missionary because the English teacher gave the young Mohegans little motivation to learn. But, as an adult, he was so drawn to reading that he taught himself, and he desired the skills to pass his knowledge on to others. Although inspired in part by his own recent conversion to New Light Christianity and by his "Desire to learn to read the Word of God," Occom noted, "At

Figure 7. Portrait of Reverend Samson Occom, by Nathaniel Smibert, ca. 1751–56. Bequest of James Bowdoin III, Bowdoin College Museum of Art, Brunswick, Maine.

the Same Time [I] had an uncommon Pity and Compassion to my Poor Brethren According to the Flesh. I used to wish I was capable of Instructing my poor Kindred. I used to think, if I could once Learn to Read I would Instruct the poor Children in Reading." Certainly a key motivation for Occom's "great Inclination to go to" Wheelock was his desire to learn about and share a newfound religious philosophy. However, we should not underestimate the effect Bollan's statement about the consequences of illiteracy may have had on the young Mohegan scholar. When Occom returned home many years later as a father, teacher, and minister, his literacy would evolve into a tool he could use to reclaim land and reconstruct the "whole" of Mohegan.[82]

=> decolonising act.

[margin: summary]

Occom's Journeys: Indian Education in the Network of Relations (Mohegan, Montauk, Iroquoia, 1749–1763)

The journey home was not an easy one for Occom. The Mohegan minister had been born into a tumultuous world at Mohegan. The son of Mohegan counselor Joshua Occom and his wife Sarah was born in 1723, the year the sachem Cesar died and Major Ben "usurped" the sachemship, while the English were calling on their allies to serve as scouts in Greylock's War. As a young scholar, he excelled under Wheelock's tutoring, but experienced difficulties with his health that prevented him from attending college at Yale. However, Occom's life took a positive turn when he joined some of his relatives on a fishing trip, traveling across the sound to visit relations at Montauk. As Occom related in his "Narrative," "The Indians there were very desirous to have me keep a School amongst them, and I consented." Occom remained at Montauk for eleven years, marrying into a leadership family, living within the community, and traveling with them in the subsistence cycle that continued to sustain Algonquian village life. Occom served the community as a teacher, minister, scribe, and healer. As Bernd Peyer has observed, "Rather than having received any employment assistance from his mentors as he may well have expected, Occom found relief by tapping the ancient sociolinguistic network among Coastal Algonquian Indian communities to find a useful application for his newly acquired skills." During these years, Occom kept a journey journal that illustrates the intertwined relationships between his "home" of Mohegan, his wife's home of Montauk, neighboring villages like Niantic and Mashantucket, and his mentor's school at Lebanon. Occom often traveled with his relations, including Robert Ashpo, Joseph Johnson, and his brother-in-law, David Fowler, building and maintaining connections between coastal communities. During these journeys, Occom began to develop a reputation as a stirring preacher, and he emerged as a leader who strengthened relationships in the larger network.[83]

While Occom was traveling and teaching, his mentor was developing his own project to educate young Indians for missionary work.

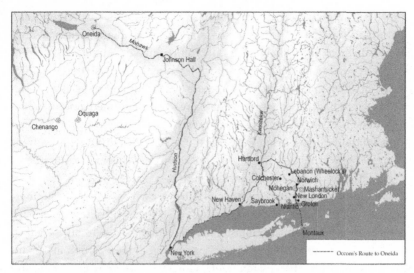

Map 8. Samson Occom and Samuel Ashpo's travels, showing Native villages and colonial towns (mentioned in the text), with Occom's route to Oneida indicated.

Occom's success may have served as the inspiration for Wheelock's "Indian Charity" school, but the motivation for Indian education also came from within. Occom was operating his school at Montauk, and Samuel Ashpo was teaching the Pequots at Mashantucket several years before Wheelock established his school at Lebanon. The majority of Wheelock's first students had close ties to Occom; they included his brothers-in-law, David and Jacob Fowler; his Pequot cousin Samson Woyboy, who had taught at Mashantucket before Samuel Ashpo; his son Aaron; as well as Augh Quant Johnson's grandson and granddaughter, Joseph Jr. and Amy Johnson, the first girl to enroll at Wheelock's school. Even Ben Uncas's son Isaiah attended for a brief period, but he proved a weak student. In addition, Samuel Ashpo eventually went to Wheelock to formally acquire a license to preach and to seek financial support to teach at the intertribal village of Chenango on the Susquehanna River, where he had received an invitation to serve as minister. So, while the school served to foster Wheelock's colonial experiment, it also provided a space of interaction for Native students who could potentially utilize their education for community empowerment.[84]

When Samuel Ashpo sought help from Occom's mentor, he probably knew that Wheelock and the missionary societies that supported him had targeted eastern Iroquoia as the best venue for Algonquian missionary-teachers. The Mohawks' and Oneidas' alliance with the English made them more likely to accept offers from New England than from northern Algonquians like the Abenaki, while the English perception of their "heathen" status and "wilderness" environment gave the project more weight than the schools that had already been formed among the acculturated southern New England Algonquians. Both Occom and Ashpo traveled to Iroquoia during the early 1760s, forging a diplomatic path for many of the young men who would follow from Wheelock's school.[85]

Occom received a commission to be a teacher and missionary at Oneida after serving many years within his own network of relations, during which time he faced increasing frustration with the lack of support he received from the missionary societies that were supposed to fund him. In comparison, as Peyer has observed, the position at distant Oneida was a "lucrative assignment." However, Occom was not entering into a territory entirely unknown. The Mohegans had a long-standing alliance with the Mohawks and Mohicans, and all three nations had recently provided scouts to the English for their forts around Lake George. As Peyer has noted, Occom's mission held great "political import" because it commenced "at the height of the French and Indian Wars." Ben Uncas himself had sent a message pledging the support of "the Mohegan tribe" to "our brethren of the Mohocks & Stockbridge Tribes" under "the old agreement made by their wise forefathers" to "defend that tree of Shelter planted by Our father the King & our ancestors." With this message, the Mohegans had promised to maintain their alliance with the Mohicans and Mohawks to defend their English brothers against the French and northern Indians, including those Abenakis who were fighting for their own land rights against the Mohegans' allies. The message was delivered only two years before Occom traveled to Iroquoia and only one year after Augh Quant Johnson's son, Captain Joseph Johnson, wrote a letter home to Mohegan, sending news on the men in his all-Mohegan company and relating a firsthand account of the siege at Fort William Henry.[86]

So, although the Oneidas may not have been acquainted with Occom as an individual, they were well acquainted with the Mohegans as a nation, and Occom's entry into Iroquoia was already grounded in alliance. Occom's first stop was Johnson Hall in the Mohawk Valley, where he met up with Sir William Johnson, the superintendent of Indian Affairs. Johnson was, in many ways, a British inhabitant of Haudenosaunee space; the Irishman's marriage to Molly Brant had solidified his place in the Mohawk kinship network, and he frequently played an intermediary role between the Haudenosaunee and the English. Johnson's ability to translate between English and Mohawk as well as his substantial education in Haudenosaunee diplomacy made him a good candidate for ushering Occom into Iroquoia. Johnson "introduced" Occom "to the Oneidas and Tuscaroras as a person sent for their Instruction in the Christian religion, and earnestly desired and recommended it to them to treat him as became one of his sacred function." Thus, Johnson represented Occom's position as something akin to that of a traditional spiritual leader, opening the eastern door to Iroquoia through an act of cultural translation.[87]

Samuel Ashpo subsequently followed in Occom's tracks to preach at the multinational villages of Oquaga and Chenango on the Susquehanna River. Oquaga was known as the "place of hulled corn soup," and these communities represented "kettles" where many traditions mixed. Combining Algonquian and Haudenosaunee families, traditional agriculture and European husbandry, longhouses and log cabins, Confederacy councils and Christian meetings, the communities at Oquaga and Chenango utilized the best of indigenous and European tools to maintain a flourishing existence in the Haudenosaunee homeland. Because Ashpo had been invited into this dish by its inhabitants, the motivation for his mission emerged, in many respects, from within Native space.[88]

The combination of alliance during the French and Indian War and the establishment of the missions created a new space of exchange between coastal Algonquians and the Haudenosaunee Confederacy, and education flowed both ways. While Occom, Ashpo, and their successors taught reading, writing, and the principles of Christianity, they learned Haudenosaunee language and diplomacy, as well as the limits of their own religious beliefs. Wheelock's school functioned as a site within this network. Occom brought his Montauk brother-in-law, David Fowler, with him to Oneida, and Fowler returned to Wheelock's school with four Mohawk students, including the young Joseph Brant. Brant had recently fought alongside his brother-in-law, William Johnson, in his first military battles and had witnessed the death of his clan chief, Hendrick, all of which had taken place on the same ground from which Captain Joseph Johnson wrote to his wife and on which his own life was sacrificed. At Wheelock's school, Joseph Brant and his Mohawk relations interacted with Johnson's son and daughter, as well as Occom's son Aaron, David Fowler's brother Jacob, and a much older Samuel Ashpo. Joseph Johnson

Jr. would eventually follow in his father's tracks toward Iroquoia, but he, like Occom, would serve as a teacher and missionary rather than as a soldier and scout, while Brant would mature into a powerful war leader and influential diplomat.[89]

Algonquian teachers in Iroquoia also learned a great deal about the circumstances that Indian people shared, including dispossession. When Occom arrived at Oneida, the clan chiefs presented him with a belt of wampum to "bind" them in "friendship," saying, "We are glad from the inside of our Hearts that you are come here to teach the right way of God." However, as a crucial part of their message and relationship, the Oneida speaker also insisted, "We desire to be protected in our lands, that none may molest or encroach upon us." During the same period, Samuel Ashpo told Wheelock of "a great concern among the Indians in those parts esp at Jeningo [Chenango] . . . that they are very unwilling that the English should get footing among them lest by & by they root them out as they have done in New England." The shared experience of dispossession provided common ground for Haudenosaunee and Algonquian people, a space in which to discuss the intricate workings of colonial systems as well as the potential routes of resistance.[90]

Re-membering the Dish: "We Shall Look upon One Another as One Family" (Mohegan, 1763–1778)

For several years, Occom and Ashpo traveled between their coastal village and the Haudenosaunee interior, but both men returned home during the winter of 1763–64, leaving Iroquoia due to the increasing threat of violence from Pontiac's War. Occom received a commission to minister at the neighboring village of Niantic and settled back in at Mohegan, where he hoped to raise his ever-growing family. Ashpo was supporting his own sizeable family through hunting, and he suffered from considerable debt. Considering his reliance on hunting and the threats settlement continued to pose to the Mohegan land base, it is no surprise that Ashpo, in line with family tradition, assumed a leadership role in renewing complaints against colonial encroachment. Occom himself had observed brewing problems with the English overseers on a visit just before his return home, especially regarding the leases to white farmers, and he was aware of Ashpo's organizing activities. In a letter to Wheelock written during one of his earlier journeys, Occom related, "I have heard Sam Ashpo and his people together, about their controversies, and I am afraid Sam Ashpo has took irregular steps, I cannot receive him yet, and I will not do contrary to my Mind; I hope I shall find him better next time I see him." Given the Ashpo family's long-standing allegiance to Mahomet and John Uncas, it is likely that "their controversies" referred to the land case, or at least to the lands that Ben Uncas and the overseers were leasing without the community's consent. The letter suggests that Samuel Ashpo and "his people" had begun taking "steps" to renew their legal case as early as 1762 and that Ashpo was attempting to persuade Occom to assist him in seeking redress. Occom's hesitancy was reflective of his own family's accustomed allegiance to Ben, as well as his unwillingness to directly challenge colonial authorities. However, his experiences upon returning to Mohegan would soon transform his position.[91]

Only a month after Occom's arrival, he joined a group of Mohegan counselors who "met at Benjamin Uncas's" house "to consult about our land affairs." They sought to regain control over the leases and make their sachem, Ben Uncas III, responsible to the whole. Ben III had succeeded his father in 1749, at least as far as colonial officials and the inhabitants of Ben's Town were concerned. Like his father, he violated the responsibilities of the sachemship, acting unilaterally and cooperating with the overseers rather than consulting with the counselors and the community. Even the English schoolteacher, Robert Clelland, had complained to Wheelock that Ben III was consuming "the profits of Mohegan" in drink. When Samson Occom, Henry Quaquaquid, and other leaders from Ben's Town gathered for a meeting on March 24, 1764, they resolved to "go unanimously in all matters," counteracting the divisive dynamic and attempting to pull Ben back into a participatory process. "But," their meeting minutes related, "our over Seers got in With our Sachem alone at Norwich on March 29 & 30: and got him to give a Lease to Mr. Ross of Banks' Farm — Contrary to the agreements between the over Seers and the Indians, and between the Sachem and his Councel."[92]

According to their minutes, "The Tribe of Mohegan got together to Consult What our over Seers, and Sachem had done, and found it altogether Disagreeable to our Minds." Occom and Quaquaquid were in attendance, along with the majority of Ben's counselors; however, at this gathering the counselors from John's Town were equally represented, including John Uncas Jr. and Samuel Ashpo. Three weeks later, the same group met at Henry Quaquaquid's home in Ben's Town and "found our Selves of one Mind Still." Counselors from both factions were once again present, including Occom, Quaquaquid, and Ashpo, as well as a number of women.[93] This reconstructed group then "constituted Trustees to Act in the behalf of Mohegan tribe of Indians" and "concluded to Send the Trustees to Benj Uncas, to talk With him in a Mild Manner, to Bring him to Consideration, that We may agree and make up Matters in an Amicable manner." The trustees "went, on 24 of April in the Morning to his house, and talkd With him, but it only Stird up fire in his Breast and was inraged against us and So We left him."[94]

After this altercation, the group gathered in John's Town to have "a Meeting of the Mohegan Indians amongst themselves" and "found many faults more against Ben Uncas." Together, they confirmed their conclusions in writing:

> First he has never regarded his Fathers Will by which he was made Sachem — 2ly he has least out Some Lands Without his Councill; and 3ly he has Sold much Tymber Wood and Whoop Poles and Stone, and Contrives a great deal to set the Indians by the Ears in stead of making peace amongst them, and he is not Contented With all the privileges he Injoys and all the help he has from the Indians he reckons as nothing, and Wants more Still, but We believe he Wont have So much in time to Come for these things[.] We think he has forfeited his Sachemship over and over again [;] Neither Can we in Conscience look upon him again as our Lawful sachem in Mohegan.[95]

From this moment on, Ben Uncas found himself with few adherents outside of colonial circles. A few remained loyal to him, but the majority of Mohegans had reconstituted themselves as a communal body, leaving Ben Uncas and his acquiescence to colonial control behind.

The records of the meetings of the Mohegan tribe reveal a movement from within to reclaim the ethic and structure of the common pot. First they endeavored to draw the sachem back into his role of responsibility within the group and to restore a commitment to unanimity. When that failed, the process of rebuilding the pot began with a meeting that united leadership from both towns and rekindled cooperative deliberation. During the course of their meetings, the Mohegan counselors began to think as "one mind" and act as one body, re-membering their social structure and perhaps even drawing on the rhetoric of Haudenosaunee councils in which Ashpo and Occom had participated.[96] The Mohegans alternated meeting locations between the two towns, ensuring that neither would be regarded as the "center" of decision making. This generation of leaders became highly cognizant that the greatest threat to the village was its division, and through their deliberation they repaired the divides between the two towns and reconstructed the social body of their village. Their next step was to address the re-memberment of their land base.[97]

On behalf of this newly united council, Samson Occom drafted a formal letter to William Johnson, utilizing his connections in Iroquoia to renew the case against the colony. He opened with eloquent phrasing that flattered Johnson as a "mediator" for "the Miserable Nations of this Land," demonstrating his literacy in the language of diplomacy. The draft among Occom's papers shows that he struggled with choices in rhetoric and metaphor so that the letter would reflect indigenous oratorical styles, including appeals to political kinship and prayers for pity and empathy. He lauded Johnson for his clarity and compassion, praising his foresight in having seen, from looking far and wide, that the "Natives" were "liable to be imposed upon by all other Nations." Occom wrote, "It moved your Heart in a way of Commiseration," and thus "God hath made you a mediator between the Natives and other nations," to whom the Mohegans, as "children," now "make our cries in your ears."[98]

Having established a space for diplomatic address, Occom related the key problem faced by his nation:

> We are imposed upon by our overseers, and what our overseers have done, we take to be done by the [Connecticut] Assembly. By what they have already done, we think they want to render us as cyphers in our own land. They want to root us out of our land, root & branch. They have already proceeded with arbitrary power over us, and we want to know from whence they got that power or whether they can maintain such power justly over us.[99]

This protest marked a renewed narration of Native rights. Like his forebear Appagese, Occom employed a metaphor for indigeneity that "rooted" Mohegans in their native land. He pointed to colonization as the main threat to the continuance of their tree and the growth of their "branch." In contrast to a developing rhetoric of gradual extinction, Occom invoked the image of a living and growing community being actively thwarted by people acting under questionable authority. Demonstrating a complex cognizance of colonial power, he contended that the colony's leaders were attempting to displace his nation both physically and conceptually — to turn the Mohegans into "cyphers in our own land." In using the word "cypher" he articulated awareness of the colonial processes through which the Mohegans were being transformed into disempowered non-entities, "wanderers" in their own land. Yet for Occom, the tree remained rooted and tangible. It was the "power" claimed by the Connecticut government that was "arbitrary" and intangible. Reinforcing the embed-dedness of the village, Occom questioned the legitimacy of a system that colonists (and some Mohegans) took for granted, and he challenged its very existence within Native space.[100]

In his letter to Johnson, Occom demonstrated keen comprehension of the colonial source of the division within his community and revealed his position, with other like-minded leaders, as a mediator between the two towns: "Understand Sir, this Tribe has been in 2 parties, the Government Pretended to befriend the Indians, and Mr. Mason pretended the Same, and each had a Number of Indians, and there is a few of us that Seems to Stand between the two parties — Deacon Henry Quaquaquid will relate the whole matter to your Honor." He also revealed the community's cognizance that Ben's sachemship was part of the divisive design, telling Johnson that the Connecticut government had "used Ben Uncas as a tool in their hands." Explaining how the tribe had reasserted their sovereignty over the sachemship, he related, "Ben Uncas was to do nothing without his Council while he was our sachem. And now we have cast him off, as your Honor may see in a Bit of Paper, and the English intend to Continue him as a Sachem over us, but we have a Law and a Custom to make a Sachem without the help of any People or Nation in the world, and when he makes himself unworthy of his Station we put him down — ourselves."[101]

Occom was invested not only in reclaiming a sense of sovereignty, but also in reasserting the Mohegans' political relationship with the Crown. Given the Mohegans' recent contribution to Britain's military success, Occom could speak from a position of alliance. In concluding his letter to Johnson, he appealed to British law, asking "whether the kings Instructions Concerning the Indian Lands, aren't as much for us as any Tribe." He was referring to the 1763 Royal Proclamation that protected the land rights of Britain's Indian allies and, in particular, to a critical passage in which the king "strictly enjoin[ed] and require[d] all persons whatever, who have either willfully or inadvertently seated themselves upon any Lands . . . which, not having been ceded to, or purchased by Us, are still reserved to the said Indians as aforesaid, forthwith to remove themselves from such Settlements."[102]

Occom's question demonstrated his literacy in the documentary record of the land case, as well as British Indian law. In his analysis, the proclamation could be applied to any Indian nation that had not ceded its territory, and by his reading of the land case, Mohegan certainly qualified.[103] Under British law, Connecticut colonists should be enjoined to "remove themselves" from the "reserved" Mohegan lands, which had not been "ceded" or "purchased" lawfully. Occom used his reading skills to interpret the laws that might secure his community's rights, and in writing to Johnson, he sought an audience with the source of those laws. Henry Quaquaquid traveled to Iroquoia to deliver the letter, along with the minutes of the tribe's meetings, which had probably been recorded by Occom. Johnson apparently cleared the way for Occom to address the King of England more directly. For, while news spread quickly through the colonies of stirrings at Mohegan, by the end of the year a report reached the governor of Connecticut that Samson Occom "has wrote a Letter agst this Colony with his own hand to the King of G Britain, and amongst many other things, he says they have not a foot of land." John Mason had recently traveled to London in order to reopen the land case, and "Had it not been for Occom," Robert Clelland told Governor Thomas Fitch, "Mason had not gone to England." Ben Uncas confirmed the rumor, and just a few months later, another settler corroborated it: "Samson wrote a letter to the King of England wherein he said these Indians joined the English when few in Number, but when they increased they took their Lands from them after they sett up stakes for their bounds, and now their widows suffered as they had no land to plant, or kept creatures on & that in truth they had not land of their own."[104]

Even this brief summary shows that Occom followed the rhetorical patterns of his forebears: he appealed to Mohegan agency, alluded to the history of alliance and wrongful dispossession, and insisted that the community needed the lands in question for subsistence. According to Clelland, Occom was not only writing on behalf of the community's Native rights, but was "stirring up the Mohegan tribe" to reclaim them. "He has behaved very ungratefully to the worthy & kind overseers who have spent no small time to protect them & manage their affairs," the schoolteacher complained. Furthermore, "Repeated complaints he has Sent up to Sir William Johnston & it is said he is gone up to him this Season, It is trew I suppose that he said he would ly down & die if he got not his Will." Colonial officials were especially alarmed that the Mohegans seemed to be coalescing against the colony around the land case. Clelland lamented,

"All the Indians but 3 ingages to stand by one another agst this Gov't," and added, "If Samson could be gain'd the rest would come easily over, at present his is all in all with them."[105]

Occom's involvement in Mohegan politics erupted into public controversy. His mentor Wheelock was especially concerned about a "breach" between him and the missionary at Mohegan, David Jewett, who was threatened by Occom's reputation as an orator. Wheelock reported, "A great number from other neighbouring parishes flock to hear Mr. Occum on Lord's Days at Mohegan & the effect of which you may easily guess." Furthermore, Jewett was "like to lose all his land in his parish, if the Indians there should gain their point in their suit against the government." These circumstances led Jewett to privately pursue actions against his rival. According to Wheelock, "Mr. Jewet wrote the Commissioners at Boston, on which they withdrew [Occom's] pension." Wheelock wrote to Jewett in January of 1765 regarding the need for a "publick enquiry" into Occom's activities and asked him to gather "evidence" for the case "against" Occom for the Board of Commissioners, but Jewett was somewhat reluctant to do so, fearing public antipathy. However, when Wheelock's own purse was directly threatened by Occom's "stirrings," he was motivated to take action. He became incensed when his petition to the General Assembly for the continued funding of the Indian school was denied "on acct of the reports & jealousies of his [Occom's] being active in the old Mason Case, as it is called, of late revived."[106]

According to Wheelock, "Clamours spread through the government, and almost every one cryed out against Mr. Occom as a very bad, mischevious, and designing man." As a result of all the "controversy," Occom was called before the Commissioners for a formal hearing. Not surprisingly, the evidence included statements from Mohegans who remained loyal to Ben. They relayed testimony about Occom's involvement in the land case and the reconstruction of the Mohegan government. Joseph Johnson's brother Zachary, Ben's closest counselor, reported that the Mohegans "had frequent meetings but never wanted Sachem & he to meet with them[;] he said they car'd not for them for they were for Govtt & English & they wanted all their lands from them." Zachary Johnson further related, "Samson said . . . I was for the Government & overseers & that these very men eat up their lands." A Mohegan woman named Sarah Mohomet testified that Occom had sent "Eliphalet Peggy" to "ask of her whether she would be for Sachem & Government or join to have him turn'd out, [and] if she would join with them they would take care of her." Peggy, she related, said the group had made an "agreement of one and all of them & that they would stand by one another as the English."[107]

For his participation in the land case, the missionary board reprimanded Occom for his "ill conduct" and forced him to make a "confession" in which he formally apologized and promised not to "act in that affair, unless called thereto and obliged by lawful authority." He wrote,

> Although as a Member of the Mohegan Tribe and, for many years, one of their Council, I thought I had not only a natural & civil Right, but that it was my Duty, to acquaint myself with their temporal Affairs; Yet I am, upon serious and close Reflexion, convinced, that as there was no absolute Necessity for it, it was very imprudent in me, and offensive to the Public, that I should so far engage, as, of late, I have done, in the *Mason Controversy*.[108]

However, Occom later told a Mohegan woman that he had "outwitted" the commissioners. Ironically, this information was revealed in a long complaint that Ben Uncas wrote along with Zachary Johnson and Simon Choychoy to demonstrate that Occom and his compatriots were still pursuing the land case. Only two months after Occom's "confession," Ben reported to the governor, "Samson told a squa he had outwitted the ministers, when she told him they were to put him down."[109] This revelation gives weight to the subtext of Occom's confession, which asserts his obligation as a councilor to his community. In an undercutting tone, Occom reminded the commissioners that he was not only a missionary under their pay but a "member" and leader of a "tribe," with a "duty" to enable his people to survive here on earth, not merely to prepare a path for them to heaven. Occom suggested that this duty was also a "right" ensured by the "natural" laws common to all humans and by the colony's own code. He spoke covertly to the missionary society's pretense of benevolence, implying that their own claims of concern for the "poor Indian" may have been rooted in hypocrisy.[110] While providing the "confession" that would enable him to retain his salary, Occom validated his actions by demonstrating his position within Native space and his literacy in common law, exposing the colony's paternalism as a duplicitous pretense with which the "ministers" appeared complicit.

Regardless of the commissioners' chastisement, Occom, along with Ashpo and Quaquaquid, proceeded to push the land case through William Johnson, seeking "authority" from the internal "obligation" to his community and appealing to the "lawful authority" of higher colonial

powers, thus remaining faithful to the letter of his promise. To demonstrate the key role Occom continued to play in Mohegan political affairs,
Uncas, Johnson, and Choychoy reported to Governor Fitch:

> The melancholy condition of this tribe for 15 months past ever since
> Samson Occum has moved here, oblidges me to lay all open to your
> Honr for relief. Presently upon Occum's arrival, he differed with
> our overseers and me for leasing Mr. Ross a piece of land, He first
> drew of the bulk of the Indians from their allegiance to me that they
> would not acknowledge me as their sachem; 2ndly He has got the
> Indians to disregard and despise this kind Government & our good
> overseers — who protect & defend us against all incroachments. . . .
> 3rdly He has brock up our School, and persuaded the Indians to
> keep back their children from School because the Master joins us he
> says with the overseers against the tribe. . . . 4ly He has join'd with
> Mason party against this Government and makes the poor Indians
> believe he will recover for them a vast tract of land 4 miles wide & 8
> miles long, he sent Hary Quaquid last summer twice to Sir William
> Johnston's & it is said hary is going again very soon, I suppose
> Mason had never gone to London had not Occum got the Indians to
> sign several papers for said Mason.[111]

Furthermore, the three reported that "our Indians have meetings by themselves on the Mason affair" and that Henry "Quaquid set
out this week for Sir William Johnston with a Pacquet." This "Pacquet,"
which Quaquaquid did indeed carry to Johnson, contained a statement
from the "Tribe of Mohegan Indians" signed by leaders from both towns,
the combined group of counselors selected during the meetings held the
year before. The only surviving copy is fragmented, but the entire letter
concerned the land case. The document suggests that it was Johnson who
had advised the Mohegans to send their petition to the king, and it contains a report on "our guardian" Mason's journey to England. The council
appealed directly to their "alliance" with the English and addressed their
concern that the case had been "postponed, which we fear & Dread Inas-
much [as it] hath been so Long delay'd already by the Government."
This delay, they wrote, "hath already Impovershed us." Insisting that
they were being "kept out of our Lands by the Government," the Mohegans reiterated that their Native rights were being violated and their
subsistence was at stake. They asked for Johnson's help in bringing the
"Case to A Speedy Determination."[112]

As Ben reported to Governor Fitch that spring, Occom himself traveled to see "Sir William with a fresh packet." Although Occom's travel back to Iroquoia was ostensibly in service of Wheelock's missionary project, his trip was clearly related to the land case as well. Occom spent a good part of the summer traveling between Oneida and Johnson Hall, even attending Joseph Brant's wedding while he was visiting.[113] Once more, Iroquoia served as a space for deliberating dispossession. While Occom was visiting his territory, the Mohawk teacher Isaac Dakayenensere wrote to Eleazar Wheelock, regarding his proposal to send missionaries and settlers to "assist" them "in setting up husbandry":

> We would have you understand Brethren that we have no thoughts of selling our Land to any that come to live among us; for if we should sell a little Land to any, by & by they would want to buy a little more & so our Land would go by Inches till we should have none to live upon — yet as those who come to Instruct us must live, we have no objections against their improving as much Land as they please; yet the Land shall remain ours.[114]

This statement reflects the exchange of knowledge that took place in the networks of Native space, a shared remembrance of the experience of colonization as a deceptively gradual process of dismemberment and dispossession. However, it also reflects the knowledge that comes from that shared experience, a re-memberment that could ultimately protect the lands, and the Native rights, that remained.

Although British magistrates ultimately decided the land case in favor of the colony, this outcome did not alter the Mohegans' conviction. Rather, the decision deepened their belief in the hypocrisy of the colonial legal system and pushed them to seek solutions from within. It also gave Occom and other leaders even greater motivation for pursuing education in order to "outwit" colonial deceit. Occom's commentary upon hearing the decision exemplifies this position:

> The grand controversy which has subsisted between the Colony of Connecticut and the Mohegan Indians above seventy years is finally decided in favor of the Colony. I am afraid the poor Indians will never stand a good chance with the English in their land controversies, because they are very poor, they have no money. Money is almighty now-a-days, and the Indians have no learning, no wit, no cunning: the English have it all.[115]

Although the Mohegans lost their case in the colonial courts, perhaps the greater accomplishment was their reclamation of an indigenous
internal organization. They brought back a sense of unity to the community
and a sense of sovereignty to the land. The renewed tradition of deliberation and consensus is especially evident in the minutes of a meeting held
on the eve of the Revolutionary War, recorded by Samson Occom:

> April 28, 1778: In the evening, the Tribe met together, to Consult
> about the Disposal of the Rent money, and as it has been agreed
> unanimously heretofore once and again, that we shall look upon
> one another as one Family, and will call or look upon no one as a
> Stranger, but will take one another as pure and true Mohegans; and
> so at this time, we unanimously agreed that the money does belong
> to the whole Tribe, and it shall be disposed of accordingly for the
> Benefit of the Whole.[116]

When the Mohegans confirmed themselves as "one Family," they were
actively engaged in the re-memberment of the common pot. Recognizing
the role colonialism played in their division, they reclaimed an Algonquian ethic of familial inclusiveness and a commitment to act in the traditional role of sachems, equally distributing resources "for the benefit of
the whole."

Conclusion: Reclaiming Native Space "at the Mouth of the River" and at Mohegan Hill

The Mohegans' reclamation of sovereignty from within enabled the leadership to continue to assert their Native rights even after the land case was
over. A petition from the Mohegans and Niantics in 1785 regarding their
fishing rights at the mouth of Kwinitekw exemplified this ongoing articulation, even after the establishment of the United States:

> To the Most Honorable General Assembly of Connecticut.... Your
> steady, close and faithful friends the tribe of Mohegan, and the tribe
> of Nahantick sendeth greeting. Sincere friends and brethren may
> talk freely together without offence. Such we concluded, the Eng-
> lish of Connecticut and Mohegans, and Nahanticks are — your
> Excellency may well remember, that we sent a Memorial to the Gen-
> eral Assembly, held at New Haven last October, requesting, not a
> Priviledge, which we never had before, but a Protection in our
> Natural Priviledges, which the King of Heaven gave to our Fathers
> and to their Children forever. When we received an answer or grant

to our petition, we were all amazed and astonished beyond measure. What? Only half a sein allowed to Monooyauhegunnewuck,
from the best friends to the best friends? We are ready to conclude,
that the meaning must be, that in time to come we must not have
only one canoe, one bow, one hook and line, among two tribes, and
we must have taxes imposed upon us also, &c., &c. Whilst the King
of England had authority over here they order no such things upon
us. Alas, where are we? If we were slaves under tyrants, we must submit; if we were captives, we must be silent, and if we were strangers,
we must be contented; or if we had forfeited our priviledges at your
hands by any of our agreements we should have nothing to say.
Whenever we went to war against your and our enemies, one bow,
and one hatchet would not do for two tribes — And what will the
various tribes of Indians, of this boundless continent say, when they
hear of this restraint of fishing upon us? Will they not all cry out,
mmauk, mmauk, these are the good that the Mohegans ever gloried
and boasted of — Certainly we cannot hurt the public by fishing, we
never had more than two seins in Mohegan and two in Nahantick
and many times not one in Mohegan for over 15 years together, and
we fish but very little in the season. We conclude your excellencies
must have mistaken our request. And therefore we earnestly pray
again, that the honorable Assembly would protect us in our Natural
Priveledges, that none may forbid, hinder, or restrain us from fishing
in any of the places where we used to fish heretofore.[117]

The petition was signed by Samson Occom, Henry Quaquaquid,
Robert Ashpo, and three Niantic leaders, Phillip Cuish and Joseph and
Isaac Uppauquiyantup. They opened their address by recalling their long-
standing friendship with Connecticut. Like their forebears, they expressed
"astonishment" and "amazement" that the colonists would dishonor this
friendship by disrespecting their "natural privileges" to fish freely in their
home territory (see Map 7). They invoked their sovereignty by demonstrating cognizance of their right to self-government and their status as
separate nations, exempt from paying taxes to the state. They also suggested that the new state might be trying to erode this status in attempting
to regulate their fishing.

The petition is important as well for its representation of the relationship between the Mohegans and the Niantics. They continued to share
space at places like fishing sites and maintained a social and political
relationship, but they also preserved their separate identities as villages.
The petition's authors balked at the colony's proposal that they should

share one sein between them, asking sarcastically if the Mohegans, the colony's ancient allies, should be "allowed" only "half a sein." The metaphor of being forced to use "one canoe, one bow, one hook and line, between two tribes" suggests a comparison to the larger village environment. Both groups had regulated their common fishing space by using particular seining sites to ensure equal distribution. By lumping all Indians in the region into one category, the colonial government threatened to break this system of balance between groups, which would inevitably lead to conflict and competition.

Furthermore, the Mohegan and Niantic leaders insisted that they had not "forfeited our privileges...by any of our agreements." They asserted fishing rights in the very same territory on Kwinitekw that previous sachems had claimed during the land case. Despite decisions made in the courts, Native rights could neither be granted nor taken away by the colonial government, but existed as a reality within Native space unless the indigenous inhabitants relinquished them. The Mohegans and Niantics bolstered this position by locating themselves within a larger network of Native nations across "this boundless continent," suggesting that a message of distrust would spread through an extensive network of communication if the state of Connecticut did not respect their rights. Like Owaneco and Mahomet II, the Mohegan and Niantic leaders insisted on placing their English, now American, allies within Native space, concluding their petition by reiterating the obligation of their "friends" to respect their "natural privileges" in their land.

Although the Mohegans continued to assert their Native rights, the material impact of the land case decision could not be denied. Their subsistence suffered, and colonial encroachment continued. Even the Mohegans' attempt to build a subsistence culture around agriculture was thwarted by continuing infringement on their planting grounds. As during the beaver and wampum wars, colonial acquisition led to scarcity and competition within and over the common pot, despite the political unity the Mohegans had built from within.

Still, the Mohegan leaders were able to learn from their experiences of the wampum wars and the land case, developing several solutions that were rooted in the renewed ethic of reconstruction and unity. Occom's strategy was to strengthen relationships within the larger coastal network and to reconstruct a new dish from among the surviving wampum-making nations, a village that could be moved along the waterways to a place with more abundant resources, away from colonial control. All of the people involved in this project were committed to the principles of Christianity that Occom had embraced as a young man, as well as to the ideals of the common pot. His partner in the development of this "utopian" vision was the grandson of Cato Johnson, Joseph Johnson Jr., who, after teaching at Oneida and the neighboring Tunxis community, had married Occom's daughter. Utilizing their connections to the Haudenosaunee, Occom and Johnson appealed to the Oneidas, who gave them land and adopted the Algonquians into the Confederacy. As Occom related in his journal, he and his followers named their newly constructed village "Brotherton, in Indian Eeyamquittoowauconnuck," recalling the relationships between all of the nations from which they came and honoring the Mohegans' commitment to "look upon one another as One Family."[118]

Henry Quaquaquid and the Ashpo brothers chose to remain at Mohegan, developing a strategy based on the lessons of the land case and exemplified by their 1789 petition, which was quoted at the beginning of this chapter. The Mohegan leaders' romanticized nostalgia for their ancestors' hunting and fishing life and their emphasis on agriculture as the new foundation of community sustenance reveals a strategic utilization of the language of property law. In asserting, "We have begun to work our land, keep horses and cattle and hogs; and we build houses and fences in lots," Quaquaquid and Ashpo appealed directly to the rhetoric of "improvement." Their petition represented a strategic reversal of John Winthrop's original justification of colonial ownership. The Mohegans argued that they clearly owned their lands not only through Native rights but by the definition of property rights as well. Furthermore, by advocating for the division of the dish into individual lots, the Mohegan leaders may have been attempting to protect the pot as a whole, because individually owned property could not be easily contested. Even as they lamented the loss of their "one large dish," Henry Quaquaquid and Robert Ashpo may have been ensuring its preservation. The petition, in this reading, represented a mastery of colonial law and rhetoric to ensure the continuance of the village.[119]

Even if this interpretation of Quaquaquid and Ashpo's strategy is valid, it was truly the Mohegan women, and especially Occom's sister Lucy Tantaquidgeon, who led the most effective movement to sustain the village dish. Unlike her brother, Lucy remained firmly planted at Mohegan. For generations, the Mohegan people had held their annual Green Corn/Wigwam festival celebrating the women's harvest at the village center, where the Algonquian transformer Moshup, "the greatest" of all the creatures of the sea, had marked this spot with his footprint. Indeed, it was at this annual gathering that the "great meeting" of the Mohegans, Niantics, and Pequots had been held in 1736, where Mahomet's mission had been confirmed and Ben Uncas had been condemned with a "black dance." Here, the Mohegan women planted the structure that would mark the village as Native space and prevent the eradication of the community and its land base. And it was primarily in community remembrance that this story was sustained.

As Mohegan tribal historian Melissa Tantaquidgeon Zobel has related in her own written history, "Four generations of Mohegan women," beginning with Lucy Occom Tantaquidgeon, "fought hard for the creation of that structure. Its purpose was to prevent Mohegans from being relocated, for by the 1830s, federal law required any unschooled or nonchurchgoing Indians to go West." By the "end of the reservation era," when plans were made by the colonial government to dissolve the Mohegan reserve entirely, the Mohegan church was the "only communally owned tribal property" and "sacred site." By planting a church at the site of Moshup's rock, the Mohegan women created a marker of property and sacred space that would be respected by their American neighbors (see Figure 8). Yet, at the same time, the church also represented a site of communal remembrance and a central space for the maintenance of a unified community. Here, leadership councils continued, community members gathered, and the wigwam festival was renewed. Here, the pounding of corn into *yokeag* with a giant mortar and pestle reminded every generation of the power of the village dish and of the women who sustained it through the tradition of transformation. Here, the Mohegan women reminded all of their relations to "come . . . home."[120]

Ultimately, the male leaders could not envision a solution that did not entail division. Occom's plan became controversial in his home community because it involved the parting of some of its strongest members to build the new village of Brotherton. While his plan entailed the division of the community, Quaquaquid and Ashpo's required the division of its lands. But Lucy Tantaquidgeon and the Mohegan women remained committed to the vision of unity. They grounded their common land in a building that marked their territory in a way that outsiders would comprehend, creating a space that served as a gathering place for the whole "family" until they were able to renew the Mohegan narration of Native rights before a colonial court, 150 years later, to reclaim their village as Native space.[121]

Figure 8. View of the Mohegan church through the trees from Moshup's rock. Photograph by the author, 2007.

According to Melissa Tantaquidgeon Zobel, the Mohegans still gather at the site of Fort Shantok, upriver from the Mohegan church. The "ruins" of this village, marked by red cedar trees and crushed shell, stand as a reminder of the "conflicts" between the Mohegans and the Narragansetts and as a testament to Uncas's ability to reconstruct and defend his village. She relates, "A large stone called Shantok Rock" once marked the site where Uncas gathered his people together after they first split from their Pequot relations. This rock, although removed to make way for railroad tracks in the nineteenth century, would remain, in the memory of Uncas's descendants, as a remembrance of "the political discord that can divide a nation." The church and the wigwam festival, which continue at Mohegan to this day, would also remain as permanent markers and reminders of the power of unity and of the strength of the village that sustains.[122]

3

Two Paths to Peace

Competing Visions of the Common Pot

From the mouth of Kwinitekw we now travel back upriver to Fort Dummer, where the Mohawk leader Hendrick and the Mohican leader Aupaumut served during Greylock's War, then to the Housatonic, Muhhekunnutuk, and Mohawk Rivers where they both had homes and kin. We follow the paths of their grandsons, who served on opposite sides in the American Revolution and developed competing visions of reconstruction in its wake.

Two Paths to Peace (Newtown, Buffalo Creek, Niagara, 1791)

In a meeting with American emissary Timothy Pickering held at Newtown Point to discuss the potential for peacemaking between the recently established United States and the "Western Indians" of the Ohio River Valley, a speaker for the Oneidas proclaimed:

> Brother, What shall we do, now you have told us the mind of the United States? We have told you that since the peace, we have sent to the Western Nations so many belts of peace as would make a very large heap. Now whatever more shall we do in the matter? Four paths for peace are already made: Brant went in the first path: The Big Gun tried to go in the second: The Stockbridge Indians go in the third: and in the fourth go the Western Army, carrying peace in their hands.[1]

The "peace" to which Young Peter referred was the treaty between the United States and Great Britain that ended the Revolutionary War. To the astonishment of Britain's Native allies, they had been left out of the treaty entirely, and the Haudenosaunee were charged with transmitting a message to the Native nations in the Ohio Valley telling them to lay down the hatchet, without being able to offer any guarantee of their land rights. Rumors spread quickly through the Ohio tributaries that backcountry settlers had resumed their ferocious drive to acquire land in the valley and that the United States claimed to own, by conquest, the full span of the continent to the Mississippi River. The Treaty of Paris left Britain's allies in a precarious position in changing political space, with both Indians and Americans embroiled in a whirlwind of frontier violence. Many on both fronts desired a solution that would lead to peace, although settlers and Indians had very different ideas about what that solution should entail.[2]

Young Peter spoke of two paths to peace led by the United States — that of the "Big Gun," Colonel Thomas Proctor, and that of the American army. Peter, like many Native leaders, expressed disapproval of the young nation for pursuing two contradictory paths at once. The American leadership had sent Proctor on a diplomatic mission to meet with the Haudenosaunee leadership at the newly reconstructed Confederacy council fire at Buffalo Creek while simultaneously moving soldiers into the Ohio Valley to fortify their military posts. Even as they met with Proctor, they received a message from military leader Arthur St. Clair inviting them to participate in an action against the Western Indians. Young Peter implied, with more than a hint of irony, that Proctor's mission had failed because the Americans were entangled in conflicting intentions. Seneca leader Red Jacket told Pickering, "Your discourse is intermixed with friendship and trouble. When we speak to you, we speak of friendship unmixed. . . . In ancient times, when we made peace, we cleared the path and made it open both ways."[3]

Although wary of American peacemaking efforts, the Six Nations expressed hope for the two indigenous paths to peace mentioned by Young Peter.[4] The Mohawk leader Joseph Brant had just attended a council at nearby Buffalo Creek where Haudenosaunee people discussed the American emissaries' proposals for peace. He had left charged with a mission to travel to the Western Indian country to discern, in the words of Seneca leader Young King, "what is the mind of these people towards the thirteen fires." The Six Nations would wait for the Western Indian response before they took any formal action. The Mohican leader Hendrick Aupaumut arrived at Newtown from New Stockbridge with the Oneidas and Tuscaroras.[5] During the meeting with Pickering, Aupaumut and his counselors pledged to travel west to mediate a peace between their American "brother" and their Algonquian relations. Oneida leaders appeared confident that these two paths could be pursued in parallel. Young Peter told Pickering, "Our minds are still strong for peace. Just before you came from home, we sent off Brant to continue the peace with the Western Indians" and "our nephews...are going on the same business with Brant. We hope they also will succeed; and that those nations may be brought to take hold of the chain of friendship with the US."[6]

At the British Fort Niagara, just north of Buffalo Creek, Aupaumut and Brant encountered each other for the first time on the path that led to the Western Indian country. Aupaumut related in his report, "I had the opportunity to talk with Brant but he never say a word to me of his business, and when he saw that these Indians were so friendly & free, he privately calls them together and tell them not to talk or walk with these Yankees." He offered to "go with" Brant to the Western Indian country, so that they might walk together, but at every turn, according to Aupaumut, the Mohawk leader "stopped" him from traveling farther. He waited for months for the path to clear, but finally "set out homewards," and returned to "find my family alive — but my business lay desolate." Brant, he related, "advise[d] me never to do anything for the United States, for they are strong & must do everything themselves."[7]

From Brant and Aupaumut's encounter at Niagara, this chapter moves in divergent directions, east to explore the transformations in Native space during the American Revolution and west to comprehend the councils of the United Indian Nations in its wake. The protection of the village dish and the preservation of the larger network are placed in relational opposition, elucidating how different leaders articulated divergent frameworks for defining that network, from Brant's commitment to the "Dish with One Spoon" to Aupaumut's effort to renew the place of his village within the Algonquian family of nations. This chapter highlights the importance of conflict and critique among Native intellectuals and analyzes the disagreement between Brant and Aupaumut, as evidenced in their writings, with a recognition that conflict itself is a force as ambivalent as wampum and writing, necessary and useful for all dynamic societies but holding the potential to cause profound damage in shared space.

Origin Stories: The Birth of Two Brothers

The crossroads at which Brant and Aupaumut met were already mired in blood. The Revolution had put them on opposing sides of a British war "between brothers." It had divided the Haudenosaunee Confederacy and split the Mohicans from their "brothers," "nephews," and "grand-fathers" to the west. Aupaumut was en route to renew those relation-ships, and Brant "stopped" him because he was suspicious of the Mohi-cans' brotherhood with the Americans. Although deeply rooted in this conflict, the clash between Aupaumut and Brant can be most fully under-stood when contemplated through a lens drawn from a narrative they both knew well: the story of Sky Woman and the next chapter of the ancient Haudenosaunee cycle, the conflict between her two grandsons.

When Sky Woman fell from the Sky World to the sea below, she carried not only the seed of the earth but the seed of its human inhabi-tants as well. In the words of John Norton, "When she had fallen on the back of the Turtle, with the mud she found there, she began to form the earth, and by the time of her delivery had increased it to the extent of a little island. Her child was a daughter, and as she grew up the earth extended under their hands."[8]

There is disagreement over exactly how it happened, but Sky Woman's daughter, "the Lynx," soon became pregnant. In Norton's ver-sion, Great Turtle himself takes on the appearance of "a middle aged man, of dignified appearance" and woos her. He enters her house at night and lays two arrows by her side, returning them to his quiver at sunrise and leaving before she wakes. Soon after, she finds herself pregnant with twins. As Norton's telling continues: "At the time of delivery, the twins disputed which way they should go out of the womb; the wicked one said, let us go out of the side; but the other said, not so, lest we kill our mother; then the wicked one pretending to acquiesce, desired his brother to go out first: but as soon as he was delivered, the wicked one, in at-tempting to go out at her side, caused the death of his mother."[9]

The son who entered the world in the natural way is known as "Teharonghyawago, or Holder of Heaven," or Skyholder.[10] The other is known as "Tawiskaron, or Flinty rock," or Flint. In common English trans-lation, the twins are known as the Good Mind and the Bad Mind, but these labels can be deceptive. As Onondaga linguist Kevin Connelly explains, the real difference between the two is rooted in the relationship between thought and action:

> In the Iroquoian telling of creation, twins are born in this world. They are beings but not human beings. Collectively, they can be

referred to as Two Minds and they go about transforming this world, creating. Eventually humans are created. Two Minds becomes two human cognitions; what I refer to as being versus analysis, and participant versus doer. Culturally, presently, the two minds are given the moral labels of Good Mind and Bad Mind in English. Culture privileges and nurtures 'the given,' that is, two created cognitions, uniquely. In Onondaga being and participant are treasured, analysis and doer are reined in tightly.[11]

Other versions of the Sky Woman story confirm Connelly's interpretation. In the Oneida translation published by Floyd Lounsbury and Bryan Gick, the Oneida storytellers Demus Elm and Harvey Antone relate, "Na?tehoti-?nikul-ó:tʌ," meaning "They had different kinds of minds/ thoughts." Skyholder walked through the land "considering" what might contribute to it, acting constructively from *within* the environment, while Flint "arrange[d]" without deliberation, acting *upon* the environment in careless and destructive ways.[12] This distinction between "participant" and "doer" is also prominent in Tuscarora David Cusick's telling in *Ancient History of the Six Nations*. He relates: "While she was in the limits of distress one of the infants in her womb was moved by an evil opinion and he was determined to pass out under the side of the parent's arm, and the other infant in vain endeavored to prevent his design."[13] In Cusick's version, Flint does not act out of inherent malice but is "moved by an evil design." The distinction is critical. He is not thinking clearly, in concert with his relations, and thus he responds rashly to impulse. In contrast, Skyholder's behavior is participatory, with a clear concern for the effect of his brother's actions on their mother.

As Connelly observes, these two ways of thinking are central to human "being," but the activity of participation is held in higher regard.[14] The continuing story of the twins emphasizes this principle. While Skyholder conceives of ways to make the world productive, Flint acts in opposition, making life on earth difficult for its inhabitants. When Skyholder creates rivers flowing in two directions, making travel as easy upstream as down, Flint creates swirling rapids, disrupting the water's flow and making movement difficult and dangerous. Yet humans are then forced to think imaginatively to counteract Flint's designs, resulting in cultural achievements like portages and birchbark canoes. A real conundrum surfaces when we realize that Flint's actions actually resulted in the creation of the earth "as we know it," and they invite rebalancing, making the inhabitants strive harder to make life continue on this island we call home.[15]

Origin Stories: A War between Two Brothers (Turtle Island, 1743–1783)

Joseph Brant and Hendrick Aupaumut were, in many ways, sons born of the same mother. The conflict between them was rooted in Sky Woman's earth, the ground of their shared history and common experience. Their paths can be tracked all the way back to Kwinitekw, where Aupaumut's grandfather and Brant's clan chief, Theyanoguin or Hendrick, had led joint scouting expeditions during Greylock's War. Hendrick had also traveled, for a number of years, between his home village of Canajoharie on the Mohawk River and the elder Aupaumut's village of Stockbridge on the Housatonic, where he had maintained a residence along with his brother Abraham and Old Town, one of the authors of the Petition at No. 2. Here Hendrick Aupaumut was born just after the Mohawk leader's death, and it is likely that his family named him in honor of their friend.[16]

Joseph Brant was born far from these familiar waterways, to a Mohawk mother in the Ohio Valley, where a number of Haudenosaunee families had established themselves among western allies. At the time of Brant's birth, the valley was a critical gathering place: a bowl of abundant resources, home to multiple "multiethnic villages," and a meeting point for many nations. However, following the death of his father, Brant's mother, Margaret, moved her family back home to Canajoharie, the flourishing "upper village" of the Mohawks. Here, there were abundant fields of corn, beans, squash, potatoes, and melons, as well as orchards of peach and apple trees. Longhouse political traditions continued alongside frame houses, like the one in which the Brants lived, and churches, like the one at Fort Hunter, near the lower village of Tiononderoge, where Joseph's sister Molly had been baptized before his birth. Mohawk clan mothers and chiefs participated in Confederacy councils and, with their villages so close to Albany, they played a critical role in maintaining the Covenant Chain alliance with the British. At Canajoharie, Joseph and Molly were drawn more closely into their mother's clan, and Margaret further secured her family's position by marrying Turtle Clan chief Brant Canagaraduncka, well regarded among Mohawks and British alike. The family frequently received visitors, including Margaret, Joseph, and Molly's

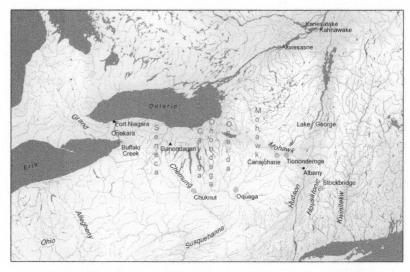

Map 9. The Revolutionary War in Haudenosaunee country, highlighting the territories of the Five Nations and showing the locations of Native villages, colonial towns, and other places mentioned in the text.

clan chief, Hendrick, and the man who would make a marriage alliance with Molly, Sir William Johnson. Joseph and Molly thus came into adulthood within an influential family, surrounded by relations and engaged in discussions of change and dispossession, talk of peace, and talk of war.[17]

Not surprisingly, brother and sister were early drawn into leadership roles. Molly accompanied her father and Hendrick on a diplomatic trip to Philadelphia in 1755 to discuss a long-standing dispute over fraudulent land sales. She was likely in training, joining the clan mothers in the formulaic process of remembering the words of the meetings in order to bring them home.[18] Shortly thereafter, young Joseph joined Hendrick and William Johnson at the Battle of Lake George. Mohegans, Mohawks, and Mohicans were present at this historic confrontation, joined in their alliance to the British. At the same time, Mohawks found themselves divided, with many warriors from Kahnawake joining Abenakis, Algonquins, and Wyandots in alliance with the French. Joseph Brant must have been present when Hendrick delivered a famous speech just before the battle. According to William Stone, the Mohawk leader looked out over the group of warriors assembled to assist the British and, seeing that they were outnumbered, remarked, "If they are to fight, they are too few; if they are to be killed, they are too many." Stone related, "When it was proposed to send out the detachment in three parties, Hendrick took three sticks and said, 'Put these together, and you can't break them; take them one by one, and you will do it easily.' Hendrick's advice was taken, and victory was the result." Hendrick might just as well have been speaking of his own nation and, perhaps, prophesying the future of the Confederacy. Although he died in this battle, the young Brant survived, carrying his clan chief's words.[19]

At Stockbridge, only one year after his death, Hendrick's namesake was born.[20] The town into which the young Hendrick Aupaumut emerged was rooted in the Deerfield Conference, where English, Abenakis, Mohawks, and Mohicans had gathered at the foot of the great beaver. The town of Stockbridge was designed to foster cooperative living between settlers in western Massachusetts and Mohicans living on the Housatonic River, many of whom had been displaced by Albany colonists. The original plan, as articulated at Deerfield, was that English settlers and Mohican converts would share space at Stockbridge and participate equally in town governance. However, as in the Kwinitekw Valley, this idealistic vision did not hold up against colonial land hunger. "As the English population grew," Colin Calloway explains, "the newcomers crowded the Indians out, and the town became divided into Indian and English neighborhoods." These "newcomers" included a "new generation of immigrants" who sought to push the Mohicans out of town governance and off of town lands, despite opposition from some of the original settler families. On the eve of the Revolution, some relations of the Mohicans, the neighboring Wappingers, joined with "rent rioters" in New York to protest dispossession by "manor lords" who "demanded rents from anyone living on lands they claimed." Like Samson Occom, Wappinger leader Daniel Nimham sought assistance from William Johnson, but, in contrast with his action in the Mohegan case, Johnson blocked Nimham's path to justice, siding with the New York land barons. Many of those dispossessed Wappingers joined the Mohicans at Stockbridge. When Daniel's son Abraham led a company of Stockbridge Indians to join their Massachusetts neighbors in resistance to the king's rule, he believed they were defending their own lands.[21]

As this conflict began brewing on Turtle Island, most Native leaders advocated for neutrality. However, the Stockbridge were among the first to pledge support to the American cause. Early in 1775, after "sitting near two days in council," they told their American "brothers," in a speech delivered by Captain Solomon Uhhaunauwaunmut, the chief sachem of the Moheakunnuk Tribe, that they were "sorry to hear of this great quarrel between you and Old England.... We never till this day understood the foundation of this quarrel between you and the Country you came from." However, the speech continued, based on the friendship they had sustained since "you first came over the great waters... when I was great and you was little – very small," the Mohicans pledged their assistance, saying, "Although I am [now] low and very small, I will grip hold of your enemy's heel, that he cannot run so fast and so light." They also offered "to take a run to the Westward, and feel the minds of my Indian brothers, the Six Nations, and know how they stand.... If I find they are against you, I will try to turn their minds. I think they will listen to me, for they have always looked this way for advice concerning all important news that comes from the rising of the sun."[22]

The Americans later responded, "Brothers.... All the chief counselors who live on this side of the great water, are sitting in the Grand Council House in Philadelphia. When they give the word, we shall all, as one man, fall on and drive our enemies out of their strong fort" at Boston. They accepted the Mohicans' offer, saying, "Though you are small, yet you are wise. Use your wisdom to help us. If you think it best, go and smoke your pipe with your Indian brothers towards the setting of the sun, and tell them all you hear, and all you see, and let us know what their wise men say."[23]

The Mohicans sent runners with wampum belts to Mohawk country and to their relations in the Ohio Valley, acting as intermediaries from the start of the war. When they attended the Treaty of Albany between the Haudenosaunee and the burgeoning American leadership in the fall of 1775, they pledged their fidelity to their American brothers: "Wherever you go we will be by your Side. Our Bones shall lay with yours.... If we are conquered our Lands go with yours, but if we are victorious we hope you will help us to recover our just Rights." In contrast, the Mohawks stressed the Confederacy's position of neutrality, telling the Americans, "We bear as much affection for the King of Englands subjects on the other side of the water as we do for you born upon this island" and warning the Mohicans against their joining impulsively in war: "If any ill Consequences should follow, you must conclude you have brought it on yourselves."[24]

While the Mohican and Haudenosaunee leaders were at Albany, Joseph Brant was in London "to feel the minds" of the British and address the wrongful acquisition of Mohawk lands. He had traveled to England with William Johnson's sons-in-law, Guy Johnson and Daniel Claus, and his nephew, Peter Johnson. While Brant enjoyed an aristocratic reception, he also listened carefully to debates on the American rebellion. Just as Wappingers joined with local settlers to oppose land grabs by the aristocracy, Mohawks called on their British allies to rein in land grabs by local settlers. In London, Brant became convinced that the only sustainable route to the protection of Mohawk lands was a firm alliance with the Crown.[25]

While Brant was in London, however, the Confederacy was holding fast to its own decision-making protocols. Many northeastern leaders viewed the brewing conflict as a dangerous battle "between brothers" and urged their relations to avoid getting embroiled in such a divisive war. Samson Occom counseled his own "beloved brethren" not to "intermeddle" with the "family contentions of the English" but to remain in "peace and quietness." The Oneida chiefs, representing the collective position of the Confederacy, initially told the Americans: "We cannot intermeddle in this dispute between two brothers. The quarrel seems to be unnatural; you are two brothers of one blood. We are unwilling to join on either side in such a contest, for we bear an equal affection to both of you, Old and New England."[26]

At the Confederacy's central council fire at Onondaga, the chiefs and clan mothers had met repeatedly, deciding firmly on a policy of neutrality. In 1774, Joseph Brant had attended the month-long Grand Council, where every nation had declared for peace and warriors who struck out on their own were chastised, and he had recorded the words exchanged in writing. However, the young Brant missed many critical councils while he was away in England. "With the Confederacy still pledged to peace and neutrality," Brant acted on his own impulse, counter to the collective decision. Barbara Graymont has suggested that this behavior represents a "classic example of a warrior chief seizing the leadership from the sachem chiefs" and clan mothers. On returning from England, Brant immediately began recruiting young men from his home village of Canajoharie and his wife's village of Oquaga, forming his own company composed of breakaway warriors and "about a hundred Loyalists from the area between the Hudson and the east branch of the Susquehanna, calling themselves Brant's volunteers." In recruiting men at Oquaga, Brant reportedly said they should "defend their Lands & Liberty against the Rebels, who in a great measure began this Rebellion to be sole Masters of this Continent."[27]

At the same time, young men in Oneida country were also breaking away from their clan leaders and joining the Americans in war. This trend was symptomatic of the erosion of women's power in particular. The decision to go to war rested with them, and the clan mothers had firmly decided for neutrality, with the goal of maintaining the Confederacy as a whole. Traditionally, their decision was enforceable because they held the harvest. They had the responsibility "to feed war parties" and the right to withhold provisions when young men acted independently. But with both the British and Americans providing supplies and a rise in the influence of warriors and war chiefs, the balance of powers became skewed. At the same time, the British were also tearing at the political fabric of the Confederacy. While leaders from New England and Albany were pulling on the eastern door, shifting from a request for neutrality to a demand for military support, the British at Niagara were pulling on the western door, insisting that the Six Nations adhere to the Covenant Chain and defend the British, and their own lands, against the rebels. In the midst of deepening chaos, disease hit the central council fire of Onondaga, and, for the first time since the Confederacy's founding, the leaders at Onondaga relayed the terrible message that the central fire had been extinguished. Finally, as Oneida warriors were moving toward the American side and Brant's company joined the British in campaigns against settlers in the Mohawk Valley, the commander at Niagara finally persuaded Seneca leaders to join the British in war, and even the clan mothers acquiesced. As warriors from both ends of the longhouse met in Oneida country, the "Iroquois civil war exploded" at the battle of Oriskany and spread throughout the country, culminating in the infamous assault known as Sullivan's campaign.[28]

At Newtown, at Chuknut: Sullivan's Campaign, 1779

This multifaceted American offensive moved north and west across Iroquoia, resulting in a devastating blow to the power of Haudenosaunee women, for the target of this campaign was the sustenance of the Confederacy, their bountiful fields of corn. George Washington, who thereafter became known as "Town Destroyer," instructed his generals "to carry the war into the Heart of the Country of the six nations; to cut off their settlements, destroy their next Year's crops, and do them every other mischief of which time and circumstances will permit.... It will be essential ... to ruin their crops now in the ground and prevent their planting more." As Calloway has written, during "the Revolution, American armies waged war against Indian cornfields." Thus, although the American Revolution is most often remembered as a liberatory resistance to British colonial tyranny, it was simultaneously a colonial war on the lifeblood of the Confederacy, the power of its women and the land they held in common.[29]

Long before their encounter at Niagara, Brant and Aupaumut's paths had crossed for the first time at Newtown, or "Chuknut," the first battlefield of Sullivan's campaign. Ironically, this place had most recently functioned as a multinational village, with Mohican, Delaware, and Haudenosaunee families living together in relationships of kinship and alliance. Now it would become a battlefield at which relations divided by the British would meet each other in war. Hendrick Aupaumut arrived at Chuknut as a captain of the Stockbridge company, newly appointed following the deaths of Daniel and Abraham Nimham on the battlefield in New York. The young Aupaumut and his men traveled with General John Sullivan and his troops, from the Delaware country in Pennsylvania up the Susquehanna to the Chemung River, where Joseph Brant's company awaited them, along with British rangers and Seneca warriors. Although Haudenosaunee leaders had provided ample intelligence that this major assault was imminent, British commanders did not heed their warning and failed to send the troops necessary to protect the Haudenosaunee villages. Although strongly resisted, particularly by Brant, the initial blow was devastating. In addition to killing men on the battlefield, the Americans destroyed the "extensive fields of crops" at Chuknut, including the "sixteen foot" stalks of corn, as well as "beans, potatoes, squash, pumpkins, cucumbers, and watermelons" that "grew in unbelievable abundance." Sullivan and his troops struck out from Chuknut, traveling north through Cayuga country and west to Seneca country, destroying fields, orchards, and houses as well as those who resisted and leaving only devastation in their wake.[30]

Simultaneously, Colonel Daniel Brodhead led an assault from the south, following the Allegheny River to Seneca country, where he reported seeing impressive villages containing large log homes and fields, as well as some "five hundred acres of corn and vegetables at the very least," which his troops subsequently destroyed. Another company struck out from the east toward Brant's home village of Canajoharie and the lower village of Tiononderoge. While most of the Mohawk families had already sought refuge, this campaign represented a physical and symbolic conquest of their coveted cultivated lands. In a message to Sullivan, Brodhead said of Canajoharie, "This Castle is in the Heart of our Settlements, and abounding with every Necessary so that is remarked that the Indians live much better than most of the Mohawk River farmers." Such statements demonstrate the degree to which the Confederacy had adapted to the changing circumstances wrought by colonization. Rather than a final blow to a "vanishing" culture, these were campaigns against nations who were successfully adapting to change and recovering from the effects of disease and war. In fact, the abundant fields of Iroquoia represented an obstruction in the path of westward expansion and a promise of the bounty to come. Rather than relics of an American past, the thriving villages of the Confederacy represented a vital, growing present, which, like the corn that grew to twice the height of any man, had to be cut down for America to grow.[31]

At Niagara, at Onakara: Maintaining an "Open House"

Both before and after the devastation of Sullivan's campaign, Haudenosaunee families flocked to the western door of Seneca territory, where they could seek shelter "at the channel" that connected Lakes Erie and Ontario and receive food and supplies at the British fort. Colin Calloway has described "Fort Niagara during the Revolution" as "a military headquarters, a trading post, a supply depot, a diplomatic hub, and a multiethnic, multiclass society." Like many Haudenosaunee people, Molly Brant made her way to the refuge of Onakara, or Niagara, where she maintained an "open house for all those Indians that have any weight in the 6 Nations confederacy." Molly had remained at Canajoharie protecting her matrilineal inheritance (as well as the wealth she had inherited from her husband) long after many had left. She abandoned her substantial house with her seven children only after the Battle of Oriskany, and even then she remained confident of her eventual return, writing to Daniel Claus, "I hope the Time is very near, when we shall all return to our habitations on the Mohawk River." As Joseph fought Sullivan's troops at Chuknut, Molly worked on diplomacy at Niagara, playing an instrumental role in maintaining Haudenosaunee support for the British cause. During the many councils held there during the Revolution, Molly Brant acted as "confidant in every Matter of Importance & was consulted thereupon." Reflecting on her influence among the male leaders of the Confederacy,

Daniel Claus related, "One word from her is more taken Notice of by the five Nations than a thousand from any white Man without exception."[32]

In truth, Molly Brant was playing a long-standing role of women leaders at the trade crossroads of Onakara. During the time before the Confederacy was formed, there lived a woman near this place who had also maintained an "open house" for war parties and traders. She was of the Attiwanderonks, a family of the Wyandots who would later be known as "Neutrals." She was one of many women who led in the cultivation of corn, and she would come to lead in the cultivation of peace. It is said that she embodied the reemergence of Sky Woman's daughter, "the Lynx," during a time similar to that of the Revolution, when brother fought against brother, threatening to destroy the body of the whole. Her name was Jigonsaseh, meaning "new leaf," and she signaled the birth of a new era. It is said that the Peacemaker, who founded the Great Law of the Confederacy, came to Jigonsaseh first. Through her, the women's role in leadership was established. Because of her, only women would have the right to declare war, and they would hold the peace in their hands. Her home became the House of Peace, where the clan mothers gathered to deliberate. From that time, the woman in each generation who held the title of Jigonsaseh served as the "head clan mother" and held the responsibility of engendering the peace.[33]

However, historically the Jigonsaseh had also served on occasion as a leader in war. It was the Jigonsaseh who in 1687 led Haudenosaunee warriors against a French assault on the Seneca known as Denonville's campaign. According to historian Barbara Mann, "She proved to have been a formidable opponent, rallying the flagging spirits of the refugees, pulling the army back together, and mounting a massive retaliatory strike against the French invader that drove Denonville out of Seneca at break-neck speed." This same Jigonsaseh, while protecting and defending "the peace town" of Ganondagan, also led raids on Fort Niagara, which at the time was controlled by the French.[34]

Molly Brant, inhabiting the same geographic space as this Jigonsaseh and descended from her people, also acted as a "conduit for information" between traveling war parties, among the Haudenosaunee leaders, and between "the British government and the Iroquois." She participated in the war herself, supplying British rangers and Indian warriors with goods, ammunition, and intelligence. In fact, Oneida warriors struck her home at Canajoharie only after she sent messengers to warn the Mohawks and British of the approach of American troops, resulting in an ambush at Oriskany. From all accounts, like Jigonsaseh, Molly also acted to "rally the flagging spirits of the refugees" at Niagara and strived to maintain the alliance with the British, even as their strength began to wane. Although there is no evidence to suggest that Molly ever served in the official capacity of Jigonsaseh, at Niagara she assumed a similar role, not only rallying the men but acting as "the head of a Society of six Natn Matrons, who ha[d] a great deal to say among the young Men in particular in time of War."[35]

Although it would seem that at the outset Joseph Brant was a young man acting independently of his clan mothers, the picture appears more complicated when we take into account the role of Molly Brant, who from the beginning advocated for maintaining a strong alliance with the British. For instance, at a critical council in Mohawk country just before the Albany Treaty, one of the American representatives observed, "The Indians pay her great respect and I am afraid her influence will give us some trouble, for we are informed that she is working strongly to prevent the meeting at Albany, being intirely in the Interests of Guy Johnson." Indeed, for Molly, her kinship ties to the Johnson family kept her firmly tied to the loyalist cause, and, like Joseph, she regarded the alliance with the British as the best path to the preservation of Mohawk lands.[36] As Barbara Mann observes, the sister–brother relationship was one of the strongest bonds in Iroquoia. Maternal uncles, not fathers, played the most instrumental role in raising young men, while clan mothers (always on the maternal side) were responsible for choosing the next generation of leaders and ensuring that they acted in the best interest of the whole. Joseph Brant's actions were completely in line with his elder sister's wishes, even if they went against the decisions of the Confederacy.[37]

Thus, even as the power of the clan mothers was increasingly eroded, women like Molly Brant continued to assert their leadership roles. In fact, Molly may have been one of the most instrumental, though unacknowledged, leaders in the war against the Americans. Yet she also recognized the critical role of women in making peace. When her brother set out toward the Ohio Valley after the war, seeking to forge a peace between the Western Indians and the United States, Molly insisted on women's involvement in that process. Thus, when Hendrick Aupaumut met Molly and Joseph at the crossroads of Niagara, carrying the words of the Americans, she chastised him as strongly as her brother, saying, "Here is another thing looks much strange — if these Indians were upon good business, they would certainly follow the customs of all nations — they would have some women with them, but now they have none."[38]

While Hendrick Aupaumut and Joseph Brant chose opposite sides in the Revolutionary War, their experience of its aftermath was strikingly similar. Canajoharie was devastated by the effects of war, and by its end, colonial settlements had overtaken the Mohawk Valley. Brant subsequently led the movement to relocate his community to Grand River, just north of Niagara in the old Attiwandaronk territory of Jigonsaseh, under the protection of the British. Aupaumut's participation on the American side did not prevent settlers from taking over his own village of Stockbridge. In fact, he returned to a level of devastation and displacement equal to that experienced by Brant. Thus, the Mohicans joined Samson Occom and the Brotherton Indians, relocating their village to Oneida, now the Haudenosaunee village closest to the American settlements. Like the Mohawk relocation to Grand River, the Stockbridge removal to Oneida may have been the only viable choice for a community devastated by both encroachment and war.[39]

The ensuing conflict between Brant and Aupaumut was thus rooted in a complicated cycle of warfare and alliance between their two nations, a history of friendship between their two "grandfathers," and a shared experience of violent loss and reconstruction.[40] Although both men may have been susceptible to the rash impulses of youth during the war, in its wake each regarded himself as a constructive participant in a delicate process of peacemaking and renewal. In turn, each man regarded the other as one who put obstacles in his way. Most important, the two paths they took to the Ohio Valley emerged from a geographic, social, and historical space inhabited by both, and their distinctive visions of peace arose from competing visions of Native space rooted in each man's particular cultural and geographic location.

The Two Paths: Competing Visions of the Common Pot

Joseph Brant's Vision: The Dish with One Spoon (Ohio Valley, 1786)

At the mouth of the Detroit River, from fall through midwinter of 1786, an enormous number of Native people — including "the Five Nations, the Hurons, Delawares, Shawanese, Ottawas, Chippewas, Powtewattimies, Twichtwees [Miamis], Cherokees, and the Wabash confederates" — gathered in council, "deliberating," in the words of Joseph Brant, "the best method we could to form a lasting reconciliation with the thirteen

United States." From within these councils an extraordinary document emerged, a communal narrative and proclamation of union agreed upon by all nations present and written by Brant.[41] "The Speech of the United Indian Nations" to the "Congress of the United States of America" challenged American claims to ownership of the continent and made it clear that the newly formed nation would have to negotiate directly with the older nations that continued to maintain this space as their own. While these confederated nations were willing to share space with their American "brothers," they were unwilling to share in a European system that constructed them as unequal inhabitants of a colonial environment.

Addressing the American Congress, the United Indian Nations opened by expressing disappointment with their exclusion from the treaty between "the King of Great Britain and you" while welcoming the opportunity to negotiate a "plan of accommodation" on their own terms. They had worked hard to "promote a friendship" with the Americans "during this time of tranquility," and, in Brant's words,

> We thought we were entering upon a reconciliation and friendship with a set of people born on the same continent as ourselves, certain that the quarrel between us was not of our own making. In the course of our councils, we imagined we hit upon an expedient that would promote a lasting peace between us ... the first step towards which should, in our opinion, be, that all treaties carried on with the United States, on our parts, should be with the general voice of the whole confederacy, and carried on in the most open manner, without any restraint on either side; and especially as landed matters are often the subject of our councils with you, a matter of great importance and of general concern to us, in this case we hold it indispensably necessary that any cession of our lands should be made in the most public manner, and by the united voice of the confederacy; holding all partial treaties as void and of no effect.[42]

The speech evoked an evolving conception of nativity, suggesting that both Americans and Indians had an investment in the shared space of their birth and a responsibility to generations of future inhabitants, even as its authors maintained Native sovereignty over the Ohio Valley. Insisting that their "rights and privileges" had "been transmitted to us by our ancestors," the United Indian Nations asserted that indigeneity was a stronger claim than conquest, that they held the responsibility for determining the best course of action for the future of their lands. The speech effectively incorporated Americans into Native space

Figure 9. Portrait of Joseph Brant by Gilbert Stuart, ca. 1786. Fenimore
Art Museum, Cooperstown, New York. Photograph by Richard Walker.

without relinquishing the rights inherent in long-standing indigenous
inhabitation.[43]

The cornerstone of the United Indian Nations' plan of accommodation was their insistence that the United States deal with the whole,
especially in matters of land. This vision was firmly grounded in the tradition of "the Dish with One Spoon." As Brant later explained the concept
to Alexander McKee, a British trader with strong ties to the Shawnee:

We have been told that such a part of the country belongs to the Six Nations. But I am of the opinion that the country belongs to the confederated Indians in common. If we say that such a part of the country belongs to one nation and such a part to another the Union cannot subsist, and we cannot more effectively serve our enemies whose whole aim has been to divide us.... Upwards of one hundred years ago a moon of wampum was placed in this country with four roads leading to the center for the convenience of the Indians from different quarters to come and settle or hunt here. A dish with one spoon was likewise put here with the moon of wampum. This shows that my sentiments respecting the lands are not new.[44]

The American leadership had a particular vision for the Ohio Valley. If Indians were to remain there at all, they would be contained on limited plots, while the bulk of the valley would be divided into lots and sold to settlers to fill the nearly empty national treasury. But the United Indian Nations sought to bolster a much older vision of the valley. The land itself was held in common, consisting of a network of shifting riverside villages within a larger shared hunting territory of grasslands and forests, all fed and connected by the Ohio River and its tributaries, enabling an efficient and diplomatic use of resources. The dish with one spoon was a geographic-social configuration and a political concept that solidified in the councils that followed the Revolution. The political vision depended on recognizing equality and building consensus among all nations who ate from the dish, a joining of minds that would enable the political system to mirror the geographic one. As Brant told the Western Indians during one of those early councils, "Let there be peace or war, it shall never disunite us, for our interests are alike, nor should anything ever be done but by the voice of the whole as we are but one with you." In speeches and in writing, Brant urged Algonquians and Haudenosaunee alike to participate in collective "deliberation" so that they might achieve "unanimity" in their dealings with the young American nation and thus preserve a large territory in the west that would remain exclusively under Native control.[45]

The United Indian Nations put the blame for continuing violence firmly on the United States and their attempts to divide the dish. Their speech continued:

Brothers: We think it is owing to you that the tranquility which, since the peace between us, has not lasted, and that essential good has been followed by mischief and confusion, having managed every

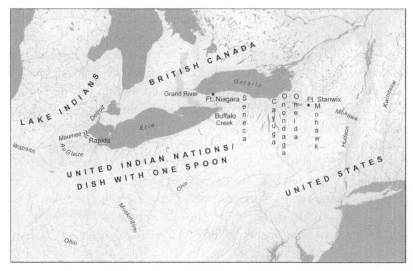

Map 10. Joseph Brant's vision: the Dish with One Spoon, demonstrating the spatial conceptualization of the territory of the United Indian Nations, with the Haudenosaunee Confederacy and the United States to the east, British territory to the north, and the territory of the Three Fires or the "Lake Indians" to the northwest. Also shown are the locations of places mentioned in the text, including Brant's village of Grand River.

thing respecting us your own way. You kindled your council fires where you thought proper, without consulting us, at which you held separate treaties, and have entirely neglected our plan of having a general conference with the different nations of the confederacy. Had this happened, we have reason to believe every thing would now have been settled between us in a most friendly manner. We did every thing in our power, at the treaty of Fort Stanwix, to induce you to follow this plan, as our real intentions were, at that very time, to promote peace and concord between us, and that we might look upon each other as friends.[46]

The United Indian Nations were particularly opposed to the Americans' orchestration of a series of faulty, forced treaties with individual nations, often represented by spurious "leaders." This course of action had begun at Fort Stanwix, where American emissaries coerced some Haudenosaunee leaders to sign a treaty when only a preliminary war council was planned. The commissioners infuriated the Haudenosaunee by taking several men hostage, including one of Brant's closest friends, the Mohawk chief Aaron Hill, to ensure compliance. When the Americans sent an invitation to the Shawnees to join them at a similar "council" at "the Mouth of Great Miami," Shawnee leaders chastised the Americans, saying, "You ought to know this is not the way to make good on lasting peace, to take our Chiefs prisoners, and come with Soldiers at your backs." Like the Six Nations, the Shawnees expressed disdain for the United States' pursuit of contradictory paths, and especially for encouraging divisiveness. "We are aware of your design, to divide our Councils," they told the American commissioners. Calling on the principles of the dish with one spoon, they insisted, "We are Unanimous and it is not right for you to kindle Council fires among Bush or Nettles.... Nothing is to be done by us but by general consent, we Act and speak like one Man."[47]

Even as they chastised the Americans for behaving like impulsive and destructive younger brothers, the United Indian Nations offered a wiser alternative, devised with "the best thoughts in our minds."[48] Their speech continued:

> Notwithstanding the mischief that has happened, we are still sincere in our wishes to have peace and tranquility established between us, earnestly hoping to find the same inclination in you. We wish, therefore, you would take it into serious consideration, and let us speak to you in the manner we proposed. Let us have a treaty with you early in the spring; let us pursue reasonable steps; let us meet half ways, for our mutual convenience; we shall then bring in oblivion the misfortunes that have happened and meet each other on a footing of friendship.[49]

The United Indian Nations proposed a middle ground rooted in the common pot and the tradition of condolence: they would meet the Americans "half ways," as equals in political and geographic space, where they might clear their minds of the storms of past violence and give thought to finding a path to mutual agreement. However, the speech also revealed another agreement embodied in the dish with one spoon. If the United States continued to act in the role of Flint and rejected their considered proposals for peace, the Native nations would "most assuredly, with our united force, be obliged to defend those rights and privileges which have been transmitted to us by our ancestors."[50]

The speech forced Congress into diplomatic action, but also alerted the congressmen to the power of the Confederation. They instructed Arthur St. Clair, the governor of the "Northwest Territory," to answer the call for a treaty, but also to "ascertain who are the head men and warriors of the several tribes, and who have the greatest influence among them; these men you will attach to the US, by every means in your power." Above all, they insisted, "Every exertion must be made to defeat all confederations and combinations among the tribes."[51]

Joseph Brant would not have been surprised by this instruction. He understood most fully the power of divisiveness: the beaver wars that had torn apart the tightly knit indigenous networks of the northeast, the Revolution that had divided the powerful Haudenosaunee Confederacy, and the current U.S. policy that sought to divide, isolate, and contain Indian nations to enable the colonization of the continent. For more than a decade, the Mohawk leader urged "unanimity" above all and worked to maintain the United Indian Nations as "one body" and "one mind" dedicated to sustaining the Native space of the dish with one spoon. Summarizing his vision, he wrote to his former classmate, the missionary Samuel Kirkland, in 1791:

> It has been my constant study since the peace between Great Britain and the United States to Unite the Indians together, and make such a peace between them and the States, as would remove all prejudices and enable us to set quietly down on our seats free from apprehensions and Jealousy. . . . You wish me to suggest my Ideas on the practicability of an accommodation between the Western Indians and the U States, to which I answer candidly that I think it still practicable, if proper measures are pursued by the States, but they must alter their system materially — Lay down the Hatchet, and call a general Treaty with the United Nations. If they are sincere in their pretensions to establish peace and live friendly with all the Indian Nations, they should cherish the Union, and make such proposals as will place the Indians on a more respectable footing than they have hitherto attempted — give up the Idea of taking possession of the country as conquered Land. Abandon that wicked mode of calling them out in separate Nations, or parties, to treat with them, which only serves to irritate and inflame their minds, instead of healing the sore, and removing the prevailing prejudices.[52]

Hendrick Aupaumut's Vision: Renewing the "Path of My Ancestors" (Western Iroquoia, 1791–1792)

Writing from his home at New Stockbridge in 1792, after completing a long journey from the Ohio Valley, Hendrick Aupaumut told American commissioner Timothy Pickering:

When I come to reflect on the path of my ancestors, the friendship
and connections they have had with these western tribes, and my
own feelings towards them, I conclude that I could acquaint them
my best knowledge with regard of the dispositions, desires, and might
of the United States, without partiality — and without groundless
opinion I could be more useful in that particular embassage than
those who have been opposing my undertaking.[53]

Aupaumut claimed a position within Native space that made him
uniquely qualified to mediate a peace between the Western Indians and
the United States. He emphasized ancient connections to his relations and
downplayed Brant's opposition by suggesting that the Mohicans' old Mohawk enemies were not to be trusted. He began his first re-port by relating that when he "arrived at Niagara" and "found the different nations of
the westward, . . . they rejoiced to see us — and we immediately begun to
speak together as our fathers & forefathers use to do."[54] Similarly, his 1792
"Narrative" opened with "a short sketch what friendship and connections,
our forefathers, and we, have had with the western tribes." At every stop
along his journey, Aupaumut described the relationship the Mohicans had
with each village and the welcoming joy the inhabitants expressed at his
arrival. Aupaumut's vision rested on renewing an older Algonquian network and reasserting a place for Mohicans within it. When his Western
relations told him about the confederation "of all who has one colar" and
asked "whether my nation would accept the plan of Union," he responded,
"It is a happy thing that we should maintain a Union. But to us it is not a
new thing. For our good Ancestors (who used to have compassion to each
other), many, many years ago, have agreed to this. And we, who are their
descendants . . . must always remind each other how our ancestors did
agree on this Subject, that we may never forego that."[55]

At the same time, Aupaumut was trying to claim a place for his
nation in post-Revolution political space, reminding his American brothers
in the east of Mohican service in the war and the ancient friendship between
them. Standing on the ground of Chuknut (now renamed "Newtown"),
recalling the shared bloodshed of Sullivan's campaign, Aupaumut told
Pickering, "I, my nation, have always been the friends of the Americans;
even from the first day they entered into the covenant of friendship. . . . I
(my nation) am your true and nearest brother. . . . My blood has been spilt
with yours: and to this day my bones lie in the fields with yours."[56]

Aupaumut traced this brotherhood to the first meeting between
the Mohicans and the Europeans on the Muhhekunnutuk (Hudson) River.

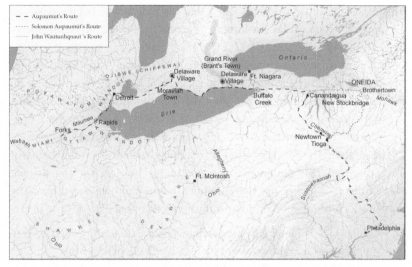

Map 11. Hendrick Aupaumut's vision: renewing the "Path of My Ancestors," demonstrating the spatial conceptualization of the same territory within a Mohican framework, highlighting Aupaumut's journey through the villages of his relations and the locations of Native territories (in caps) in the Ohio Valley and adjacent to New Stockbridge. Also shown are the side routes taken by his counselors and the locations of places mentioned in the text.

He called to mind a shared mortality, a mixing of bodies in war, and a shared nativity, the mingling of bones that would eventually transform into earth. While the Mohicans had acted as good brothers in defending the Americans against the British, the Americans had not participated fully in the relationship of reciprocity required by brothers in the Algonquian network:

> I lost many lives in your defence: I stood by you in all your troubles. . . . But I had no territory to fight for, nor had I to fight for liberty, for liberty I always possessed. But friendship, pure friendship, induced me and my nation to join you. But sometimes I feel sorrow, and shame, that some of my great brothers have forgotten me — that all my services and sufferings have been forgotten, and that I — my nation — remain neglected. What are the reasons I cannot say. Perhaps I am too small to be regarded. My friendship however is strong: my friendship I do not forget.[57]

Like the United Indian Nations, Aupaumut insisted that the Mohicans stood on equal footing with the Americans, conveying that they cherished their ancient "liberty" as much as the Yankees valued their newfound freedom. Aupaumut acknowledged that his nation had been weakened by warfare, yet he was requesting not patriarchal protection but reciprocity between allies.

Refusing containment within colonial space, Aupaumut also insisted that he did not follow an American road to peace but traveled on the path of his ancestors. When the British commander at Niagara interrogated him, the Mohican leader responded: "I did not come to this Country in order to see you.... My business is with my own color, that we might brighten the Chain of friendship which has subsisted between our forefathers."[58] This statement was not merely a ruse for the British. Aupaumut told Pickering, too, that his mission had originated from the deliberations of his own mind and the councils of his nation:

> For some time past I have felt a disposition to use my endeavors to effect an accommodation; seeing the Shawanese are my younger brothers, the Miamis my fathers, the Delawares my grandfathers, the Chippewas my grandchildren, and so on: They have always paid great respect to my advice.... Brother, my mind is now ripe. I am appointed by my nation: and these are my men who would go with me. I would undertake to visit the Shawanese and the other hostile tribes with a view to persuade them to make peace with the United States.[59]

Although American leaders were hoping for an Indian agent to represent their cause, Aupaumut asserted indigenous motivations, even if the United States was supplying the means. Aupaumut's declaration "My mind is now ripe" is particularly evocative. Much of the conference at Newtown centered on condolence for the loss of both American and Indian lives. Pickering spent several days brightening the chain of friendship with the Mohicans, Tuscaroras, Oneidas, and Senecas, burying "everything that was bad" and clearing their minds for peace. Aupaumut's "ripe mind" was one that had deliberated carefully, in the manner of Skyholder, and was prepared to embark; his was a mind that was full, ready for harvest, but also, a mind that was open and clear, ready to hear the stories of his relations.

Mapping Spatial Relations: The Eastern Door

Brant and Aupaumut both claimed a position for their nation as the eastern door — between the United States and the Western Indians, within the Haudenosaunee Confederacy, and within competing visions of alliance.[60]

Both worked to keep open the paths created by their ancestors. Brant's was one of four established paths to the dish with one spoon. Aupaumut's was the path between the eastern and western Algonquians, critical to maintaining that network, especially as colonial settlement threatened to split it in two.

The Revolution had divided the Haudenosaunee and had cost Brant and the Mohawks their lands on the Mohawk River, thereby weakening their geographical position as the eastern door of the Confederacy. Haudenosaunee space itself was reconfigured after the Revolution. The central council fire was rekindled in Seneca territory at Buffalo Creek, where Senecas, Onondagas, and Cayugas reconstructed new villages even as those who followed Brant sought to rekindle a fire at Grand River. Brant strove to create a position for the new center of Buffalo Creek/ Grand River as the door to the eastern path of the dish with one spoon. At the same time, he was repositioning himself within Haudenosaunee political space, using his military success and his ties to the British to support his ambitions. He frequently appeared as speaker for the Six Nations at Buffalo Creek and at Western Indian councils, circumventing traditional Haudenosaunee sachemship customs to make his position as war chief more substantial in diplomatic affairs.[61]

Mohicans traditionally served as mediators and messengers between eastern and western Algonquian villages. As Aupaumut related to Pickering, "It was the business of our forefathers to go around the towns of these nations to renew the agreements between them, and tell them many things which they discover among the white people in the east."[62] The Revolution had divided the Stockbridge community from its western relations. Too much time had elapsed between councils of renewal, messages had stopped traveling between them, and their political alliances had put them on opposite sides of the conflict. Aupaumut sought to repair this rift in the network and to reclaim an old role by weaving a new relationship between his American brothers to the east and his Algonquian relations to the west. His first task was to open the way for clear communication.

The Narrative of False Treaties: Cutting Up the Pot

Aupaumut went west bearing a message from the United States along with his impressions of President Washington's sincerity, but he returned bearing a message from the Western Indians.[63] In his 1791 journey journal,

Aupaumut communicated a narrative of false treaties, relaying Algonquian perceptions of recent history to the American leadership:

> They told me that by the transactions of the big knifes, at the treaty
> [of] McIntosh 6 years ago was the beginning of the displeasure of
> the Indians — that the big knifes did wrong the Indians in taking
> unlawfully of their best hunting grounds. Further they upon my
> querie tell me that if the big knifes [are] willing to restore the hunt-
> ing grounds to the Indians, they would have peace immediately,
> and further, they say that they would exchange lands with them . . .
> "but now, [as] long as they take our lands [in] such [a] manner as
> they have done we will never have peace with them for this reason.
> The great Spirit did give us that land and fill it with abundance of
> wild creatures for our living."[64]

Aupaumut, like Brant, pointed to the false treaties as a root cause
of current violence on the frontier. While Brant had referred to the Fort
Stanwix Treaty of 1784, which involved his Haudenosaunee relations,
Aupaumut cited the Fort McIntosh Treaty of 1785, which concerned his
Delaware "grandfathers."[65] As he explained to Pickering, his relations
were willing to compromise, but the invalid treaties would impose conditions that were not viable in the Ohio Valley environment. The American leadership, in their ignorance of the social and geographical landscape, made impossible demands for lands on which Native families
depended for subsistence. The Western Indians, Aupaumut related, were
willing to "cut a large slice" for American settlement, but only if their
hunting and planting grounds were confirmed. Like the United Indian
Nations' speech, Aupaumut's report also asserted the claim to indigeneity, quoting the Algonquians' statement that this land had been given
to them by the "great Spirit" and suggesting that his relations were as
embedded in the valley as the "wild creatures" on which they relied.

One of the foremost characters in Aupaumut's narrative of false
treaties was Joseph Brant. Although critical of Brant's opposition to his
mission, Aupaumut constructed the Mohawk as a praiseworthy leader,
perhaps implying that their paths were not so far apart. As he told it,
Brant had attempted to broker an important compromise preceding the
Fort Harmar Treaty of 1789, which followed the United Indian Nations'
speech. Aupaumut related:

> Before this, the Western Indians had been displeased with the treaty
> at Fort McIntosh, by which their land had been taken away. Brant
> proposed this to them — Whether in order to get those lands back

(as they were their best hunting grounds) they would give other lands in exchange? They were pleased with the idea, and told him they would. Then he mentioned a place, where he thought it best to have the line run. To wit — To follow the Muskingum to its head, where it approaches Cayahoga: then to run to the Head of Cayahoga river, & follow it down to its mouth; and that the Indians should relinquish all the land eastward of this line to the United States. This proposition greatly pleased the Western Indians and they asked Brant to assist them in getting that line settled.[66]

Aupaumut referred to Brant's Muskingum Compromise, a proposed boundary between the United States and the Western Indian country that allowed for the continuance of the "dish with one spoon" and extant American settlements.[67] The line along the Muskingum River represented a compromise between the Ohio River boundary established during the original Fort Stanwix Treaty in 1768, which many of the Western Indians wanted to maintain, and the boundaries set by the United States through the false treaties, which delineated nearly all of the Ohio Valley as American space (see Map 12).[68] Brant worked diligently to bring the nations into a "unanimous" agreement to offer the Muskingum Compromise to the Americans at the proposed treaty. In the midst of the indigenous councils he wrote to a British officer:

> I still have my doubts whether we will all join or not, some being no ways inclined for peaceable methods. The Hurons, Chippewas, Ottawas, Pottawattamies, and Delawares, will join with us in taking lenient steps, and having a boundary line fixed; and, rather than enter headlong into a destructive war, will give up a small part of their country. On the other hand, the Shawanese, Miamis, and Kickapoos, who are now so much addicted to horse-stealing that it will be a difficult task to break them of it, as that kind of business is their best harvest, will of course declare for war, and not giving up any of their country, which, I am afraid, will be the means of our separating. They are, I believe, determined not to attend the treaty with the Americans. Still I hope for the best.[69]

Brant's overriding concern was for unanimity among all nations in the Confederation, and, as Aupaumut's narrative intimated, Brant finally achieved enough support to move forward with the compromise. The "Address of the Chiefs of the Six Nations & Western Confederacy to Gov. St. Clair," which Brant recorded, stated that the Confederation had been working "for several years past, to bring the whole of the Indian

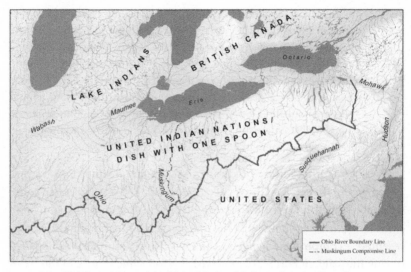

Map 12. The territory of the United Indian Nations, showing Brant's proposed Muskingum Compromise boundary line and the original Ohio River boundary line established by the Fort Stanwix Treaty of 1768.

Nations of this Country, to agree to come to some terms of peace with the US" and asserted that it was American "backwardness" that thwarted their efforts. Confronting the false treaties, the "Address" continued:

> This is our last and full determination, it being what was agreed upon by the Confederate Indian Nations that were lately Assembled at the Miami River, and ... differs widely from the Councils held by Gen. Butler, which was only with a few Nations and those not authorized to transact any Business which Concerned the whole, therefore any thing that was done with him we lay aside, as we cannot agree to abide to the unreasonable demands that were made by him & agreed to by those few who attended, and it must have been well known would never meet with the concurrence of all of us. Brother, as it is our wish to live in peace with all men, and to put an end to any further uneasiness on either Side, to convince the world that it is from our desire to enter into a War without the Greatest reason. Indeed, As the Great Spirit Above has been pleased to place us in this Country, which until the late unhappy War Between great Britain and America we enjoyed peaceably, We look upon ourselves to be Masters and only true proprietors of it, to avoid further trouble we propose to give to the US all the Lands lying on the East side [of the] Muskingum.[70]

The confederated Indians reasserted the claim to indigeneity and expressed their determination to maintain the dish as a "whole" in terms of both the land and its inhabitants. If lines were to be drawn, they would do the drawing, as the "only true proprietors," and such lines would concern the boundaries of the pot, not its division into smaller pieces. Indeed, it was their concern for the land and the community it contained that prompted them to offer a generous compromise in order to prevent the valley's destruction by war. Still, in their conclusion they made clear that Americans would face the full force of the Confederation if they persisted in claiming sovereignty over the pot. In laying out the parameters of the compromise, they emphasized, "This is the Boundry line . . . which we cannot Exceed."

Aupaumut's journal related the events that followed:

> The Commissioners sent an answer that they were willing to settle the dispute about the boundary line: But a Wyandot Chief [Half King] & Captain Pipe [Delaware], who had been concerned in the treaty at Fort McIntosh, privately left the Body of Indians, and went to the Commissioners. . . . These Chiefs told the Commissioners that they might not mind Capt. Brant; but attend to the Chiefs of the Western Indians. For (said they) this Brant has parted with all his land; and has no business to meddle with ours. They then told the Commissioners they would stand to the agreement made at Fort McIntosh.[71]

Brant related his own version of the events in a speech to the Western Indians in 1793, which he recorded in his journal:

> In consequence of [the series of false treaties], we advised you to attend a Treaty at the Muskingum. . . . We had then agreed on that river as the Boundary. . . . [Then] the Hurons [Wyandots] here present and some Delawares had sent word to the American Commissioners that their Nations would at all events agree to [the Commissioners'] terms, which afforded General Sinclair an opportunity of taking the advantage of us and making what terms they Pleased with those who attended.[72]

In fact, St. Clair happily reported the treaty a success to Washington: "I am persuaded their general confederacy is entirely broken: indeed, it would not be very difficult, if circumstances required it, to set them at deadly variance."[73]

According to Aupaumut, after St. Clair sent a message rejecting the Muskingum Compromise, Brant "told the Indians that those people did not desire peace; but were upon bad designs," and the gathered nations decided to leave for home. On the way, they "met a large body of Shawanese & Miamis, & other nations, to the amount, as well as I remember from my cousin's information, of near a thousand, many on horseback, and looked, he said, very grand." This group had already expressed reluctance to negotiate with the Americans; after hearing Brant's story, they solidified their position, and the Mohawk leader could not disagree with their sentiments. Aupaumut wrote, "Brant told the whole that they could do nothing — that the Commissioners were on bad designs — and that they had best go back, and the next day they all set out for their homes."[74]

In calling attention to Brant's phrase "bad designs," Aupaumut echoed the insinuations of the United Indian Nations that American representatives were acting on "bad-minded" thinking that threatened the peace. Although he presented his report in a detached, factual tone, Aupaumut concluded with a veiled accusation that "the Commissioners" were implicated in a deceitful division of the common pot, making the American leadership accountable for answering to "the whole" of the land's inhabitants.

The Common Pot: Competing Visions of Native Space

The Muskingum Compromise illustrates Brant's particular conceptualization of Native space, which formed the foundation of his peacemaking vision. Although he may have ceded control of the east to the United States — by the first Fort Stanwix treaty, the violent land claims of the Revolution, and continuing negotiations — he was not willing to relinquish the idea that Native space could exist independent of American space. As he told the U.S. commissioners at Buffalo Creek in 1794:

> We are of the same opinion with the people of the US; you consider yourselves as independent people; we, as the original inhabitants of this country, and sovereigns of the soil, look upon ourselves as equally independent, and free as any other nation or nations. This country was given to us by the Great Spirit above; we wish to enjoy it, and have our passage along the lake, within the line we have pointed out.[75]

Through the Muskingum Compromise he sought to solidify and legalize this conceptualization. The only path to peace, as he saw it, was for the United States to acknowledge the continuing existence of Native space and deal directly with the confederation that represented it.

Yet Brant's conceptualization was problematic for those Native people who remained in New York and New England. The Mohawk leader was apparently willing to concede that Native space no longer existed in the East. As his Wyandot and Delaware adversaries observed, he had relinquished his Mohawk River lands to the Americans and occupied a place at Grand River under British protection. In Brant's spatial configuration, the Mohicans and their village of New Stockbridge were contained by American space. He even defined them as "Yankees," tying their geographic location to their participation on the U.S. side in the war. In contrast, Aupaumut insisted that New Stockbridge remained Native space and that the Mohicans were an "independent" nation. Even when the Western Indians questioned his claim to sovereignty, saying they had heard "for several years" that the Yankees had the Mohicans "surrounded in arms" and "shut up like so many hogs in a pen," he told them this was false rumor, that "we were an independent people, and could go where we pleased."[76]

Aupaumut's sense of the spatial relations between Indians and the United States was complicated by his own position in the network of relations, including New Stockbridge's geographical location and his ties to Algonquians who remained in New England. He believed that Native communities needed to secure particular village territories bound by treaty, as he had done for New Stockbridge, because land encroachment, in his experience, was unstoppable. Aupaumut's vision could be interpreted either as pragmatic forethought or as acquiescence to a nascent colonial policy that claimed "Indian tribes" as part of American space.[77] In either case, this belief made him more supportive of individual treaties. He strove to explain the deceitful and impractical nature of previous agreements with a view to making legitimate ones in order to retain lands that could realistically support communities. As he explained to Pickering, his Western relations

> said, all last summer, that they did not choose to sell their lands; because they wanted to get their living out of them. They are uneasy where they are. They are anxious to get back to the waters running into the Ohio. There the country is better watered. There are hills

bearing berries and roots & supporting game. The heads of those waters afford the best hunting grounds. The lands are also good for corn. Perhaps a few tracts restored for towns with a right of hunting at large might induce them to confirm in the main the former treaties.[78]

These competing visions were rooted in distinctive cultural traditions. Algonquians conceptualized Native space as a network of villages connected by rivers and relations. This concept is especially evident in the structuring of Aupaumut's journal as a journey through waterways, with the Mohican delegation moving from village to village, encountering friendly kin. Aupaumut bolstered his position in Algonquian space by emphasizing his ties to Mohican relations who lived in western villages. He frequently referred to his cousin Aaron, who lived in the Delaware village at Grand River, and to his "uncle" Pohquannoppeet, a Mohican who had lived "with these nations since he was a boy."[79] In writing his community's history, Aupaumut described "Muhheakunnuk our nativity" as the place where his ancestors "agreed to kindle a fire" and "hang a kettle, whereof they and their children after them might dip out their daily refreshment." Algonquian identity was grounded in the place where you lived, the pot that fed you. Each village was both a "kettle" unto itself and a part of the larger common pot that linked the communities together. The greatest motivation for Aupaumut's mission was to secure a place for Stockbridge in the networks that would enable its continuance.[80]

Haudenosaunee construction of space was more complicated and less fluid. The Confederacy longhouse consisted of five nations (later six, with the adoption of the Tuscaroras) who occupied particular geographic spaces, with clan identity tying each person to maternal relations within the other nations. Land was held in common by the clans and, more specifically, by the clan mothers. Identity was defined by maternity: individuals belonged to the nation and the clan of their mother, while membership in the Confederacy could be acquired only by birth to a Haudenosaunee woman or adoption by a particular family, clan, and nation.[81] The political life of the Confederacy was highly structured, with specific roles assigned to individuals based on clan, nation, and aptitude.[82] Entire nations could be absorbed by the Confederacy, but only through formal incorporation into the longhouse's complex kinship structure. Brant's vision adapted the Algonquian dish to the Haudenosaunee longhouse, transforming the Ohio's network of rivers and villages into a political space that could be more strictly ordered and a geographic space that could be contained.[83]

Peacemaking protocols were tied to these spatial frameworks. The Mohican tradition involved reinforcing connections between nations in the network of relations. For New Stockbridge to be secure, ruptures had to be repaired. Therefore, Aupaumut's first task on arriving at Buffalo Creek in 1792 was to acquire the tools he would need for the job. He wrote: "I dispatch[ed] my brother to go cross the woods to Oneida to fetch my bag of peace, in which there is ancient wampum, and to get two of my best counselors and a young man to meet me at Chapins, in order to have them with us, that the western nations may see that we are upon important business."[84] (See Map 11.)

As Aupaumut explained in his history, this "bag of peace" contained "all the belts and strings which they received of their allies of different nations." They were used "to establish peace and friendship" between nations and would also establish the weight and sincerity of his mission. "This bag is, as it were, unmoveable," Aupaumut related, meaning that it was always kept at the sachem's house. The bag symbolized his leadership as both hereditary and "elective," demonstrating that he was a man who had earned respect and responsibility.[85]

Furthermore, he insisted on having his "best counselors" with him, not only for protection and consultation but to represent the village and emphasize his place in the network of relations. Aupaumut was accompanied by his brother Solomon and his brother-in-law John Quinney, young leaders from prominent families, as well as Captain David Neshoonhuk, who had served in the Revolutionary War and was familiar with both American and Algonquian diplomacy. Finally, he chose a "young man" named John Wautunhqnaut to serve as a runner.[86] With this group, Aupaumut not only demonstrated the continuance of diplomatic tradition — by bringing the appropriate leaders and a messenger — but reinforced the Algonquian roots of his peacemaking mission.

Brant drew heavily on Haudenosaunee history in cultivating the United Indian Nations, relying on the Great Law in particular. Oral tradition, embedded in wampum belts, attests that the Confederacy formed in response to uncontrollable fratricidal warfare. A version of the story published by Seneca Arthur Parker relates, "Men were ragged with sacrifice and the women scarred with the flints, so everywhere there was misery. Feuds with outer nations, feuds with brother nations, feuds of sister towns and feuds of families and of clans made every warrior a stealthy man who liked to kill." In envisioning the Great Law, Dakanawida, the "Peacemaker," told Hayonhwatha: "Our people are weak from warring and weak from being warred upon. We who speak with one tongue should combine against the Hadiondas instead of helping them by killing one another." Hayonhwatha responded, "I, too, am of the same mind.... I believe that we should be as brothers in a family instead of enemies."[87] Dakanawida envisioned a "union of all the nations" who would act as "one head, one body, and one mind." Hayonhwatha contributed the ceremony of condolence to clear their minds of grief and "evil thoughts," and together with Jigonsaseh they shaped a Great Law that would enable the nations to maintain a "Great Peace." Leaders were obliged to "work in unity," not for their "own interests" but "to benefit the people and for the generations not yet born."[88]

The Great Law directly invoked the common pot. According to Parker, the chiefs were directed to "eat together from one bowl" and to refrain from using any "sharp utensils" so they would not "accidentally cut one another.... All measures must be taken to prevent the spilling of blood in any way." When people eat from the same bowl, the possibility of violence always looms — in the potential to get in each other's way or to fight over food. So the Peacemaker instructed leaders to restrain themselves from acting on these impulses and to focus their minds on cooperative, "calm deliberation."[89]

In promoting an Indian union, Brant sought a return to the principles of the Great Law, but he had to assure his Algonquian allies that participating in the "United Indian Nations" would not signify submission to a Haudenosaunee Confederacy that they had come to regard as a hierarchical and often oppressive body.[90] To build a common language, Brant invoked the Algonquian metaphor of the "dish with one spoon" to articulate his vision. Since the continuance of the common pot was threatened, the people who shared in its sustenance needed to unite together to work as "one head, one body, and one mind," "deliberating" on the best strategy for its preservation.

Narratives of the Common Pot: The Two Paths Collide

Two distinct narratives emerged from the Ohio Valley that show these two peacemaking traditions in action. Hendrick Aupaumut's journal of his 1792 journey, "Narrative of an Embassy to the Western Indians," published by the Massachusetts Historical Society in 1827, and "Captain

Brant's Journal of the Proceedings at the General Council Held at the Foot of the Rapids of the Miamis" from 1793, published within the *Correspondence of Lieutenant Governor John Graves Simcoe* in 1923, stand as the most comprehensive indigenous accounts of these councils. These texts provide critical counternarratives to the colonial version of events, representing not simply alternate "perspectives" on history but testimonies to the fictionalization of U.S.–Indian relations.

Two Paths to Philadelphia, 1792

Before Brant and Aupaumut proceeded west on the journeys that resulted in these narratives, their paths converged at the center of American space, the new capital of Philadelphia. George Washington sent invitations to both, along with other Haudenosaunee leaders, to meet with him in the spring of 1792, ostensibly to discuss American charitable contributions to Indian "civilization." When Brant and Aupaumut crossed paths at Niagara that winter, the Mohawk leader expressed skepticism. According to Aupaumut, Brant showed him the part of the invitation where Washington discussed "plowing & sowing," saying that "he already knew how to plough and sow. If (said he) I had been desired to be an instrument for the purpose of making peace with the Western Indians — I would go to Philadelphia." Brant told the Haudenosaunee leaders that "the business for which they were invited to Philly was not on the face of the paper, but *behind it* — out of sight." As Brant intimated, Washington's main concern was Haudenosaunee and Mohican mediation. American leaders were well aware of these nations' geographic and political positions and hoped to draw them closer by offering guarantees of their land rights, as well as annual payments and gifts to enable them to cultivate the land and achieve a more "civilized" state.[91]

Brant insisted on meeting separately from the "Five Nations" and Mohicans, and he was courted with greater zeal. Concerned over his rising influence, Secretary of War Henry Knox had asked Samuel Kirkland to renew his correspondence with Brant to ascertain his position and his susceptibility to American influence. Although Knox remained anxious about Brant's "dangerous" ideas "relative to a general confederation of Indians," he also believed "it would be wise to conciliate Captain Brandt, and if within the power of a reasonable sum of money, to attach him warmly to the United States." Brant's opinions proved influential on American policy. Soon after Kirkland sent him Brant's correspondence, Knox replied, "Col. Brandt is right as to the principles of the boundaries. The idea, in future, of conquest, ought to be relinquished, and fair purchase and optional sale take place."[92]

Aupaumut expressed concern that Brant's expanding influence disrupted the balance of power and bewilderment at American tolerance of the Mohawk's interference with his mission. In reporting their encounter at Niagara, Aupaumut portrayed Brant as pretentiously complaining that "he was not properly invited" to the meeting in Philadelphia, and he later asked Pickering, "What occasioned the so urgent desire of the UStates to get Brant down to Philadelphia, that they sent for him repeatedly? I ask this because it hurt and surprised me: for the UStates must know that Brant is their enemy."[93]

Whatever Aupaumut and other leaders may have made of Brant's arrogance, the Mohawk leader was also motivated by his allegiance to the dish with one spoon. In response to Knox's invitation, he wrote, "Visiting you as an individual, would be by no means tending to the accomplishing any good end; as those meetings must show, that have hitherto been held with people not deputized by the nations, in general, to transact business. . . . This has been too much the case, of late years, and, in my opinion, principally the cause of the present disturbances."[94] Brant was most concerned that Washington would use American money and influence to divide the dish. As Aupaumut related, "In the course of our conversation, I asked Brant if he saw any danger to the Five Nations, in going to Philadelphia? He paused a while, and answered – 'I see no danger, except in this way – that the United States will harden the Chiefs on their side. That is always the way of the white people; to disunite the Indians, and set them to fighting one with another.' "[95]

Brant was not too far off. In Philadelphia, Washington guaranteed "the yearly appropriation of the sum of one thousand five hundred dollars, for the use and benefit of the Five Nations – the Stockbridge Indians included" in return for their promise to mediate a peace. Brant viewed Washington's offers as outright bribery. When he visited Philadelphia later that year, he offered to listen to Washington and Knox's perspective and relayed his willingness to work toward peace but maintained his position with regard to the Muskingum boundary. He told Knox, "Peace will not be easily established, without relinquishing part of your claim." He later alleged that the American leadership had offered him "a thousand guineas down, and to have the half-pay and pension I receive from Great Britain doubled, merely on the condition that I would use my endeavors to bring about a peace. But this I rejected." During councils that summer, the Western Indians praised Brant for joining with them to interrogate the Seneca leader Cornplanter about "the bundle of American speeches under [his] arm."[96]

In inviting Aupaumut, Brant, and Cornplanter to Philadelphia and sending them west with separate messages, the Americans played on their ambitions and put them in competition for the same place in the network of relations. Brant told Aupaumut that summer, when the councils fell apart and the Shawnees began to mobilize for war, that "he had blamed the Great Men of the U States for sending so many messengers to the Western Indians, at the same time, which could only have distracted them."[97]

For Aupaumut, however, the Philadelphia meeting represented a great accomplishment. As he told the Western Indians later that summer, "Last winter was the first time I had invitation from the great man of the United States to attend Council in Philadelphia." When Mohican representatives had traveled to Philadelphia in 1785 to press their land claims in New York and Massachusetts, they were pacified with blankets and empty words, "forgotten." However, their mediation efforts bolstered their position, ensuring that the Mohicans would have a voice and a secure place in post-Revolution Native space.[98]

Renewing the Algonquian Alliance: Aupaumut's Narrative (Ohio Valley, 1792)

Aupaumut's diplomatic efforts proved effective not only in Philadelphia but in the Ohio Valley. His "Narrative of an Embassy to the Western Indians" testified to his success in renewing his ancestors' path and their place in the network of relations (see Map 13). Beginning in Philadelphia, Aupaumut endured a "stormy" journey, encountering high winds as his small delegation traveled by canoe from Buffalo Creek across Lake Erie. Approaching Grand River, Aupaumut sent his runner, John Wautunhqnaut, to the Delaware village upriver to fetch his cousin Aaron, who then guided the Mohican delegation west. Despite the challenging weather, the Mohicans were welcomed at villages along the way; Aupaumut reported that their relations were always "happy to see us" and exchange "news." Arriving in the Ohio Valley in July, Aupaumut was greeted enthusiastically by Miamis at the Detroit trading post. When they reached the "Grand

Council Fire" at the Maumee "Rapids," the delegation was met by their Munsee "brothers," who invited them to set up camp in their town, near their Delaware "grandfathers" in Captain Pipe's town and near Alexander McKee's trading post, which was located near the camps of McKee's kin, the Mohicans' Shawnee "younger brothers." The Delawares, many of whom had traveled from other towns upriver, formally brought the Mohicans through the ceremony of condolence, giving them strands of white wampum, and Aupaumut reciprocated, "rehears[ing]" the Delawares' speech and "deliver[ing]" an "answer, to manifest my friendship to them as they did to us."[99]

Over the course of several months, Aupaumut exchanged news with his relations, re-embedded himself in these networks, refamiliarized himself with the social geography, and relayed and received messages and speeches, including the controversial message from "the 15 sachems of the United States." He moved more deeply into the political and geographic territory, traveling to "the Forks or Naukhuwwhnauk, where the Shawanese, Delawares, and part of the Miamies had towns," and was then invited to stay in Big Cat's Delaware town on the AuGlaize River, where the Mohican leader Pohquannoppeet lived. Aupaumut noted the numerous nations that had set up towns and camps, many leaving their home territories to discuss the best course for the extensive space they shared.[100]

As the Grand Council began in late September, the Mohican delegation joined their relations and traveled to the Forks, led by their Delaware "grandfathers." From there, Aupaumut wrote, "the Delawares, Monthees, Wenuhtkowuk, Kuhnauwautheew, five Nations of us called Eastern Nations or Wauponnuhk," which included all of the peoples who had inhabited the region from the Housatonic to the Susquehanna, "went together on single file to attend the Council at Shawanny village." He explained, "We went in one body to show that we have been in good friendship this great length of time."[101]

However, both Aupaumut's position and his mission were challenged by the arrival of a message from Joseph Brant:

> My friends, I now tell you do not believe what Message the Muhe-
> conneew brought to you; neither believe what he says, if you do
> you will be greatly deceived. I have myself seen Washington, and
> see his heart and bowels; and he declared that he claims from the
> mouth of Miamie to the head of it — thence to the land of the Wabash
> river, and down the same to the mouth of it; and that he did take up

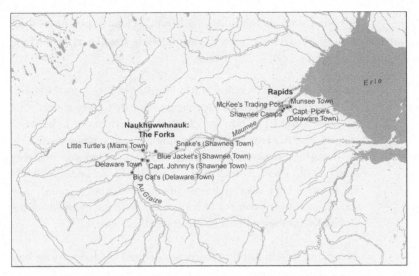

Map 13. Aupaumut's travels: the Rapids and the Forks. Inset of the territory on the Maumee and Auglaize Rivers through which Aupaumut traveled, showing the locations of Algonquian villages where he visited, camped, and participated in council.

dust and did declare that he would not restore so much dust to the Indians, but he is willing to have peace with the Indians.[102]

Aupaumut counteracted the message by directing suspicion away from himself and back toward Brant. Having grown ill on his way west, Brant had entrusted his son to carry this message for him. However, Aupaumut and his relations suspected the young man of bad-minded intentions. Aupaumut reported that "Tawalooth" was keen on war and had spread "many lies," including his insinuation that their mission was to provide military intelligence so the United States could strike more effectively.[103] "This he told to frustrate peace, and that we may be hated or killed," Aupaumut concluded. "He is a proper Liar or Emmissary of the Devil."

Nevertheless, Brant and his son may indeed have been relaying Washington's own words, for the lines described in the message did match those in the false treaties, on which the American leader remained firm. Yet Aupaumut preferred to believe that the accusations arose from Brant's own guilt for "going alone to Congress, contrary to what he recommended to those nations, that no individual nation or person should go to speak to the Big knifes."[104] Brant, Aupaumut asserted, was himself acting against the principles of the dish with one spoon.

In addressing his relations, the Mohican leader put Brant's actions in the context of a long history of Mohawk betrayal and evoked the Algonquian common pot in his defense:

> Let us consider the meaning of this Brant's Message — by the sound of it, he point[s] at me as a deceiver or roag, that every nation must be warned. But let us now look back in the path of our forefathers, and see whether you can find one single instance wherein, or how my ancestors or myself have deceived you, or led you one step astray.... But you look back and see heaps of your bones, wherein the Maquas have deceived you repeatedly. I think I could have good reason to tell you not to believe the Message or words of the Mohawks, for they will deceive you greatly as Usual.[105]

According to Aupaumut, suspicion of the Haudenosaunee had become a key issue in public councils, especially when the Algonquian "body" met on its own. In particular, leaders recalled the Haudenosaunee role in drawing them into the American war. Aupaumut reported that they concluded, "The English and the Five Nations did lay a foundation for our ruin...[so they] must settle all this difficulties with the Big knifes. But we must retain all our lands just as much as before the war. Let the English and Five Nations lose their lands."[106] From this council at the Shawnee village, Aupaumut related, "we set out about five hundred of us, on a single file, to the camp of the Senacas" to "have a council with them, and drive away their minds." There could be no greater symbol of the renewed alliance than five hundred Algonquians marching, "on a single file," to chastise the once powerful Six Nations. According to Aupaumut, their "head warrior, Puckoncheluh," said to the Seneca leaders, "In our publick council you tell us, we who are one colar, now have one heart and one head. If any Nations strikes us, we must all feel it. Now you must consider whether this is true what you told us."[107]

Aupaumut placed himself and Brant in a historical narrative that pitted a long-standing Algonquian network against a destructive Mohawk brother, effectively exploiting his relations' suspicions and their common language to reinforce his position in the network.[108] Brant's main concern, however, was maintaining unity in the dish, which rested on a precarious Haudenosaunee–Algonquian alliance. Aupaumut, despite his claims to independence, represented a certain acquiescence to the invaders and a solution that came from the Americans rather than the United Indian Nations. Furthermore, Aupaumut's attempts to forge a stronger Algonquian alliance counteracted Brant's own efforts to maintain the Confederation. As Aupaumut himself reported, Brant told him "that perhaps the Western Indians thought I had come to divide them; as that had always been the aim and practice of the White People. I answered him I had come with no such intention."[109]

While Brant accused him of dividing the dish with one spoon, Aupaumut charged the Mohawk leader with blocking the paths of the Algonquian network. According to Aupaumut's report, when Brant finally arrived, the Western Algonquians chastised him:

> The Western Indians had heard that I had been stopped by the British at Niagara, & by Brants orders at Grand River the year before, when I was going to the Westward. . . . To the Five Nations they said, "You Five Nations must open the path between us and the Eastern nations, you must make it wide, and let no stumbling blocks be again thrown in the way, but keep it smooth and clear, thus our friends the Muhekonnucks and others may pass and repass freely."[110]

Aupaumut described this encounter in response to Timothy Pickering's query, "What passed between Brant & the Indians at the Rapids?" The Mohican leader may have privileged this moment to bolster his own position, but he may have also been covering for the larger story. In his reports to Pickering, Aupaumut failed to mention the numerous discussions about the need to renew the Indian Union and the threat Americans posed to it. According to British records of the proceedings, the Seneca leader Red Jacket explained, "The white people are now looking at us and know what we are about, they were always the instigators of our quarrels," while the speaker for the Western Indians, Messaquakenoe (Painted Pole), reminded the Six Nations that the Americans only wanted "to divide us, that we might not act as one Man." Nor did Aupaumut reveal that the Haudenosaunee speakers took pains to describe the difficult situation that they all faced in the wake of the Revolution. Seneca leader Farmer's Brother explained, "From that moment our lands were torn to pieces and the Americans triumphed as the greatest people on this island."[111]

Still, the Seneca leadership believed Washington was sincere in his "desire of cultivating peace and Friendship with all nations of our Colour on this island," even as Brant insisted that "General Washington is very cunning, he will try to fool us if he can — He speaks very smooth, will tell you fair stories, and at the same time want to ruin us." Brant warned them again to be wary of division: when the Americans "send out a flag" of peace, he said, it "will not do for one man to turn about and listen to that flag — We must be all be at it, as we are all united as one man."[112] Aupaumut found it difficult to dismiss Brant's words, even as he endeavored to persuade his relations of Washington's good intentions: "Many Indians came from time to time to seek information about the White people. Many mentioned the injuries they had received from them. . . . They mentioned many instances of deception. In answering these enquiries, and endeavours to remove their prejudices, I was continually employed."[113]

Aupaumut devoted three pages of his "Narrative" to explaining the lengths to which he had gone to advocate for his American brothers as the Western Indians related their experiences of dispossession and deceit, their apprehension about the Americans' desire for domination, and their doubts about the inability of the American leadership to control its settlers on the frontiers. At the end of this account, a frustrated Aupaumut declared:

> In all my arguments with these Indians, I have as it were oblige to say nothing with regard of the conduct of the Yorkers, how they cheat my fathers, how they taken our lands Unjustly, and how my fathers were groaning as it were in their graves, in loseing their lands for nothing, although they were faithful friends to the Whites, and how the white people artfully got their Deeds confirmed in their Laws. I say had I mention these things to the Indians, it would aggravate their prejudices against white people.[114]

Aupaumut's charged language unmasked his realization that the Western Indians' story was his own. He was not just a messenger of the narrative of false treaties, but a character within it. His own role in assisting the United States seemed increasingly questionable. Samuel Kirkland later reported to Pickering that Aupaumut seemed dejected on returning from the Ohio: "Since his tour to the westward last summer, he has greatly altered. He has been a lover of the intoxicating draught & duplicity begins to mark many steps of his conduct. He is not so friendly to the cause & character of the white people as formerly." Kirkland blamed this transformation on "his intercourse with Capt. Brant" and his friendship with Samson Occom. In making his assessment, Kirkland did not even consider the harsh realities that Aupaumut was forced to confront in the valley or the parallel to his land troubles at home.[115]

British accounts of the councils reveal a part of Aupaumut's story that he concealed from his own "Narrative." As Brant himself knew, during the course of their journey the Mohicans began to envision a new path. Even if Aupaumut kept silent about their land troubles as he claimed, the other Mohicans did not. The Western Indians informed Brant, "The Mohickens have told us...that they find themselves hampered among the white people and wanted to get into a place where they could be more at their liberty." Unbeknownst to those who had funded their journey, the Mohicans were also securing their position within the Algonquian network so they might have a place to move their pot, away from American encroachment and control.[116]

Renewing the Dish with One Spoon: Brant's Journal (Ohio Valley, 1793)

By the summer of 1793, both Aupaumut and Brant were emissaries of a boundary line compromise. Aupaumut traveled once more to the Ohio Valley to ascertain whether his relations would agree to a resolution based on his understanding that the American leadership might be willing to "give up a part of the lands southward of the line settled by the treaties of fort McIntosh and fort Harmar" and allow for hunting rights on any of the lands "retained" by the United States. On the other hand, Haudenosaunee leaders told the Americans that they must follow the "road for peace," led by the Six Nations: "You can come by no other road, as only this one is open." All other roads, they said, had been "turned miry and swampy, by the spilling of blood, for which we blame the Americans." They related that the Shawnees were willing to make peace only if the Americans agreed to the Ohio River boundary. Knowing the Americans would never agree to retain the old line, Brant desired an open council about the location of the boundary "between us & the Americans" and sought to renew discussion of the Muskingum Compromise. With positive changes in American policy due to the efforts of Native leaders, the establishment of a more trustworthy commission (including Timothy Pickering), and the defeat of American military expeditions in 1790 and 1791, the Americans, Brant believed, "now seem earnestly inclined for peace."[117]

The American goal remained confirmation of previous treaties and monetary compensation for land, but for the first time a compromise on the boundary line was a real possibility. Knox instructed the commissioners: "If the relinquishment of any lands, in the said space, should be an ultimatum with the said Indians, and a line could be agreed upon which would be free from dispute, you may, in order to effect a peace, make such a relinquishment." Still, the United States strove to divide the Indian Union. Knox urged the commissioners "to form separate contracts" with the "tribes" and to avoid "as much as possible, to confirm the idea of union," to which, he acknowledged, "the said Indians are much attached."[118]

Aupaumut, whether he realized it or not, was being used as an instrument of this strategy. The communications between Aupaumut and the American leadership during 1793 demonstrate that while both he and Brant had made progress in negotiations, the Mohican leader was being coerced into increasing complicity with a divisive policy. The American leadership instructed Aupaumut not just to carry a message or mediate but to present their arguments to the Western Indians "as of yourself, in order to discover how far they may be persuaded to depart from their rigid demands." Aupaumut expressed growing concern that he would be perceived as a spy. Pickering noted that "Hendrick proposed to translate" the commissioners' instructions "into his own language, and then destroy the original paper." From his camp at the Rapids, Aupaumut wrote to Pickering: "The Shawanese, Wyandots, & Miamis and part of the Delawares have deep prejudice against the Whites, also to us. They expect that I will inform you everything in writing for which I did not sent letters to you before — had they knew that I have sent every necessary intelligence to you they would condemn me."[119]

Brant was especially wary of the tightrope on which Aupaumut was walking. In council, the Mohawk leader warned the Western Indians: "There are bad Birds amongst us or there soon will be, whom it is our business to guard against. They will say that they know the Minds of the Commissioners but we must not listen to Spies, who we ought to Banish, as we mean to Meet these Commissioners we will hear from them what they have to say."[120] In his journal Brant added, "At this time I was informed that Capt. Hendrick was at Detroit & to whom I alluded." He also took further steps to banish the Mohican leader from councils. As Aupaumut reported to Pickering: "Brant brought & deliver[ed] a Message to me which was said from Wyondots Shawanese & Miamis — the substance of it was this — you the Muhheconnuk nation came from among the big knifes — You must not enter into our councils." Aupaumut insisted these words came "from Brant alone." He said the message angered his

Delaware relations, fostering anti-Iroquois sentiment. Meanwhile, he continued to advocate for the United States' proposals in private meetings, which angered Brant even more.[121]

Brant's "Journal of the Proceedings at the General Council Held at the Foot of the Rapids of the Miamis" thus began with a dish in rupture. The Mohawk leader arrived at the Rapids "with the Indians of the Six Nations and Delawares from the Grand River" to confront "evil reports" that he was a "traitor." To Brant's dismay, the nations had neither gathered for council nor begun the condolence ceremonies that would clear the way for deliberation. The nations were divided, with some moving toward the American proposals and others hot for war. According to his journal, Brant organized a council himself, telling the Western Indians, "We are come here with good intentions, but if you have received bad impressions respecting me I request you will now explain it and let nothing remain upon your Minds that may be in the Way of our Public Business." The Shawnees responded that they entertained no "bad thoughts" toward him and wanted to proceed. Brant reminded them all of the critical moment they faced in their maintenance of the dish: "We have had various meetings with the Americans, but none of such importance as this Will be, it therefore Stands us in need to give it the most serious Attention, and requires the greatest Prudence & Unanimity amongst ourselves." Brant emphasized that they all needed to "coolly consider our true Interest" and "pursue that, which is the only means of rendering real service to our Country." Despite the "friendly council," "evil reports" continued to circulate against him, while the "Shawanoes, Delawares and Miamis held Private Councils many nights, to which none of the Six Nations were invited."[122]

Brant appealed for dialogue on the location of the boundary "between us & the Americans." At Alexander McKee's suggestion, Brant organized a delegation to ensure that the American commissioners were authorized to "make a New Boundary Line." The commissioners answered affirmatively, and Brant believed the time was ripe for discussion of the Muskingum Compromise. However, when he returned, a whole new set of misunderstandings erupted. Although Western Indian leaders had authorized the trip, some of them — especially McKee's relations, the Shawnees — suspected Brant of negotiating with the commissioners in private and remained wary of any conciliation with the Americans.[123]

The Shawnees, Miamis, Delawares, and Wyandots living in villages along the Maumee and Wabash Rivers, many of whom had already relocated in response to dispossession and war, faced an immediate threat if the American treaties were allowed to stand or if American settlement continued to push past the Ohio. While the Shawnees' response was to advocate for armed defense of their territories, Aupaumut's "eastern" relations were especially wary of war. Referencing both their geographic and their political positions, the Delaware war chief Puckonchelah told the Wyandots, "You use me as your front door, now let us exchange our seats, let me live or set yonder, and you set here as my front door see whether you would not rejoice to hear the offers of peace." Most of the "Lake Indians" or Three Fires (Ottawas, Pottawatomies, and Ojibwes) lived on the northwest side of Lake Erie. While their villages were not as directly threatened as were those of their southern relations, they knew that if the Americans moved into the Ohio Valley, a threat to their lands would not be far behind.[124]

Therefore, it was the Lake Indians who stepped forward to support Brant and rekindle the Union, saying, "We . . . give our head, our hands, and our hearts to yours, to be firmly united ought to be the Business of the Confederacy and by that Bond prolong the Days of our Women and Children." Brant accepted on behalf of the Six Nations. "We are sorry," he said, "that some tribes will not pay attention to any thing that opposes their View of War, but it is our Business to put them right, and if we can by a peace obtain our just rights, it ought to take place." Offering a belt of wampum, he asked the Lake Indians to make known their "sentiments to the rest of the Confederate Indians."[125]

Even as Brant strove to renew the Confederation, the Shawnees, Wyandots, and Delawares accused Brant, the Six Nations, and the Lake Indians of "breaking" it, especially in advocating against the Ohio River boundary. Brant insisted that they desired only an open council on the location of the line, so that they might speak "with one Voice" to the commissioners. He continued to emphasize the possibility for peace in his original vision, insisting that "the Six Nations and Lake Indians" had "come here at your request to assist you in making peace for this *our* Country. . . . We assure you before the Great Spirit that we do not mean the least Deviation from the Confederacy, and our hearts are true to their Interest." Laying down a white belt, Brant noted, "At this time, we placed a Moon of Wampum and a Dish with one Spoon in the Council which Signified that the Country was in Common."[126]

The Shawnees and their allies broke off to "consult," leaving the Haudenosaunee and Lake Indians to talk among themselves. When the council resumed, the Shawnee sachem said, "We are withdrawn here to form another Message to the Commissioners, we must Strike a Boundary line, that line must be the one agreed upon at the Treaty of Fort Stanwix." In his journal, Brant commented,

> I must here observe that the opinion of the Six Nations was not Asked, which I thought strange as in a matter of such importance the opinion of all the tribes should have been asked. The Shawanoes Chief then asked me to put down in writing the Words that were to form the Message. But afterwards the Chief of the Wyandots formed the Message & Lieut. Selby put down the Words in Writing, I was then asked to Sign the Message which I refused as I disapproved it.[127]

Meanwhile, "an alarming voice" had arrived with Creek warriors from the southeast, who told of further threats to the south. They were advised in General Council "what the Six Nations had said some days ago respecting the Moon of Wampum and the Dish with One Spoon." Their speaker related that they had come "to strengthen the Union," but their chief concern was its defense: "Our Confederacy is like a house with four Doors and all the Indian Country is in common, it appears to be most exposed to the Eastward but we are determined that no part of it shall suffer if in our power to support it... The White people to the Eastward are encroaching on our lands, we are Determined to oppose them." They said a pipe would be sent to the north and south, "and those who do not smoke it, we shall look upon as not belonging to the Union & who do not join to Defend their Country."[128]

In General Council the following day, the Shawnee speaker Captain Johnny recalled the history of the union, telling the Six Nations, "You recommended the strictest union as the only means of Preserving our Country.... You advised us that... as the whole Country was in Common, whatever was done" in the councils of the "Confederacy would remain firm." He related that the nations had decided in council the previous year to stand firm on "the old boundary line" of "the Ohio" and insisted, in concert with the Creeks, that if the Six Nations were committed to the principles of the dish, they were bound to defend it.[129]

Brant, sending white belts to symbolize his desire for peace, was unwilling to commit to war without a fair discussion of his compromise, which, he told the Western Indians, had failed to come to fruition largely because of division and jealousy within the union. He spoke of the need for clear thinking and "comparing our ideas together." In his final plea to his western relations, Brant advocated for his path to peace and the preservation of the dish:

> It is well known that for these many years past, we have exerted ourselves for the Confederacy and no part of their situation has escaped our Notice, but after the most serious Attention to their Affairs and after Deliberating & Maturely Weighing in our Minds our Force, Resources, and every local advantage we possess, we declare our sentiments from the bottom of our hearts that the Boundary of the Muskingum[,] if adopted in General Council, is for the interest of us all and far preferable to an uncertain War, you must likewise consider my Brethren that you referred this line to Lord Dorchester two years ago. I therefore beg of you not to be rash and consider the Consequence of a War in which we are not unanimous.[130]

The next day, according to Brant, "the Chiefs of the Shawanoes and those of the Hurons, Delawares and the 7 Nations of Canada come to the Six Nations and spoke as follows": "Brothers, We have since yesterday been thinking seriously of your opinion in the last Council, we know that your knowledge of the White People exceeds ours, and that you are from that enabled to form a better Judgment of our Affairs than we can for which reason we are now come to tell you that we mean to adopt your opinion respecting the Boundary line."[131] Having "deliberated" carefully, the nations unanimously adopted Brant's Muskingum Compromise and laid down wampum to seal their words. Hendrick Aupaumut happily reported to Pickering: "I think you will receive invitation from the whole confederate nations to meet them near the mouth of this river this week, where highly probable you will establish a permanent peace — for the greater nations sincerely desire. And for the terms of peace I think with no difficulty a new line will be drawn — and taking yearly rent is very acceptable to all."[132]

However, Brant related, "After this meeting . . . Col McKee had a private meeting with the aforementioned chiefs at twelve o'clock at Night." To Brant's surprise, the next morning, when "we met in General Council," Captain Johnny reported their "final Resolution" to "unite our Warriors" to defend the Ohio boundary. According to Brant, the Delaware leader Buckongehalis pointed to McKee, saying, "That is the Person who advised us to insist on the Ohio River for the line." Brant later blamed the breakdown of the peace effort on the trader's manipulation of his Shawnee relations.[133]

The British wanted to maintain an Indian "buffer zone" between Canada and the United States; in essence, they wanted the Western Indians to be their "front door."[134] Brant had initially insisted that Confederation councils should be an exclusively Native space because he feared this kind of interference. The British, on the other hand, feared Indian independence. As Lieutenant Governor John Simcoe wrote in a letter to his deputy, he disliked Brant's insistence on Indian-only councils: "I am not without suspicion that both this previous meeting and that of the 6 Nations is of Brant's suggestion. The independence of the Indians is his primary object; his views are extensive, and he speaks most contemptuously of the Superintendent General and his Deputies, and indeed, of every body."[135] Ironically, the British-Shawnee association may have done more to divide the dish than the Mohican–U.S. partnership, and Brant may have had more to fear from McKee than from Aupaumut.

Brant painted the final scene of his journal as a picture of division:

> When the Council was over a War feast was prepared, and the Chiefs of the Shawanoes singing the War Song encouraging the Warriors of all the Nations to be active in defending their Country, saying their Father the English would assist them and Pointed to Col. McKee. When we arrived at Detroit a Deputation of the Lake Indians overtook us and repeated what they had before said[;] they gave us a Belt with a Number of Streaks across it and said the tribes which these Streaks represent have made Peace with the Americans, and that they would go to Post Vincent and make Peace also.[136]

Timothy Pickering, writing from Detroit as well, sent the following letter to Aupaumut:

> My Friend & Brother, When I first saw you, about two years ago, I remember you proposed to make a visit to the Western Indians, to try to bring about a peace between them and the US: and I recollect you mentioned as the motive of your attempt to promote peace – "That you were a friend to the US, and also a friend to the people of your own color." You will therefore be very sorry, as I am, that peace can not now be made. You know that in our speech delivered the 31st of last month to their Deputies, we told them that we could not make the Ohio the boundary: and yesterday their answer arrived, insisting that the Ohio should be the boundary. The negotiations for peace are therefore over; and we are going home immediately.[137]

Conclusion: The Process of Making Peace

The Iroquois chief had received these presents himself, and looked at the Sun and then at all who were assembled there, Onontio, he said, you have dissipated all the clouds, the air is serene, the sky seems to open, the Sun is shining brilliantly, and we see no more trouble, the peace has put all of us in the calm, my heart is in repose, and we will go on in a state of contentment.[138]

Bernd Peyer has observed that leaders like Aupaumut and Brant "consciously followed the paths they sincerely believed would lead their people out of the colonial situation."[139] Unfortunately, each legitimately believed that the other posed a threat to his vision of peace. Aupaumut maintained that Brant, by blocking his path, was denying him access to the Algonquian alliance. In his view, Brant took advantage of his position in geographic space, preventing Aupaumut from fulfilling his traditional role as a mediator in order to dominate that role himself. Brant initially blocked Aupaumut's way at Niagara to keep the path to the Ohio Valley clear. He wanted to deal with Native space first, forging a compromise that emerged from within Indian councils and with which all could agree. Because of Aupaumut's divided loyalties, he could not fully participate in the dish with one spoon. Ultimately, Brant could not take the risk of inviting the United States — in any form — into Confederation space. Brant was certain that the American strategy was to divide the Union, and he regarded Aupaumut as an agent of this strategy, whether he was complicit or not.[140]

In the narratives Brant and Aupaumut created, their representations of each other reflect the ways of Sky Woman's "bad-minded" son. As the Six Nations had explained to the United States, the road from the American settlements to the Western Indian country was mired in brambles and blood, so clearing the path would be a painstaking and delicate process. Each man believed he had the tools and vision required and that the other was "moved by an evil opinion" and "endeavouring to prevent his design," to the detriment of their common mother.[141]

Yet each man keenly understood Young Peter's original criticism of the United States for the grave mistake their younger brother was making in following two paths at once. During that initial meeting at Newtown, Aupaumut told Pickering, "I have said that I would go to the Western Indians, but there is one difficulty in the way: You have an army assembling in that quarter.... If I proceed, the operations of your army must be suspended." The Mohican leader continued to assert this opinion, writing to Pickering in 1793: "In order to establish lasting peace between US and the different Tribes of Indians — and in order to have peaceable treaty — US ought to withdraw their troops from Fort Jefferson, and that without delay." Brant was an active participant in the councils where this particular brand of American duplicity was discussed with bewilderment, and he also expressed great disappointment that some of his relations were "addicted" to war.[142]

The problem, as both leaders understood it, was that a mind clouded by war could not focus on the process of making peace. Brant was particularly upset, upon arriving in the Ohio Valley, that condolence had not taken place: "No business was transacted and the evil reports against me still continued; — I must here remark that it has always been an invariable Rule amongst Indians when they meet, to go through the Ceremony of Condolence." Brant made a direct connection between the chaos at the council grounds and the failure to conduct condolence. The effect of the "addictive" power of war on the effort to make peace cannot be underestimated. Both Brant and Aupaumut expressed concern that the Shawnees were especially afflicted. Brant's concern over their neglect of protocol is directly related to this predicament. Condolence was necessary to dispel destructive words and thoughts, to make the way clear for the "business" of diplomacy. Brant finally initiated the process himself: "I went through the usual Compliments with a large Belt and removed all obstructions, that there might be no impediment in the Way of Public Business. — This they should have done," he remarked.[143]

The ceremony played a prominent role in Aupaumut's "Narrative" as well. At the first stop on his journey, the council fire at Buffalo Creek, his Haudenosaunee "uncles" condoled him before giving him a message for the Delawares. Then, meeting with a Munsee chief from Grand River, Aupaumut said he could not answer their invitation to join them at their village until the "winds" had cleared: "My friends — I Find that our eyes are not fully open — we could not see things clear, for the reason of high winds and dark clouds. . . . Friends — compose your minds in peace and exercise patience. By and by we shall see things clear. When the wind cease and clouds are removed, and the earth lay in silence, then we shall be able to contemplate this subject better."[144]

Aupaumut's use of natural metaphors is not merely symbolic. In his "Narrative," the physical environment reflects the social landscape. His evocative word pictures make clear that the two are irrevocably

intertwined. In recounting his journey with his counselors across waterways, he frequently described the "high winds" that "obliged" them to
"wait" until it was safe to travel and the storms that obstructed their
way, paralleling his depiction of the challenges he faced in the network
of relations. When Aupaumut reached the Delaware village at the Rapids,
his "grandfathers" were obliged to clear his mind and body of the damage these winds had caused:

> You have come from great way off to see and visit us — you have
> seen many dismal objects for which your tears are dropping down.
> Our good ancestors did hand down to us a rule or path where we
> may walk. According to that rule I now wipe off your tears from
> your eyes and face that you may see clear. And since there has been
> so much wind on the way that the dust and every evil things did fill
> your ears, I now put my hand and take way the dust from your
> ears, that you may hear plain — and also the heavy burden on your
> mind I now remove, that you may feel easy, and that you may con-
> template some objects without burden.[145]

In exchange, Aupaumut returned the condolence, describing the
chaos of war in which his relations were embroiled and delivering "six
white strings of wampum" with his empathetic words:

> Grandfather — As I come to you, when I beheld your face, I saw
> your tears flowing down, for the reason of much difficulties and
> crosses. I now put my hand on your face and wipe off your tears, so
> that you may see things clear, and that to a great distance. Grand-
> father — Since there is so much wind, and much dust flying about,
> your ears are stop'd, you are almost deaf. But I now stretch my
> hand and take away all the dust from your ears, that you may now
> hear. And I also put my hand and clean your throat, and take away
> all the heavy burdens which hangs on your mind, and cast it away,
> that you may now understand what is good for your children, and
> that you may have comfort.[146]

Then Aupaumut exchanged condolences with his "younger brother," the
Shawnees, "wip[ing] away" their "tears" and opening their "eyes that you
may see clear and discern what is good."[147]

The paths Aupaumut and Brant traveled were full of storms and
briars, in the waterways they navigated and the networks in which they
participated through many cycles of war. They understood that before
peacemaking could begin, nations had to acknowledge and clear each

other's grief and call for a halt to immediate combat. One of the biggest questions that the Peacemaker's vision answered was how to alter the course of violence, sorrow, and warped thinking that justified the cycle of war. Condolence played a crucial part. Both Brant and Aupaumut had experienced severe ruptures in their home communities and the larger networks to which they belonged. They understood all too well the grief that followed participation in war. But each man knew that peace could develop only if all participants were able to clear their minds of fury and set them to deliberate on the best course for all the land's inhabitants.

Ultimately, Aupaumut and Brant's narratives are testimonies to a long-standing tradition of peacemaking in Native space: the dish with one spoon and the old Algonquian network were both ways to ensure cooperation and equity between those born in and nourished by the same common pot. Both accounts attest to the continuing operation of these indigenous systems. Both men worked tirelessly to foster peace, and each participated fully in the councils designed to clear minds and renew the relationships that would allow for the continuance of Native space. Unfortunately, the United States, in believing that its own plans for the continent outweighed indigenous attempts to share space and assuming that its diplomatic and military traditions were superior to Native ones, failed to grasp an opportunity to learn from its elder brother. In following two paths at once, the American leadership chose a course for the island that ensured its trails would be mired in brambles and blood for decades to come.

Yet perhaps the most glaring mistake made by all parties was the failure to fully engage the original cultivators of peace. The women's roles in this process, and in particular the role of the Jigonsaseh, are strikingly absent from the council records, leaving open the question of how the process might have been different had the women been more involved. Perhaps the most telling aspect of the encounter between Aupaumut and Brant was the moment when Molly Brant asked, "Where are your women?"

Even so, the decision-making processes of the clan mothers still remained within the Confederacy, and despite the erosion of their power, they held onto their right to declare war. In fact, it appears that this tradition, established by the Great Law, was strengthened by the hard lessons of the Revolution. As John Adlum, a settler traveling through Seneca territory, related just after Brant and Aupaumut's journeys, "If the Indians go to war without the consent of the great women the mothers of the

Sachems and Nation, The Great Spirit will not prosper them in War, but will cause them and their efforts to end in disgrace." The clan mothers of the reconstituted Confederacy had expressly decided against war in the Ohio Valley and were apparently "adamant" in their resolve. Thus, both Brant's and Aupaumut's missions were in line with the wishes of the women. Despite opposition from some of the male leadership, one of whom went so far as to advocate for the eradication of this tradition, "the women's judgment," according to Barbara Mann, "was vindicated rather quickly... as news arrived at Seneca that the resistance warriors had been decisively defeated at [the battle of] Fallen Timbers."[148]

Although Brant and Aupaumut's visions failed to produce a lasting peace in the Ohio Valley, both made deep contributions to the common pot. Hendrick Aupaumut secured a place for the "kettle" of New Stockbridge within the "Five Nations," with the newly formed United States, and, most important, within the Algonquian family of nations, opening space for the kettle in the west in case the brotherhood with the United States or the newly developed relationship with the Oneidas failed.[149] During his journeys, Aupaumut reconstructed the "path of my ancestors," reconnecting his village to the larger network that the Mohicans needed to sustain them. Even if Brant did not ultimately achieve union among the Western Indians, his efforts did help to reconstruct the Six Nations. Developing the dish with one spoon enabled him to take lessons learned during the horrific breakdown of the Confederacy to reconstruct his ancestors' vision of unity. He wrote to British Indian Commissioner Joseph Chew just months before the historic Treaty of Canandaigua: "[I] am happy to say that there never was greater Unanimity prevailed amongst the Six Nations than appeared at this Council, being to a man determined in One Opinion."[150]

Most significantly, the two leaders eventually made peace with each other. The only surviving communication between them is a letter Aupaumut wrote in sympathy with Brant's land troubles with the Canadian government. The letter, which arrived at Grand River just two months before Brant's death, reveals a commonality of vision and the development of a friendship between them. Both men were struggling with division in their communities and difficulty in securing their land bases from encroachment. These troubles would eventually lead the majority of the Mohicans, along with their Brotherton neighbors, to move their "kettle" along the waterways and relocate among their western relations. In 1818, the Stockbridge leadership would petition the New York government to "buy a part of their dish" but "keep the other part for the use of those who remained in the State, and keep away their people from it."[151] However, when Aupaumut wrote to Brant in the fall of 1807, he still had hope that he might protect New Stockbridge through writing, by acquiring legal title to their land at Oneida, and he encouraged Brant to do the same.

The Mohican leader was en route to renew the alliance with the Western Algonquians when he stopped at Buffalo Creek and wrote to Brant. As in his "Narrative," Aupaumut began the letter by locating himself within the network of relations:

> My friend, This is to inform you that I am arrived here with my companions on the 3rd inst., on our way to visit our friends of the different tribes of Indians on the Indiana Territory, on purpose to renew the covenant of friendship that was subsisted between my ancestors and theirs — which friendship we and they have renewed four years ago. My friend, I am sorry to hear that there are so many envious men in your neighborhood who create division among your nations. I understand that they constantly oppose the measures you have taken to secure their lasting benefit — that is, you wish to obtain such writing for the land, that you may look upon it as your own property, and not to live on that country merely as poor tenants. And I am sorry to hear that many of my Uncles are willing to be as such. And for my part I will never live on a land which can be taken away from me without my consent. And I hope you will exercise patience and keep good courage, that you may at length succeed in your wishes. May the God of heaven bless you![152] Farewell! Your friend, Hendrick Aupaumut.[153]

Long before the time of Aupaumut and Brant, a Seneca woman who held the title of Jigonsaseh had developed an innovative strategy for conflict resolution. She utilized her position at the crossroads and her responsibility to feed the war parties to cultivate the art of peace. According to Barbara Mann,

> This Jigonsaseh would conduct warring factions in through either the ceremonial Eastern or Western Door of her longhouse, which was partitioned down the middle, with the East screened off from the West, so that neither side could glimpse who was eating across the way. At the end of the meal, the Jigonsaseh would draw aside the bark curtain separating the longhouse in half, so that the enemy sides could see that they had just partaken of food from the same source, or "eaten from the same bowl." ... Since it was forbidden to

make war on one's own kin, by feeding both sides from the same pot, the Jigonsaseh had effectively used this provision of the Great Law to make peace between warring factions. This "one bowl" strategy should not be considered a ruse on her part, however, as anyone who ate in her Gaustauyea longhouse had to have had an inkling beforehand who might have been on the other side of the curtain. Voluntarily partaking of her food was, consequently, a de facto petition for her to broker a peace.[154]

Although they had acted rashly at times, following in the tracks of Flint, and had not always paid her the deference she was due, they were still her sons, born from her body and mind. By the end of their lives, Jigonsaseh, the Lynx, the First Mother, had lifted the partition between her sons Hendrick Aupaumut and Joseph Brant. As they faced the predicament that joined them, the partition and destruction of the land from which they both fed, they understood all too well that they had, all along, been eating from the same dish, the Mother that sustains us all.

4

Regenerating the Village Dish

William Apess and the Mashpee Woodland Revolt

Moving from the interior of the Ohio Valley, in this chapter we return to
Sobakw, the sea, and to Kwinitekw, where the Pequot preacher, writer,
and intellectual William Apess was born just upriver from Ktsi Amiskw,
on a branch of Pocumpetekw in Colrain, Massachusetts. We return to
the Mohegan hunting grounds and to the town of Colchester, Connecticut, where Apess was raised, then travel with him to the territory near
Brant's Grand River, to the mountain of his rebirth. Finally, we follow
him to the southeast coast and to Mashpee, in Wampanoag territory,
where the descendants of Weetamoo and King Philip sought to reconstruct and reclaim their village dish. Thus, this chapter will also bring us
back to the microcosm of the village before we move on, in the next chapter, to an exploration of Apess's grand vision of New England's place in
the network of relations.

William Apess represents an apex of the Native northeastern intellectual tradition, writing his relations into a narrative of continuance
at a time when the rest of New England was heavily invested in the tragic
story of extinguishment. Of all his published writings, *Indian Nullification
of the Unconstitutional Laws of Massachusetts Relative to the Mashpee Tribe;
or, The Pretended Riot Explained* is the least used in critical inquiry and
teaching. Yet this multivoiced narrative probably has more significance
for Native New England communities than all of his other publications
combined. *Indian Nullification* tells the story of the "Mashpee Woodland
Revolt," a moment in the early nineteenth century when the Mashpee
Wampanoags declared their reserve Native space and "nullified" the
laws enacted by the Commonwealth of Massachusetts to manage them
as dependents of the state. During the "Revolt," Apess and the Mashpees

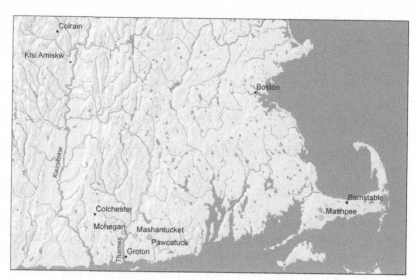

Map 14. Apess's travels, showing the locations of places mentioned in the text.

enacted their claim to self-governance, organizing councils and implementing regulations regarding "outsiders" who were encroaching on their village and its resources. Apess's text functioned not only as a narration of the revolt but as a tool of transformation, an extensive petition designed to effect change in the social, political, and geographic environment.[1]

Entering Native Space (The Mashpee Meetinghouse and Pitch-Pine Forest, Spring 1833)

When Apess traveled to Mashpee in 1833, he went looking for his "brethren." He had heard conflicting reports about this Indian town on Cape Cod; some people suggested that the Mashpees were "well provided," while "others asserted they were much abused." He related, "I resolved to visit the people of Marshpee and judge for myself." Arriving at the village center in a horse-drawn carriage, Apess was moved by the scene he saw before him, at the center of which was an old Indian meetinghouse:

> The sacred edifice stood in the midst of a noble forest and seemed to be about an hundred years old, circumstances which did not render its appearance less interesting. Hard by was an Indian burial ground, overgrown with pines, in which graves were all ranged

north and south. A delightful brook, fed by some of the sweetest streams in Massachusetts, murmured beside it. After pleasing my eyes with charming landscape, I turned to meet my Indian brethren and give them the hand of friendship.[2]

However, this pastoral portrait of idealized Native space was suddenly disrupted by the intrusion of colonial encroachment, symbolized by the stream of white parishioners who began to make their way toward him, in place of the "Indian brethren" he expected: "I was greatly disappointed in the appearance of those who advanced. All the Indians I had ever seen were of a reddish color, sometimes approaching yellow, but now, look to what quarter I would, most of those coming were pale faces, and in my disappointment, it seemed to me that the hue of death sat upon their countenances."[3]

Playing on the trope of the "vanishing Indian" that appeared prominently in popular American narratives, Apess related that the Indians seemed to have disappeared from the forest.[4] "Pale faces" had displaced the Natives, and the remaining Indians were already dead. Yet, as Apess told the story, those advancing "pale faces" were out of place in this idyllic forest scene; they were the ones who displayed a telling "hue of death" under the surface of their countenances.[5] Beneath the illusion of disappearance lay the morbid truth of displacement. Dispossession is not destiny but rather a disjuncture.

As Apess related in *Indian Nullification,* he went on to preach to this strange audience at the invitation of the local missionary, Phineas Fish, who had been appointed by Harvard College to minister to the Indian community. Apess noted that when he "cast" his "eyes at the gallery...paleness was upon all their faces. I must do these *Indians* justice to say they performed their parts well."[6] Apess's ironic voice implies a critique of narratives of Indian vanishing, including the claim to nativity to which they were often linked. The parishioners' "performance" as "Indians" and their pretension of ignorance masked the reality of dispossession.[7] Portraying colonial displacement in the microcosm of the meetinghouse, the Pequot minister reflected, "'It is written that my house shall be called the house of prayer, but ye have made it a den of thieves,' for these pale men were certainly stealing from the Indians their portion of the Gospel, by leaving their own houses of worship and crowding them out of theirs."[8]

The meetinghouse was an apt symbol to represent the colonization of Native space. The building had been constructed in 1684 with
funds raised specifically for Indian ministry and education and had
hosted a number of politically active indigenous ministers who preached
in the Wampanoag language and conducted services that arose from a
unique syncretic tradition. Simon Popmonit, for instance, had emerged
from a leadership family to become Mashpee's first Native preacher,
occupying the pulpit only one year after the meetinghouse was built and
holding that position until his death. As the son of a sachem and brother
to a community leader, Popmonit served as a political and spiritual ad-
viser and was, according to historian Daniel Mandell, "highly respected
by both Indians and colonists." In 1700, he joined with other leaders to
make the Mashpees' first protest to the colonial court, against forced servitude in settler households, and ten years later participated in remonstra-
tions against Barnstable settlers who made claims on Mashpee lands.
When Popmonit died, the Mashpees threatened to boycott the church
unless the English minister who replaced him promised to preach in their
language, and when he was removed for selling liquor, the Mashpees
refused the missionary society's attempt to send another of their own.
They insisted on restoring an Indian minister to their meetinghouse and
selected Solomon Briant, who had been preaching at a neighboring Indian church for twenty years. Briant remained at Mashpee until his death
in 1775 and played an instrumental role in preserving community governance and Native rights. This tradition had been carried on into Apess's
generation. When the Pequot minister asked Phineas Fish "where the
Indians were," the missionary reluctantly admitted that the Mashpees
were in the schoolhouse conducting their own services, led by a Native
man named Blind Joe Amos.[9]

Apess's portrayal represents his recognition of a familiar scene.
This is what Native space looked like in New England during Apess's
time. The Indian meetinghouse, as in the example of the Mohegan church,
became an embedded part of the landscape: it visibly marked the village
territory and provided a central place for maintaining the communal
body. Its physical presence embodied the longevity of the community
and its particular identity, its gatherings provided psychological sustenance and cultivated group unity, and its structure gave authority to the
community's internal decision-making process. Furthermore, Native
preachers like Popmonit, Occom, Briant, and Apess traveled between

these meetinghouses, strengthening ties between communities and creating a space for regional identity based on "shared language and religious
rituals." This shared space of worship that developed in the common
pot of the Algonquian coast combined "Christian and traditional ways,"
emphasizing individual testimony and group participation and thereby
fortifying oral culture and community cohesion. As Mandell has written,
"The religion introduced by English invaders," ironically, was transformed to act "as a cement for native enclaves." Fish's crime, therefore,
had been not the preaching of a "foreign" religion, but the displacement
of the Mashpees from their political and spiritual space, which by the
time of Apess's arrival was occupied almost exclusively by white parishioners from the neighboring towns.[10]

Continuing with his story, Apess related, "The next day, I paid
the people of that place a visit in their meetinghouse." He gave an "address" to the Mashpee audience, concluding with a prayer that "the Lord
[would] have mercy on them and relieve them from the oppressions under
which they labored. Here," Apess interjected, "Mr. Fish cautioned me not
to say anything about oppression, that being, he said, the very thing that
made them discontented. They thought themselves oppressed, he observed, but that was not the case. They had quite liberty enough." Need-
less to say, Apess did not heed the missionary's advice. For the next few
days, Apess and the Mashpees made the schoolhouse an open space for
the very talk of oppression that the missionary had hoped to suppress.
The Mashpees told Apess that Fish had been "placed over them" by Harvard College, without their consent, and had taken over their meetinghouse and parsonage grounds. Contrary to his mission, Fish was preaching to the local white population, partly because the Mashpees had no
interest in his sermons. Yet the minister lived off the fund designed for the
Mashpees, occupied Mashpee space, and increased his income by selling
wood from the Mashpee forest. Apess had been told that the Mashpees
had a missionary "who took care of their lands," but he found that in
reality their lands had been taken over.[11]

The forested land that surrounded the meetinghouse was the
foundation of the community's sustenance and the focus of those rumored
"abuses" of which the Pequot writer had heard. Like many Massachusetts "Indian towns," the Mashpee village was established within Wampanoag territory as a haven for Native people who embraced Christianity, but it had become a refuge for the dispossessed. The town was able

to support its sizeable population, according to Mandell, "in large part because of [its] large, resource-rich environment."[12]

At Mashpee, a combination of controlled burning and limited cutting of firewood helped to produce an abundant open forest for game animals, birds, and human inhabitants. Tall oak trees and scrubby pitch pines remained under such practices, but the spacious canopy allowed much light to come through, encouraging the growth of blueberry, huckleberry, and other edible plants. Fire provided ash to balance the effects of acidic pine on the soil, facilitating cultivation in cleared areas while removing the litter and undergrowth, providing space for native plants and shrubs to regenerate from the forest floor. The grasses, berries, and saplings that flourished in this forest were inviting to game animals, while ground cleared of slash and undergrowth facilitated travel and provided long-range visibility for hunters. The space was also ideal for women gatherers, providing not only the berries and plants essential to their families' spring and summer diet but also ease of movement and comfortable ground on which to perch while picking.[13]

Burning was especially beneficial to the indigenous pitch pine, a "fire-dependent" tree uniquely adapted to the dry soils of Cape Cod. Its seeds not only are fire-resistant, but are often released from their cones only by the heat of fire. Furthermore, to establish themselves in the ground, pitch pine seeds require nearly bare soil, as well as an open canopy that allows plenty of light. Without the presence of fire, the pitch pine is usually superseded by white pine and oak. For the pitch pine, fire is a force not of destruction but of regeneration. It has a "dramatically thick, layered bark" that is "fire resilient," and, unlike any other conifer in New England, even if the crown or part of the trunk is destroyed, the tree will resprout from buds at its base, drawing sustenance from its deep roots.[14]

The Mashpee community was like the pitch pine forest on which it depended, regenerating, despite the devastating impacts of colonization, from the roots of shared tradition and adaptive creativity. Although surrounded by deforested Massachusetts towns, the Mashpee reserve remained a sustainable woodland environment. The continuance of an indigenous land tenure system in which the land was held in common and could not be sold without collective consent played a crucial role. While many Massachusetts "Indian towns" had been divided into individual parcels, most of the Mashpee reserve still consisted of shared space that people used in a variety of ways, including for hunting, fishing, gathering, planting, pasturing, and cutting firewood. At Mashpee, the village operated as a common pot from which many relations drew.[15]

Origin Stories: "Taking the Forest"

While Mashpees were striving to maintain a forest on which they could depend for many generations, the American settlers who surrounded them were still trying to recreate European space.[16] Clearing the land of its trees was deemed necessary not only for the products that land might provide, but for the "progress" of "civilization." Forested land was unused space in need of improvement. Mandell explains the difference between indigenous and settler constructions of space in eighteenth-century Massachusetts thus: "Most native enclaves divided only a small percentage of their lands into small farming plots. All continued to depend heavily on their still-large commons for fish, wood, game, and building materials. By comparison, their English neighbors had divided most if not all of their common lands by the early eighteenth century and faced a shortage of precisely the resources still plentiful on Indian reserves."[17]

By the mid-nineteenth century, New England was "more than three-quarters cleared land." As an example of the dire situation in which Massachusetts settlers found themselves, consider that in addition to the lumber required for building houses and the requisite fences, a "typical New England household" burned "as much as 30 to 40 cords of wood per year." For this amount of wood, each household had to cut over an acre of forest annually. According to Timothy Dwight, president of Yale College and a direct descendant of the commander of Fort Dummer during Greylock's War, in journeying across the whole of Massachusetts on the road from Boston to New York, "twenty miles of wood, made up of fifty or sixty parcels is all the wooded land" a traveler would see. "Our forests," Dwight observed, "have for a century been so extensively felled as scarcely to have left sufficient timber and fuel for the necessary use of the inhabitants."[18]

At the time of Apess's arrival in the spring of 1833, the Mashpees faced increasing pressure to divide their common lands, as well as intensified poaching of their "woodlot." Gideon Hawley, a missionary assigned to "oversee" the Mashpees, had reported in 1795, "Their lands are yet preserved in good degree.... But they are more coveted by the white people than formerly.... Wood in many of the lower towns on the

Cape is scarce.... At Mashpee it is plenty." Hawley estimated that Mashpee space included ten thousand acres of pine and oak forest, with only two thousand acres actively farmed, while "much of the land in neighboring towns had been denuded." In neighboring Barnstable and Sandwich, in particular, the forests had been "universally cut down." In Mashpee, settlers saw an untapped source of timber begging for domestication.[19]

The Massachusetts government had received complaints against wood poaching and land grabs on Indian reserves throughout the eighteenth century. As early as 1710, the Mashpees had protested to the General Court that Barnstable settlers had claimed "a considerable part of their lands." In 1714, a group of "Cape Cod Indians" protested that settlers disregarded their exclusive right to "cut wood in their undivided commons," and in 1715 Natick Indians in mainland Massachusetts sought to legally ban the sale of their wood to English settlers. In 1727, another inland group, the Punkapoags, complained to the General Court that "some of our English Neighbors are too ready to Incroach upon our timber and our wood, cutting it down to make coal with, and damnifying us greatly thereby." Historian Jack Campisi has noted that repeated protests by the Mashpees, in particular, were significant not only "because [the] land disputes occurred but for the vigor with which the Mashpees prosecuted their claims and defended their rights." The Wampanoags at Aquinnah also vigorously "defended [their] resources against intrusions." According to Mandell, the "success" of communities like Aquinnah and Mashpee "came from their ability to maintain wide cultural boundaries against Anglo-American settlers." Like the Mohegans, these communities maintained their villages through the adaptation of "native land tenure to colonial law," allowing for the usage rights of individual families (as "proprietors") but maintaining ownership as a whole. And, also like the Mohegans, they used writing to retain their Native rights and reserved lands with petitions that "stressed communal landownership" and depicted encroachment on their lands and their wood as illegal violations of "proprietary" rights.[20]

The colonial government's response to these complaints was to create a guardianship system for "protecting" the Indians. In 1746, the Massachusetts Assembly passed an "Act for Better Regulating the Indians." The language of the law implied that it was Indians who required better "regulation," when in fact, as Campisi has observed, the real problem "was the inability or unwillingness of the state to enforce its own laws against non-Indians who trespassed on Mashpee land."[21] Rather than criminalizing colonial encroachment, the act empowered state-appointed guardians to regulate Indian bodies and resources. Under the auspices of protection, they collected Mashpee men's pay for their service on whaling ships, rented out Mashpee children and adults as servants, leased "unimproved" land to neighboring settlers, distributed wood-cutting permits to both settlers and Mashpees, and sold fish and wood from the reserve. As Mandell has pointed out, "The guardians did not understand, or were not interested in understanding, Native reliance on undivided resources" and instead instituted management models based on European land tenure, further undermining the Mashpees' effort to maintain a distinct land base.[22]

Not surprisingly, conflicts with the new system immediately arose throughout Massachusetts. In 1747, leaders from Aquinnah sent a petition to the General Court, "telling the assembly that the guardians had rented out their best woodland, [and] were denying them critical firewood." In 1748, a Nantucket Indian "was fined for trying to stop a white man from taking wood from the Indian reserve." At Punkapoag, clearcutting ultimately obliterated the community. The members of the community complained of the guardians: "Since they were set over us our woodlands have been plundered by many people so that our Cedar Swamps & Timber Trees have been destroyed." Most disturbingly, the Punkapoag complainants were put in prison for a month, "for no apparent reason." The prisoners included a wife and husband who, prior to their arrest, had been living with their children in a remote wigwam. The children died in their absence. The Punkapoag example is particularly significant because, unlike at Mashpee and Aquinnah, self-governance and traditional land tenure on the mainland reserve had eroded, and the guardianship system facilitated the displacement of the entire community.[23]

According to Mandell, "The Mashpees refused to accept subordination and fought the guardianship system from its inception. For nearly a century...the Cape Cod enclave sought every opportunity to reclaim its autonomy." Soon after the guardianship was established, the Mashpees protested against it in a petition to the legislature, reporting that they were "almost ruined by having our lands and Medows taken from us." They explained, "English men use our land and it will soon be Worn out, they Cut off our Wood, and some set their houses upon our land, we are allowed to use some small pieces of land but these will soon be worn out." The Mashpees were especially concerned that English "use" of their land would result in "worn out" soil and "cut" forests that would not support future generations at Mashpee. In April 1752, "no longer able to ignore 'the great hurt and damage done by English men invading their marsh and Land and culling their wood,'" the Mashpees "appointed a committee to 'look into means of getting [the] English out.'" In June, they petitioned the General Court, saying: "Against our will these Englishmen take away from us what was our land. They parcel it out to each other, and the marsh along with it, against our will. And as for our streams, they do not allow us peacefully to be when we peaceably go fishing. They beat us greatly, and they have houses on our land against our will." Regarding their reserve, the Mashpees insisted, "We shall not give it away, nor shall it be sold, nor shall it be lent, but we shall always use it as long as we live, we together all our children, and our children's children, and our descendants, and together with all their descendants."[24]

In 1753, the Mashpee community demanded that either the guardianship system be abolished or they be permitted to elect their own guardians. Like the Mohegans, they emphasized their recent service in King George's War. When the Massachusetts government failed to act, the Mashpees sent a representative to England to petition the king. Ruben Cognehew, a Mohegan living at Mashpee, endured kidnapping and enslavement before completing his voyage overseas, but ultimately persuaded the Royal Council to hear the Mashpee case. He protested "that the English inhabitants of the said Province of Massachusetts Bay have of late years unjustly encroached upon the said [Mashpee] Lands, and have hindered and obstructed the Indians in the exercise of" their "just rights." Parallel language suggests that Cognehew was drawing on his own community's land case in bringing the Mashpee protests to the king.[25] Indeed, Samson Occom would send his own remonstrance overseas only three years later. Cognehew was apparently persuasive, for after hearing the petition and an account of his arduous journey, the Royal Council ordered the governor and General Court of Massachusetts Bay to examine the petition and urged them to rectify the situation.[26]

After enduring two years of indifference from the Massachusetts government and direct opposition from their guardians, the Mashpees sent Cognehew and the "Indian pastor" Solomon Briant to protest this inaction directly to the General Court at Boston. Their efforts resulted in the 1763 "Marshpee Act," which restored self-government to Mashpee and banned both settlement and wood poaching. However, this success proved temporary. After the Revolutionary War, in which many Mashpee men served and died, the new state of Massachusetts reinstated the guardianship system, at which point the Mashpees began a whole new series of complaints. Their petitions were largely ignored, while Mashpee faced the continual threat of poachers, settlers, missionaries, and guardians, which constituted an encroachment of the colonial land tenure system and an assault on the forest itself.[27]

Origin Stories: Reclaiming the Forest and Its Sons

William Apess's first publication, *A Son of the Forest*, has received considerable attention as the first Indian autobiography, and critics have noted the irony of his title, given the popular use of this romantic phrase in American literature and the fact that, by his own account, Apess was largely raised by a white family as an indentured servant after suffering abuse at the hands of grandparents. Yet none have noted the ironic use of this title in light of the surrounding environment: in Apess's New England, there was little forest that remained. In Connecticut in particular, Timothy Dwight wrote, "Although the inhabitants have begun to be frugal with respect to their wood, it has already become dearer in several towns than could be wished, and is purchased by the poor at the expense of too great a proportion of their labor." Like the Mohegans and the Mashpees, the Pequots faced a "shared struggle" against dispossession, division, and deforestation. The Pequot leadership at Mashantucket and Pawcatuck also presented petitions against the "destroying of their timber and c[row]ding upon their lands," expressing their perception that Connecticut governors, nearly one hundred years after the Pequot War, still demonstrated "that thare Chefest Desir is to Deprive us of the Privelidg of our land and drive us off to our utter ruin." The deforestation and dispossession at Mashantucket may have been one of the reasons that Apess's family was living up north in the backwoods of Colrain, one of the few forested areas remaining in Massachusetts, when Apess was born.[28]

Tellingly, one of the most climactic moments of Apess's autobiography, the scene of his rebirth, took place in the copious woods of the Bay of Quinte, an area with substantial Mohawk and Mississauga communities not far from Joseph Brant's home. After serving in the military, Apess led a sort of wandering life, traveling through upstate New York and Canada, visiting with Native communities, and taking work where he could find it. Eventually, he was led north to "the Bay of Quinte" on Lake Ontario, where "the scenery was diversified." He remarked on

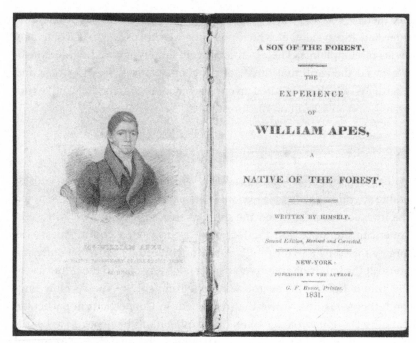

Figure 10. William Apess and the title page of his first publication,
A Son of the Forest, 1831. Widener Library, Harvard University.

the substantial Native population there, observing that "my brethren were all around me, and it therefore seemed like home." It was there that Apess had the epiphany that enabled him to reclaim his identity as a "son of the forest":

> On the very top of a high mountain in the neighborhood there was a large pond of water, to which there was no visible outlet — this pond was unfathomable. It was very surprising to me that so great a body of water should be found so far above the common level of the earth. There was also in the neighborhood a rock that had the appearance of being hollowed out by the hand of a skillful artificer; through this rock wound a narrow stream of water: It has a most beautiful and romantic appearance, and I could not but admire the wisdom of God in the order, regularity, and beauty of creation; I then turned my eyes to the forest, and it seemed alive with its sons and daughters.[29]

In this passage, Apess connected the Christian God to the spirit of creation, to the forest and its network of relations, which contained all the Native inhabitants of the region, including Apess himself. The water is "alive" and active in this passage, as is the forest, and "its sons and daughters" are participants in creation. The reference to a "skillful artificer" alludes to Algonquian stories of Moshup and his transformations in the landscape. In this moment, Apess found a sense of belonging. In reclaiming his identity as a "son of the forest," he recovered a conceptual interdependence. The son reclaimed the forest as the place of his birth and the pot that sustained him, thereby reclaiming his identity as a "Native," in accordance with Wzokhilain's sense of being human and being born of this land. Yet, in Apess's telling, the forest also appeared to reclaim him as its son. Although he had been separated from his Native community, abused by and removed from his family, seemingly displaced, the land still recognized him as one of its own. This relationship, he understood, entailed an obligatory reciprocity to the forest that gave him birth and to its sons and daughters, whom he now fully recognized as his relations.

Bernd Peyer has remarked that this moment "marked a turning point in his life." Soon after, Apess returned home to claim his place in the Pequot community. As Barry O'Connell has observed, "When [Apess] decide[d] to return to Connecticut after his postwar sojourn in Canada, it [was] to go 'home.' And he [spoke] of missing his brethren. . . . Home now [became] seeing and being with his fellow Pequots." Once home, he joined religious meetings led by his Aunt Sally George, who, according to O'Connell, "seems to have been . . . one of several Pequot women who led the nation, keeping it and its precariously held land base together." She would preach in the forest at Mashantucket, most likely in her "native tongue," and drew many relations from neighboring communities to these woodland gatherings. Apess wrote that "her organic power of communication . . . was delightful, charming, and eloquent. I never knew her to speak unless the congregation was watered by an overwhelming flood of tears." Sally George was an influential force in the life of the young Apess, who even lived with her for a time, and "when Apess convert[ed]," O'Connell has suggested, "he [became] simultaneously Christian and Pequot." Of the gatherings, Apess observed, "We had no house of divine worship, and believing 'that the groves were God's first temples,' thither we would repair when the weather permitted. The Lord often met with us, and we were happy in spite of the devil. Whenever we separated it was in perfect love and friendship."[30]

Apess's Native identity was deeply rooted in this forest where his community worshipped in unity. Roger Williams's understanding that the Narragansetts "say themselves, that they have sprung and growne up in that very place, like the very trees of the wildernesse" encapsulates the notion of indigeneity that Apess invoked on the mountain near the Bay of Quinte. To be "of" a place is to be born of it, to originate from the land, and to rely on it for sustenance and continuance. Such narratives of emergence do not relate a single moment of origin but rather reveal a continuing process of growth and transformation in a particular place.[31] The Abenaki leader Polin described this relationship by referring to "the river which I belong to" when he addressed the Massachusetts governor in 1739. Correspondingly, Thomas Wallcut, a Dartmouth-trained missionary, wrote regarding the Abenakis at Odanak, "The notion which the Indians have imbibed respecting the origin of the human race, is, that they grew out of the soil like trees." What all of these statements capture is the relationship between a forested place and its inhabitants and an understanding of the word *indigenous* as that which grows from within.[32]

Regenerating the Sons of the Forest (Mashpee, Spring 1833)

Writing just eleven years before Apess, Timothy Dwight boasted of the resilience of New England's native forests, commenting on their "perpetual self-restoration" even in the face of deforestation. Like most of his contemporaries, however, Dwight failed to comprehend that the same might be true of its indigenous people, whom he viewed as being in a state of "rapid decay." Dwight's words echoed the myth of the "vanishing" New England Indians, the most prevalent narrative for explaining their "degradation." For example, after traveling through Massachusetts in 1765, Hector St. John de Crevecoeur observed that Indians "appear to be a race doomed to recede and disappear before the superior genius of the European." In 1820, the missionary Jedidiah Morse reported to the secretary of war that New England Indians need not be of concern to the War Department because they were "gradually wasting away" and would soon be extinct. Another contemporary lamented, "A few only remain, like the spared trees of an ancient forest."[33]

Amid this chorus of concurring voices, one rose with a resounding dissonance. When William Apess emerged from the forest and began lecturing on the popular topic of "Indian degradation," he demonstrated that "degradation" was the result neither of racial character nor of an inherent tendency to vanish in the wake of civilization but rather of "acts" designed to dispossess Indians of their land.[34] While Anglo-American writers like Timothy Dwight nostalgically mourned the loss of "proud, heroic" leaders like "Miantonomo, Philip, Sassacus, Uncas, or the great Hendrick," concluding that their descendants were mere "remnants" who had "shrunk" into "the torpor of reasoning brutism," Apess composed a remarkably different story: the Natives of New England stemmed from such "heroes" and "ancient trees," and, just like the pitch pine forest that sustained it, a community like Mashpee could regenerate from within.[35]

When Apess "turned" his "face toward Mashpee, to preach the word there," he found an audience that recognized his voice and applauded his message of regeneration. But before the Mashpees could act to reclaim their forest, Apess led his kin to undergo their own conceptual homecoming, to reclaim their identity as the "freeborn sons of the forest." According to his own narrative, when Apess took the pulpit at the meetinghouse to address his "brethren" for the first time, he concluded his address by reading from a "small pamphlet that contained a sketch of the history of the Indians of New England." We cannot be sure of Apess's words on that day, but the "pamphlet" was likely a draft of his most potent oratorical essay, the *Eulogy on King Philip*.[36] Thus, the "sketch" probably began with the initial welcoming of the Puritans by the Wampanoags at Plymouth, then related the series of kidnappings and violations that explorers and settlers perpetrated against New England's Native population and, after raising the horrific specters of the burning of the Pequot village and King Philip's War, inevitably demonstrated the continuity of colonial "oppression" up to Apess's day. Furthermore, Apess likely connected the Mashpees' specific struggles to those of Indians across the Americas, from the arrival of Columbus to the Removal Act that was so hotly debated at the time. Apess probably discussed the ironies of Revolutionary rhetoric, portraying the sons of the Revolution as tyrants against the country's original inhabitants. Most important, he surely reminded the Wampanoags, again and again, that Mashpee, as well as the whole of New England and the Americas, was Native land and that their struggle was a shared space in which they were survivors and fighters, not victims destined to fade away. Apess later recalled that, as he was reading from his pamphlet, "an individual among the assembly took occasion to clap his hands, and with a loud shout, to cry 'Truth, truth!'"[37]

"This gave rise to general conversation," Apess related, "and it was truly heartrending to me to hear what my kindred people had suffered at the hands of the whites." "Then," Apess continued, "wishing to know more of their grievances, real or supposed, and upon their invitation, I appointed several meetings; for I was requested to hear their whole story and to help them." At the final meeting, "the house was well filled," and each person rose and gave testimony to their "distresses." "Tears flowed freely," he said, and at the end of the day "I counseled them to apply for redress to the governor and Council. They answered that they had done so, but had never been able to obtain a hearing; the white agents had always thrown every obstacle in their way."[38]

After Apess gave another rousing speech, which his audience "listened to with profound attention," the Mashpees agreed to adopt him as a member of their tribe so that he might help them seek a just solution. "Ebenezer Attaquin, being one of the prayer leaders... said, If we get this man to stand by us, we must stand by him." In return, Apess pledged to "unite" his "efforts" with those of the Mashpee leadership, including the preacher, Blind Joe Amos, saying, "had I but half a loaf of bread, I would gladly divide it with him." Apess added, "It was then agreed that we should unite and journey together on the road toward heaven."[39] Apess and the Mashpees were using a diplomatic dialogue familiar in Algonquian circles. Through their words they were building unity, and Apess, as the outsider, made clear his intention to be an equal participant by appealing to the ideal of equal distribution.[40] As Apess related, under adoption customs, "our rights and interests would become identical," and the united community could then act as one body.[41]

As Steve Pike observes in *Geographies of Resistance*, the "repositioning" of subjectivities occurs not only in "overt political spaces" but also in "inner spaces." Building on the ideas of Frantz Fanon, Pike suggests that this reconstruction of conceptual space is akin to "setting up garrisons within the conquered city of the mind." If an oppressive situation "is to be changed," he writes, the participants in that change "will need to have their fears devalidated, their guilt, shame, and embarrassment overcome, and their desires given the resources of hope."[42] Apess delineated the markers of communal history and created an open space for voicing the shared experience of oppression, leading the Mashpees to wage their internal battle together and to imagine an alternate route to community survival, regenerating Native space from within.

Reclaiming Native Space (Mashpee, May 1833)

From within this "inner space" the Mashpees were able to stand up as "the red children of the soil of America" and address "the White People of Massachusetts" as "the descendants of the pale men who came across

the big waters to seek among [us] a refuge from tyranny and persecu-
tion." At the conclusion of their "council" with Apess, they "drafted"
three "papers": a petition to the state, a petition to Harvard College, and
a set of "resolutions" to be posted, just like *awikhiganak*, for all of the neighboring communities to see. All of these texts were subsequently embedded within *Indian Nullification*.[43]

The petition to the "Governor and Council of the State of Massachusetts" began by using the trope of the "poor Indian" to call attention
to a long history of oppression:

> Gentlemen, Your Honors —
>   Permit us poor Indians who for the space of two hundred and
> ten years or ever since this country has been settled. Who ever have
> been degraded or imposed upon more or less by the white man, to
> address you thus, and as we Marshpee Tribe speak as the voice of
> one man we would wish to be heard, and as former attempts has
> been fruitless and overruled by design men that cared not for the
> Indians any thing further than what they could cheat or rob them
> out of we trust we shall be heard by your honors.[44]

While establishing themselves as occupying a place in Massachusetts colonial history which would be familiar to the governor and
council, the Mashpees also presented a contrasting identity that emphasized the rhetoric of the common pot, representing themselves as "we
the Marshpee Tribe," who "speak as the voice of one man." The petition
also addressed the guardians' complicity in their ongoing oppression,
pointing to the "design men" who "cheat and rob" them while inviting
the council to act with more "honor" toward the original inhabitants of
their state. In a diplomatic rhetorical move, they also absolved the counselors of guilt for not responding to their previous "attempts" to "be
heard" by blaming the guardians for interference.[45]

The petition continued by addressing the guardianship system
more directly:

> We say as the voice of one man that we are distressed, and degraded
> daily, by those men, who we understand were appointed by your
> Honor. That they have the rule of every thing, that we are not con-
> sulted is true, and if we are, they do as they please, and if we say
> one word, we are then called poor drunken Indians, when in fact
> we are not, that we have joined the temperance cause and wish to
> be counted so and heard to by your honors.

Here is the clear hand of William Apess, who had transformed the trope of "Indian degradation" so that it was an activity in which "men" were engaged, not an intrinsic state of being. The Mashpees exposed the "poor drunken Indian" stereotype as a tool that served to justify unethical actions, and they even reversed the image to give greater weight to their request for a hearing. Their "complaints," they continued, were "as follows":

> First, There is something like six or seven who pretend to be our Masters and spend and dispose of our property as they please.... Our Meadows are set up at auction and sold, and only is reserved enough for the wintering of one cow, and if we want more we have to buy it the same as our white neighbors. Our wood shares the same fate, sold at Auction, and we have to pay one dollar upon every cord we sell. Much of our Land is also rented out and white people have the pre-eminence, and the overseers will not rent our own lands to us, and we can not turn our own sheep or what little stock we have without a noise from these Lordly men. These white men take the liberty to turn their cattle upon our plantation if they please, and no body must say a word. Even our fishing streams are over run daily with many who are whites, so that all of our privileges are in a matter taken from us, our people are forsaken many of them sleep upon the cold ground, and we know not why it should be so, when we have enough if properly managed to supply all our wants.[46]

This rhetoric echoes earlier petitions from Mohegan. Through verbal repetition the Mashpees claimed the land and its resources as "our property," and, in a clever appropriation of abolitionist speech, they portrayed the guardians as "pretend[ed]...Masters." In other words, these assertions of white ownership were a pretense without moral or legal authority. The resulting encroachment on Native "property" interfered directly with their "privileges" and threatened the limited resources of the environment on which they were dependent. If left alone, they insisted, they would "have enough...to supply all our wants," including both subsistence and trade. But under these bewildering conditions, they said, "our people are forsaken," prevented from using what was theirs by birth and law. The Mashpees asserted that they had the knowledge to "properly manage" their land so that it would support them indefinitely, but they now faced rapid resource depletion, which was the direct result of the guardianship system and the disregard for the boundaries of Native space.[47]

In concluding, the Mashpees insisted, "There is much more, but we think that this is sufficient for your honors, to satisfy you, knowing that if we were whites, one half would be enough for redress." They then reasserted their position "as Proprietors of the soil," connecting their "property" rights to their indigeneity, just as their predecessors had done. They diplomatically expressed their desire "that we one day should take care of ourselves" before reporting that they had already taken measures to enact it: "We have several good trusty men who are capable men who are about to be chosen officers by us." They then asked the governors to "discharge" the guardians, and, like the Mohegans, they rooted their request in urgent subsistence needs and cloaked it in the language of the law: "If we do not take such measures in five years our property will be gone."[48]

The Mashpees formally closed their petition with the following signature, "Yours most obediently, as the voice of one man we approve of the above; as the voice of one man we pray you hear." In their final words, the Mashpees strategically used the language of colonial diplomacy, humbling themselves before the council, but also brought Native oratory into play, reiterating their communal voice and asking the governors to listen with clear ears. And, as if with wampum, they marked the authority of that voice and the weight of their request with the written word.[49]

The petition was signed by 101 men and women, along with the newly "chosen officers," Israel Amos and Ebenezer Attaquin, who attached the council's "Resolutions." They read:

> Resolved, That we, as a tribe, will rule ourselves, and have right to do so; for all men are born free and equal, says the Constitution of the country.
> Resolved, That we will not permit any white man to come upon our plantation to cut or carry off wood or hay, or any other article, without our permission, after the 1st of July next.
> Resolved, That we will put said resolutions in force after that date, with the penalty of binding and throwing them from the plantation, if they will not stay away without.[50]

The Mashpees had drafted their own "Declaration of Independence," and the mimicry was not merely an act of appropriation. A large proportion of Mashpee men had served during the Revolution, and the majority had died for the American cause.[51] The Constitution was as much theirs to cite as it was that of any of the men who had fought with them. As Apess observed in *Indian Nullification,* "Often and often have our tribe been promised the liberty their fathers fought, and bled, and died for; and even now we have but a small share of it," echoing Hendrick Aupaumut in suggesting that settlers seemed content to share the space of war but not that of freedom and equality.[52] If Americans had the natural right to be free from British colonial rule, the Mashpees had the same right to be free from the laws imposed on them by Massachusetts. But, like their neighbors in Boston, the Mashpees understood that such rights had to be asserted from within. As their first act of self-governance, they addressed the problem of wood poaching by posting resolutions strategically around "our plantation," marking the forest as Mashpee territory. Furthermore, by appointing a date for the institution of the resolutions and a penalty for defying them, they created clear political boundaries between the commonwealth and Mashpee space. With their resolutions they publicly proclaimed their internal reconstitution "as a tribe" and communicated their position by using a persuasive rhetorical framework familiar to all Americans.

The Mashpees' petition to Harvard College echoed the other council documents, but it addressed the issue of the meetinghouse and the missionary Phineas Fish. The petition repetitively emphasized the rhetoric of the common pot, using phrases such as "we do say, as the voice of one," "we, as a body," "we, as a tribe," and "we, as a people" to address "our white brethren of Harvard College." The Mashpees insisted they had no objection to sharing space with "our white neighbors, provided they come as they ought to come." However, Fish and his congregation had come "as thieves and robbers, and we would ask all the world if the Marshpee Indians have not been robbed of their rights." Here we see in play the same metaphor Apess used to begin *Indian Nullification,* connecting Fish and his congregation with colonial "thievery."[53]

For the Mashpees, history was taking place not in linear time but in the space of Native New England, where the dynamic between the desire to share space and the activity of colonial dispossession seemed to recur wherever resources remained. The petition asserted that the missionary had taken "possession of five or six hundred acres of the tribe's best woodland ... pretending that his claim and right to the same was better than that of the owners themselves." Like the guardians and the governors, Fish asserted a "pretended claim" over Native land. The Mashpees protested this entitlement, saying,

We were never consulted as to his settlement over us, as a people. We never gave our vote or voice, as a tribe, and we fully believe that we are capable of choosing for ourselves, and have the right to do so, and we would now say to you, that we have made choice of the Rev. Wm. Apes, of the Pequot tribe, and have adopted him as one of ours, and shall hear him preach, in preference to the missionary, and we should like to have him aided, if you can do it. If not, we cannot help it — he is ours — he is ours.[54]

With this petition, the Mashpees reclaimed both their meeting-house and the parsonage woodlot as Native space. But they also claimed the position of preacher and community leader as "ours." The traditions of the meetinghouse and of indigenous ministers — those men like Pop-monit, Solomon Briant, Samuel Ashpo, and Samson Occom, who brought families together and helped them to protect their land — belonged to the Mashpees and their relations. The meetinghouse belonged to this place.

After "publishing" their petitions and posting their resolutions, the internal gathering at Mashpee continued. Apess journeyed with Blind Joe Amos to the seaport to call in his brother Daniel, who was working "in the coasting business." According to Apess, he "had done much to teach the Indians and to bring them to a right knowledge of their degraded condition." Years after his passing, Daniel Amos was remembered as "the smartest man we ever had among us." Upon hearing about the recent events, "he said that he would willingly relinquish his business and join in the efforts of his brethren to shake off the yoke which galled them." Together they "resolved to hold a convention" at Mashpee "for the purpose of organizing a new government." Upon their return, Apess related,

> We now, in our synagogue, for the first time, concerted the form of a government, suited to the spirit and capacity of freeborn sons of the forest, after the pattern set us by our white brethren. There was but one exception, viz., that *all* who dwelt in our precincts were to be held free and equal, *in truth*, as well as in letter. Several officers, twelve in all, were elected to give effect to this novelty of a government, the chief of whom were Daniel Amos, president, and Israel Amos, secretary. Having thus organized ourselves, we gave notice to the former board of overseers, and the public at large, of our intentions.[55]

The "National Assembly of the Marshpee Tribe" announced with their "proclamation" that they were determined to halt the "distress" and "robbery" to which they were subjected "daily." They declared that they had chosen "our own town officers to act instead of whites" and intended to "enforce" their "resolutions." "Now," they said, "we would say to our white friends, we are wanting nothing but our rights betwixt man and man." However, according to Apess, after the publication of this notice, "the missionary and agents and all who put their faith in them combined together to work our destruction."[56]

Reclaiming the Woods (Mashpee, July 1833)

Fittingly, the "climax" of the Mashpee Revolt occurred in the forest on the day appointed in the resolutions for the resumption of self-rule. While "walking in the woods" on July 1, Apess and several other Mashpee men discovered two brothers, members of Fish's congregation, loading up their "teams" with timber. In Apess's words, "They came, in defiance of our resolutions, to take away our wood in carts." He calmly informed the poachers of the tribe's resolutions and "begged them to desist, for the sake of peace, but it was to no purpose...they were resolved to load their teams." He reminded them that the "men who owned the wood were resolved to carry their resolutions into force, and asked if they had not seen the notification we had posted up. One of them replied that he had seen but had not taken much notice of it." Apess had "previously cautioned the Indians to do no bodily injury to any man, unless in their own defense, but to stand for their rights and nothing else." On Apess's advice, his Mashpee companions proceeded to unload the wood from the carts. He related that one of the white men, "who was a justice of the peace, forbade them and threatened to prosecute them for thus protecting their own property." This threat, he wrote,

> had no other effect than to incite them to work more diligently. When they had done, I told the justice that he had, perhaps, better encourage others [not] to carry away what did not belong to them and desired the teamsters to depart. They said they would, seeing that it was useless to attempt to load the carts. Throughout this transaction the Indians uttered neither a threat nor an unkind word, but the white men used very bitter language at being thus, for the first time, hindered from taking away what had always been as a lawful spoil to them hitherto.[57]

Apess constructed this moment in *Indian Nullification* so that the "wood" metonymically stood in for the "woods." In a brilliant reversal of the rhetoric of Manifest Destiny and Indian vanishing, the Indians reclaimed the woods from those who had thought their own claim was most "lawful" and forced the interlopers to confront the fact that the "property" that they had taken so easily for so long did, in truth, "not belong to them." The Mashpees' physical reclamation of the "wood[s]" followed organically from the reorganization of their council. Both physically and conceptually, the Mashpees were in the process of reclaiming Native space, and the rights inherent to that space justified their acts of repossession. Furthermore, as they had pledged to each other in council and sealed with writing, they were obliged to follow through on their resolutions. In introducing the woodlot incident, Apess wrote, "We did even as we had pledged ourselves to do, having in view no other end than the assertion and resumption of our rights. Two of the whites, indeed, proved themselves enemies to the Indians, by holding themselves in readiness to break up the new government and daring them to carry it into effect."[58]

Although Apess depicted the poachers as violators of indigenous rights, the colonial government responded by treating the woodlot incident as an act of Native rebellion against the state. Apess and his companions were arrested on the ironic date of July 4 for "riot, assault," and most absurdly, "trespass." Apess suggested that the poachers had "hurried off to get the aid of legal might to overcome right," and a message arrived from the governor shortly after the incident, requesting a hearing. The governor's agent, Josiah Fiske, suggested a meeting at a local tavern, but the Mashpees insisted on gathering at their meetinghouse. The governor agreed, but invited the guardians to respond to the Mashpees' accusations. The guardians arrived with the local sheriff and a number of settlers. Apess wrote, "The excitement which pervaded Cape Cod had brought these people to our council, and they now heard such preaching in our meetinghouse as they had never heard before — the bitter complainings of the Indians of the wrongs they had suffered." By insisting on holding the "council" at their meetinghouse, the Mashpees were calling on an old tradition of northeastern treaty protocol. Apess's narration mirrored this political move: the governor, guardians, and settlers entered into the Mashpee "council." Like their forebears, they were portrayed as coming into Native space. Not only had the Indians reclaimed their meetinghouse, but they filled it with the voices of "truth." Where talk of "oppression" had formerly been excluded, it now ran freely, and the captive audience was forced to listen.[59]

The government responded by attempting to reassert an image of Indianness that would contain the Mashpees within colonial space. Fiske first advised them of "the laws...and the consequences of violating them." Apess related, "He told us that merely declaring a law to be oppressive could not abrogate it." While subtly raising the threat of physical force, the governor's agent reasserted the control of law by using language that presumed that the Mashpees, as individuals, were subjects of the state and therefore subject to its laws. At the same time, Fiske also invoked the Mashpees' special status as Indians, reminding them of the "parental feeling of government for the remnant of a once mighty and distinguished race." The agent sought to recontain the Mashpees within the boundaries of American discursive space, restoring them to the comfortable category of "the Indian," both a "remnant" of a "noble race" that had existed in the past and a dependent ward of the state.[60]

While Fiske used familiar tropes to counteract the authority of the Mashpees' written resolutions, Apess unmasked the agent's efforts with his own rhetorical skill. His derisive narration of the agent's assertions alongside eloquent descriptions of Mashpee self-determination functioned to expose these images, so carefully constructed in American courtrooms and publishing houses, as fallacies that served only to deprive Indians of their rights.

Reclaiming Discursive Space (Massachusetts, Summer–Fall 1833)

The "woodland revolt" sparked a dialogue in the local press that mirrored national debates. Typical of the editorials written by Massachusetts citizens in the early days of the "Mashpee Revolt" was an article published in the *New Bedford Press*. It began thus: "The remnants of that race of men who once owned and inhabited the forests and the prairies of the Old Colony that have now given place to large and populous villages and the busy hum of the civilized man, are, it would seem, somewhat dissatisfied with the manner in which they are governed." Indians, in this construction, were part of the past. The prophecy of Manifest Destiny had already been realized. The Indians of New England had already been contained, either by history or under the jurisdiction of a "civilized" government. In contrast to this common narrative, the Mashpees asserted a continuing presence within a particular place that they had the right to maintain without interference. Another editorialist, in the

Barnstable Journal, demonstrated a clear comprehension of this perspective: "All the Indians want in Marshpee is to enjoy their rights without molestation. They have hurt or harmed no one. They have only been searching out their rights, and in so doing, exposed and uncovered, and thrown aside the mantle of deception, that honest men might behold and see for themselves their wrongs."[61]

Having acquired the power of writing for themselves, the Mashpees decided to add their own voice to the national and local debate.[62] In *Indian Nullification,* Apess related that it was "common opinion" that his "imprisonment" would put fear in other Mashpees and "cause them to forego their efforts to recover their rights." In fact, it had quite the opposite effect. After instituting their resolutions, Apess and the Mashpees moved the site of their conceptual battle from the inner space of their own minds "into [the] public prints." They published articles and notices in newspapers from Barnstable to Boston, figuring that their neighbors in Massachusetts might want "to hear the Indians speak for themselves."[63]

The Mashpees specifically asked New Englanders to recognize the shared space of their past and its relation to the current struggle. In the *Barnstable Journal,* they compared their revolt to the Revolution, saying, "We unloaded two wagons of wood" in place of "English ships of tea." Using rhetoric similar to Aupaumut's, they asked the citizens of "Massachusetts, the boasted cradle of independence, whom we have petitioned for a redress of wrongs, more grievous than what your fathers had to bear," whether they were willing to play the role of the British tyrant to those who had once assisted them in gaining their independence:

> And now, good people of Massachusetts, when your fathers dared to unfurl the banners of freedom amidst the hostile fleets and armies of Great Britain, it was then that Marshpee furnished them with some of her bravest men to fight your battles. Yes, by the side of your fathers they fought and bled, and now their blood cries to you from the ground to restore that liberty so unjustly taken from us by their sons.[64]

The Mashpees also hit a nerve in abolitionist circles when they posed the following question to "our brethren, the white men in Massachusetts," who had "recently manifested much sympathy for the red men of the Cherokee nation": "How will the white man of Massachusetts ask favor for the red men of the South, while the poor Marshpee red men, his near neighbors, sigh in bondage? Will not your white brothers of Georgia tell you to look at home, and clear your own borders of oppression, before you trouble them?"[65]

By using such words as "brethren" and "neighbors" repeatedly, the Mashpees reminded their American "brothers" that they were born of the same land. They suggested that "oppression" between brothers was an indisputable injustice, one that many Massachusetts citizens seemed able to recognize in other regions but not in their own state. Apess and the Mashpees continually asked New Englanders to imagine themselves in the "place" of their Indian neighbors: "We wonder how the good citizens of Boston... would like to have the Indians send them a preacher and force him into the pulpit and then send other Indians to crowd the whites out of their meetinghouse, and not pay one cent for it. Do you think the white men would like it? We trow not."[66]

Similarly, in *Indian Nullification* Apess made the following proposal to "the government of Massachusetts," exposing the roots of "Indian degradation" once again:

> Let them put our white neighbors in Barnstable County under the guardianship of a board of overseers and give them no privileges other than have been allowed to the poor, despised Indians. Let them inflict upon the said whites a preacher whom they neither love nor respect and do not wish to hear. Let them, in short, be treated just as the Mashpee tribe have been: I think there will soon be a declension of morals and population.[67]

The Mashpees wrote to the *Boston Daily Advocate*, "We are hard to believe... that any people, served as we have been here, would more kindly submit to it, than we have. We think now we have submitted long enough, and we thought it no crime to look, or ask after our rights." Such pieces not only drew outsiders into Native space but also thrust the Mashpee case into public space, sparking a debate that raged in the press for nine months. In this forum, Mashpees found not only a venue in which to voice their oppressions but a strategy for building a coalition. With strategic reversals and calls for brotherhood, they invited their "neighbors" to occupy a position of empathy and unity with the oppressed rather than inhabiting the role of the oppressor: "You think the men you give us do us good, and that all is right. Brothers, you are deceived; they do us no good. We do them good. They like the place where you have put them. Brothers, our fathers of this State meet soon to make new laws; will you help us to enable them to hear the voice of the red man?"[68]

Reclaiming Native Rights (Boston, Winter 1833–1834)

During the winter of 1833–34, a "delegation" traveled from Mashpee to Boston to present their petition before the House of Representatives. Yet, before the Mashpees were even allowed to speak at the State House, an unprecedented debate ensued on Beacon Hill over whether they should even be allowed to have their petition read. Some wanted to wait for a statement "on the subject of the difficulties with the Indians" from the governor and council, and one legislator objected that it might be too "long [and] it would take up time unnecessarily to read it," while another blatantly stated that he "hoped the motion to read the petition would not prevail," because it might "prejudice the House" against the forthcoming governor's statement. However, several representatives insisted that the House had never refused to hear a petition, even "of the humblest individual." One asserted, "The petitioners have a constitutional right to be heard. I know not of what value that provision is which gives a right to petition, if the House can refuse to hear the petition." A legislator from Boston said that, "due to the character of the House, and to our native brethren the petitioners," the petition "should be heard, and heard patiently." The Mashpees had challenged their neighbors to examine their democratic claims and the grounds on which they differentiated themselves from their British ancestors and their southern contemporaries, making it much more difficult to dismiss the Mashpees' complaints on the basis of their second-class standing as Indians. The petition was finally read, and then, according to Apess, the Mashpee "delegates . . . were privileged to tell their own story."[69]

The Mashpee "delegation," consisting of Isaac Coombs, Daniel Amos, and William Apess, followed the path of their predecessors, Solomon Briant and Reuben Cognehew, in bringing their case to the colonial center. In addition to the legislature, they addressed "crowded houses" at Boylston Hall and the Tremont Theatre, where their speeches were interrupted by "applause." On Beacon Hill, Isaac Coombs spoke to legislators about the increasingly "intolerable" problems the entire community faced with the current system, remarking on the pressure imposed on them to cooperate with the guardians. The Mashpee leader insisted that, "although by taking side with the overseers, he might have advanced his own interests, he nevertheless chose to suffer with his people, and to plead in their behalf." Here, Coombs illustrated the ethical system that governed his actions, emphasizing faithfulness to the whole and expressing suspicion of those who encouraged self-interest over the needs of the group. Daniel Amos spoke diplomatically about the long history of the community's oppression and related his own personal experience of the "severity of those laws" imposed upon his "native home." He, too, emphasized the unity of the tribe, insisting that nothing had been included in their petition "but by their unanimous consent." William Apess followed by presenting "a fearless, comprehensive, and eloquent speech" about the relationship between the current system and the Mashpees' "degradation." He related his opinions on the current state of affairs and explained the full context of recent events, including the woodlot incident for which he had been arrested. In a statement that contained echoes of the questions Samson Occom posed to William Johnson, "Mr. Apes" said he "wished to know from whence the right to tax them without their consent, and at pleasure, and subject them to the arbitrary control of a Board of Overseers was derived?" The reporter for the *Liberator* who summarized the speeches noted, in conclusion, "In several instances, the speakers made some dexterous and pointed thrusts at the whites, for their treatment of the sons of the forest since the time of the pilgrims, which were received with applause by the audience." This reception symbolized the effectiveness of the Mashpees' strategy. Massachusetts citizens were eager to express their support for the "sons of the forest," to cleanse themselves of the crimes of their Puritan ancestors and to assure their Indian neighbors that they would pursue a more just course, in keeping with their republican values.[70]

"About this time," Apess wrote, "the opposition of our enemies increased into a flood," and their opponents were not afraid to use the time-honored strategy of division. Phineas Fish himself presented a memorial to the legislature to subvert the Mashpees' campaign. The document purported to represent a different group of "inhabitants and proprietors...of Marshpee," who said they were "well satisfied" with Fish and insisted that the current protests had all originated from Apess. The Mashpee council counteracted this memorial by publishing in the *Advocate* their own statement, which had been composed at "a regular meeting at Marshpee" and recorded by Daniel Amos: "It is unfair to attempt to prejudice the public against us, while we are petitioning for our rights. It is not true that the Indians are satisfied. The Legislature ought not to be deceived by such stories from interested men. There is a universal dissatisfaction with our condition, and unless something is done to relieve us, the whole tribe must suffer."[71]

The Mashpees firmly rejected the suggestion that Apess had been responsible for instigating the revolt and made clear that he was just a part of the village, not its leader:

> Now we know something of our rights without being told by Mr. Apes, or anyone. We have confidence in Mr. Apes, and have seen no reason to doubt that he means well; but our dissatisfaction with the laws and the overseers was the same as it is now, long before Mr. Apes came among us, and he will have our confidence no longer than while we are satisfied he does right.... He is only one of us, and has no more authority over the tribe than any other member of it.[72]

The council's statement reiterated the rhetoric of the common pot, insisting that the current conditions affected the "tribe" as a "whole" and that they were united in their effort to restore their "rights." They recalled the circumstances under which Apess had been adopted into the tribe as a member equal to others, responsible to the community, and insisted that the current resistance had emerged from within. Furthermore, they insisted that any claims to the contrary were merely the "stories" of men who had interests in their land, drawing a parallel to the popular American poems and dramas that eradicated Native existence with the power of the pen.[73]

Citing the authority of indigenous authorship, the Mashpees' neighbor and attorney Benjamin Hallett dismissed the opposition's memorial entirely, stating, "This remonstrance was not prepared by the Indians. It came wholly from the Rev. Mr. Fish, and the Overseers.... No one who signed it had any voice in preparing it." Furthermore, he related that some who had signed the memorial had been told it was merely a "petition for Mr. Fish, to retain his salary, but that they are entirely opposed to having Overseers and to the present laws." In contrast, Hallett insisted, the petition presented by the Mashpee delegation to the House of Representatives "comes directly from the Indians. It was drawn up among them without the aid of a single white man." Contrary to Fish's "remonstrance," he asserted, "They are all united in wishing to have a change in the laws, and removal of the Overseership, but desire that their land may not be sold without the mutual consent of the Indians and the General Court."[74]

The Mashpee council directly addressed the problem of division in their petition, explaining the manipulation behind the opposition memorial:

> We can assure your Honors that there is not one enlightened and respectable Indian upon the plantation, that wants Overseers or the present minister, Mr. Phineas Fish. We say that all of our rulers, and he who is said to be our preacher, was placed here amongst us without our consent; and it has been the policy of these interest men to work upon the feelings of some of our most ignorant and dissipated men and women, to keep us divided. We are sure that none but those who are in the habit of drinking, have signed this paper, to hear him preach; and many of them said they did not know what it contained. Why we mention this, is because we have discharged him, and passed Resolutions that we will not hear him preach; and we are of the same mind still.[75]

Like Occom and the Mohegans or Brant and the United Indian Nations, Apess and the Mashpees demonstrated a clear understanding of the motives and tactics of colonial division and countered it by reasserting their commitment to unity and self-determination. While colonial leaders and many of the writers who had followed in their tracks often assumed that the most intelligent and educated Indians would naturally follow a course of submission and acceptance, intelligence and sobriety demanded that leaders honor the wishes and needs of the whole, necessitating their defense of Native lands and Native rights.

Massachusetts citizens were themselves divided on the issue of Mashpee rights, and the debate grew heated while the Indian delegation was in Boston. In the *Boston Daily Advocate*, Benjamin Hallett proclaimed the Mashpees the "native owners of the soil," who possessed a "better title than the whites hold to any land in the Commonwealth." Invoking shared space, he wrote, "These Indians fought and bled side by side, with our fathers, in the struggle for liberty; but the whites were no sooner free themselves, than they enslaved the poor Indians." The "descendants" of these "martyrs to liberty," Hallett continued, were "placed under a despotic guardianship, and their property wrested from them to enrich the whites." To contradict such editorials, the opposition used the press to reinscribe the Mashpees within a controlled colonial space. Former governor Levi

Lincoln depicted them as a tribe "under the protection and guardian-ship of this Commonwealth," who had committed an act of sedition. He suggested that they were a "misguided" and "deluded" people who "as-sumed" a pretended right to "self-governance" but were in fact "in a state of open rebellion against the government of the State." Lincoln sent this piece to the *Boston Courier* shortly after the famous abolitionist William Lloyd Garrison denounced the state's role in keeping the Mash-pees "in servile dependence." In the *Liberator*, Garrison proclaimed, "Dep-recating partial and occasional injustice to them on the part of individuals, it has shrewdly deemed it lawful to plunder them by wholesale, continu-ally." The abolitionist leader celebrated "this spontaneous, earnest, up-ward movement of our red brethren," insisting, "It is sedition, it is true; but only the sedition of freedom against oppression; of justice against fraud; of humanity against cruelty."[76]

Emerging from within the space of their council and expanding into this environment of vitriolic opposition and rallying support, the Mashpees presented their final petition with sensitivity and force. Fol-lowing a diplomatic opening in which they appealed to the desire of all "inhabitants of this Commonwealth" for "justice and equity" and flat-tered the "enlightened and judicious Representative[s]" before them, they pulled their audience abruptly into Native space:

> While ye are filled with the fat of our fathers' land, and enjoy your
> liberties without molestation, will not this Honorable Body be as
> benevolent to us, poor Marshpee Indians, who are sighing and weep-
> ing under bondage, as ye are to the poor Cherokees? And have we
> not groaned under the weight of degradation long enough? Are ye
> willing that we should go down to the grave with sorrow and dis-
> grace, as our fathers have before us, when we are willing to try to
> take care of ourselves? And we fear that our petitions have been
> laid aside without much notice heretofore; and our complaints that
> come before common Courts, as well as this Honorable Body, have
> been looked at as being mere ciphers. But we hope that this indiffer-
> ent spirit is dying away, and that the true spirit of the Christian phi-
> lanthropist is beginning to reign in the hearts of the people, and
> those who compose their Legislative Bodies. If so, may we not ex-
> pect to share a part, although we are looked upon to be but poor
> and insignificant creatures.[77]

The Mashpees began by asserting their indigeneity, destabiliz-ing the position of those in power, who, as they portrayed it, were eating greedily from their ancestors' dish. Then they immediately called to mind issues of injustice common to the broader political space, comparing their situation to that of the Cherokees and enslaved African Americans, suggesting that guardianship was a system as oppressive as slavery or forced removal.[78] Building on those images of disempowerment and dis- location, the Mashpees reversed the rhetoric of vanishing, expressing hope that it was the "indifferent spirit" of colonialism that was "dying away," not the Native population. If Indians appeared to be dying, they insisted, it was the result of this unjust system, and if the legislators would only listen to their complaints and remove the restraints that bound them, they would be able "to take care of ourselves."[79]

Drawing the legislators into the common pot, the Mashpees expressed a desire to "share a part" of the "true spirit of the Christian philanthropist" and the democratic process. Legislators, if truly benevo- lent, would lend an ear to the "Voice" of "the Mashpees" and engender respect for Native people rather than regarding them as "insignificant creatures" or "ciphers" without rights. Echoing Occom's rhetoric, the Mashpees accused the republic of failing to treat them as equals. Colonial discourse and law placed them under the jurisdiction of the federal and state governments yet denied them the entitlements of citizens, as well as the rights of nations.

Before introducing their lengthy "bill of complaints," the Mash- pees revealed the irony of their second-class status as "ciphers" by re- minding their audience of Beacon Hill's location in Native space: "We purpose only to give you a few statements of facts, such as generally can be sustained by us, whose fathers were the original proprietors of the soil where this stately edifice now stands, and whose laws have ground us to the dust." The "edifice" in which the Mashpee delegation presented their case stood on their ancestors' property, and the laws that had been made within its walls had been used to clear the land of its inheritors, serving the expansion of the state. The Mashpees thereby implied that the legislators should consider whether the current policy, for which they must take responsibility, was merely a continuation of the practices and laws that resulted in the dispossession of the original inhabitants and whether the advocates of that policy were motivated by the desire to clear more Native space for colonial "edifices."[80]

In fact, the Mashpees argued that the guardianship system itself was an insidious form of encroachment. They related that the missionary Fish and the overseer Gideon Hawley occupied "ministerial farms upon our plantation," including "about fifteen hundred acres of our best land, and do us no essential service whatever, but contrawise, a bill of expense, and as destructive to us as a famine would be, in gradually wasting away the people before it." The village, therefore, was "maintain[ing]" its overseers, rather than vice versa. And the overseers were being well fed: the guardians, they insisted, "all find such good picking they are loth to leave us."[81]

Not only were the guardians living "off the fat" of Mashpee, but they allowed "unholy and unprincipled men, that prowl around our borders" to plunder the streams, woods, and fields, sinking the land and its people into poverty. Even if the guardians were not allowed to divide the land into parcels for sale, they were dividing it by selling its resources, including "just as much wood" as they had "a mind to cut and sell." In a strategic reversal, the Mashpees portrayed these Massachusetts settlers as the "prowling savages" who threatened "our plantation." And while the maintenance of Indian paupers was one of the purported reasons for maintaining a "fund" from the sale of resources, the Mashpees made clear that for them, poverty was a condition not of individuals but of the village as a whole. "As to the poor, we are all poor together," they said. Furthermore, the central cause of their poverty was neither a lack of ability or interest in maintaining their village nor a lack of resources to sustain them but a system that encouraged others to invade their village and take from it at will, with no restrictions imposed from within or without.[82]

"This law," they continued, "discourages our people, so that many of them have left their homes, and say they will not live under such oppressive laws." They concluded, as Occom and the Mohegans had before them, that such laws were rooted in colonial motivations: "We believe it is the design of the Overseers to so oppress us as to drive all our people from the plantation." Apess refined this argument in *Indian Nullification,* writing, "The laws were calculated to drive the tribes from their possessions and annihilate them as a people; and I presume they would work the same effect upon any other people.... Degradation is degradation, all the world over." In fact, Apess and the Mashpees discerned, the image of "degradation" served the purpose of dispossession. The overseers, they observed, had tried to oppose their petitions by representing them "as a set of indolent, drunken Indians; but we say it is not the case," they continued, "for many, very many of our people, are temperate, and sober, and industrious.... And now, if we wish to take care of ourselves, we cannot see why we may not have that privilege."[83]

"We do not want Overseers," they asserted, "as for them, we want them discharged, and never want their names mentioned amongst us again." The only aspect of the law they wanted to retain was the protection of communal ownership and the prohibition against land sales. They requested "that our Town may be incorporated, and called Marshpee," and they desired the freedom "to form a Municipal Code of Laws amongst ourselves." The petition concluded with the following charge to the House of Representatives:

> We have made these requests, believing the white men are knowing to our oppression in the general; and that if such laws are still enforced upon us, it is still murdering us by inches. And we do not know why the people of this Commonwealth want to cruelize us any longer, for we are sure that our fathers *fought, bled, and died for the liberties* of their now weeping and suffering children, the same as did your fathers for their children, whom ye are, who are now sitting to make laws to suit your own convenience, and secure your liberties. *Oh, white man! white man!* the blood of our fathers, spilt in the Revolutionary War, cries from the ground of our native soil, to break the chains of oppression, and let our children *go free!*[84]

Restoring the Forest to Its Sons (Boston, Spring 1834)

In March of 1834, the *Boston Daily Advocate* reported, "The Mashpee Act, restoring the rights of self-government, in part, to the Mashpee Indians, of which our legislation has deprived them for 140 years, passed the Senate of Massachusetts yesterday, to the honour of that body, without a single dissenting vote." Under the Act, Mashpee was incorporated as an "Indian District," and the Mashpees were "granted the right to elect selectmen," empowered with the authority to make their own laws and the responsibility for regulating their resources, as well as a "clerk" to record the meetings and a "constable" to enforce community laws. The act also directly addressed the Mashpee forest, stating that "no person other than the proprietors or inhabitants of said District, shall ever cut wood, or transport the same therefrom."[85]

The Mashpees' moment of triumph in the colonial courts, although somewhat short-lived, represented a victory for the village, for the common pot, and for the narration of Native rights. Writing was used not only to fight the case, but to record it. Apess published the multifaceted *Indian Nullification* only a year after the restoration of the Mashpees' rights. While much of the book related details and documentation of the "revolt," the final third addressed the continuing problem of Phineas Fish and his control of the meetinghouse and established the legal basis on which he should be expelled. In writing *Indian Nullification*, Apess was not only publishing an account of the case for the public interest but was enacting a pledge the community had made during their first meeting in the spring of 1833. In their "resolution" to Harvard College, they had "resolved that we will publish this to the world; if the above reasons and resolutions are not adhered to, and the Rev. Mr. Fish discharged." Apess, in concert with the community, was fulfilling this final resolution in the hope that the Mashpees' story would inspire further public action and that the meetinghouse would be fully restored.[86]

When Apess and the Mashpees put their resolutions in writing, they bound themselves together in a promise to enact them. The tribe utilized writing to pledge commitments and actions, to persuade political bodies, to communicate to neighboring communities, to record communal decisions, and to clearly delineate Native space. Thus, well into the nineteenth century, writing was operating in forms similar to those of wampum and *awikhiganak*. More important, the Mashpee petitions and resolutions, as well as *Indian Nullification* itself, demonstrate the continuing use of writing as an instrument for communal re-memberment and land reclamation, as well as a powerful means of narrating Native continuance.

The title of William Apess's *Indian Nullification* contained elusive multiple meanings. While it alluded to the national "nullification" debate regarding states' rights that would erupt into the Civil War, it also evoked issues that were critical to the Native northeast.[87] The title testified to the power of a Native nation to "nullify" unjust laws while also challenging the very concept of "Indian nullification." What no "American" writers could imagine at the time was the reemergence of Native communities from those "spared trees of the ancient forest." To them, such reemergence seemed contradictory to the very notion of progress on which their own succession depended. Yet, like the pitch pine that was the center of their sustenance, the Mashpees demonstrated a remarkable ability to regenerate and reclaim the forest that was their home. Despite the rhetoric of vanishing that pervaded the discursive space of the American nation, "Indian nullification" would be resisted at Mashpee.

5

Envisioning New England as Native Space

William Apess's Eulogy on King Philip

> We often hear of the wars breaking out upon the frontiers, and it is
> because the same spirit reigns there that reigned here in New Eng-
> land; and wherever there are any Indians, that spirit still reigns; and
> at present, there is no law to stop it. What, then, is to be done? Let
> every friend of the Indians now seize the mantle of Liberty and
> throw it over those burning elements that have spread with such
> fearful rapidity, and at once extinguish them forever. . . . We want
> trumpets that sound like thunder, and men to act as though they
> were going at war with those corrupt and degrading principles that
> robs one of all rights, merely because he is ignorant and of a little
> different color. Let us have principles that will give everyone his
> due; and then shall wars cease, and the weary find rest. Give the
> Indian his rights; and you may be assured war will cease.

Two years after William Apess joined the Mashpee leadership in addressing the Massachusetts legislature, he returned to Boston, taking the stage
at the prestigious Odeon lecture hall to deliver the words above. The
"Eulogy on King Philip," Apess's final and most provocative petition,
emerged, in many respects, from his experience at Mashpee. Most likely
an extension of the "pamphlet" he read at the schoolhouse, the *Eulogy*
was published in 1836 after Apess presented the oratorical address in
Boston and was compelled to deliver an encore performance. At Mashpee, Apess had facilitated the construction of an empowering conceptual
space that united the members of the community, then helped to extend
that space to include those who had the power to help them recover their
rights. In the *Eulogy*, he attempted to build a conceptual space from
within New England that could potentially include all of the lands' inhabi-

tants and would serve justice to those who were disempowered within it, including his closest relations. With his final publication, Apess reclaimed New England as Native space and used the power of words to entice his audience into that space so that, together, "we" might reverse the legacy of colonial violence that had "spread with such fearful rapidity" not only in New England but throughout America.[1]

Apess presented his "Eulogy on King Philip" at a moment when Americans had begun to claim and mourn the fallen Wampanoag leader as part of their national past. For both contemporary narrators and subsequent historians, Philip's death in 1676 at the hands of English soldiers and an Indian scout had marked the end of the conflict between Indians and whites and the death of Native New England.[2] One hundred and fifty years later, that symbolic death was enacted repeatedly, on the Boston stage and in the minds of sympathetic American readers. As Jill Lepore has demonstrated, plays like *Metamora, or The Last of the Wampanoags* and romantic novels such as James Fenimore Cooper's *The Last of the Mohicans* and *The Wept of Wish-ton-wish* were at the height of popularity while Apess was writing. Authors and audiences invested in the creation of an American national identity that would distinguish them from their European ancestors were quite willing to embrace Indians as poetic, tragic figures within a uniquely American landscape as long as they were contained by the discourse of vanishing. However, as Lepore points out, "by his mere existence," a writer like William Apess "gave the lie to *Metamora*'s subtitle, 'Last of the Wampanoags.' Standing in front of the Odeon before, presumably, a largely white audience, Apess was himself, in his physical presence, evidence that New England's Indians did not die out with Philip." Furthermore, the popularity of plays like *Metamora* opened up a space through which a Native orator like Apess might stage his own performance. William Apess exploited the sympathy engendered by literary representations of Indians to take a critical stand for contemporary Native rights and to attest to the persistence of Native people as political beings who, even in New England, continued to occupy contemporary space right alongside those who preferred to have them contained by a mythologized past.[3]

In composing the *Eulogy*, Apess drew on a long indigenous tradition by establishing New England as Native space into which Europeans entered, by invoking the centrality of Native rights, and by seducing his audience into the conceptual space of the common pot. Through a persuasive rhetorical strategy, Apess called on his listeners and readers to participate in communal deliberation, to recognize the shared space and shared history of New England (and America), and to see themselves as agents within it. He challenged Anglo-Americans in particular to acknowledge the legacy of destruction "planted" by their Puritan forebears and to confront the continuing violence that had "grown up" from it. He asked his audience to act as brothers within a familial network: to think and act in a way that would benefit the whole rather than allowing the Puritans' perilous quest for power to determine the future of the space shared by all.

Reclaiming the Native Stage (The Odeon, Boston, 1836)

Addressing his New England audience directly and intimately, Apess commences the *Eulogy* by stating that his purpose in raising the specter of King Philip is neither to celebrate an individual nor to glorify war, but

> to bring before you beings made by the God of Nature, and in whose hearts and heads he has planted sympathies that shall live forever in the memory of the world, whose brilliant talents shone in the display of natural things, so that the most cultivated, whose powers shown with equal luster, were not able to prepare mantles to cover the burning elements of an uncivilized world. What, then? Shall we cease to mention the mighty of the earth, the noble work of God?[4]

Apess centers the trope of indigeneity in this opening passage, referring to Philip, his contemporary relations, and his descendants as beings simultaneously "of the earth" and "planted" by "God." The realm of the earth is also "God's" sphere, and the Christian God is merged with the "God of Nature," so that nature, nativity, and divinity are interconnected. In Apess's vision, the biblical God and "the Indian's God" are one and the same, and the "noble work" of this "great Spirit" can be seen in, and is enacted by, the inhabitants of earth. The use of tense in this passage suggests that Apess is purposefully ambiguous about the identity of these indigenous "beings," speaking as if they are still here by using phrases like "he *has* planted" in the same sentence with phrases that locate them in the past: they are part of "the memory of the world"; their "talents shone." Joining the past and present, he makes clear that their light, though no longer bright, has not been extinguished: the "burning elements" remain despite the efforts of "the most cultivated" to "cover" them. The word "cultivated" here is used ironically, in mimicry of colonial constructions of the civilized/uncivilized binary. Yet "cultivated" is

also used in opposition to indigeneity, so that the Natives are "the nations of this soil," those who were planted by God and grew up from the
earth, while the "cultivated" are foreigners, domesticated individuals
transplanted into a landscape that was already inhabited and flourishing.
The "mantle" the "cultivated" used to "cover" the "burning elements of
the uncivilized world" directly refers, in one sense, to the replacement of
forests with fields and farms. It may also refer to the violence through
which one people sought to succeed another, and especially to those fires
that destroyed Native villages during the Pequot War and King Philip's
War, but it also suggests that "cultivated" people have sought to conceal
the fiery brightness of Native "elements" with images, beliefs, and the
very rhetoric of vanishing that Apess is subtly interrogating here.[5]

   As Apess's experience attested, colonial violence and rhetoric,
although powerful forces, could not conceal the continuance of places
like Mashpee. "Sympathies" live on in communal memory and practice,
and the Native landscape is evident in the "display of natural things."
The existence of the forest at Mashpee reveals the "talents" of its inhabitants: the ability to "fire" and sustain their "wood" amid mass deforestation. The "few remaining descendants," Apess relates, are living "monu-
ment[s]" to the "cruelty" of colonization but also markers of indigenous
"memory." These "degraded yet grateful descendants" still remember
Philip as the "all-accomplished son of the forest" and a "hero of the
wilderness." By painting such an evocative portrait, Apess is bringing
communal remembrance to his audience, asking them to participate in
this process, to see the landscape through Native eyes. Apess reveals that
he feels charged by King Philip, by his ancestors, and by "humanity" to
"melt the prejudice that exists in the hearts of those who are in possession of his soil, and only by right of conquest." This task, Apess claims,
can be accomplished only by one who has "the blood of a denominated
savage run[ning] in his veins."[6]

   Maureen Konkle suggests that Apess, like the Cherokee memorialists and many African American abolitionists, utilizes the trope of
"nature" to make a political argument that roots Native sovereignty in
"natural law." She observes of this passage:

   The "natural sons of a civilized being" . . . are not the sentimental-
   ized noble savages of primitivist representation, a representation
   Apess explicitly rejects, but people whose formation of autonomous
   political entities precedes their relationship with British colonial authority, and its successor, the U.S. government. Even to be uncivilized

marks Indians as belonging to a state of nature that is not inferior but socially and politically autonomous.[7]

Apess thus manipulates romantic associations of Indians with "nature" to build a base for addressing Native rights.

In developing his case, Apess establishes New England both as Native space, into which Europeans entered from another world, and as shared space in which Natives, "people of color," and the "sons of the Pilgrims" must coexist.[8] Playing with the portrayal of Puritans as the fathers of New England and America, Apess refers to the English as "comers from the new world" and "pilgrims" who "came among them."[9] As he is developing this Native-centric perspective, he uses an intriguing rhetorical strategy to draw his audience into participatory deliberation. In the first four pages of the *Eulogy*, Apess gradually persuades his readers to think as a body, raising speculative questions and suggesting that intelligent, moral people will see his arguments clearly, then inviting them to examine the history and character of King Philip with him. He accomplishes this, in part, through his use of the inclusive and exclusive "we."

In Algonquian languages like Apess's native Pequot, there are two forms of *we*.[10] In Abenaki, an easy way to distinguish between the two forms is by looking at the words *ndakinna* and *kdakinna*, which both translate to "our land." If we wanted to speak of "our land" as ours exclusively, to make a statement about Wabanaki being Native land, we would use *ndakinna*. If we wanted to speak inclusively, to make a statement about common responsibility for the land, we might use *kdakinna*.[11] Any time *we* is used in Algonquian languages, there is a clear reference to inclusivity or exclusivity. Similarly, in the *Eulogy*, Apess uses the word "we" quite strategically. His "we" can range from including all of humanity to implying an exclusive space that contains only New England Natives. In the first few pages of the oratory, Apess uses the inclusive form to pose questions to an assumedly unified body in which he includes the entire audience, and then he moves to suggest that "we" consist of people with "common sense," seducing his listeners to pride themselves on their inclusion in the group.[12]

Only after building this common base does Apess turn to the shared history of New England. Portraying the transformation of the idyllic forest in a manner that echoes the Mohegan "dish" petition, he suggests that the landscape has been irrevocably altered by violence, turned into blood-soaked fields. Most chillingly, Apess insists that these fields are growing still. Referring directly to contemporary policy, he remarks: "There are many who are said to be honorable warriors, who in the wisdom of their civilized legislation, think it no crime to wreak their vengeance upon whole nations and communities, until the fields are covered with blood and the rivers turned to purple fountains."[13] Apess's spatialized history is not a tale of tragedies that have taken place in the past, progression toward an improved present, or the vision of a utopian future. Violence has been "cultivated" in the land and continues to grow in place, working through its human inhabitants and spreading through the "fields" and "rivers," as if it is a living force that feeds its cultivators.

Apess is careful to make allowance for natural defense, for he must justify Native resistance even as he condemns settler aggression. He notes, "Nature always has her defense for every beast of the field; even the reptiles of the earth and the fishes of the sea have their weapons of war." Still, he insists emphatically that human significance should not be located in war: "Frail man was made for a nobler purpose — to live, to love, and adore his God, and do good for his brother."[14] For Apess, the human's ability to choose and to discern "God's will" is what makes him able to restrain himself from acting on violent impulses even in his own defense, a position he consistently maintained in *Indian Nullification*. He sets this distinction up, in part, to construct violence against Indians as a violation of both human nature and divine will:

> How inhuman it was in those wretches, to come into a country where nature shone in beauty…sheltering beneath her shades those natural sons of an Almighty Being, that shone in grandeur and luster like the stars of the first magnitude in the heavenly world; whose virtues far surpassed their more enlightened foes, notwithstanding their pretended zeal for religion and virtue. How they could go to work to enslave a free people and call it religion is beyond the power of my imagination and outstrips the revelation of God's word.[15]

Apess reiterates his portrait of Native space, presenting America as an idealized interweaving of nature and divinity into which Europeans brought their destructive powers. As a literate being, Apess asserts that he has read the Bible and can find no evidence that "God's word" justified the explorers' and Puritans' acts of destruction. To the contrary, their "work" vastly contradicted the precepts of the religion they claimed to follow. Ironically, Apess points out, the heathen "sons" of the Americas "naturally" demonstrated more human "virtues" than those who professed the religion of Christianity. He continues: "O thou pretended hypocritical Christian, whoever thou art, to say it was the design of God that we should murder and slay one another because we have the power. Power was not given us to abuse each other, but a mere power delegated to us by the King of heaven, a weapon of defense against error and evil; and when abused, it will turn to our destruction."[16]

This passage represents the first time that Apess uses "we" to represent the shared space of history. Apess is quite strategic here in not pointing directly at anyone, while inviting all of his listeners into private self-examination regarding "our" beliefs. Denaturalizing the colonial project, he reveals the fallacy that the Puritans and their descendant historians have perpetrated in asserting that the destruction of Native people could be destined by either God's will or natural processes.[17] Ability to conquer, he insists, does not imply an imperative to do so. He connects the "inhuman wretches" of the past to those "hypocritical Christians" who continue to justify their injurious policies and actions through religion. Yet he also makes an important strategic move in suggesting that all humans are vulnerable to this misuse of power and to its consequences. While he makes a distinction between "thou pretended hypocritical Christian" and himself, Apess shifts immediately into shared space, emphasizing a collective burden of responsibility by using the inclusive "we" repeatedly in the sentences that follow. In switching from the binary to the inclusive, Apess suggests that within this shared space there are two groups (Indians and whites) that have falsely been put in opposition. At the same time, he is purposefully vague, so "we" might refer to any humans who are engaged in destroying each other.

The relationship between "power" and "destruction" is crucial to understanding Apess's point. "Power" here is directly related to the concept of Manitou. This Pequot descendant is applying the lessons of the wampum and beaver wars to a much wider history of the continent. Although all humans are given "power" for "defense," if abused, the power of defense can easily "turn" to "our destruction." Apess's use of "our" here is clearly inclusive. Violence is a force that takes on a life of its own; it can "turn" into destruction of others and can just as easily "turn" back on the self. As Apess so eloquently reveals, "we" all inhabit these bloodied fields. His strategic use of "we" serves to connect whites and

Indians, past and present. The legacy of Puritan violence continues in its representation and in the process through which such representations affect policy. The ways in which we tell history, Apess insists, hold power. He suggests that in self-examination, any of "us" may discover that we are participants in this legacy. Yet, having created an atmosphere in which inclusion is desirable, Apess begins, in this passage, to suggest that his white listeners may want to exclude themselves from the "we" of their Puritan forebears to oppose the legacy of destruction.[18]

From here, Apess begins his own narration of history, including the kidnapping of Indians on the coast and the arrival of the Pilgrims in Native space, using strategic reversal to put his listeners in the place of the Natives. He relates a series of violations, including a portrayal of how the Puritans "without asking liberty from anyone possessed themselves a portion of the country," proceeded to build settlements, "made a treaty, and commanded" the Indians "to accede to it." Apess then asks the Americans in his audience to consider whether they would withstand such an invasion: "This, if now done, it would be called an insult, and every white man would be called to go out and act the part of a patriot, to defend their country's rights.... And yet the Indians (though many were dissatisfied) without the shedding of blood or imprisoning anyone, bore it." Apess thus supports his earlier assertion that the Natives had more "virtue" than their invaders in their demonstrated ability to resist the impulse toward violence, but he also makes his American audience understand Native resistance as national defense.[19]

The passage continues: "And yet for their kindness and resignation toward the whites, they were called savages and made by God on purpose for them to destroy. We might say, God understood his work better than this." This is where Apess's use of "we" becomes tricky. He separates the contemporary moment from the past by calling the Indians "they," but then uses a seemingly exclusive "we" to refer to the contemporary Indian community, whose history is being relayed. This "we" appropriates the role of communal narrator from the Puritans and their descendant historians while putting into question the otherness of Indians as historical figures. The contemporary Indian "we" is not an object to be cleared away, but a living witness to history. Yet, with rhetorical ambiguity, Apess simultaneously leaves room for his audience in this "we," especially for those who would distinguish themselves from the Puritans. He thus opens an alternative route through which his contemporary audience might enter Native space: not through the "founding fathers" but as supporters of "American" virtues.

For the next several pages of the *Eulogy*, Apess continually switches back and forth between an inclusive and an exclusive "we." There is a "we" that is "present[ing]" history "before you," which suggests a communal Native voice, as if Apess is taking on the role of speaker for the larger Indian community. This "we" carries authority and invites the audience to examine the historical acts and narrations of "white people" who behave "more like savages than Christians." Apess, as spokesperson, encourages his listeners to participate in deliberation on the case he presents, asking, "What say you, judges, is it not so, and was it not according as they did? Indians think it is." The structure of the narrative makes it appear as if Apess is putting the Puritans on trial, and he asks the audience, as "judges," to confirm his narration of history and to acknowledge his condemnation of their forebears. Up to this point, in relating history he has often used "them" to describe "Indians," but in this passage, listeners can begin to see that Indians not only are included in the "we" but constitute its base. "They" are not others but the primary subjects of Apess's historical narrative. The audience has entered Native space.[20]

Apess continues to employ this strategy in his relation of Philip's story, often conflating Indians of past and present with his use of tense while simultaneously exposing the fallacy of the Christian/savage binary. In disrupting this construction of difference, he creates greater possibility for sharing space. The clear outsiders to the communal "we" are the perpetrators of historical violence, and he draws the audience in by occasionally invoking inclusivity, suggesting that "we are led to believe," together, by the facts of history and the Puritans' own narrations, that "if it had been in the power of the Pilgrims, they would have butchered them out and out, notwithstanding all the piety they professed." Here, both historical Indians and Puritans are "they," whereas "we" represents the audience and the speaker as a whole, in the present moment, reflecting on the past. It offers his contemporary audience an opportunity to distance themselves from the past, to separate themselves from the Puritans — as Christians, as humans, and as those who stand to inherit their legacy.[21]

Then Apess addresses "the sons of the Pilgrims" directly as he exposes the venom present in the words of founding forebear Increase Mather, who labeled Philip one "of cursed memory." Apess critiques Mather, a learned theologian, for not looking to the source he claimed as his guide when he cursed "God's works." Apess asserts:

He ought to have known that God did not make his red children for him to curse; but if he wanted them cursed, he could have done it himself. But, on the contrary, his suffering Master commanded him to love his enemies and to pray for his persecutors, and to do unto others as he would that men should do unto him. Now, we wonder if the sons of the Pilgrims would like to have us, poor Indians, come out and curse the Doctor, and all their sons, as we have been by many of them. And suppose that, in some future day, our children should repay all these wrongs, would it not be doing as we, poor Indians, have been done to? But we sincerely hope there is more humanity in us than that.[22]

Apess makes a daring move here, connecting Indians of the past with Indians of the present and connecting the prejudicial beliefs of the Pilgrims with those of their "sons," exposing this hypocritical brand of religion as an inherited legacy. Yet, at the same time, he grants both the "sons of the Pilgrims" and Indians choice and agency as "humans," defining the value of "humanity" in the virtue of its birth from "God" and from the earth.

Following this passage, Apess's rhetoric rapidly alternates between an exclusive "we," defining Indians as "our tribes," and the more inclusive form, saying, "Let us look" together, with one mind. Apess asks "us" to look with clear eyes at the process through which "our tribes," who were once "large and respectable" according to the audience's own "New England writers," have "been destroyed." "Is it by fair means?" Apess asks. "No," he answers for the audience. "Then how?" Apess asks. And the communal voice answers, "By hypocritical proceedings, by being duped and flattered; flattered by informing the Indians that their God was going to speak to them, and then place them before the cannon's mouth in a line, and then putting the match to it and killing thousands of them."[23]

In this passage, Apess refers not to a particular historical event, but to the communal history of Indian New England, to the villages that were "fired" by the colonists under the guise of religion, cleared as if they were brush. Using the communal "we" to address the audience and using "they" to refer to both Indians and whites of the past, Apess sets up this scene and its commentary so that the audience is looking with him at the past on display, much as they may have watched popular plays like *Metamora*, in sympathy with the "poor Indians," with tears of grief flowing down their cheeks.[24] "What an awful sight!" Apess remarks, in concert with them, before abruptly charging the whites in his audience with their own hypocrisy:

> And who is to account for those destructions upon innocent families and helpless children? . . . Let the children of the Pilgrims blush, while the son of the forest drops a tear and groans over the fate of his murdered and departed fathers. He would say to the sons of the Pilgrims . . . let the day be dark, the 22nd day of December, let it be forgotten in your celebration, in your speeches, and by the burying of the rock that your fathers first put their foot upon. For be it remembered, although the Gospel is said to be glad tidings to all people, yet we poor Indians never have found those who brought it as messengers of mercy, but contrawise. We say, therefore, let every man of color wrap himself in mourning, for the 22nd of December and the 4th of July are days of mourning and not of joy. . . . Let them rather fast and pray to the great Spirit, the Indian's God, who deals out mercy to his red children, and not destruction.[25]

Here, Apess makes a clear move against American romanticism and nostalgia. In his portrayal, the domestic space of history is occupied by Indian "families" and "children" rather than by Puritan settlements. It is neither the right nor the privilege of the "children of the Pilgrims" to "drop a tear" over the "vanished" Indians they have claimed as part of New England's past. Let them acknowledge their shame, Apess says, and the grief of the descendants who live facing the continuing legacy of "hostilities" and forced to see the demise of their ancestors celebrated by the same people who claim to mourn the tragedies of the past. Apess makes clear that inclusion in this greater whole will require self-reflection and sacrifice on the part of the Pilgrim descendants. They cannot separate themselves from the "they" of the Puritans simply through divorcing themselves from the past. They must look carefully at the roles they occupy in the larger network of New England and America, especially vis-à-vis its indigenous "descendants."

Apess also makes a clear distinction between the "children of the Pilgrims" and people "of color." Building the space of inclusivity, Apess begins with Native space and Native grief, then expands the circle to include all people of color in that mourning, because they have also suffered from the Puritan legacies of blind violence. Apess's America is first and foremost a space shared among people of color, and it is the children of the pilgrims who are excluded from this space. However, it is from here, Apess says, that change can begin to take place: rather than mourning dead Indians and celebrating the Puritan fathers, he insists, the children of the Pilgrims ought to take action to reverse their legacy:

> O Christians, can you answer for those beings that have been destroyed by your hostilities, and beings too that lie endeared to God as yourselves?... Although in words they deny it, yet in the works they approve of the iniquities of their fathers. And as the seed of iniquity and prejudice was sown in that day, and so it still remains; and there is a deep-rooted popular opinion in the hearts of many that Indians were made, etc., on purpose for destruction, to be driven out by white Christians, and they to take their places; and that God has decreed it from all eternity. If such theologians would study the works of nature more, they would understand the purposes of good better than they do.[26]

With these words, Apess asks his audience to join with him in confronting the shared space of bloodied fields. He asks the "Christians" in his audience how they will answer for the continuing "destruction," challenging not only their actions but their "deep-rooted" beliefs that European colonization and Native dispossession represent the continent's inevitable destiny. He insists that no such lesson can be learned from either the Bible or the natural world. Indeed, although "popular opinion" suggested that not just Indians but much of the forest and its inhabitants were destined to be cleared for civilization, there is no process or being in nature that would enact wholesale eradication to make room for one species alone. Even fire, perhaps the most potentially damaging force in the forest, enables more Native inhabitants to grow. Harkening back to the metaphors with which he began his oratory, Apess contrasts the seemingly foreign forces of "prejudice" and "iniquity" that have taken root in the soil with his idealized indigenous landscape. He insists that dispossession is justified neither by nature nor by God, ardently asserting that humans were not made to "drive and devour each other." Rather, he reveals that at the "root" of colonial violence are human actions and doctrines, many of which have been planted in the minds of the descendants by their forefathers, enabling them to continue the established course without fully realizing the consequences of their acts.[27]

To demonstrate that "the spirit of the Pilgrims still remains," Apess provides evidence of these "deep-rooted" beliefs in a contemporary quote from a western missionary, which glorifies colonization as God's plan: "The desert becomes an Eden.... The savage has left the ground for civilized man; the rich prairie, from bringing forth all its strengths to be burned, is now receiving numerous enclosures, and brings a harvest of corn and wheat to feed the church. Yes, sir, this is now God's vineyard; he has gathered the vine, the choice vine, and brought it from a far country, and has planted it on a goodly soil."[28] The missionary's language masks colonial violence by making the American advance appear to be a natural process led by God, in which settlements grow up, as if indigenous, from the prairie. The Indians, of course, have "left." They are both passive and past. The cleared land is a receptive mother for God's seed. Still, the missionary's own words belie his peaceful portrait of the prairie, revealing that its natural "strengths" have been "burned." The fire of violence that cleared the land of its Native inhabitants (human, animal, and plant) is naturalized as part of the divine plan.

Apess further reveals that this same missionary has expressed an interest in converting "the poor heathens, as if," he observes sardonically, "God could not convert them where they were but must first drive them out." In response, he calls on "my brethren" to turn their attention to the real problems of "the red men" who continue to live in their midst rather than pursuing their removal and conversion. Such "missionaries," Apess protests,

> have injured us more than they have done us good, by degrading us as a people, in breaking up our governments and leaving us without any suffrages whatever, or a legal right among men. . . . We poor Indians want no such missionaries around us. But I would suggest one thing, and that is, let the ministers and people use the colored people they already have around them like human beings, before they go to convert any more.[29]

Once more uniting the Native "we" with all people of color, Apess also opens the door through which whites might once more take their place within the human family, allowing his listeners to distinguish themselves from advocates of Manifest Destiny and providing the opportunity for just action. From within this communal space, Apess moves swiftly to the subject of Native rights: "I trust that the Great Spirit will stand by me, as also good and honorable men will . . . standing as it were upon the graves of his much injured race, to plead their cause and speak for the rights of the remaining few." Apess realizes, though, that he first must prove that "Native rights" exist. Using the documentary record, he cites Roger Williams's argument on hunting grounds and his descriptions of Native leaders to suggest, "Although it is said by many that the

Indians had no rights ... it does appear that Indians had rights, and those rights were near and dear to them, as your stores and farms and firesides are to the whites, and their wives and children also." Here, he uses the trope of domesticity and national defense, especially popular in post-Revolutionary America, to provide a space in which his audience might come to comprehend Native rights by grounding them in the notion of home, with all its domestic implications. Native rights are part of the reality of the landscape, Apess asserts. Even when not fully recognized by colonial governments, they are inherent and precious to Native people.[30]

Apess directly connects King Philip's resistance to the long line of Native rights cases that had appeared before the New England courts and to contemporary struggles like the Mashpee Revolt. Apess asks his audience: "Who stood up in those days, and since, to plead Indian rights? Was it the friend of the Indian? No, it was his enemies who rose — his enemies, to judge and pass sentence. And we know that such kind of characters as the Pilgrims were, in regard to the Indians' rights, who, as they say, had none, must certainly give verdict against them, as generally speaking, they always have."[31]

In referring to the "friend of the Indian," Apess implies a critique of the missionary project, through which oppression was masked as benevolence, and of contemporary fiction, which concealed both the truth of colonial history and the continuance of Native communities. True "friends of the Indians," Apess insists, would "stand up" for Native rights, not fund worthless missions or write stories of Indian disappearance. He also exposes the hypocrisy of the colonial legal system, where settlers are designated to "judge and pass sentence" on the very people they seek to displace. Apess is asking his audience to enter Native space perceptually by imagining the domestic scene and by putting themselves in the place of the Natives who know their own rights, regardless of what colonial courts decide *about* them. Apess's arguments align almost perfectly with those made by Occom and the Mohegans. It is likely that he had heard stories from the neighboring tribe, and he may have even reviewed the records of their land case. Like Occom, Apess based his arguments on extensive historical and legal research, as any review of his writings will demonstrate, and this knowledge in itself gave urgency to his pleas for recognition of the realities of Native space.[32]

Concluding his own narration of Native rights, Apess asserts that "not one" of the promises made during Philip's time, even to those Indians who sided against him, "have as yet been fulfilled by the Pilgrims or their children." Again Apess conflates the past and the present, but now it is the Pilgrims and "their children" who are united. The responsibility for repairing their ancestors' mistakes lies with these descendants, who inhabit a land that is marked not by a free and sanctified American space but by stolen Native ground. "It was only, then, by deception," Apess insists, "that the Pilgrims gained the country, as their word has never been fulfilled in regard to Indian rights."[33]

At this point in the *Eulogy*, Apess returns to his narration of Philip's story, laying scenes before the audience in a manner that allows them to be spectators along with the larger group. Then he begins once again to use the inclusive "we" to draw them into the circle. After fully censuring the conduct of the Pilgrims and their descendants, making much of his audience believe, perhaps, that they are completely excluded, he once more includes them in the group by inviting them to condemn their forefathers with him. Using this "we" vaguely several times in one paragraph to make general observations, he concludes by denouncing the behavior of the Puritan forebears toward Philip and his relations, remarking, "We presume that no honest men will commend those ancient fathers for such absurd conduct." With this deceptively flippant remark, Apess makes it clear that the all-encompassing "we," which certainly includes Indians and people of color, also might include all "honest" men, regardless of who their fathers may have been. This represents a direct challenge to his audience: it is clear that "we" should align ourselves against the Puritan fathers and embrace our "brethren" in the space we share now.[34]

Yet, in order to do so "we" must thoroughly confront the shared space of the past. When Apess next presents a difficult scene, he nearly apologizes to his audience on behalf of the Native community for which he speaks: "But we have another dark and corrupt deed for the sons of Pilgrims to look at." After relating the story of the kidnapping and enslavement of Philip's wife and son, Apess soliloquizes:

> While I am writing, I can hardly restrain my feelings, to think a people calling themselves Christians should conduct so scandalous, so outrageous, making themselves appear so despicable in the eyes of the Indians; and even now, in this audience, I doubt but there is men honorable enough to despise the conduct of those pretended Christians. And surely none but such as believe they did right will ever go and undertake to celebrate that day of their landing, the 22nd of

December. Only look at it; then stop and pause: My fathers came here for liberty themselves, and then they must go and chain that mind, that image they professed to serve.[35]

Just as Apess makes his audience switch perspective, here he puts himself in the place of the Puritans' descendants to empathize with their position and to direct their vision. Those who would "serve" the "image" of God, he insists, would honor the intent for which they were made by treating all people as equally worthy of liberty and respect. Having seduced his listeners into desiring inclusion, Apess uses carefully worded rhetoric to challenge them to respond that they are indeed such honorable men, that they will turn from the paths of their fathers and follow the course of justice.

With his audience now on board in the common space he has created, Apess brings the past and the present into union for "us" to examine together, revealing that King Philip's prophecy that "white people would not only cut down their groves but would enslave them" has seemingly come to pass: "Our groves and hunting grounds are gone, our dead are dug up, our council fires are put out, and a foundation was laid in the first Legislature to enslave our people, by taking from them all rights, which has been strictly adhered to ever since." Apess uses the romanticized rhetoric of vanishing strategically to reassert his argument for Native rights. He employs a narrative that his audience will recognize, but diverges from the accustomed tragic ending to make them "look" directly at the contemporary landscape:

> Look at the disgraceful laws, disfranchising us as citizens. Look at the treaties made by Congress, all broken. Look at the deep-rooted plans laid, when a territory becomes a state, that after so many years the laws shall be extended over the Indians that live within their boundaries. Yea, every charter that has been given was given with the view of driving the Indians out of the states, or dooming them to becomes chained under desperate laws, that would make them drag out a miserable life as one chained to the galley; and this is the course that has been pursued for nearly two hundred years. A fire, a canker, created by the Pilgrims from across the Atlantic, to burn and destroy my unfortunate brethren, and it cannot be denied.[36]

Apess returns to the planting metaphor with which he began the *Eulogy* to reveal the cancerous growth that has arisen from within

Native space from the seeds sown by the original immigrants from "across the Atlantic." He addresses a catalog of unjust policies and contemporary issues, from states' rights debates to removal to the guardianship system, then characterizes current policies as symptomatic of an ongoing syndrome with a long history. Apess takes the imagined progress of Manifest Destiny and turns the trope on its head, painting European colonization as a fire that spreads across the landscape, waging destruction. It is, he says, a "cancer," an out-of-control, self-replicating disease that has infected the land and will continue to spread, perhaps the very worst of the pathogens that were brought over from Europe, and it affects us all. He emphasizes that neither this fire nor its creators are indigenous or natural to the landscape, directly opposing those American narratives that painted European colonization as part of the destiny of the continent.

Still, Apess insists, these "plans" have deep roots, hidden beneath the ground, and those who grew up from these roots may be participating in the dispossession and destruction of Native land without fully realizing it. Like a cancer, this disease is often difficult to see on the surface of the being that it infects. Apess deliberately avoids pointing directly to human agency in contemporary policy, using the passive voice to describe the continuance of the Puritan legacy. This allows him to portray colonization as a force that seems to have a life of its own and to put agency in the hands of those who would fight its spread. It is in suggesting a unified human opposition to this abstract destructive force that Apess once more takes up the inclusive "we" to challenge his audience to prove Philip's prophecy wrong. The "son of the forest" insists that the fate of this shared space lies not in destiny or God or nature, but in the hands of all the land's inhabitants: "What, then, shall we do? Shall we cease crying and say it is all wrong, or shall we bury the hatchet and those unjust laws and Plymouth Rock together and become friends? And will the sons of Pilgrims aid in putting out the fire and destroying the canker that will ruin all that their fathers left behind them to destroy?"[37]

Having joined the past with the present in one space, Apess directs the eye of his communal audience to the future and to the possibilities of *human* will. The fate that might seem inevitable, in both Puritan narratives and Philip's prophecy, will take place only if the land's inhabitants allow the destructive course to continue. Apess locates his listeners quite firmly in the space they currently inhabit rather than privileging the progression of time. Philip's prophecy may be foreseeable because of the "deep-rooted" violence that has been planted in this soil, but this place, Apess asserts, also has another, deeper legacy to which its current inhabitants can now turn.

As if speaking in council, Apess continues to address his newly constructed community:

> We often hear of wars breaking out upon the frontiers, and it is because the same spirit reigns there that reigned here in New England; and wherever there are any Indians, that spirit still reigns; and at present, there is no law to stop it. What, then, is to be done? Let every friend of the Indians now seize the mantle of Liberty and throw it over those burning elements that have spread with such fearful rapidity, and at once extinguish them forever.... We want trumpets that sound like thunder, and men to act as though they were going to war with those corrupt and degrading principles that robs one of all rights, merely because he is ignorant and of a little different color. Let us have principles that will give everyone his due; and then shall wars cease, and the weary find rest. Give the Indian his rights; and you may be assured war will cease.[38]

As Anne Marie Dannenberg observes, Apess insists that, "'wherever there are Indians,' the same legacy of colonial racism prevails. Focusing on the racialist dynamics of Indian–white relations 'from Maine to Georgia,' Apess' writings redraw the frontier as the color line, and in so doing lift the veil of invisibility that cloaks indigenous groups remaining east of the Mississippi." The violence on the frontiers is thus joined with the continuing violation of Native rights in New England. They are part of the same space and the same process of colonialism. Yet, in building a conceptual common pot, Apess also lifts the ideological lines that bolstered the belief that Indians and whites could not share the same space, an ideology that justified forced removal and military violence and propagated the myth of disappearance.[39]

Only through acknowledgment of shared space and through cooperative action, Apess insists, can such a destructive fire be extinguished. The land can be renewed only if "we," as a unified body, use an equally powerful force to counteract the effects of the disease. The wording in this passage parallels and reverses the metaphor Apess used to open the *Eulogy:* the "mantle of liberty," he says, should be thrown over the "burning elements" of the colonial apparatus, in opposition to the "mantle" with which the Puritan attempted to conceal "the burning elements of an uncivilized world." Here, Apess is using a common trope from Native oral tradition: when faced with a force of destruction, a community must turn the power of that force back on itself so that balance can be re-stored and the world can be transformed.

The "mantle of liberty" refers to Native liberty, the legacy of King Philip and one of the "elements" that the Puritans attempted to "cover." Yet, it is also the mantle of American liberty. Apess insists that the free-doms that white Americans celebrate as theirs should be extended to all other inhabitants of the continent. This, Apess suggests, is a cause and a fundamental right we all share. Still, Apess is not merely requesting in-clusion in the new American vision, but is establishing Native space, with its long history of colonial violence, as the very foundation of the coun-try.[40] In this passage, Apess brilliantly connects both the ideology of the common pot and the call for respect of Native rights. He envisions for New England, and for America, a political space that is similar in prin-ciple to Brant's dish, but at the same time he wishes to see those rights honored that are particular to the preservation of the village "kettle." Indians, he insists, want only freedom and justice in "our" own country, not the so-called benevolence of colonizing "friends." Respect for Na-tive rights, as Brant and Aupaumut argued so eloquently in the Ohio Valley, is the only means through which "frontier" violence will "cease."

Unlike the controlled burning that the Mashpees used to renew their forest, this fire, Apess warns, is spreading west with "fearful rapid-ity," and only "laws" that enable "liberty" hold the power to stop it. The "mantle of liberty" will smother the fire, making the soil ready for new seeds and allowing the land itself to regenerate. Once the ground is cleared of the "doctrines" that have "grown up" to choke out the inhabi-tants, Native plants may, if left unhindered by colonial restraints, spring up once again in their soil to grow alongside the diverse plants that have "come into" this land. Then, the work of reconstructing the forest can begin.

"Having now given historical facts, and an exposition in rela-tion to ancient times, by which we have been enabled to discover the foun-dation which destroyed our common fathers in their struggle together," Apess continues, "we" can see, as a group, that "it was indeed nothing more than the spirit of avarice and usurpation of power that has brought people in all ages to hate and devour each other." He warns that if people continue to be led by these forces and the fires are left to burn, the conse-quences for the common pot could be dire. Earlier in the narrative, Apess had noted, "We find that, of late, Pilgrims' children have got to killing and mobbing each other." Now he appeals to "ye fathers...who are white": "Have you any regard for your wives and children, for those delicate sons and daughters? Would you like to see them slain and lain in heaps, and their bodies devoured by the vultures and wild beasts of prey, and their bones bleaching in the sun and air, till they molder away or were covered by the falling leaves of the forest, and not resist?"[41]

With this passage, Apess reveals the ultimate connection between this force of colonialism and the colonizers, maintaining that violence against Indians will be transformed into violence against and between whites and asking his listeners whether they will have to experience this pain in their own families before they can fully empathize with their neighbors of color. He pleads, "Can or do you think we have no feeling?" Although here "we" refers to Indians and perhaps to all people of color, having created a shared conceptual space, Apess is able to use the word to call on the compassion and empathy of the larger human "we." He places all of his listeners in the shared space of violence and makes them understand that the feelings of grief, violation, and injustice that "we" feel are one and the same for all. Through his portrayal of an imminent future, white bodies become part of the bloodied landscape, too. He asks the "Pilgrims' children" if they want to continue to root themselves in the false dichotomy that allows them to believe that some people have "no feeling," do not suffer so much from the devastation of war, or are destined to die. Apess brings his whole audience together to consider the most important lessons of the common pot: to think as a body about the consequences to the whole — of greed versus equal distribution, of unexamined action versus deliberation, and of division versus unity.[42]

Native Origins: Reclaiming the Common Pot of New England

For William Apess, the labels that the Puritans developed to define other human beings ultimately served the purpose of division, enabling the conceptual separation that justified the colonization of his native home, as well as the debilitating injustice that his relations continued to face. "Indian" was, according to Apess, merely an "opprobrious epithet" that whites "threw" at the "sons of the forest." "The proper term that ought to be applied to our nation," Apess wrote, "to distinguish it from the rest of the human family, is 'Natives.'"[43] To Apess, "Indian" represented an identity marked by scorn and shame, marked by the "degradation" of which so many whites had written as a fall from nobility to disgrace that was the result either of nature or of Indian character. In reclaiming his identity as a "Native" and a "son of the forest," Apess re-rooted himself in the once vibrant forests of New England, in their strength, their oft-romanticized nobility, and their very real regenerative ability. Reversing the constructed image of the degraded "Indian," he insisted that any human being living under the conditions imposed by colonization would become degraded. If Americans would remove their destructive policies and laws from the land rather than removing the indigenous people themselves, the "Natives" would be able to grow and flourish once again.

In reclaiming his own identity as a "son of the forest," Apess felt compelled to return to the place of his birth and to the kinship network of his native New England. He listened to the voices from his own village first, then brought his own voice into the larger Algonquian community. Once Apess had developed an even grander vision, his experience at Mashpee revealed that in extending Native conceptual space to the wider New England audience, he might be able to persuade them through inclusion.

Thus, in the *Eulogy* Apess invited the "sons of the Pilgrims" to see themselves, in being born of this land, as part of a wider, Algonquian-centric family. He asked them to act in a manner that befitted the grand forests that they had begun to celebrate and the Native leaders whom they had begun to mourn, and to treat their "colored" "brethren" with the respect due the land's original inhabitants, with the respect due to family, in the spirit of equality that Philip had demonstrated and the American Revolution had claimed as its hallmark. Yet, Apess's subtly argued vision was not a request for inclusion in American space. Rather, he asked Americans to step into Native space, to bravely join him in the forest, to extinguish the fires set by their Puritan forebears, and to allow the forest to recover itself. He asked them to acknowledge the shared history of destruction and to join with the Natives and all people of color as a body to end its continuing legacy. But, he insisted, in concluding the *Eulogy*, "our" focus should be turned not to the frontiers but to the place in which "we" are rooted and from which the legacies of Philip and the Puritan fathers were born: "This work" Apess insisted, "must begin here first, in New England."[44]

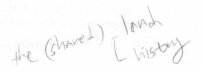

the (shared) land
[history

6

Awikhigawôgan

Mapping the Genres of Indigenous Writing in the Network of Relations

awikhigan is an instrument, something that is manifested, stillness

awikhigawôgan is an activity, something that is in process, flowing and moving

awikhigawôgan is an activity that is on its way to being an instrument: an activity that can transform, an activity that has power/ Manitou

awikhigan is an instrument that can be used for communication, for recording and remembering, for persuasion, for marking a journey, for telling a story, for sealing a promise

awikhigan is an instrument that is an active agent in Native space

We have to be cautious in the act of writing because what we write has power, what we write will become manifest, and our writing has the potential to transform.[1]

In the recently published dictionary of the contemporary Western Abenaki language, Gordon Day defines the word *awikhigan* as "book" or "letter" and *awikhigawôgan* as "writing," while the root word *awigha-* denotes "to mark, draw, or write."[2] The word *awikhigan* has come to encompass a wide array of texts, and its scope is still expanding. It has proven to be an adaptable instrument. The forms that indigenous texts took in the northeast during the eighteenth and nineteenth centuries arose from a utilitarian aesthetic rooted in the instrumentality of writing. The aesthetic achievement of these literary forms was dependent on their rhetorical and material ability to effectively communicate a message, to persuade someone of the importance of an issue or idea, to map the route of an interior or exterior journey, to bind words to deeds, or to embed evocative mnemonic images that would transfer communal memory across time. In short, the success of the literary endeavor would be evaluated based on its capacity as a carrier or catalyst within the network of relations.

These texts reflect what postcolonial scholar Bill Ashcroft terms a "poetics of transformation":

> A poetics of transformation is concerned with the ways in which writers and readers contribute constitutively to meaning, the ways in which colonized societies appropriate imperial discourses, and how they interpolate their voices and concerns into dominant systems of textual production and distribution. Transformation recognizes that power is a critical part of our cultural life, and resists by adapting and redirecting discursive power, creating new forms of cultural production; but above all, a poetics of transformation recognizes the transformative way in which post-colonial texts operate, even those which pose as simply oppositional.[3]

As European writing entered Native space, it was transformed, both in interaction with indigenous systems of communication and in response to the needs of indigenous communities. This chapter serves as a map of those transformations, tracing the genres that were most commonly in operation within the Native networks of the northeast.

Communication: Letters and Messages

Just as birchbark *awikhiganak* were employed as traveling communication, the form of the letter was adopted by Native people as an instrument that could carry words across the network of rivers and relations. Among Mohegans, for instance, letters were used to send news and maintain relations, particularly with family traveling outside the village. An illustrative example is Captain Joseph Johnson's letter to his wife, written from the warfront after the battle of Lake George:

> Dear and loving wife. I received your letter, dated the 9th day of this month. I am glad to hear you are well and all my friends. I am not so well, as I have been: I am afraid [I am] going to be sick with the camp distemper. But I pray God to preserve me from all evil, from sickness, and from the danger of the enemy, and, if it be his will, return me in safety to you and my friends. Should be glad you would send me a letter by the post, and tell me if you have received five shilling bill and two pistareens, which I sent in my last letter. Solo-

mon Cheebucks is sick. I am afraid he will die with it. The French
have taken our fort at lake George and killed and carried captive a
great many Indians. But none of our Connecticut are taken this
time. I remain your loving husband, Joseph Johnson. . . . I hope you
will find two dollars and one six penny piece, which I have sent in
this letter, which I got for a deer skin, that I killed yesterday.[4]

Johnson used writing as a tool to communicate with his family,
to maintain his connection to Mohegan across a long distance, and to relate information about the men in his company to the community back
home. The letter reveals that Johnson was using his tracking skills to
earn money for his family, through both scouting and hunting. The letter
also provides a Native perspective on the siege at Fort William Henry
that contrasts markedly with colonial narratives of the event. As Laura
Murray has observed, "Johnson's emphasis on the violence of the French
and the cost to the Indians at the surrender of Fort William Henry is particularly interesting since other accounts emphasize the violence of the
Indians and the cost to the British." Johnson's letter centers Mohegan
even in the midst of a colonial war.[5]

Johnson's son, Joseph Jr., also used writing to communicate with
fellow Mohegans. Whereas a young man may have traditionally sent
wampum to propose a marriage alliance, Johnson sought approval for a
union with Samson Occom's daughter by writing a letter to his mentor,
including a request to "speak in favor of poor me to your Worthy Con-
sort," Samson's wife, Mary. Writing about their daughter, Tabitha, Johnson assured him, "My heart is fixed upon her . . . and I have promised by
my all to have her, and She also has promised to give herself to me if
Possible. So, I humbly beg that no denial be given hereafter, seeing that
we truly love each other."[6]

In an earlier letter, Johnson had expressed his growing attachment to the family, saying, "I wish you all well, from the bottom of my
heart, and love all perhaps, with sincere love. I reverence you as a kind
Father, and respect your Hon'd wife, as a fond Mother, & your Children
dear, as my beloved Brothers, & sisters." Thus, Johnson's appeal was also
a request to become part of Occom's family. In this same letter, the young
Johnson related how much he missed his "native place," because he was
teaching at the Tunxis community in Farmington. Most of his family had
passed away by this time, giving greater weight to his appeal for marriage into another Mohegan family. When Johnson wrote his proposal,
he was near home, in the town of Norwich, so he could have easily made

Lisa ef close reading

the request in person. However, the young Mohegan was using writing not only to communicate but to solidify his pledge and to propose a formal tie in the network of relations that had already begun to take shape from within.[7]

Writing was used among the Mohegans to communicate practical matters as well. For instance, Occom's sister, Sarah Wyacks, sent a letter to him at Montauk relaying a message from their mother. She wrote, "Mother says if you intend to come over and live to come over in season in sowing time & getting hay." If Occom was going to return home for a visit, his sister insisted, he should honor their mother's request and the cycles of seasonal subsistence by arriving at a time when he could be of use. Under other circumstances, letters carried news of great weight between family members, such as Jacob Fowler's message from his teaching post at Groton to Occom at Mohegan: "Here comes melancholy news to you — Behold the Hand of him who has all Power both in Heaven and on Earth, for We are bereaved of our only *Child*, that lay so folded up in our Hearts. . . . Do dear Brother come over *speedily*. I am your little brother that is bereft of my only Darling — Jacob Fowler."[8]

Writing was also used to communicate messages from the community to outsiders, as is evident in Occom's correspondence with William Johnson during the land case. To elucidate the relationship between this mode of writing and the traditional role of wampum, we might compare the use of wampum among whites living in Native space with the use of writing by Native people. For example, when Samuel Kirkland initially arrived in Iroquoia, William Johnson sent him toward Seneca country with two guides who carried a wampum belt and a "long speech" from Johnson designed, in part, to introduce the missionary. Such runners had a special ability to memorize and carry oral messages, facilitated by the use of mnemonic devices, and men like Johnson had to be literate in this mode of communication if they were going to function in Native space. In comparison, when Henry Quaquaquid traveled to Iroquoia during the same year carrying the message of the Mohegan council, he delivered a written letter to Johnson. Writing provided a highly effective vehicle for relaying information and decisions but functioned as a complement to an oral report. As Occom conveyed in the letter to Johnson, "Henry Quaquaquid will Relate the Whole Matter to your Honor."[9]

Writing was also used in a complementary manner as a form of communication between Native nations. During Greylock's War, the Mohawks sent oral messages with wampum to the Abenakis inquiring about possible terms of peace with the English. Likewise, in 1739, a message accompanied by wampum passed among the Mohawks, Mohicans, Schaghticokes, and Abenakis encouraging their mutual commitment to avoid the burgeoning war between French and English. By the time the dish with one spoon emerged in the Ohio Valley, Mohawks, Mohicans, and Western Indians were sending messages in writing *and* wampum to communicate news and pledges. Diplomatic leaders and runners carried written messages along old routes from the Susquehanna to Lake Erie to the Ohio tributaries relating the results of meetings with U.S. representatives, reports of violence on the frontier, and speeches made in council. Both Joseph Brant and Hendrick Aupaumut were in high demand for their writing skills. For instance, as Aupaumut related, when he stopped at Buffalo Creek en route to the Ohio Valley, the Seneca leader "Farmer's Brother delivered five strings of wampum — and desired me to write his speech and deliver it to the Western Delawares." Once he arrived in the valley, the Delaware sachem instructed him, "You my Grandchild must be here with us, and write our speech to the great man at Fort Jefferson." Joseph Brant often acted as scribe for the Six Nations and the United Indian Nations. His role was so well established that even at the tumultuous conclusion of the 1793 councils, the Shawnee chiefs "asked" Brant "to put down in writing the Words that were to form the Message" to the commissioners, despite his opposition to their resolution. Aupaumut further related:

> Many times those nations desired us to stay all the Winter, and the day before we left the Glaize they delivered a Speech with five strings, desiring that some of us might stay all the winter, to assist them in their endeavors to bring about a peace; particularly to read any messages which should come to them from the White People: for (said they) we have many times rec'd messages from the White People; and the traders read them & gave wrong interpretations.[10]

As Aupaumut observed, Native writers were especially valued because colonial officials — whether British or American — could not be relied on to translate the written word accurately. In speaking of the Great Miami treaty, Shawnee leaders told the Six Nations that the Americans "induced us to sign their proposals, but we find we have been ignorant of the real Purport of them till we returned here." Without ready access to Native writers, communities were forced to seek interpretive assistance from men who were not bound by the network of relations. As the Seneca leader Red Jacket told Timothy Pickering, "We had told you that our old way was to use wampum and not writing. . . . You know there is not one in our nation who knows writing. Therefore we are obliged to turn our faces to the British to know what the writings are when we receive them." Pickering had in fact urged the Six Nations to educate their children at places like Wheelock's school in order to avoid such deceptions. The Oneida chief Good Peter recalled, "You wished that we would send our children to read and write; and if we did this, you said we need never be cheated."[11]

As Red Jacket's statement suggests, Native leaders recognized the similarity between writing and wampum as modes of communication. Aupaumut related that a message sent without "wampum, or writing" was an "empty message" that he would "not regard." Writing gave weight to the message and validated the integrity of the messenger. However, as both Brant and Aupaumut's journals amply demonstrate, writing was being used in parallel with wampum, not as a replacement for it. Indeed, the Six Nations rejected Pickering's dualistic and temporal view of abandoning old ways for new. They insisted that they were "willing that both shall live," with the "new rules" to "live along side" the old.[12]

Protest and Persuasion: Petitions

Communication between Native communities and colonial centers was formalized in written petitions. Although they took their form from the legal template that was common in colonial America, Native petitions can be viewed as a genre unto themselves, corresponding to formal messages from one nation to another that were delivered with wampum. Native people clearly regarded the petition as a form they had to adopt to protest encroachment directly to its source. A petition, they learned, required a response. While the Abenaki "Petition" at No. 2 resembled an *awikhigan*, the Mohegan petitions followed the colonial form more closely, yet still retained particular conventions of Native oratorical protocol.

The most striking difference between these two nations' petitions resulted from the petitioners' positions in relation to their colonial addressees. While the Abenaki *awikhigan* represented a haughty message to a disempowered enemy, the Mohegan memorials represented pleas to an ally who had power over their circumstances. Although Native petitioners often adopted self-deprecating tones, this approach should be understood in the context of the relationship between a "petition" and a "prayer," terms often used interchangeably in colonial America. Occom's use of "petition" and "prayer" in the *Sermon on Moses Paul* exemplifies his own understanding of the similarity between the two, and John Norton frequently used the word "petition" in his journal to mean "prayer," noting, for example, that the Onondagas offered a "petition to the Great Spirit" for his good travels. As David Murray has observed, the act of demonstrating great need in order to request assistance from a divine being, an animal or plant helper, or a human relation was common in the Native northeast. In writing about the fur trade in the Ohio Valley, Richard White has noted:

> In referring to exchange, Algonquians spoke of their *besoins* — their needs or necessities. . . . *Besoin*, as used by the Algonquians, was not simply a statement of desire; the term has a particular resonance in their society because, once an appropriate relationship had been established, as assertion of need for something could become a special claim on the thing needed. To be needy is to excite pity and thus to deserve aid. Just as in addressing manitous Algonquians sought to portray themselves as weak and miserable, so in addressing Onontio, Jesuits or traders, they usually stressed their own misery and need. . . . According to Algonquian cultural logic, the French, as allies, should act as if they were kinspeople of the Algonquians. Each side would supply the other's needs. Each side would graciously bestow what the other lacked.[13]

If the English understood the petition as a prayer, and Native people understood prayer as the pitiful application to a being that held *Manitou*, and furthermore understood alliance in terms of mutual obligatory reciprocity, the written Native petition becomes an intriguing form in which a community uses a tool that has power, writing, to make a "prayer" to a political body that has power in relation to themselves, both the power to change that which afflicts them and the power of a relationship between them, on which the Native group could call. All of the Mohegan petitions contained these facets of the form: calling on a historical relationship of alliance, flattering their ally's power to transform, and emphasizing a dire need for a change in the conditions that oppressed them. In expressing their abject state, the Mohegans asserted that it was their English allies' *obligation* to relieve their suffering, especially because they had the means to do so.

Conversely, the petition can also give way to satirical protest, as exemplified by the Petition at No. 2 and the Mashpee writings, as well as Occom's and Apess's writings in general. Both Bernd Peyer and Jace Weaver have discussed Occom's and Apess's ironic use of the trope of "the poor Indian." Weaver has dubbed this strategically subversive style "Occom's guileful rhetorical razor," while Peyer has compared Apess to "later masters of Indian satire such as Alexander Posey, Vine Deloria, Jr., and Gerald Vizenor." Even as Native students and scribes were obliged to use the language of subservience in addressing colonial officials, their writings often subverted it, exposing the pretentiousness of the convention. Indeed, this tradition of satirical writing may very well be rooted in texts such as the Petition at No. 2 and the oral traditions from which it emerged, reflecting a Native space of humor as "survivance" in the face of colonization.[14]

The parallel between Occom and Apess also extends to their roles in the Mohegan and Mashpee cases. Both used their oratorical skills to help their communities reconstruct from within and recover collective forms of governance. Both asserted the right to self-government, challenging the overseers and missionaries who had fostered division and dispossession even as they claimed the ministerial role for themselves. Finally, both used their writing ability to compose petitions on their community's behalf to the political bodies that had the power to transform the conditions that oppressed them.[15]

Mapping and Relating Travels: Journey Journals

Writing not only traveled among communities but mapped the ties between them. Both Occom's and Aupaumut's journals exemplify the continuance of a spatialized writing system, suggesting a relationship between journey maps written on birchbark, pictographic journey stories marked on bark or stone, and written "journey journals" that documented the network of relations. The early forms were graphic texts with mnemonic geographic and social markers that often correlated with communal narratives. Some scholars have remarked on the sparseness of Occom's journals, but they are a rich source for understanding the relationships between people and places. Occom's first journal reads as a log of his travels between his "home" of Mohegan and Wheelock's school at Lebanon, with trips to other villages, such as Niantic and Montauk, in between. Often traveling with relations, Occom demonstrated a keen understanding of geographic and social ties. As he wrote on a return trip from Montauk, "We all returned home again to Mohegan, to several places where we belonged." While some scholars have mined Occom's journals looking for evidence of Mohegan culture, they may have missed the most crucial aspect — Occom's relational understanding of indigenous identity, mapped quite clearly by his entries.[16]

In the first entry of the second Journal, Occom recorded that he had traveled to Shinnecock from Montauk, and several days later, "John Ashpo came to me from Montauk... and we immediately set out for South Hampton [another Shinnecock village]," where they "stayd... amongst our Country men." During a trip home to undergo his final examination at Wheelock's school, Occom related, "I went on my Journey and got to Mohegan... and found my Relatives well in general[.] July 15th my Brother and I went Down to New London in a Canoe, and I tarried there that night" before returning to his wife and children at Montauk. During another journey to "New England," Occom traveled to Mohegan, then to Lebanon to visit with Wheelock and his relations at the school, and from there, he related, "David Fowler accompanied me to Farming Town [Tunxis], and we got there about just after sun set and there were found our Friends some from Mohegan, some from Nahantick, and some from Groton [Mashantucket], and we held a meeting at one Solomon Adams House." Each volume details one or more journeys between Occom's "home" of Mohegan and the villages, towns, and encampments of his relations. The journal as a whole could be mapped spatially, a network with Mohegan at the center. Occom consistently depicted Mohegan as his "home" village, even during his long stay with his wife's family at Montauk. Therefore, the decision to remove to Brotherton was a critical decision for Occom. He marked the transformation in his journal, proclaiming that he would "make this town my home and center." In moving to Brotherton, he was keenly aware of the act of leaving one village to construct another, to which he and his reconstructed family of "brothers" would belong.[17]

The pain of this act of separation is especially evident in the writing of Joseph Johnson Jr., who experienced conflict and grief in contemplating removal from the "womb" of Mohegan. Writing in his journal at Tunxis, in the midst of planning for emigration to Brotherton, he lamented,

> Well I remember home — O Mohegan O Mohegan — the time is long before I shall be walking my wonted places which are on thee — once there I was but perhaps never again, but Still I remember thee — in you is lodged my father & Mother dear — and My Beloved Sisters — and brothers. ... Perhaps in due time I may once more come on thy borders — but first I have to go, to distant Lands; and far Country — and Different Nations I have to walk through — before I see thee. Thus O Mohegan I must bid you farewell, and Shut the door of my Heart against thee — for I have a truer friend — to entertain my Heart — So good night.[18]

Johnson's journals are most valuable for the deep expressions of his relationships with the people and places in his network, as well as for the conflict, expressed so eloquently here, between his embodied attachment to Mohegan and the ideal of heaven presented by his Christian faith. As these journals demonstrate, journeys had internal landscapes as well. In their autobiographical writing, both Johnson and Apess related similar circular journeys from home to Iroquoia during which they experienced challenges to their character and harsh lessons in human fallibility, and after long journeys to remote places they returned home as humbled sons who were accepted as participants in the communal activities of the whole. This moment of return and belonging marks a central place in each of their texts.[19] Both also found mentors in their communities' preachers: for Apess, Aunt Sally George; for Johnson, Samson Occom, who eventually became his father. They assumed roles as teachers and community mobilizers only after each found a clear place within the map of his relations.

The same can be said for Hendrick Aupaumut. The importance of finding his place in the neglected Algonquian network is clear in the urgency of his celebratory tone as he traveled from village to village and described his reception. In the *Narrative* of his journey, Aupaumut repeatedly situated himself in relation to the places and people of Iroquoia and the Western Indian country. He emphasized his direct relationships with family such as his "cousin Aaron" and his "Uncle" Pohquannoppeet while highlighting the Mohicans' location in the family of nations. Yet, as his journal makes clear, when Aupaumut returned to his center of New Stockbridge, he faced his own community's land struggles, as did Occom, Apess, and Johnson, with a humbled resolve.[20]

Occom's journals of his journeys to Oneida mirror aspects of Aupaumut's journal of his journey to the Ohio Valley. Occom described

the places where he stopped, the conditions of the wind, and his meetings with "my relations." He described Confederacy councils and the
continuing use of wampum to make pledges, to "bind" people in "friendship," and to communicate needs and desires. A deep concern for fostering right relations in the network to which one belonged was shared by
Occom and Aupaumut, and the difficulty of maintaining such relations
under the pressures of colonial division may have solidified the bond
the two men shared late in Occom's life. Just as the maps and pictographic stories depicted on birchbark and stone related both internal and
external journeys, the journey journals composed by Native writers in
the eighteenth and nineteenth centuries reflected the intertwining of psychological, social, and physical travel within the layered geographies of
Native space.[21]

Binding Words to Deeds: Treaty Literature

Indigenous forms of writing often resemble a map more than a chronological, event-centered narrative. Apess, Aupaumut, and Brant all wrote
in a style that provided multiple routes into their stories rather than presenting a logical flow of causal events. The roots of this stylistic convention may be located in the literary form of the treaty, with its origins in
both wampum belts and best-selling publications in Europe and colonial America.

"Treaty literature" is a genre of early American literature that has
been almost entirely neglected by literary scholars. This "native American literary form" preceded European writing in Native space. It consisted of an oratory protocol guided by mnemonic wampum belts and
birchbark scrolls that contained the records of international exchange.
These graphic texts could be read only by "rememberers" trained in
recording and recalling the words associated with them. However, when
Europeans came to council, they brought their own political customs and
forms of recording, even as they were obliged to adopt Native conventions. Thus, published treaties represent the interaction between indigenous council protocol and European political discourse, between Native
oratory and the written literature of the "encounter."[22]

Some fifty treaties were published as "small books" during the
eighteenth century, beginning with *Propositions Made by the Sachems of
Three Maquas Castles, to the . . . City of Albany* in 1690, gaining in popularity
with Cadwallader Colden's *History of Five Nations* in 1727, and culminating

in Benjamin Franklin's treaty publications issued from 1736 to 1762. In his essay "The Indian Treaty as Literature," Lawrence Wroth concluded that there must have been a "good market" for treaties because they were published "as private ventures at the charge of the printer" and not by the colony or crown. In a dissertation on this "neglected genre," Augustus Pham observed that the "popular appeal" of Indian treaties was evident in the financial success of Franklin's publications in Boston and London, which included the printing of hundreds of volumes at a time, as well as translations into other European languages. According to Pham, these treaties "became landmarks in colonial printing and publishing ventures." Carl Van Doren, in his introduction to the collected Franklin *Treaties*, asserted that they were "in both matter and manner... the most original and engaging documents in their century."[23]

In style and content, according to Van Doren, published treaties resembled "diplomatic dramas," a "form... prescribed by Iroquois ritual." Treaty councils required Europeans to engage in indigenous diplomatic discourse, particularly because of competition for allegiances in trade and war. William Fenton has remarked that "the patterns that had governed Iroquois life for centuries" compelled colonial leaders to participate "in a highly ritualized [form] that was completely foreign to European ways and thinking." Native orators, Pham related, "obliged the English to adopt the same manner of public speech and respond to the memory of the same ceremonies." Thus, the symbolic and ontological maps of Native council traditions formed the base of the written treaties that were published in Europe. As Pham noted, "The ceremony of condolence, the solemn opening of the council, and much else in traditional, symbolic language of the Indian tribes, was incorporated into the Indian treaties with the English colonists. They become the most obvious characteristics of the Indian treaty as literature." These indigenous forms, Van Doren has observed, "grew familiar to the English, and they became expert in the practice of them." Through this cross-cultural venue, Native "patterns of imagery, formulaic utterances, allusions," and "recollections of... elaborate mythology" were introduced into English, which also became a shared language in Native space. "In the treaties," Pham has contended, Indians "emerged as rational being[s], capable of sitting down along side of Europeans to discuss affairs of state." By the time Franklin's treaties were published, Native northeastern oratory was well established, and admired, as a "literary convention."[24]

Thus, when Native writers like Hendrick Aupaumut and Joseph Brant began reading and recording treaties themselves, they were part of an intellectual tradition that had emerged from within indigenous councils to circulate throughout the world. And, as Maureen Konkle has argued in *Writing Indian Nations*, "The struggle over treaty rights motivated the emergence of the first significant body of Native writing in English in the first half of the nineteenth century."[25]

Before turning to this genre of indigenous writing, it is worthwhile to consider what the earlier treaty literature, recorded by non-Native scribes, reveals about the role of writing in Native space. We begin in Mohegan territory, with their relations, the Delawares. When Samson Occom's mentor Eleazar Wheelock wrote his *Plain and Faithful Narrative of the Indian Charity School*, he explained the challenge posed by the education of "our Heathen Natives" by describing the downfall of his first pupil, John Pumshire. In Wheelock's portrayal, the young Delaware man left the school on his horse, dejected and terribly ill. "Pumshire set out on his Journey, November 14th 1756 and got Home," he reported, "but soon died." The pressures of civilization had been too much, and the Indian had succumbed to the tragic fate of his nature. The ending of Pumshire's story evoked an image of the "dying Indian" that would permeate American literature for centuries to come.[26]

Scholars who have written about the history of Wheelock's school have taken this report at face value. However, the treaty literature of the period reveals that John Pumshire did not die at all. In fact, he appeared as an interpreter, on the exact day he had supposedly left the school, at an important council in Easton, Pennsylvania. Rather than going home to perish, Pumshire assumed an active leadership role in his community, pushing the colony of New Jersey to make the sale of Delaware land illegal without the consent of a preselected council of Delaware men, and used his skills in literacy and diplomacy to support the larger Delaware confederation.[27]

Pumshire served as the Delaware interpreter for two critical councils held at Easton during 1756 and 1757, the minutes of which were published as treaties by Benjamin Franklin. Pham has observed that colonial officials were reluctant to allow the Easton Treaties to go to print because they "dealt with sensitive matters relating to the serious charges made against the proprietors of land fraud." As Pumshire explained during the 1757 council, "The Land is the Cause of our Differences; that is, our being unhappily turned out of the Land, is the Cause." The Delawares were particularly persistent in addressing the infamous "Walking Purchase," through which the sons of William Penn had attempted to defraud the Delawares out of their lands.[28]

Two decades before the Easton Treaties, the Penn brothers had produced a fraudulent deed and map that delineated lands supposedly granted to their father, with the bounds measured by a walk of a day and half. The map was particularly deceptive because the geographic markers showed lands outside the Delaware villages, while the words implied a much larger expanse. The Penns and Delaware leaders had agreed to meet to measure out the "walk," but, unbeknownst to the Delawares, the Penn brothers had preselected runners and trained them to move at the fastest pace possible, and they had already blazed a straight trail through the forest rather than following the long-standing trail by the Delaware River. The walk ended at a point much farther north than the Delawares had read on the map, and they were infuriated with the Penn brothers' attempt to claim lands that would encompass their villages and hunting grounds. The Penns not only had "taken advantage of Indian illiteracy," but had used writing to purposefully distort the spatial text of the map. The contest over these lands continued for twenty years, reaching its height at the councils for the Easton Treaties. In 1756, when the governor of Pennsylvania invited the Delawares to speak to the issues that concerned them most, the Delaware leader Teedyuscung announced dramatically, "This very Ground that is under me (striking it with his Foot) was my Land and Inheritance, and is taken from me, by Fraud." Having witnessed the "Walking Purchase" as a young man, Teedyuscung had experienced displacement by paper firsthand.[29]

When the Delaware leader began his speech, Conrad Weiser, the official recorder for the colony, "threw down his Pen, and declared he would take no Minutes when the King [Teedyuscung] came to complain of the Proprietaries" (that is, the Penn brothers and the settlers who had moved onto the land, to whom Weiser was closely tied). According to Francis Jennings, "When he threw down his pen in 1756, [Weiser's] purpose was simply to suppress Teedyuscung's charge from official records. But [a Quaker named] Charles Thomson among the observers continued to write, so [Governor] Denny ruled that Thomson's notes should be adopted officially 'as the most perfect.'" This was the version that Franklin published.[30]

At the beginning of the second Easton council, Teedyuscung insisted on having his own "secretary" to record the proceedings because, according to Thomson, he was afraid that when he raised the issue of the Walking Purchase, Weiser would once again "throw down his pen." Initially, the governor balked at the suggestion, but Teedyuscung refused to participate without this stipulation and announced he was going to "break up and go home." As Thomson reported, "This being made known to the Governor, he told Teedyuscung, that...no Indian Chief before him ever demanded to have a Clerk," but as "Proof of [his] Friendship and Regard," he would allow it, and, not surprisingly, the Delawares chose Thomson. Although the debate over Teedyuscung's request went on for four days, it was omitted from the official minutes recorded by Weiser.[31]

Weiser did, however, record Teedyuscung's request to present a written speech composed by the Delaware council. As he told the governor, "This Morning early, when we came to sit down by ourselves, and our secretary with us, when we had done, and had fully understood one another, and agreed on every Word, we then ordered our Secretary to write it down." John Pumshire added, "I will just mention this in Addition; we ordered him to read it over four Times, and approved it." Teedyuscung continued, "Having done that, we have the Words already written down, and if it please the Governor to hear it read, this that is written down is what was concluded on." According to Weiser, "The Governor, in Answer, told him, Brother, you know that this is quite a new Method, and was never before practiced. I well know the Indians have good Memories, and can remember what was transacted twenty years ago, as if yesterday." Another huge discussion ensued over this request, and Teedyuscung offered to recite the speech from memory because the governor was so insistent on maintaining the oral tradition.[32]

The history of the Easton Treaties that has passed down to us was directly impacted by Teedyuscung's request for his own secretary and John Pumshire's literacy. Although Weiser threw down his pen and refused to record Teedyuscung's narrative of land fraud, Thomson continued writing, and it was his version that Benjamin Franklin, a witness to these proceedings, published. Weiser tried to use writing to erase the history of dispossession, and Teedyuscung, well aware of the power of paper, demanded that his words be recorded and "published," saying, "It depends much on you, Brother, that it may be openly and publickly declared and published to the Province or provinces under the Government of the Great King." Furthermore, Pumshire's role as a multilingual and literate interpreter was critical to the accuracy of the minutes. Not only was he was called on to elucidate Teedyuscung's complaints for the governor and the record, but, as Wheelock himself had observed, Pumshire had "made uncommon Proficiency in writing," so he would have been able to read and review Thomson's minutes to ensure that they matched the English words he had spoken for Teedyuscung.[33]

Not surprisingly, Teedyuscung also insisted that Delaware ownership of the "Wyoming" lands to the west of their original villages, where he and his followers "intend[ed] to settle," should be recorded in writing. During the 1757 council, he drew on the table a map of this territory, which would later be drafted on paper, and said, "We would have the Boundaries fixed all around, agreeable to the Draught we give you, that we may not be pressed on any Side, but have a certain country fixed for our own use, and the use of our Children for ever." Having learned a harsh lesson during the Walking Purchase, Teedyuscung insisted on drawing his own map to delineate their territory and solidify their rights. He also made a request for a teacher "to instruct our Children in Reading and Writing." The Delawares, like their relations, recognized the links among literacy, land, and sovereignty. If a man like Pumshire had been present for the Walking Purchase, the fraud would have failed.[34]

Events like those surrounding the Walking Purchase, in which dispossession was accomplished through falsified documents, necessitated the adoption of writing in Native communities. In the Lancaster treaty of 1744, also published by Franklin, the Six Nations complained vehemently about the problem of fraudulent deeds, protesting, "We are being impoverished by pen and ink work." The Penobscot leader Loron responded to the falsification of his words in the printed Treaty of Casco Bay by crafting a rebuttal to counteract the version distributed by the Colony of Massachusetts. The Casco Bay conference had been held to set terms for the cessation of Dummer's (or Greylock's) War, and Loron had participated along with representatives from multiple Wabanaki communities. In his written statement, likely translated and transcribed by a local priest, Loron noted "the diversity and contrariety of the interpretations" he had "received of the English writing in which the articles of peace are drawn up" and protested, "These writings appear to contain things that are not, so that the Englishman himself disavows them in my presence, when he reads and interprets them to me himself."[35]

Loron quoted directly from the printed treaty, then challenged nearly every point, vehemently insisting that he (that is, his nation) did not "become [a] subject" of the British King, "or," he said, "give my land, or

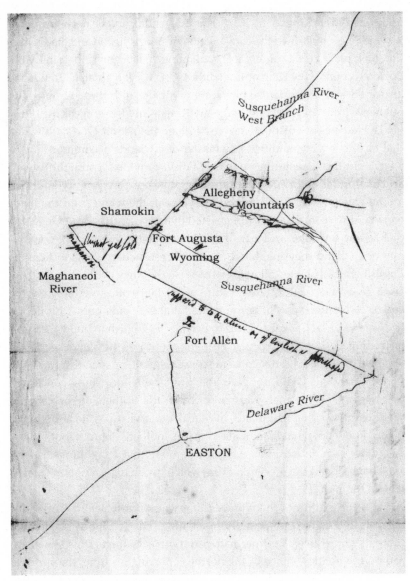

Susquehanna River,
West Branch

Allegheny
Mountains

Shamokin

Fort Augusta

Wyoming

Maghaneoi
River

Susquehanna River

Fort Allen

Delaware River

EASTON

Figure 11. Teedyuscung's map: "Draught of land desired by the
Delawares July 30 1757." Pennsylvania State Archives, Record Group
26, Records of the Proprietary Government, Provincial Council.

acknowledge his King as my King. This I never did, and he never proposed it to me." Loron clarified the conversation over jurisdiction and land tenure that took place at the conference, explaining, "He again said to me — But do you recognize the King of England as King of all his states? To which I answered — Yes, I recognize him King of all his lands; but I rejoined, do not hence infer that I acknowledge thy King as my King, and King of my lands. Here lies my distinction — my Indian distinction. God hath willed that I have no King, and that I be master of my lands in common."[36]

In this concluding sentence, Loron provided a straightforward articulation of the principles of the common pot. Sovereignty and land tenure were vested in the communal voice of the whole, and the lands were held "in common." Loron insisted that his nation had no king. Neither he nor any other leader held that kind of authority over the community or the land they inhabited. As speaker, his charge was to take the English words back to "all my relatives" so that they could discuss them "in a general assembly," then return with their collective reply. At the end of his written speech, Loron related that the "only point" his nation had agreed to "at Caskebay" was to permit the English to build a "store," or trading post, at St. Georges, near the mouth of the Kennebec River. On their behalf, he did not consent to a settlement, or even to a fort, and, Loron reiterated, "I did not give [the king] the land." Loron concluded by asserting, "What I tell you now is the truth. If, then, anyone should produce any writing that makes me speak otherwise, pay no attention to it, for I know not what I am made to say in another language, but I know well what I say in my own. And in testimony that I say things as they are, I have signed the present minute which I wish to be authentic and to remain for ever."[37]

Loron did not mention sending wampum to seal these words, but instead used the European form, "signing" his "testimony" to demonstrate its authenticity and permanence. Whatever impact his statement had on the political space of the northeast during his time, the survival of his statement in the colonial archive makes it impossible for any historian to take the Treaty of Casco Bay at face value. Writing ensured that this "authentic" voice has "remained," as Loron wished, to communicate his "Indian distinction" regarding continual Wabanaki sovereignty over the "lands in common."

Native people quickly learned that writing could enact their dispossession, but they also realized that it had the potential, like wampum, to reverse that destructive course. Likewise, as the Easton Treaties suggest, some Europeans regarded Indian illiteracy as an advantage. While many missionaries encouraged their Native students to read and write in order to draw them closer to Christianity, others neglected or even prevented the acquisition of these skills. Apess's *Indian Nullification* contains the most vocal indictment of this obstruction. "Much" has been "said," he wrote, "about the pains that [have] been taken to educate the Marshpees, and it was averred that, instead of going to the schools opened for them, they preferred going about the country picking berries and basket making." However, Apess insisted it was colonial legislators who did not want the Mashpees to be educated. As proof, he cited a Massachusetts law: "Let him who has been prejudiced against the Marshpees, by such argument, look at the legislative act of 1789, section 5, for the regulation of the plantation, prohibiting the instruction of the Marshpees in reading and writing, under pain of death. Who, then, dared to teach them?" Ironically, it was Apess's own ability to read and write that allowed him to expose the mythology surrounding Native illiteracy.[38]

Apess insisted that neither "the former missionary," Gideon Hawley, nor Phineas Fish, who "succeeded Mr. Hawley . . . set up schools" that enabled literacy, even though both received funds for teaching. Furthermore, "when the Marshpee children were put out to service," as Apess was, "it was with the express understanding, as their parents all agree, that they should not be schooled." Comparing the laws and practices that prohibited education with those that facilitated dispossession, Apess asked, "Is not depriving them of all means of mental culture the worst of all robberies?"[39] Apess himself received only "six winters" of schooling, so he must have acquired his remarkable rhetorical dexterity through other avenues. Clearly, missionary schools were not the only routes to acquiring literacy. In fact, Apess insisted that most Mashpees had "learned to read and write" when they "lived abroad among the whites" and that, "on returning to the tribe, they have taught others what they knew themselves, receiving pay from those who had the means and teaching the rest gratuitously."[40]

Challenging his "brethren" in Massachusetts, Apess insisted that dispossession, literacy, and the law were linked:

> The laws were calculated to drive the tribes from their possessions and annihilate them as a people; and I presume they would work the same effect upon any other people; for human nature is the same under skins of all colors. Degradation is degradation, all the world over. If the white man desires the welfare of his red brethren,

why did he not give them schools? Why has not the state done something to supply us with teachers and give us places of instruction? I trow, all the schooling the Marshpee people have ever had they have gotten themselves.[41]

Apess's *Indian Nullification* addressed many of the same issues that appeared in the treaty literature — in which he was undoubtedly well read — and its form reflects that tradition. Peyer has noted that the "array of pertinent documents such as newspaper articles, letters, appeals, minutes, and resolutions," presented in dialogue with Apess's narration, make *Indian Nullification* "a complex ethnohistorical collage that presents the case from several points of view, both in concurrence with and in opposition to his own." Building on Peyer's insights, Theresa Gaul has remarked, "By placing all these materials together in one text, Apess emphasizes the existence of multiple and contradictory viewpoints." Taking "the textual spaces of the written word as exemplified in the press and writings by whites about American Indians," Apess "enters *Indian Nullification* into their debates, even as the text enacts such debates within its own pages."[42]

Gaul has observed that *Indian Nullification* "eludes easy classification," particularly within the genres of American literature. However, Apess's "strategic use of intertextuality" and tendency to place multiple voices "in dialogue" does correspond to the literary form of the treaty. According to Pham, published treaties followed a format of "dialogue" between multiple parties, and, as Fenton has observed, these texts could claim "no single author." The structure of *Indian Nullification* resembles the participatory deliberation of a council and the polyphonic form of a treaty, with its orchestrator drawing oral testimonies and printed texts into discursive exchange through oratorical convention. Even as Apess wove multiple voices in contradiction and collaboration, he spoke as a dynamic participant. Furthermore, he actively engaged his readers in deliberation, inviting them to consider the evidence and contribute their own response, which, if he fulfilled his own role, would bring them to consensus with the whole.[43]

The literary form of the treaty is evident in the structure and content of other Native-authored texts as well, including Aupaumut's and Brant's journals. Their narratives represent an important shift that occurred in the treaty literature tradition when Native writers took up the role of recorder and interpreter for themselves. Brant's *Journal* is nearly identical in form to the treaties published by Franklin. The text resembles a dramatic dialogue because Brant recorded, word for word, speeches and responses from multiple nations from the councils he attended at the Rapids. However, Brant's *Journal* diverges from earlier treaties by incorporating commentary on the context surrounding the councils and analysis of the problems and proposals that arose from within them, written from a perspective entrenched in Haudenosaunee principles and protocol. In this sense, Brant's text seems a precursor to Apess's *Indian Nullification.*

Brant's and Aupaumut's narratives also contain innumerable textual parallels to the "symbolic language" of Franklin's treaties. The language through which Brant articulated the union of the dish with one spoon, as well as the speech conventions that Aupaumut and his relations exchanged, mirrored almost exactly the rhetoric of the earlier treaty publications, demonstrating the persistence of indigenous diplomatic traditions. Aupaumut's *Narrative* also demonstrates that American leaders were fluent in treaty diplomacy and council protocol. For example, the message of the United States that Aupaumut carried emulated Native oratorical rhetoric and was accompanied by a wampum belt with "15 square marks, which denote 15 United sachems, and path of peace goes thro the marks." In his *Narrative,* Aupaumut recorded the message, the council at which he delivered it, and the deliberations and responses of his relations, as well as his own remarks and his opinions of American diplomatic strategy. All of this was accomplished through writing.[44]

Brant and Aupaumut were trained to write by educators who sought to transform Indians into "useful" servants to the colonial project. Ostensibly, the skill of literacy was tied to proper conversion. At the Indian Charity School in Lebanon, where Brant, Joseph Johnson Jr., and John Pumshire were educated, Eleazar Wheelock used writing to ingrain English values, rules, and obedience into their consciousness.[45] However, writing also took its own course in indigenous networks, and it even became a tool with which to counteract colonization. As Native people began to read, land acquisition through deceptive writings became increasingly difficult. It is no coincidence that Brant was not present at any of the meetings that produced the false treaties. Such treaties simply could not be made with him there, unless he was made complicit. He was too effective a witness. His leadership and literacy combined made him a real threat to the United States; thus, the extraordinary efforts of U.S. representatives to woo him to their side. Yet, both Brant and Aupaumut used their skills to perform their traditional roles more effectively: Aupaumut delivered messages between the various nations with which he was connected, recording and relating the words of each side for the other, and successfully transmitted his relations' perspective on the false treaties to the American leadership. Brant recorded messages, speeches, and treaties and witnessed councils to make sure that the written words matched the spoken ones. Each man played an instrumental role in creating writings that ensured words would be bound to deeds.

While Aupaumut and Brant composed their journals primarily for colonial officials, they also utilized writing, along with Apess and Occom, to record the deliberations and decisions of Native councils for internal use. This is evident in Apess's *Indian Nullification*, which incorporates numerous proclamations of the Mashpee council, often recorded by Daniel Amos as "secretary," and in Occom's papers, which contain the "Records of the Mohegan tribe," including multiple references to "unanimous" decisions regarding their "common" lands. While Occom recorded the meetings of the Mohegan council, Joseph Johnson Jr. recorded meetings with the Oneida leadership regarding the Brotherton removal. Like Brant's and Aupamut's journals, Johnson's council records demonstrate the continuance of treaty protocol, as well as the Mohegans' cross-cultural fluency in multiple Native traditions. Likewise, the Mohicans had a long tradition of rememberers, including Aupaumut, who recorded councils and composed petitions and correspondence on behalf of the Stockbridge community. The papers of Brant and his nephew John Norton contain voluminous records of councils, from the multinational gatherings in the Ohio Valley to the Confederacy meetings at Buffalo Creek and Grand River. The speeches they recorded often addressed the problem of "divisions" and the goal of "unity" that had been set by "the Ancient Chiefs."[46]

Records of indigenous councils, as exemplified in the writings of Apess, Occom, Johnson, Aupaumut, Norton, and Brant, reveal the power of participatory thinking, as Native communities deliberated to make collective decisions for the "benefit of the whole." Like the treaty literature, council records illuminate the ways in which the common pot was torn apart and reconstructed, and they demonstrate the strength of thought and commitment that was required for such transformation to take place. Writing worked to solidify a community's decisions while providing a record for future generations. Throughout northeastern networks, writing took on a role that was complementary to that of wampum, ensuring that spoken words would be honored and that agreements would be remembered. Writing generated and recorded transformations in Native space.

Recording and Remembering: Communal Histories

From within these councils, communal historical narratives emerged that were spatial and relational, written texts drawn from oratorical traditions that delineated the relationships between people, mapped the relationship between people and place, and marked important transformations in Native space. In writing a local history of Stockbridge, Anglo-American author Electa Jones recalled the process of remembering among the Mohicans: "The History, and perhaps we may say the entire literature of the Muh-he-ka-ne-ok, was treasured in the minds of a succession of 'historians,' each of whom trained one or more to fill the office after his death. When a mission had been established among them, and youth had been sufficiently instructed, a portion of this literature was written down for preservation."[47]

During the same year that Jones's *Stockbridge Past and Present* was published (1854), on the fourth of July, the Stockbridge Mohican leader John W. Quinney addressed a crowd of New Yorkers, who, he said, were "now standing upon the soil which once was, and now ought to be, the property of this tribe." He related that his education had enabled him "to read your histories," including "the documentary papers of this State," and that "the many traditions of my tribe, which are as firmly believed as written annals by you, inform me that there are many errors." He then proceeded to tell his audience, "without, however, intending to refer to, and correct those histories," how the Mohicans had adapted the tool of writing for the preservation of their own historical tradition. He related that during the time when his great grandfather, Ben Kokhkewenaunaunt, was sachem at Stockbridge,

> A Grand Council was convened of the Mu-he-con-new tribe, for the purpose of conveying from the old to the young men, a knowledge of the past. Councils, for this object especially, had ever, at stated periods, been held. Here, for the space of two moons, the stores of memory were dispensed; corrections and comparisons made, and the results committed to faithful breasts, to be transmitted again to succeeding posterity. Many years after, another, and a last Council

of this kind was held; and the traditions reduced to writing, by two of our young men, who had been taught to read and write in the school of the Rev. John Sergeant, of Stockbridge, Massachusetts. They were obtained, in some way, by a white man, for publication, who soon after, dying all trace of them became lost. The traditions of the tribe, however, have been mainly preserved.[48]

As Quinney observed, the purpose of recording this history was not to relay a Mohican story to a non-Native audience but to "convey... a knowledge of the past" from one generation of Mohicans to another. The importance of relaying and remembering communal history is evident in the amount of time and the number of people required to relate this narrative in full, as well as in the meticulous process through which the written account was created. The telling of history was a collective, participatory activity in which writing was made to play a part.

The history that Quinney subsequently related to his New York audience mirrored, in many respects, a Mohican-authored narrative published in the *Collections of the Massachusetts Historical Society* thirty years earlier, which has been attributed to Hendrick Aupaumut. Although some scholars have assumed that Aupaumut composed this narrative for an American audience, it is likely that this text is the communal history of which Quinney spoke and that Aupaumut was one of the recorders. A. Holmes, who published the "Extract from an Indian History" under his own name, may have been the "white man" who "obtained it," perhaps without the full knowledge of the community. He most likely acquired the history from John Konkapot, the Mohican "secretary," who was probably the other designated recorder. In the same volume of the *Collections*, Holmes cited Konkapot as his primary source for a vocabulary of the Mohican language, referring to him as "a young and intelligent Indian, of the Stockbridge tribe," who was responsible for recording the councils of the nation.[49]

Konkapot had attended Dartmouth College with Peter Poquanopeet, and both men emerged along with Aupaumut and Quinney's father to serve as leaders during the turbulent process of relocation to Oneida. By the time Aupaumut reached maturity, literacy was one of the most important attributes of a Mohican leader, and this tradition continued into the next generation. John Quinney cited his own education as the main reason he was selected to "attend to the affairs of the nation."[50]

Both Aupaumut and Quinney centered Native space in their histories, emphasizing a Mohican identity that was tied to the "ebb and

flow" of tidal waters, relating the village's movements along the waterways of the northeast. Quinney even characterized the Stockbridge
removal west, to the Great Lakes, as a return to the places from which
they had originated. The Mohicans, Mohegans, and Delawares share a
common origin story conveying that they came from flowing waters in
the "northwest," in contrast with nations like the Wabanakis and Wampanoags, whose origin stories root us firmly in New England. Mohican
identity was tied to the possibility of movement within the network of
waterways and relations. Thus, during their migration east, Aupaumut
related, it was only when they arrived at "Hudson's river," where they
found waters "flowing and ebbing like Muhheakunnuk," that "they said
one to another, this is like Muhheakunnuk our nativity." Only there did
they "agree to kindle fire... and hang a kettle." Quinney's version con-
curred: "The tribe, to which your speaker belongs... occupied and possessed the country from the sea-shore, at Manhattan, to Lake Champlain.
Having found an ebb and flow of the tide, they said: "This is Muh-he-
con-new" — "like our waters, which are never still."[51]

This trope of movement is directly related to the concept of
transformation, which Aupaumut's narrative connected to "nativity," in
a way similar to Wzokhilain's rendering of the Abenaki concept of
alnôbawôgan and the many Haudenosaunee recordings of the Sky Woman
story. Native communal histories are records of transformations within
Native space. The world is in a constant state of activity, and the telling
of history operates as a force that can make sense of transformation and
can empower people to be constructive participants.

This tradition is exemplified in the Haudenosaunee histories of
the nineteenth and early twentieth centuries. These include John Norton's *Journal*, which he wrote and submitted to Scottish patrons for publication in 1816;[52] David Cusick's *Ancient History of the Six Nations*, initially
published in 1825 and widely considered the first Haudenosaunee-
authored history in print; and Arthur Parker's *Constitution of the Five
Nations* and *Seneca Myths and Folk Tales*, published in 1915 and 1923, re-
spectively. All presented the key oral narratives of the longhouse in written form: the creation story of Sky Woman, the account of the formation
of the Confederacy through the Great Law, and, from within the Great
Law, the description of the ongoing ceremony of condolence.[53]

Like the Mohicans, the Six Nations had a long tradition of historical recitation in which the entire community participated. Norton
drew on the many versions of the narrative cycles that he heard from Six

Nations elders both within and outside the longhouse, as well as from the history that his "uncle" Joseph Brant had always wanted to write. Brant, in a letter to Kirkland, expressed his belief that had his effort "to Unite the Indians together" been successful, he might "have had the leisure to visit the distant Nations and collect matter to proceed upon with my History," which he regarded as a vehicle not only for recording narratives of the past but for communicating "the Ideas entertained by the different Nations of the Creation of a future State." After Brant's death, Norton continued to undertake projects in translation and education along with the Mohawk interpreter, minister, and doctor (and Brant's son-in-law) Henry Aaron Hill. This tradition was carried on by David Cusick, a respected doctor, and his brother James, a minister, who published a book of "Indian hymns." James's Onondaga grandson Albert Cusick, who served as *tadodaho* of the Confederacy, later assisted Arthur Parker in interpreting, translating, and revising the version of the Great Law meticulously recorded by Seth Newhouse, "the native scribe" from Brant's Six Nations reserve. Like Brant, Newhouse viewed the Great Law as a living tradition that contained the keys to solving contemporary problems. He made it his life's work to create a collective recording of this foundational narrative, speaking with many elders to form the best possible version, which he urged the Grand River leadership to adopt in council, even sending them written petitions to communicate his appeals. Drawing on Newhouse's manuscript, along with other oral and textual sources, Parker created a definitive *Constitution of the Five Nations,* "a compilation of native manuscripts of which Parker is in reality the editor," according to Fenton, and a "culmination" of the effort "by native annalists," beginning with Joseph Brant, "to codify" the Great Law of the Confederacy.[54]

Alongside the effort to record the communal narratives of Haudenosaunee history, the use of wampum to recall and preserve it continued. In his *History,* Cusick described wampum belts as the "record[s] of alliance," while his contemporary Thomas Webster, an Onondaga wampum-keeper, related to the New York legislature that he was responsible for "keep[ing] the treaties of the nation." He told them that the wampum belts held in New York's museums and archives "mean nothing to the white man, all to [the] Indian." Wampum reclamation took place beside the recording of communal histories. Parker and Newhouse worked together to try to retrieve belts from commercial traders and to connect them with treaties that had been published or stored in state archives. Abram Hill, an Oneida leader, told the anthropologist William

Beauchamp that wampum gave him "credentials" and gave his words credence: "If he sent a man without it, but with an official message, no attention would be paid to it; if he bore wampum his words would be heard." Hill told Beauchamp that "Indian wampum [is the] same as [the] white man's letter." Thus, the Hills, along with Brant, Norton, Newhouse, Parker, and the Cusicks, were part of an ongoing tradition of using writing *and* wampum to remember, relate, and *enact* the narratives of Haudenosaunee history.[55]

The forms that these histories took are comparable to those of the written petitions, journals, treaties, and council records that preceded them, as multivoiced, participatory narratives that recorded and relayed the voice of the whole. Furthermore, they are part of an active, living tradition. The texts themselves participate in community. Thus, Apess's *Eulogy on King Philip* acts both as a petition, an instrument that seeks to communicate and enact a transformation, and as a communal history of New England as Native space. The ways in which communal histories were created and continue to contribute to our understanding of ourselves reflect the meaning of the word for "history" in Abenaki, *ôjmowôgan*, which implies that "history" is not an object that can be contained or a subject that we can master but is rather the collective activity of telling or relating a story that belongs to the common pot.

7

Concluding Thoughts from Wabanaki Space

Literacy and the Oral Tradition

In a classic scene from James Fenimore Cooper's *The Last of the Mohicans*, the white scout Natty Bumppo, aka "Hawkeye," ruminates on the conflict between "books" and the oral tradition in speaking to his "adopted" father, Chingachgook:

> I am willing to own that my people have many ways, of which, as an honest man, I can't approve. It is one of their customs to write in books what they have done and seen, instead of telling them in their villages, where the lie can be given to the face of a cowardly boaster, and the brave soldier can call on his comrades to witness for the truth of his words. In consequence of this bad fashion, a man who is too conscientious to misspend his days among the women, in learning the names of black marks, may never hear of the deeds of his fathers, nor feel a pride in striving to outdo them.[1]

Natty Bumppo's words reflect the characteristic nineteenth-century American perspective on Indians and writing, with its diametric opposition between oral and literate cultures and its obsession with cultural purity. Writing is a "white" way, while Indians have an oral tradition, and the two ways cannot mix. Chingachgook is marked in the novel as a pure, "unmixed" Indian, so he is not only illiterate but completely unfamiliar with books. To take up writing, in this view, was to be marked as not Indian. The belief became so prevalent in the nineteenth century, alongside the myth of disappearance, that it nearly erased the long tradition of writing in the Native northeast. Even now, when so many Native people are utilizing this tool, it is often taken for granted that writing is part of a coercive colonial enterprise and that literacy is inherently antithetical to the oral tradition.[2]

Cooper's fellow "friend of the Indian," Henry David Thoreau, confronted his own conflicts between the oral and written traditions while in the company of his Indian "guides" in *The Maine Woods*. While he delighted to hear "the purely wild and American sound" of his Penobscot and Abenaki companions as they conversed over the campfire, Thoreau was left out of the conversation because of his own illiteracy in Wabanaki language. Like many writers before and after him, the Concord philosopher could only "guess at their subject," imagining the words exchanged by "the Indians":

> These Abenakis gossiped, laughed, and jested, in the language in which Eliot's Indian Bible is written, the language which has been spoken in New England for who shall say how long? These were the sounds that issued from the wigwams of this country before Columbus was born; they have not yet died away; and, with remarkably few exceptions, the language of their forefathers is still copious enough for them. I felt that I stood, or rather lay, as near to the primitive man of America, that night, as any of its discoverers ever did.
>
> In the midst of their conversation, Joe suddenly appealed to me to know how long Moosehead Lake was.[3]

The Penobscot leader Joe Aitteon interrupted Thoreau's romantic reverie, interjecting a Wabanaki question into the narrative space of American colonial fantasy and disrupting Thoreau's "transhistorical escape" with a reference to a specific and contemporary place. Earlier in the evening, the Penobscot and Abenaki hunters had discovered that Thoreau had an obsession with the measures of things that might prove useful in planning their journeys. Disappointingly to Thoreau, his guides were discussing the practicalities of travel, devising a conceptual map of the next day's journey. Thoreau found that these Wabanaki men not only spoke their "Indian language" but had at least rudimentary knowledge of reading and writing. During the same evening, one of the Abenakis, Tahmunt Swasen, asked Joe Aitteon "for a *wighiggin*," a copy of a recent law that recognized unrestricted hunting rights for the "Indians of Maine." Swasen "lived near Sorel," but traveled all over Wabanaki territory, from northern Maine to the Adirondacks, and, as Thoreau saw, he was familiar with all the "Indian names" of the lakes and rivers in the region. Thoreau observed that Swasen "could write his name very well."[4]

Thoreau's most influential journey through the "Maine Woods" was led by Joe Polis, who was not only literate but had brought Penobscot politics to Augusta and Washington and had traveled in New York and Boston. Thoreau admired Polis's social dexterity, remarking, "Thus you have an Indian availing himself cunningly of the advantages of civilization, without losing any of his woodcraft, but proving himself the more successful hunter for it." Polis's literacy, however, posed a challenge to Thoreau's representations of Indian life. Polis, Thoreau knew, would be able to acquire, read, and contest any story he wrote about him.[5]

During Aitteon and Polis's lifetime, literacy emerged as a contentious issue within the Penobscot community at Old Town, and *The Maine Woods* contains a story that Polis told to Thoreau about his role in the dramatic climax of the controversy. Both Polis and the governor, John Neptune, were advocates for education, and, not surprisingly, their position was tied to land. Polis related to Thoreau that "he thought a great deal about education and had recommended it to his tribe," advocating that it was the only "way" they could "keep" their "property." Their opposition, the "anti-school party," was dominated by people who remained loyal to the priest who told his followers they would "go to the bad place at last" if they attended the Protestant-run school. Interestingly, one of the first Protestant teachers at Penobscot was Peter Paul Wzokhilain, the Abenaki preacher (mentioned at the beginning of chapter 1). A tradition recorded by Fanny Eckstrom suggests that some of the Penobscots threatened to throw him in the river for proselytizing. Speaking of his successor, Joe Polis told Thoreau that the Penobscots had previously had a schoolteacher whom they "liked very much," but the Catholic priest had insisted that "they must send him away." Polis related, "The school party, though numerous, were about giving up." To bolster their resolve, Polis "told his side that they must not give up, must hold on, they were the strongest. . . . At length he persuaded them to make a stand." A "liberty pole" had been set up beside the schoolhouse, and the priest had organized a party to take it down. Polis and his followers dressed and painted up "like old time," and launched a mock Indian raid from within their hiding place in a nearby home, bursting in on the priest's faction as they moved to disengage the liberty pole. "There was a great uproar," he related, "and they were about coming to blows, but the priest interfered, saying, 'No war, no war,' and so the pole stands, and the school goes on still."[6]

In the decades after the publication of Thoreau's *Maine Woods,* an educated generation of Wabanaki men began publishing their own books.

These texts focused almost exclusively on bringing the oral tradition to the written word. While Polis's relation Joseph Nicolar published translated oral narratives from Old Town, Wzokhilain's relations Joseph Laurent and Henry Masta, who served as teachers and leaders in their community, published language texts from Odanak that followed directly on Wzokhilain's *Wobanaki Kimzowi Awikhigan,* or Wabanaki teaching book[s]. Nicolar's versions of Penobscot stories reflect the depth and complexity of Native oral traditions and leave much room for nuanced historical and literary interpretation, in stark contrast to the simplistic Wabanaki "myths" and "legends" published by anthropologists and folklorists like Frank Speck and Charles Leland. Nicolar's *awikhigan* takes the form of a grand and sweeping narrative of communal history with interlocking stories rather than that of a collection of individual folktales, which was popular at the time.[7]

Laurent's and Masta's language books were also successful in translating Wabanaki cosmology, demonstrating the continuance of names and stories associated with particular places in communal memory, even for those families who lived in northern villages like Odanak, outside the original home territory. For example, Joseph Laurent's section on place-names in *New Familiar Abenaki and English Dialogues* subtly echoes the journey journals of writers like Aupaumut and Occom and resembles the linguistic maps used by innumerable Wabanaki people as they traveled in their home country. Rather than a random listing of place-names, it reads like a journey map through Wabanaki space. Laurent starts out at Montreal, the city closest to the "village" of Odanak, and travels to the north, telling us the Abenaki names for cities, villages, and rivers, along with the names for the people who dwell there, whether French or Indian.[8] He then moves west of the village, naming the Mohawk town of Kaanawagi (Kahnawake) and the city of Ottawa, along with the Abenaki names for the Haudenosaunee *(Magua)* and the "inhabitants of Ottawa" *(Otawaiiak).* Then he turns to the south and essentially maps out the territory of Wabanaki, traveling from Koattegok (Coaticook, in southern Canada), to Mamlawbagak (Lake Memphremagog) in northern Vermont to Paliten (Burlington, on Lake Champlain) and to the western place of Salatogi (Saratoga, New York). From the mineral springs of Nebizonbik (Saratoga Springs) Laurent turns back toward the east and the long river, Kwenitegw, then continues into the interior, up into Koasek territory, where one can portage from the river Passumpsic to the river Winoski,

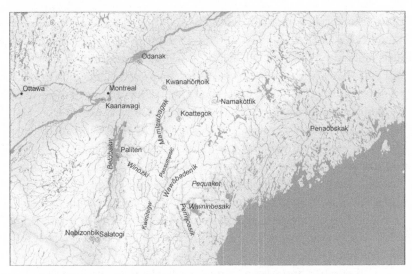

Map 15. Laurent's map, demonstrating a conceptual map of Wabanaki
space, showing the locations of the places mentioned by Laurent.

then travel back to Betobakw (Lake Champlain), or turn east to the
waters of Pemijoasik (the Pemigewasset River) and Wiwninbesaki (Lake
Winnepesaukee), which lead us directly into the sanctuary of the White
Mountains, or Wawôbadenik. Although not fully documented by historians, all of these places are well known in Abenaki oral traditions as areas
where families gathered during the nineteenth century.[9] From the mountains where his son Stephen later set up an "Indian store" near the old
village of Pequaket, Joseph Laurent continues north, traveling upriver
through Wigwômadensisek (St. Hyacinth) and Wigwômadenik (Yamaska)
to Kwanahômoik, or Durham, Quebec, where Abenakis had a hunting reserve, then on to Namakôttik (Megantic), another tradtional Abenaki community, and finally following old riverside trails south into Penaôbskak
territory in the east, which Abenakis recognized as the territory of the
Penaôbskaiiak, or "People (Indians) of Penobscot." All of these place-
names stand out in Laurent's listing as places where Abenaki people live, as
continuing Abenaki space, as part of a conceptual map of the territory that
continued in the language long after Americans claimed these spaces as
their own. This was the map Thoreau got a glimpse of in *The Maine Woods*
in the discussion of place-names, in Swasen's familiarity with this larger
territory of home, and in the dialogue between Wabanaki hunters, all of
which revealed the continual use of the land for subsistence and the con-

tinuing travel through waterways to rekindle relationships with people and places. The language was the map that Wabanaki families used in returning to and traveling through the space they still recognized as home.[10]

But Laurent does not stop here. Expanding from this center, he continues to the land of the Pastonkiak, otherwise known as Americans or "Boston" people (those who originated in a village known as Boston, then got way out of control), to Europe with its various nations, and then to "the globe." It becomes clear that the Abenaki language has come to encompass all of "Earth, the world" as *aki,* and, like William Apess, Laurent uses the inclusive form of "we" to describe "our earth," "our ground," as *kdakinna,* a land that contains all. However, Laurent also includes a conceptualization of land that denotes bounded space (or even property), *n'daki,* meaning "my land," or "my farm," and an explanation of the inclusive and exclusive "we" (which appears in the pages that follow the section on place-names). *Ndakinna,* therefore, represents an understanding of "our land," Abenaki land, as a bounded, exclusive space. The language itself contains multiple intertwined understandings of land as the common pot of the village, inhabited by a particular people, whether it refers to the village of Ottawa, Odanak, or Kahnawake; the common pot of the world, *kdakinna,* in which we are all interacting and affecting each other; the common pot of Abenaki space, *ndakinna,* Native land, which is inclusive of the concepts of indigeneity and sovereignty; and the common pot of Wabanaki, which can mean, interchangeably, Wabanaki land or Wabanaki people and suggests not merely the land itself, or even all of its inhabitants, but a particular way of seeing and being in the land that is the Wabanaki "world."[11]

As Wzokhilain, Nicolar, Masta, and Laurent recorded place-names, stories, and vocabularies in writing, they were, perhaps unknowingly, producing maps of Wabanaki space for communal use. The language is currently in the midst of regeneration, and as families have gathered together on the waterways of northern New England and southern Quebec, they have passed around photocopies of these language texts, marked with notes in script drawn from other sources, both oral and written, both private and public, from family conversations and language classes, from university archives and tribal records, engaging in an exchange of *awikhiganak* that mirrors that first circulation of birchbark prayers witnessed by Le Clercq and enacting, in both word and deed, a reclamation of the geographic, social, and linguistic space of the common pot.[12]

For families who have remained in New England and retained a sense of the larger space of Wabanaki but lost the knowledge of the language, its return has been particularly powerful. Abenaki poet Cheryl Savageau relates that, for her, relearning the language has been an experience of "reclaiming an internal landscape, which itself comes from the land," drawn from generations of living in Wabanaki. This move to reclaim the language within the community is not an act motivated by "preservationist" goals but arises from "the struggle to articulate our experience in a language that doesn't have the words.... When you're struggling to find those words to articulate your experience of the world, and then you find a word or phrase in the language that encapsulates it, it's like a relief, like coming home."[13]

Origin Stories

In Arthur Parker's communal recording of the Sky Woman story, the birth of the two brothers and the death of their mother is followed by a critical transformation in Haudenosaunee space:

> Good Mind watched at the grave of his mother and watered the earth above it until the grass grew. He continued to watch until he saw strange buds coming out of the ground. Where the feet were the earth sprouted with a plant that became the stringed-potato, where her fingers lay sprang the beans, where her abdomen lay sprang the squash, where her breasts lay sprang the corn plant, and from the spot above her forehead sprang the tobacco plant. Now the warty one was named Evil Mind, and he neglected his mother's grave and spent his time tearing up the land and seeking to do evil. When the grandmother saw the plants springing up from the grave of her daughter and cared for by Good Mind she was thankful and said, "By these things we shall hereafter live, and they shall be cooked in pots with fire, and the corn shall be your milk and sustain you. You shall make the corn grow in hills like breasts, for from the corn shall flow our living."[14]

Parker's rendering marked the first appearance of Sky Woman's daughter as a generator of corn in a published version of the Haudenosaunee story. Likewise, the Wabanaki version of the corn mother story appeared in print for the first time in Joseph Nicolar's *Life and Traditions of the Red Man*. In his telling of the creation narrative, the First Mother came into the world proclaiming:

I have come to stay, and I have brought all the color of life on my brow; Love is mine, and I will give it unto you, and if you will love me, as I love you, and grant my wish, all the world will love me, even the beast will love me, and will steal my body because they love it. Strength is mine, and those who can reach me will get it. Peace is mine and I will bring content to the heart that seeks it; but woe unto the man, who does not heed its power, he is a brute. There will be many seventy times seven persons who shall share in it, therefore keep it pure. Because I have no other place to go, and I know no other but you. I have come; I am young in age and I am tender, yet my strength is great and I shall be felt all over the world, because I owe my existence to the beautiful plant of the earth.[15]

After many cycles of time passed, the husband of the First Mother noticed a transformation in her state of mind. She was "very much agitated and her action gave much alarm; nothing seemed to give her relief, and she showed a discontented mind day after day." One evening, as he stood with her watching the sun set in the sky, the children of the First Mother came to her saying, "We are in hunger and the night will soon come; where is the food? Upon hearing this," Nicolar related, "Water came from the woman's eyes, seven drops came and dropped upon the earth. The man reached forth his right hand and wiped away the tears from the woman's brow. It moved him so much that his hand shook. Seeing this the woman said to the little ones, 'Hold your peace little ones, in seven moons you shall be filled and shall hunger no more.'"[16]

The husband pledged to do anything in his power to restore the First Mother's happiness, and after a long deliberation, she told him that he must "take the stone implement, with it slay me unto death." Her husband, knowing her deep grief, reluctantly consented to her request. She gave him special instructions on how to treat and tend her body, and after "seven moons" he found growing from her flesh corn, enough to feed all of her children, and from her bones grew tobacco, which would "give strength" to their thoughts. The husband shared her message with all of the people, telling them, "As we are all brothers, divide among you the flesh and bone of the first mother, and let all shares be alike, then the love of your first mother will have been fully carried out."[17]

From the conflict between two seemingly contradictory brothers grew the three sisters — corn, beans, and squash — from the body of their mother. Out of the great need of the people grew the corn and tobacco from the flesh and bones of their mother to feed hungry bodies and strengthen anxious minds. Both stories mark transformations of Native space through the body of a woman, known in Abenaki as Nigawes, "our mother," the common pot that births and feeds us all. Indigenous writing, like corn, emerged from within Native space out of a great need. Native languages contain the map of the common pot, but writing in English is the means through which its boundaries have been maintained, asserted, and reclaimed. The oral and written traditions have become interrelated and intertwined, not in a contest between two brothers diametrically opposed but in a manner that reflects the relationship between the three sisters of the northeastern tradition, each contributing to the sustenance and growth of the other and reliant on their interdependence for the continuance of the whole.[18]

> She picked up the charred sticks
> and then drew on the bark,
> drew all the lost stories,
> the old life of her tribe.
>
> It's that way for us all,
> we must find the old fires
> before we can draw
> out the tales of our tribes.
>
> Then the Dreamtime will find us
> in those stories that draw us
> in those stories that shape us
> and give us back our names.
>
> —JOSEPH BRUCHAC, excerpt from
> "The Paperbark Tree"

Notes

Introduction

1. Louise Erdrich, *Books and Islands in Ojibwe Country* (Washington, D.C.: National Geographic Society, 2003), 5, 11.

2. Leslie Marmon Silko, *Yellow Woman and a Beauty of the Spirit* (New York: Simon and Schuster, 1997), 21, 157. Note that this is also true of ancient Greek; the root word, *graphos,* denotes "(something) drawn or written." See "-graph," *Webster's College Dictionary* (New York: Random House, 1996), 566.

3. Joseph Aubery and Stephen Laurent, *Father Aubery's French Abenaki Dictionary* (Portland: Chisholm Brothers, 1995), 341; Gordon M. Day, *Western Abenaki Dictionary* (Hull, Quebec: Canadian Museum of Civilization, 1994), 1: 50; Joseph Laurent, *New Familiar Abenaki and English Dialogues* (Quebec: L. Brousseau, 1884), 61–62, 93, 500.

4. Craig S. Womack, *Red on Red: Native American Literary Separatism* (Minneapolis: University of Minnesota Press, 1999), 15–16 (emphasis in original).

5. Ellen L. Arnold, ed., *Conversations with Leslie Marmon Silko* (Jackson: University Press of Mississippi, 2000), 66.

6. Womack, *Red on Red,* 2, 16–17 (emphasis in original).

7. As Kanienkehaka scholar Taiaiake Alfred points out, "Onkwehonwe languages are structured on verbs; they communicate through descriptions of movement and activity.... Onkwehonwe recall relationships and responsibilities through languages that symbolize doing." Taiaiake Alfred, *Wasáse: Indigenous Pathways of Action and Freedom* (Peterborough, Ontario: Broadview, 2005), 32.

8. Keith Basso, *Wisdom Sits in Places* (Albuquerque: University of New Mexico Press, 1996), 6.

9. Ibid., 33.

10. Ibid., 45 (emphasis in original).

11. Vine Deloria Jr., *God Is Red: A Native View of Religion* (Golden, Colo.: Fulcrum, 2003), 71, 121; Waziyatawin Angela Wilson, *Remember This! Dakota Decolonization and the Eli Taylor Narratives* (Lincoln: University of Nebraska Press, 2005); Marge Bruchac, "Earthshapers and Placemakers: Algonkian

Indian Stories and the Landscape," in *Indigenous Archaeologies: Decolonising Theory and Practice,* ed. H. Martin Wobst and Claire Smith (London: Routledge, 2005).

12. Deloria, *God Is Red,* Wilson, *Remember This!* 31; Basso, *Wisdom Sits in Places,* 31.

13. Basso, *Wisdom Sits in Places,* 32–33.

14. Peter Kalifornsky, *K'tl'egh'i Sukdu: A Dena'ina Legacy* (Fairbanks: Alaska Native Language Center, 1991), xvi, 454–55. Special thanks to Jenny Davis, who introduced me to Kalifornsky through her outstanding senior thesis. Wilson, *Remember This!* 23; Greg Sarris, *Keeping Slug Woman Alive: A Holistic Approach to American Indian Texts* (Berkeley: University of California Press, 1993), 30. Such theories intersect with many of those in spatial and postcolonial studies, particularly with the notion that nothing is outside; people and places cannot be viewed from "the outside." As Timothy Mitchell argues in *Colonising Egypt,* "Believing in an 'outside world,' beyond the exhibition... the modern individual is under a new and more subtle enchantment. The inert objectness of this world is an effect of its ordering, of its setting up as though it were an exhibition, a setup which makes there appear to exist apart from such 'external reality' a transcendent entity called culture, a code or text or cognitive map by whose mysterious existence 'the world' is lent its 'significance.'" Mitchell's words correspond with Leslie Marmon Silko's critique of the term "landscape," which is, she writes, "misleading" because it "assume[s] the viewer is somehow outside or separate from the territory he or she surveys. Viewers are as much a part of the landscape as the boulders they stand on." My own use of the word "landscape" should be interpreted in line with Silko's refined definition. Timothy Mitchell, *Colonising Egypt* (Berkeley: University of California Press, 1991), 62; Silko, *Yellow Woman,* 27.

15. Robert Warrior, *The People and the Word* (Minneapolis: University of Minnesota Press, 2005), xiv (emphasis mine); Basso, *Wisdom Sits in Places,* 38.

16. Linda Tuhiwai Smith, *Decolonizing Methodologies: Research and Indigenous Peoples* (London: Zed, 1999), 28 (emphasis in original).

17. Simon Ortiz, "Towards a National Indian Literature: Cultural Authenticity in Nationalism," *MELUS* 8, no. 2 (Summer 1981): 8.

18. Ibid., 10. Ortiz's ideas correspond to those of postcolonial scholar Bill Ashcroft, who argues for understanding the term "resistance" in a framework of transformation rather than a binary of opposition and domination. He writes, "Transformation describes the ways in which colonized societies have taken dominant discourse, transformed them and used them in the service of their own self-empowerment... [and] the ways in which [they] have transformed the very nature of the cultural power that has dominated them. This is nowhere more obvious than in literary and other representational arts, but it remains a strategic feature of all cultural practice." Bill Ashcroft, *On Post-Colonial Futures* (New York: Continuum, 2001), 1.

19. Daniel Justice, "Not Just Shoveling Smoke: Indigenous Literary Nationalism and the Rhetorics of Recognition," paper delivered at the conference Native American Literature: Nationalism and Beyond, Institute of Native American Studies, University of Georgia, Athens, April 21, 2006.

20. Robert Warrior, *Tribal Secrets: Recovering American Indian Intellectual Traditions* (Minneapolis: University of Minnesota Press, 1995), 2.

21. See Jace Weaver, *That the People Might Live: Native American Literatures and Native American Community* (New York: Oxford University Press, 1997), 38–43 (emphasis in original); Warrior, *Tribal Secrets,* xix–xx, 119–22.

22. Womack, *Red on Red,* 1–5. See also Wilson, *Remember,* 42, 46–47.

23. Daniel Justice, *Our Fire Survives the Storm: A Cherokee Literary History* (Minneapolis: University of Minnesota Press, 2006), 7.

24. Siobhan Senier, "'All This/Is Abenaki Country': Cheryl Savageau's Poetic Awikhigan," paper presented at the American Indian workshop Place in Native American History, Literature and Culture, University of Swansea, Wales, March 2006. *early scholar*

25. William Apess, *On Our Own Ground: The Complete Writings of William Apess, a Pequot,* ed. Barry O'Connell (Amherst: University of Massachusetts Press, 1992); Joanna Brooks, ed., *The Collected Writings of Samson Occom, Mohegan: Literature and Leadership in Eighteenth-Century Native America* (New York: Oxford University Press, 2007); Helen Jaskoski, ed., *Early Native American Writing: New Critical Essays* (New York: Cambridge University Press, 1996); Joseph Johnson, *To Do Good to My Indian Brethren: The Writings of Joseph Johnson, 1751–1776,* ed. Laura J. Murray (Amherst: University of Massachusetts Press, 1998); Bernd Peyer, *The Elders Wrote: An Anthology of Early Prose by North American Indians, 1768–1931* (Berlin: Reimer, 1982), and *The Tutor'd Mind: Indian Missionary-Writers in Antebellum America* (Amherst: University of Massachusetts Press, 1997); A. LaVonne Brown Ruoff, *American Indian Literatures: An Introduction, Bibliographic Review, and Selected Bibliography* (New York: Modern Language Association of America, 1990); Hilary E. Wyss, *Writing Indians: Literacy, Christianity, and Native Community in Early America* (Amherst: University of Massachusetts Press, 2000). See also Arnold Krupat, *The Voice in the Margin: Native American Literature and the Canon* (Berkeley: University of California Press, 1989); David Murray, *Forked Tongues: Speech, Writing, and Representation in North American Indian Texts* (Bloomington: Indiana University Press, 1991); Margaret Szasz, *Between Indian and White Worlds: The Cultural Broker* (Norman: University of Oklahoma Press, 1994), and *Indian Education in the American Colonies, 1607–1783* (Albuquerque: University of New Mexico Press, 1988); and Cheryl Walker, *Indian Nation: Native American Literature and Nineteenth-Century Nationalisms* (Durham, N.C.: Duke University Press, 1997).

26. Maureen Konkle, *Writing Indian Nations: Native Intellectuals and the Politics of Historiography* (Chapel Hill: University of North Carolina Press, 2004),

27, 7, 34. Konkle builds on the work of Vine Deloria Jr. and David Wilkins, as well as Robert Warrior, Jace Weaver, and Craig Womack.

27. See, for instance, Konkle's critique of Arnold Krupat in *Writing Indian Nations*, 28–29, 35.

28. Konkle, *Writing Indian Nations*, 2, 6; Lee Maracle, "Beyond Myth and Legend: Looking at Oratory from Beyond Story," paper presented at The Politics of Intangible Cultural Heritage conference, Harvard University, Cambridge, Mass., May 4–6, 2006; Womack, *Red on Red*, 31.

29. Peyer, *Tutor'd Mind*, 5; Alfred, *Wasáse*, 29.

30. Womack, *Red on Red*, 26.

31. Warrior, *People and the Word*, xvii.

32. See Colin G. Calloway, *After King Philip's War: Presence and Persistence in Indian New England* (Hanover, N.H.: University Press of New England, 1997), and *The Western Abenakis of Vermont, 1600–1800: War, Migration, and the Survival of an Indian People* (Norman: University of Oklahoma Press, 1990); Colin G. Calloway and Neal Salisbury, eds., *Reinterpreting New England Indians and the Colonial Experience* (Boston: Colonial Society of Massachusetts, 2003); Amy Den Ouden, *Beyond Conquest: Native Peoples and the Struggle for History in New England* (Lincoln: University of Nebraska Press, 2005); Robert Steven Grumet, ed., *Northeastern Indian Lives, 1632–1816* (Amherst: University of Massachusetts Press, 1996); Evan Haefeli and Kevin Sweeney, *Captors and Captives: The 1704 French and Indian Raid on Deerfield* (Amherst: University of Massachusetts Press, 2003); Daniel R. Mandell, *Behind the Frontier: Indians in Eighteenth-Century Eastern Massachusetts* (Lincoln: University of Nebraska Press, 1996); Jean M. O'Brien, *Dispossession by Degrees: Indian Land and Identity in Natick, Massachusetts, 1650–1790* (Cambridge: Cambridge University Press, 1997). Two earlier landmarks are William Cronon, *Changes in the Land: Indians, Colonists, and the Ecology of New England* (New York: Hill and Wang, 1983), and Neal Salisbury, *Manitou and Providence: Indians, Europeans, and the Making of New England, 1500–1643* (New York: Oxford University Press, 1982).

33. See, for instance, Joseph Bruchac, *Dawn Land* (Golden, Colo.: Fulcrum, 1993), *Hidden Roots* (New York: Scholastic Press, 2004), and *Ndakinna: New and Selected Poems* (Albuquerque: West End, 2003); Marge Bruchac, "Earthshapers"; Calloway and Salisbury, *Reinterpreting*; Richard G. Carlson, ed., *Rooted Like the Ash Trees: New England Indians and the Land* (Naugatuck, Conn.: Eagle Wing, 1987); Thomas L. Doughton, "Unseen Neighbors: Native Americans of Central Massachusetts: A People Who Had 'Vanished,'" in Calloway, *After King Philip's War*; Melissa Fawcett [Tantaquidgeon Zobel], *The Lasting of the Mohegans* (Uncasville, Conn.: Mohegan Tribe, 1995), and *Medicine Trail: The Life and Lessons of Gladys Tantaquidgeon* (Tucson: University of Arizona Press, 2000); Daniel N. Paul, *We Were Not the Savages* (Black Point, Nova Scotia: Fernwood, 2000); Ruth Wallis Herndon and Ella Wilcox Sekatau,

"The Right to a Name: The Narragansett People and Rhode Island Officials in the Revolutionary Era," in Calloway, *After King Philip's War;* and Cheryl Savageau, *Dirt Road Home* (Willimantic, Conn.: Curbstone, 1995), *Mother/land* (Cambridge, Mass.: Salt, 2006), and *Muskrat Will Be Swimming* (Gardiner, Me.: Tilbury House, 2006).

34. Womack *Red on Red,* 4–5.

35. Tuhiwai Smith, *Decolonizing Methodologies,* 29–30.

36. Jonathan Boyarin, *Remapping Memory: The Politics of Time-Space* (Minneapolis: University of Minnesota Press, 1994), 11.

37. Donald Pease and Robyn Wiegman, eds., *The Futures of American Studies* (Durham, N.C.: Duke University Press, 2002).

38. Konkle, *Writing Indian Nations,* 2–3.

39. Ibid., 2, 7; Chadwick Allen, *Blood Narrative: Indigenous Identity in American Indian and Maori Literary and Activist Texts* (Durham, N.C.: Duke University Press, 2002), 4.

40. Ashcroft, *On Post-Colonial Futures,* 8, 20–21. See also R. Radhakrishnan, "Postmodernism and the Rest of the World," in *The Pre-Occupation of Postcolonial Studies,* ed. Fawzia Afzal-Khan and Kelpana Seshadri-Crooks (Durham, N.C.: Duke University Press, 2000), 47, 40. Although many have taken issue with the application of the word *postcolonial* to Native America, Ashcroft's particular definition of the phrase seems applicable: "If we understand the post-colonial to mean the discourse of the colonized, rather than a discourse post-dating colonialism, then post-colonial analysis becomes that which examines the full range of responses to colonialism, from absolute complicity to violent rebellion and all variations in between" (p. 19).

41. Tuhiwai Smith, *Decolonizing Methodologies,* 34.

42. David Harvey, *Justice, Nature, and the Geography of Difference* (Cambridge, England: Blackwell, 1996), 306.

1. *Alnôbawôgan, Wlôgan, Awikhigan*

1. Peter Paul Wzokhilain, *Wobanaki Kimzowi Awighigan* (Boston: Crocker and Brewster, 1830); Chrestien LeClercq, *New Relation of Gaspesia* (Toronto: Champlain Society, 1910), 88. The term *Wabanaki* refers to the related "dawnland" peoples, including the "Western" Abenakis (of present-day Vermont, New Hampshire, and Southern Quebec) and the "Eastern" Abenakis (of present-day Maine and the Maritimes), comprised of the Penobscot, Passamaquoddy, Mi'kmaq, and Maliseet. *Abenaki* commonly refers to Western Abenaki peoples. Wabanakis are part of the larger group of Algonquian language speakers.

2. Arthur Caswell Parker, *Seneca Myths and Folk Tales* (Lincoln: University of Nebraska Press, 1989), 62. For a more recent telling, see Joanne Shenandoah and Douglas M. George, *Skywoman: Legends of the Iroquois* (Santa Fe: Clear Light, 1998).

3. Lytwyn notes that agreements referencing the land as a shared dish, bowl, or kettle "have been used since time immemorial" and "have been preserved in oral traditions, wampum belts, and written records." Although it predated colonial settlement, the concept appears more frequently in the written record "after 1701." Victor P. Lytwyn, "A Dish with One Spoon: The Shared Hunting Grounds Agreement in the Great Lakes and St. Lawrence Valley Region," in *Papers of the Twenty-Eighth Algonquian Conference*, ed. David H. Pentland (Winnipeg: University of Manitoba, 1997). *Wliwni* to Marge Bruchac for recommending this article.

4. Joseph Laurent, *New Familiar Dialogues* (Quebec: L. Brousseau, 1884), 61.

5. Cecile Wawanolett, personal communication with the author during her Abenaki Language class, spring 1993, Mazipskoik. *Wliwni* to John Moody for further clarification of the linguistic relationships.

6. Arthur Caswell Parker, "The Constitution of the Five Nations," in *Parker on the Iroquois*, ed. William Fenton (Syracuse: Syracuse University Press, 1968), 32.

7. Roger Williams, *A Key into the Language of America* (Boston: George Dexter, 1643), 16.

8. Samuel Hopkins, *Historical Memoirs, Relating to the Housatunnuk Indians* (Boston: S. Kneeland, 1753), 12.

9. Neal Salisbury, *Manitou and Providence: Indians, Europeans, and the Making of New England, 1500–1643* (New York: Oxford University Press, 1982), 42; Kenneth M. Morrison, *The Embattled Northeast: The Elusive Ideal of Alliance in Abenaki–Euramerican Relations* (Berkeley: University of California Press, 1984), 65–66. See also Joseph Bruchac, *The Faithful Hunter: Abenaki Stories* (Greenfield Center, N.Y.: Greenfield Review Press, 1988), and *The Wind Eagle and Other Abenaki Stories* (Greenfield Center, N.Y.: Bowman Books, 1985), and William A. Haviland and Marjory W. Power, *The Original Vermonters: Native Inhabitants, Past and Present* (Hanover, N.H.: University Press of New England, 1994), 200. On the Haudenosaunee creation story, see chapter 3.

10. Morrison, *Embattled Northeast*, 69; Ruben Gold Thwaites, ed., *The Jesuit Relations and Allied Documents*, 73 vols. (Cleveland: Burrows Brothers, 1896–1901), 1: 173.

11. Williams, *A Key into the Language of America*, 59.

12. LeClercq, *New Relation of Gaspesia*, 106.

13. Williams, *A Key into the Language of America*, 118.

14. Karim M. Tiro, *Words and Deeds: Natives, Europeans, and Writing in Eastern North America, 1500–1850: An Exhibition* (Philadelphia: Rosenbach Museum and Library, 1997), 7.

15. LeClercq, *New Relation of Gaspesiav*, 135.

16. Ibid., 130. See also G. Malcolm Lewis, ed., *Cartographic Encounters: Perspectives on Native American Mapmaking and Map Use* (Chicago: University of Chicago Press, 1998); David L. Schmidt and Murdena Marshall, *Mi'kmaq*

Hieroglyphic Prayers: Readings in North America's First Indigenous Script (Halifax, Nova Scotia: Nimbus, 1995); and William F. Ganong's introduction to LeClercq's *New Relation of Gaspesia,* 1–41.

17. LeClercq, *New Relation of Gaspesia,* 126.

18. Thwaites, *Jesuit Relations,* 38: 27. Both *Gaspesia* and *Gaspe* are corruptions of the Mi'kmaq word *Kespek.* Daniel Paul, "Mi'kmaq Territory," http://www.danielpaul.com/Map-Mi'kmaqTerritory.html (accessed January 3, 2007).

19. LeClercq, *New Relation of Gaspesia,* 136.

20. Ganong, "Introduction," 22; Lewis, *Cartographic Encounters,* 2–14; Garrick Mallery, "Picture-Writing of the American Indians," *Bureau of American Ethnology Annual Report* 10 (1889): 330–50; Mark Warhus, *Another America: Native American Maps and the History of Our Land* (New York: St. Martin's Griffin, 1997), 9–16.

21. Parker, "Constitution of the Five Nations," 20, 29, 37, 45, 48; Thwaites, *Jesuit Relations,* 22: 291; Mallery, "Picture-Writing," 32; David Murray, *Indian Giving: Economies of Power in Indian–White Exchanges* (Amherst: University of Massachusetts Press, 2000), 120–21, 133–35.

22. Lewis, *Cartographic Encounters,* 2, 11.

23. Gordon M. Day, *Western Abenaki Dictionary* (Hull, Quebec: Canadian Museum of Civilization, 1994), 50; Lewis, *Cartographic Encounters,* 11. See also Warhus, *Another America.*

24. Indian Petition to the General Assembly, 1747 April 1, Ayer Ms. 423, Edward E. Ayer Manuscript Collection, Newberry Library, Chicago. New Hampshire and Massachusetts had only recently resolved their boundary dispute, which included the towns they claimed on the upper Connecticut River. The writers, who could have been quite aware of the conflict, may have intentionally left the name of the province blank in order to satirize the colonists' obsessions with boundaries and property claims.

25. Ibid.

26. George Aldrich, *Walpole as It Was and as It Is* (Claremont, N.H.: Claremont Manufacturing Co., 1880), 9; Elizabeth Chilton, Tonya B. Largy, and Kathryn Curran, "Evidence for Prehistoric Maize Horticulture at the Pine Hill Site, Deerfield, Massachusetts," *Northeast Anthropology* 59 (2000): 23–24; Elizabeth Chilton, "'Towns They Have None': Diverse Subsistence and Settlement Strategies in Native New England," *Northeast Subsistence-Settlement Change, A.D. 700–1300,* ed. John P. Hart and Christina B. Rieth (Albany: New York State Museum, 2002); Edith De Wolfe et al., eds., *The History of Putney, Vermont, 1753–1953* (Putney, Vt.: The Fortnightly Club of Putney, Vt., 1953); Michael J. Heckenberg, James B. Petersen, and Nancy Asch Sidell, "Early Evidence of Maize Agriculture in the Connecticut River Valley of Vermont," *Archaeology of Eastern North America* 10 (1992): 125; Evan Haefeli and Kevin Sweeney, "Revisiting *The Redeemed Captive:* New Perspectives on the 1704 Attack on Deerfield," in Colin G. Calloway, *After King Philip's War: Presence and*

Persistence in Indian New England (Hanover, N.H.: University Press of New England, 1997), 37; Westmoreland History Committee, *The History and Genealogy of Westmoreland, New Hampshire* (Westmoreland: Westmoreland History Committee, 1976), 7; Frederick Matthew Wiseman, *The Voice of the Dawn: An Autohistory of the Abenaki Nation* (Hanover, N.H.: University Press of New England, 2001), 197–98. For Sokwakik history, see Colin G. Calloway, *The Western Abenakis of Vermont, 1600–1800: War, Migration, and the Survival of an Indian People* (Norman: University of Oklahoma Press, 1990); Gordon M. Day, *The Identity of the Saint Francis Indians* (Ottawa: National Museums of Canada, 1981); Haviland and Power, *The Original Vermonters*.

27. Evan Haefeli and Kevin Sweeney, *Captors and Captives: The 1704 French and Indian Raid on Deerfield* (Amherst: University of Massachusetts Press, 2003), 12; Day, *Western Abenaki Dictionary*, 1: 508; Joseph Bruchac, *Roots of Survival* (Golden, Colo.: Fulcrum, 1996), 30.

28. Hendrick Aupaumut, "Extract from an Indian History," *Collections of the Massachusetts Historical Society* 1, no. 9 (1804): 100. Over time, I have consulted a variety of sources on the phonetic spellings of place-names; therefore, my own usage represents an amalgamation, although I have strived for consistency in my spellings of critical morphemes. My sources include Joseph Aubery and Stephen Laurent, *Father Aubery's French Abenaki Dictionary* (Portland: Chisholm Brothers, 1995); Calloway, *Western Abenakis*; Gordon M. Day, *Identity of the Saint Francis Indians, Western Abenaki Dictionary*, "The Eastern Boundary of Iroquoia: Abenaki Evidence," *Man in the Northeast* 1 (1971), and "The Name Contoocook," *International Journal of American Linguistics* 27, no. 2 (1961); Laurent, *New Familiar Dialogues*; Henry Lorne Masta, *Abenaki Indian Legends, Grammar and Place Names* (Victoriaville, Quebec: La Voix des Bois-Francs, 1932); Wzokhilain, *Wobanaki Kimzowi Awighigan*; and Marge Bruchac, "Pocumtuck History in Deerfield: Homeland, Trade, and Diaspora," unpublished manuscript held by the author. My rendering of the language has also been influenced by classes with Cecile Wawanolet, study with Cheryl Savageau, and conversations with Marge Bruchac and John Moody, as well as dialogue with other Abenaki people over the years. I am grateful to them for sharing this project of language revitalization with me. Any mistakes in orthography are my own.

29. Cheryl Savageau, *Mother/land* (Cambridge, England: Salt, 2006), 15. The "Legend of the Great Beaver as related by a Pocumtuck Indian" is recorded in Katharine Abbott, *Old Paths of the New England Border* (New York: Putnam, 1907), 163–64. See also Marge Bruchac, "Earthshapers and Placemakers: Algonkian Indian Stories and the Landscape," in *Indigenous Archaeologies: Politics and Practice*, ed. Claire Smith and Martin Wobst (New York: Routledge, 2005). *Wliwni* to Cheryl and Marge for bringing this story home and for careful readings of this chapter and to Marge for linguistic reconstruction of the name of the Great Beaver formation.

30. Calloway, *Western Abenakis*, 41–42, 61–62; Patrick Frazier, *The Mohicans of Stockbridge* (Lincoln: University of Nebraska Press, 1992), 4–5; George Hunt, *The Wars of the Iroquois* (Madison: University of Wisconsin Press, 1940); Peter Thomas, *In the Maelstrom of Change* (New York: Garland Publishing, 1990), 149–51; Bruce Trigger, *Natives and Newcomers* (Kingston: McGill–Queen's University Press, 1985), 177.

31. Calloway, *Western Abenakis*, 65; Haviland and Power, *The Original Vermonters*, 151; Hunt, *Wars of the Iroquois*, 33; Haefeli and Sweeney, "Revisiting *The Redeemed Captive*," 50; Thomas, *Maelstrom of Change*, 49. Note that the Haudenosaunee also gained access to the abundant resources of this area by exacting tribute from Pocumtucks, Sokwakik, and other Kwinitekw peoples, which would "protect" them from further raiding.

32. Gordon M. Day, *Identity of the Saint Francis Indians*, and "The Ouragie War: A Case History in Iroquois–New England Indian Relations," in *Extending the Rafters: Interdisciplinary Approaches to Iroquoian Studies*, ed. Michael K. Foster, Jack Campisi, and Marianne Mithun (Albany: SUNY Press, 1984), 40–41; Thomas, *Maelstrom of Change*, 211; Calloway, *Western Abenakis*, 70–73; Haefeli and Sweeney, *Captors and Captives*, 14–15; Neal Salisbury, "Toward the Covenant Chain: Iroquois and Southern New England Algonquians, 1637–1684," in *Beyond the Covenant Chain*, ed. Daniel Richter and James Merrell (Syracuse: Syracuse University Press, 1987).

33. Calloway, *Western Abenakis*, 73; Haefeli and Sweeney, "Revisiting *The Redeemed Captive*," 58; Bruchac, "Earthshapers and Placemakers," 13; Bruchac, "Pocumtuck History in Deerfield." Note that these settlers were "given" Deerfield in compensation for their lands at "Dedham," to make room for John Eliot's "praying village" for Indians at Natick. See Haefeli and Sweeney, *Captors and Captives*, 15–19.

34. Salisbury, "Toward the Covenant Chain," 65. On the Penacook context, see Colin G. Calloway, "Wanalancet and Kancagamus: Indian Strategy and Leadership on the New Hampshire Frontier," *Historical New Hampshire* 43, no. 4 (1988); Jere Daniell, *Colonial New Hampshire: A History* (Millwood, N.Y.: KTO Press, 1981), 10–13; and John Pendergast, *The Bend in the River* (Tyngsborough, Mass.: Merrimac River Press, 1992), 50–65. News also would have traveled upriver of the infamous attack on the Pequot village (see chapter 2), the restrictive laws passed against Indians in the Massachusetts Bay Colony (see chapter 4), the increasing English encroachment on Narragansett and Wampanoag lands, and the impact of large-scale logging on the coastal forests. See William Cronon, *Changes in the Land: Indians, Colonists, and the Ecology of New England* (New York: Hill and Wang, 1983).

35. Harry Andrew Wright, *Indian Deeds of Hampden County* (Springfield, Mass.: 1905), 74.

36. Marge Bruchac, personal communication. Bruchac has also noted that Mashalisk and other *Kwinitekw* natives who signed deeds during this period

reserved "Indian hunting, fishing, gathering, and camping rights." Bruchac, "Pocumtuck History in Deerfield," 2.

37. Morrison, *Embattled Northeast*, 29.

38. Haefeli and Sweeney use the term "Anglo–Abenaki Wars" to describe the Abenaki–English front of the wars most often referred to as King Philip's War, King William's War, Queen Anne's War, and Greylock's, Lovewell's, or Dummer's War. Although they were often associated with imperial wars that originated in Europe, in an Abenaki context these were "overlapping war[s] fought to resist English invasion of their lands." Haefeli and Sweeney *Captors and Captives*, 2.

39. Wright, *Indian Deeds*, 120–33; Haefeli and Sweeney, *Captors and Captives*, 15. See also Calloway, *Western Abenakis*, and John A. Strong, "Algonquian Women as Sunksquaws and Caretakers of the Soil: The Documentary Evidence in the Seventeenth Century Records," in *Native American Women in Literature and Culture*, ed. Susan Castillo and Victor DaRosa (Porto, Portugal: Fernando Pessoa University Press, 1997).

40. In terms of Abenaki kinship, Francis was Pinewans's brother, not his cousin, because he was Pinewans's mother's sister's son. Note that Francis may be the "Prik Sare" who also signed the petition at Fort No. 2. According to John Moody, this name may be a transliteration of *Plaswa*, an Abenaki form of *Francis*, a common name among Wabanaki families. This particular man may have been Francis Titigar, who captured John Stark (John Moody, personal communication, July 26, 2006).

41. Neal Salisbury, *The Sovereignty and Goodness of God . . . a Narrative of the Captivity and Restoration of Mrs. Mary Rowlandson and Related Documents* (Boston: Bedford Books, 1997), 32, 330; Calloway, *Western Abenakis*, 78–79, 83; Day, *Identity of the Saint Francis Indians*, 19–20; Frazier, *Mohicans of Stockbridge*, 5–6; Haefeli and Sweeney, "Revisiting *The Redeemed Captive*," 37, and *Captors*, 20–21. *Wliwni* to Marge Bruchac for leading a trip to the site and for explaining the significance of Peskeompscut as a protected place.

42. Calloway, *Western Abenakis*, 96; Day, *Identity of the Saint Francis Indians*, 78. Day also relates an account of an "Indian named Choos (or Cohas or Cohause)" who reported to the English the large number of refugee Indians who were being "sheltered by the Mahicans" (Day, *Identity of the Saint Francis Indians*, 19). See also Edmund O'Callaghan, ed., *Documents Relative to the Colonial History of New York*, 15 vols. (Albany: Weed, Parsons, 1855–61) (hereafter NYCD), 3: 715, 380. John Moody has observed that "Chee Hoose" may instead have been "little horse," a "diminuative" that is common in Abenaki families, with "Chee" being a Wabification of the French "petite" (John Moody, personal communication, July 26, 2006). On the relationships between Schaghticoke and Abenaki communities, see also NYCD, 3: 380, 3: 562–65, and 5: 721–23, and 799, and Haefeli and Sweeney, "Revisiting *The Redeemed Captive*."

43. Haviland and Power, *The Original Vermonters*, 200; Thomas, *Maelstrom of Change*, 49; Haefeli and Sweeney, "Revisiting *The Redeemed Captive*," 50.

44. Morrison, *Embattled Northeast*, 31; Haefeli and Sweeney, "Revisiting *The Redeemed Captive*," 58, and *Captors*, 28–29.

45. I draw this phrase from Lytwyn, who cites LeClercq's *Premier établissement de la foy dans la Nouvelle France* (1691) as the first reference in the documentary record. Creating a "kettle of peace" refers to the process through which nations recognize that they inhabit a shared space and commit to the pursuit of peaceful relations, making agreements to "eat from the same kettle" when they "meet up during hunting." When they meet, in hunting parties or formal councils, they will "consider" each other as "brothers" and will "eat together." This denotes a recognition of and respect for shared resources, shared space, and a formalizing of relationships through terms of kinship. However, this does not necessarily mean that the entire territory that they occupy is shared, but may refer to overlapping areas of utilization, areas in which multiple nations have interests, or a recognition that each of their territories constitutes part of a greater whole. Lytwyn, "Dish with One Spoon," 212, 218. There are also a number of references cited by Lytwyn in which Haudenosaunee and Algonquian peoples attempt to incorporate the French and English into the "dish."

46. Jonathan Belcher, *At a Conference Held at Deerfield in the County of Hampshire, the 27th Day of August, 1735* (Boston, 1735). Thanks to the John Carter Brown Library for access to the original publication.

47. Marge Bruchac, "Abenaki Connections to 1704: The Sadoques Family and Deerfield, 2004," in *Captive Histories: English, French, and Native Narratives of the 704 Deerfield Raid*, ed. Evan Haefeli and Kevin Sweeney (Amherst: University of Massachusetts Press, 2006), 262–78; Haefeli and Sweeney, "Revisiting *The Redeemed Captive*," 50, and *Captors and Captives*, 87, 137–41, 148; Calloway, *Western Abenakis*, 104–5; Thomas, *Maelstrom of Change*; Francis Jennings, "Iroquois Alliances in American History," in *The History and Culture of Iroquois Diplomacy*, ed. Francis Jennings and William N. Fenton (Syracuse: Syracuse University Press, 1985). On Williams and Wattanummon, see Haefeli and Sweeney, "Wattanummon's World: Personal and Tribal Identity in the Algonquian Diaspora, c. 1660–1712," in *Papers of the 25th Algonquian Conference* (Ottawa: Carleton University, 1994), 212–24; "Journal of Rev. Stephen Williams," in John Williams, *The Redeemed Captive*, ed. Stephen W. Williams (Northampton: Hopkins, Bridgman, 1853), 149.

48. Joseph Kellogg's brother Martin also became an interpreter and trader. Rebecca later lived at the multitribal community of Oquaga and served as an interpreter. "A Letter from Rev. Gideon Hawley of Marshpee, Containing an Account of His Services among the Indians of Massachusetts and New York . . . ," *Collections of the Massachusetts Historical Society*, 1st ser., 4: 56–57;

Mary R. Cabot, *Annals of Brattleboro*, 2 vols. (Brattleboro, Mass.: E. L. Hindreth, 1921), 1: 12; Calloway, *Western Abenakis*, 119, 138, 278; *Massachusetts Archives* 114: 598, 606; Timothy Hopkins, *The Kelloggs in the Old World and the New* (San Francisco: Sunset Press, 1903), 1: 25–28, 35–38, 63; Haefeli and Sweeney, "Revisiting *The Redeemed Captive*," 52–53, and *Captors and Captives*, 6, 149–57, 195, 224, 261, 266.

49. De Wolfe et al., *History of Putney*, 5; Colin G. Calloway, *Western Abenakis*, 130, 113–31, and "Gray Lock's War," *Vermont History* 54 (Fall 1986): 197–228; Haefeli and Sweeney, *Captors and Captives*, 229–30; NYCD, 5: 721–23, 799, 869–70. Wawanolewat lived until he was an old man, among family at Mazipskoik, the location of which remained unknown to the English leadership throughout his lifetime.

50. Josiah Temple and George Sheldon, *History of the Town of Northfield* (Albany, N.Y.: Joel Munsell, 1875), 199–202; Haefeli and Sweeney, *Captors and Captives*, 230, 265. Frazier describes Stoddard as "the richest and most powerful figure in Western Massachusetts" (Frazier, *Mohicans of Stockbridge*, 14, 19). Haefeli and Sweeney note, "Before the Deerfield raid the English never ranged more than twenty or thirty miles above Deerfield. Now they went as far as Cowass, the shores of Lake Champlain, and even to the banks of the Richelieu River. Deerfield became the western base of operations for scouts and ranging companies." In fact, the geographic knowledge and skills gained by young men during their captivities led to their recruitment as scouts. Haefeli and Sweeney, *Captors and Captives*, 195, 260.

51. *Massachusetts Archives* 29: 187; Cabot, *Annals of Brattleboro*, 10–12; Temple and Sheldon, *History of Northfield*, 206–7; Haefeli and Sweeney, *Captors and Captives*, 212.

52. Calloway, "Gray Lock's War," 213–14, and *Western Abenakis*, 116; Frazier, *Mohicans of Stockbridge*, 9; Sweeney, "Revisiting *The Redeemed Captive*," 50–53, 68.

53. NYCD, 5: 724; *Massachusetts Archives* 29: 173.

54. Haefeli and Sweeney, *Captors and Captives*, 266–68; Daniel Richter, *The Ordeal of the Longhouse* (Chapel Hill: University of North Carolina Press, 1992), 29.

55. Calloway, *Western Abenakis*, 59; Lytwyn, "Dish with One Spoon," 213, 218, 220; Robert W. Venables, "Some Observations on the Treaty of Canadaigua," in *Treaty of Canadaigua 1794*, ed. G. Peter Jemison and Anna M. Schein (Santa Fe: Clear Light Publishing, 2000), 95, 118. Lytwyn and Venables cite both Haudenosaunee and Algonquian explanations of the bowl of beaver tail, which could entail an agreement to hunt in the same space and share the resources equally or an invitation extended by one nation to another to come into their territory to hunt and/or set up camp. Note that Abenakis rejected an invitation from the Fox in 1723 "to go to their country, to eat the beaver's tail there," meaning "to pursue our hunting, and make

our abode there." Their reason, in part, was that they perceived it as a quid-pro-quo offer in which they would be obligated to assist the Fox in their war against "the upper nations," a prospect they abhorred because it "would be... to declare themselves against...their brothers," besides which, they said, they had "another war to sustain, a just and necessary one, against the English." Thwaites, *Jesuit Relations*, 67: 128–31. *Wliwni* to Marge Bruchac for relaying the people's insistence on Deerfield as the meeting place. Belcher had originally proposed Northampton.

56. Greylock's War is also referred to as "Dummer's War" after the Massachusetts colony lieutenant governor William Dummer, who led the campaign to move aggressively into Abenaki territory.

57. Jonathan Belcher, *At a Conference Held at Deerfield in the County of Hampshire, the 27th Day of August, 1735* (Boston: 1735), 2–3.

58. Belcher, *Deerfield Conference*, 8. Haefeli and Sweeney note that the locations of trading posts was a particular "cause for concern as both the French and English sought to increase their influence and presence in the Champlain valley" during the 1730s (Haefeli and Sweeney, *Captors and Captives*, 268).

59. Ken Mynter, "Leaving New England: The Stockbridge Indians," in *Rooted Like the Ash Trees: New England Indians and the Land*, ed. Richard G. Carlson (Naugatuck, Conn.: Eagle Wing Press, 1987), 31. For more on Stockbridge and Mohican participation in the conference, see Frazier, *Mohicans of Stockbridge*, 18–19 and 28–56, and Belcher, *Deerfield Conference*, 10, 15–16.

60. Belcher, *Deerfield Conference*, 7, 16.

61. Sixty-six Schaghticoke "men and women" attended the conference, including most of the twenty-four people who signed the deeds. These included Mascommah, who served at the fort as a lieutenant to Massoqunt. Cabot, *Annals of Brattleboro*, 14; Colin G. Calloway, *Dawnland Encounters: Indians and Europeans in Northern New England* (Hanover, N.H.: University Press of New England, 1991), 161; *Massachusetts Archives* 91: 280; Belcher, *Deerfield Conference*, 1. Both colonial records and town histories support the idea of continual, even if seasonal, occupation of Kwinitekw by the descendants of the Pocumtuck and Sokwakik families who escaped to Schaghticoke after the Peskeompscut massacre. For example, Northfield historian Josiah Temple and George Sheldon related that, following the Deerfield Conference, "for a series of years the Indians had come to trade at the Truck-house, and were free to hunt and rove at pleasure. They lived in all the towns, and went in and out of the houses of settlers — often sleeping at night by the kitchen fire." Temple and Sheldon, *History of Northfield*, 236. See also Aldrich, *Walpole as It Was and Is*, 21–29; Belcher, *Deerfield Conference*, 1 and 16; Calloway, *Western Abenakis*, 83, 96–8, and 103–7; De Wolfe, *History of Putney*, 4; Frazier, *Mohicans of Stockbridge*, 15; Haefeli and Sweeney, "Revisiting *The Redeemed Captive*," 43–45, 51, and 58–59; Temple and Sheldon, *History of Northfield*, 205 and 216; and Wright, *Indian Deeds*, 120–33.

62. Massoqunt's deed covered the large northern expanse from the Green Mountains to Penacook territory, including the Great Meadow and Ktsipôntekw. Wright, *Indian Deeds*, 125–28; *Massachusetts Archives* 31: 191.

63. See Cronon's discussion of usufruct rights in *Changes*, 62–63. For examples in southern New England, see Douglas Edward Leach, *Flintlock and Tomahawk: New England in King Philip's War* (New York: Macmillan, 1958), 15–20; N. Shurtleff, ed., *Plymouth Colony Records* (Boston: William White, 1855), 12: 237; and Margaret Wickens Pearce, "Native Mapping in Southern New England Indian Deeds," in Lewis, *Cartographic Encounters*. For northern New England, see Emerson Baker, "'A Scratch with a Bear's Paw': Anglo–Indian Land Deeds in Early Maine," *Ethnohistory* 36, no. 3 (1989): 235–56. For the importance of gift exchanges and speeches in negotiation, see Salisbury, *Manitou*, 116.

64. *Massachusetts Archives* 91: 280, 29: 333. Note that Kellogg's family ties to Kahnawake were likely influential in his decision to recruit Mohawks from his sister's village to work with him at Fort Dummer.

65. Westmoreland History Committee, *Westmoreland*, 6; Cabot, *Annals of Brattleboro*, 8–9; *Massachusetts Archives* 31: 191. The scheme also included plans to build a line of "defense towns" up the river Molôdemak to the central Penacook village. On parallel developments at Stockbridge, see Frazier, *Mohicans of Stockbridge*, 14, 19, 40–43, 46, 110, and 147.

66. "James Johnson — His Captivity," in *New Hampshire Provincial Papers*, ed. Nathaniel Bouton (Concord: 1867–73) (hereafter NHPP), 6: 330–31; Colin G. Calloway, *North Country Captives: Selected Narratives of Indian Captivity from Vermont and New Hampshire* (Hanover: University Press of New England, 1992), 67; NYCD, 6: 909.

67. Calloway, *North Country Captives*, 48.

68. Temple and Sheldon, *History of Northfield*, 195, 229, 233–34; Calloway, "Gray Lock's War," 214; *Massachusetts Archives* 31: 99; Calloway, *Western Abenakis*, 138; NHPP, 13: 652; Cabot, *Annals of Brattleboro*, 15, 21; Westmoreland History Committee, *Westmoreland*, 6–9; Charles Henry Pope, ed., *Willard Genealogy* (Boston: Willard Family Association, 1915), 4, 26, 34. Josiah Willard was descended from the Indian fighter, trader, and land speculator Samuel Willard, who was notorious among the Penacooks. Samuel's son, the Reverend Joseph Willard, was killed during the same raid that made Phineas Stevens a captive. Josiah Willard brought James Johnson to Fort Dummer from Boston as a ten-year-old Irish servant, and Johnson later relocated to Fort No. 4. Calloway, *North Country Captives*, 47; Temple and Sheldon, *History of Northfield*, 195; Cabot, *Annals of Brattleboro*, 21.

69. Hopkins, *Historical Memoirs*, 77; Electa F. Jones, *Stockbridge, Past and Present; or, Records of an Old Mission Station* (Springfield, Mass.: S. Bowles, 1854), 81.

70. Calloway, *Western Abenakis*, 148; Alexander Hamilton, *Hamilton's Itinerarium*, ed. Albert Bushnell Hart (St. Louis: William K. Bixby, 1907), 137; Haefeli and Sweeney, "Revisiting *The Redeemed Captive*," 55. Note that *Eastern Indians* almost always refers to Wabanaki people; they may have even been Schaghticokes.

71. Calloway, *North Country Captives*, 3–4.

72. Ibid., 14.

73. NYCD, 6: 289–305; Frazier, *Mohicans of Stockbridge*, 73, 75.

74. NYCD, 6: 291, 298.

75. Ibid., 6: 291, 293, 300, 317–26, 366.

76. Calloway, *Western Abenakis*, 153–55; *North Country Captives*, 51; Temple and Sheldon, *History*, 227, 245.

77. The story of the "Great Bull Frog" is told in Maine Indian Program, *The Wabanakis of Maine and the Maritimes: A Resource Book About Penobscot, Passamaquoddy, Maliseet, Micmac, and Abenaki Indians; With Lesson Plans for Grades 4 through 8* (Bath, Me.: American Friends Service Committee, 1989).

78. See Charles Leland, *Algonquin Legends* (New York: Dover, 1992); Bruchac, *Faithful Hunter*; William Apess, *On Our Own Ground: The Complete Writings of William Apess, a Pequot*, ed. Barry O'Connell (Amherst: University of Massachusetts Press, 1992).

79. The petition provides a contrasting narrative to Phineas Stevens's report from Fort No. 4 during the siege, in which he referred to his attackers as "an army of starved Creatures." Calloway, *Western Abenakis*, 155.

80. Ibid., 143.

81. Calloway, *North Country Captives*, 51, *Dawnland Encounters*, 121–26, and *Western Abenakis*, 160–63; *Massachusetts Archives* 31: 99.

82. *Massachusetts Archives* 32: 251–54. On Dwight, see Frazier, *Mohicans of Stockbridge*, 100–106, 110–13, and 147–52.

83. Calloway, *Dawnland Encounters*, 121.

84. Ibid., 122. When four Abenaki leaders visited Stevens at Fort No. 4 in the winter of 1754, they confirmed the words spoken by their chiefs in Montreal and "manifested great uneasiness at our people's going to take a view of Cowass meadows.... For the English to settle Cowass was what they could not agree to." They emphasized that "the English had no need of that land, but had enough without it, they must think the English had a mind for war, if they should go there." Calloway, *Dawnland Encounters*, 123. See also Calloway, *Western Abenakis*, 160–63. Timothy Woodbridge also reported from Stockbridge that at the Albany truckhouse he had spoken with Kahnawake Mohawks, who told him that "the Onuhgungos" (Abenakis) had gone to see the governor of Canada and said, "The English have abus'd us, in driving us from our Lands, and taking them from us." Woodbridge noted that "the Onuhgungos was inhabitants on Connecticut River, formerly drove away as

I take it in Phillips war, are the same originally with the Scatecooks." *Massachusetts Archives* 32: 547.

85. Calloway, *Western Abenakis*, 153; Pendergast, *River's Bend*, 46; NHPP, 583–84; David Stewart-Smith, "The Penacook Indians and the New England Frontier, 1604–1733," Ph.D. diss., Union Institute, 1998, 87, 181–83, 190, 200, 202; Haefeli and Sweeney, "Revisiting *The Redeemed Captive*," 43.

86. NYCD, 5: 663.

87. Hopkins, *Historical Memoirs*, 10.

88. Ibid., 127.

89. Frazier, *Mohicans of Stockbridge*, 14.

90. Belcher, *Deerfield*, 10, 15.

91. Ibid., 8.

92. Hopkins, *Historical Memoirs*, 67; NYCD, 6: 88, 315; Hawley, "Letter"; CMHS, 4: 50.

93. "A Letter from Rev. Jonathan Edwards...Relating to the Indian School at Stockbridge," *Collections of the Massachusetts Historical Society*, 1st ser., 10: 143–53; Hawley, "Letter," 51–54; Frazier, *Mohicans of Stockbridge*, 99–102; *Massachusetts Archives* 31: 290, 32: 251–57. Note that the Mohawks said they were glad to see Pynchon there because of "their acquaintance with his ancestors" ("Letter from Edwards," 143). Joseph Kellogg participated as an interpreter in councils with Old Town and Abraham, while his brother Martin was the Mohawks' schoolmaster for a brief time.

94. NYCD, 6: 315.

95. Wentworth had instituted increasingly high scalp bounties during the war, raising them to 200 pounds per scalp. After the war, Wentworth issued a series of township grants intended to recolonize Abenaki territory, including the former grants on Kwinitekw. NHPP, 5: 231, 375, 441.

96. Calloway, *Western Abenakis*, 164; Haviland and Power, *The Original Vermonters*, 212, 181.

97. Thanks to Susan Morse for sharing her knowledge of beavers and her theory about the longstanding effects of their work. Thanks also to Gordon Russell for bringing her to the Piscataquog and for many extraordinary tracking trips on its waters.

2. Restoring a Dish Turned Upside Down

1. Josiah Temple and George Sheldon, *History of the Town of Northfield* (Albany, N.Y.: Joel Munsell, 1875), 27; Evan Haefeli and Kevin Sweeney, *Captors and Captives: The 1704 French and Indian Raid on Deerfield* (Amherst: University of Massachusetts Press, 2003), 14, 20, 141, 265.

2. Indian Papers 2: 230, Connecticut State Library, Hartford, Connecticut.

3. Melissa Fawcett [Tantaquidgeon Zobel], *The Lasting of the Mohegans* (Uncasville, Conn.: Mohegan Tribe, 1995), 19. Neal Salisbury has discussed

the Narragansett leader Miantonomo's "depiction of a pre-English utopia" in his 1642 call to alliance (discussed later in this chapter) as representative of a real experience "within the memories of most adults." Neal Salisbury, *Manitou and Providence: Indians, Europeans, and the Making of New England, 1500–1643* (New York: Oxford University Press, 1982), 232, 13.

4. Hendrick Aupaumut, "Extract from an Indian History," *Collections of the Massachusetts Historical Society,* 1st ser., 9 (1804): 9–102. My description of "the village" pertains to the larger village "territory," not to the location of a particular village center. See William Cronon, *Changes in the Land: Indians, Colonists, and the Ecology of New England* (New York: Hill and Wang, 1983), 60–62, and William A. Starna, "The Pequots in the Early Seventeenth Century," in *The Pequots in Southern New England,* ed. Laurence M. Hauptman and James D. Wherry (Norman: University of Oklahoma Press, 1990), 36–39, 42. On locations of village sites, see Laurence M. Hauptman, "The Pequot War and Its Legacies," also in Hauptman and Wherry, *The Pequots,* 71, and Kevin A. McBride, "The Historical Archaeology of the Mashantucket Pequots, 1637–1900: A Preliminary Analysis," 97–102, in the same volume.

5. Record of Tribal Meeting, "April 28, 1778," Folder 16: Records of the Mohegan Tribe, Samson Occom Papers, Connecticut Historical Society, Hartford, Connecticut.

6. Frank Speck, "Wawenock Texts from Maine," *Annual Report of the Bureau of American Ethnology, 1925–6* 43 (1928): 195–96; Aupaumut, "Extract"; Lynn Ceci, "Native Wampum as a Peripheral Resource in the Seventeenth-Century World System," in Hauptman and Wherry, *The Pequots;* Colin G. Calloway, *The Western Abenakis of Vermont, 1600–1800: War, Migration, and the Survival of an Indian People* (Norman: University of Oklahoma Press, 1990), 43. Cronon, *Changes in the Land,* 92; Kevin A. McBride, "The Source and Mother of the Fur Trade: Native–Dutch Relations in Eastern New Netherland," in *Enduring Traditions: The Native Peoples of New England,* ed. Laurie Lee Weinstein (Westport, Conn.: Bergin and Garvey, 1994); David Murray, *Indian Giving: Economies of Power in Indian–White Exchanges* (Amherst: University of Massachusetts Press, 2000),116–40; Neal Salisbury, *Manitou and Providence,* 35, 43–49, and 148–50, and "Toward the Covenant Chain: Iroquois and Southern New England Algonquians, 1637–1684," in *Beyond the Covenant Chain,* ed. Daniel Richter and James Merrell (Syracuse: Syracuse University Press, 1987), 61–65; Lois Scozzari, "The Significance of Wampum to Seventeenth-Century Indians in New England," *Connecticut Review* 17, no. 1 (1995): 59–69.

7. Ceci, "Native Wampum," 48–50, 55, 58–59; McBride, "Source and Mother of the Fur Trade," 35; Neal Salisbury, *Manitou and Providence,* 147–50, "Toward the Covenant Chain," 61–65, and "Indians and Colonists in Southern New England after the Pequot War: An Uneasy Balance," in Hauptman and Wherry, *The Pequots,* 88–89, 94; Scozzari, "The Significance of Wampum"; Mashantucket Pequot Research Library, "Connecticut Tribes and Bands

Mentioned in Historical and Contemporary Sources: A Bibliography," http://www.pequotmuseum.org/uploaded_images/8564D213-7519-4055-B791-ADD058B62EA7/ConnecticutIndianTribesPart1.htm (accessed July 18, 2006).

8. William A. Haviland and Marjory W. Power, *The Original Vermonters: Native Inhabitants, Past and Present* (Hanover, N.H.: University Press of New England, 1994), 200; Paul A. Robinson, "Lost Opportunities: Miantonomi and the English in Seventeenth-Century Narragansett Country," in *Northeastern Indian Lives, 1632–1816*, ed. Robert Steven Grumet (Amherst: University of Massachusetts Press, 1996), 14; Salisbury, *Manitou and Providence*, 50–57, 109.

9. Salisbury, *Manitou and Providence*, 147–48; Starna, "The Pequots," 45; Paul A. Robinson, "Lost Opportunities," 18–20, and "A Narragansett History from 1000 B.P. to the Present," in *Enduring Traditions*, 82.

10. Ceci, "Native Wampum," 59; Hauptman, "The Pequot War," 71; Kevin McBride, "Historical Archaeology," 97, "Source and Mother of the Fur Trade," 35–36, and "The Pequot War and Massacre," in Fawcett, *Lasting of the Mohegans*, 13; Michael Leroy Oberg, *Uncas: First of the Mohegans* (Ithaca, N.Y.: Cornell University Press, 2003), 34–39; Salisbury, *Manitou and Providence*, 147–50, 203–4; Starna, "Pequots," 34. The Dutch, at this point, were the most powerful European brokers in the wampum trade. They had an exclusive trade with the Pequots and coerced the English to "stay out of" the trade at "Narragansett Bay." Abenakis were able to acquire wampum through the northern networks that extended into Iroquoia and then to trade it to the English for European goods. Because the Dutch were dominating the trade in southern New England, the English at Plymouth looked north and brought "the 'wampum revolution' to Abenaki country." Salisbury, *Manitou and Providence*, 149–52.

11. Hauptman, "The Pequot War," 71; Oberg, *Uncas*, 39–49; Salisbury, *Manitou and Providence*, 148, 205–11. The sachem was Tatobem.

12. Salisbury, *Manitou and Providence*, 206, 263–64; Melissa Fawcett [Tantaquidgeon Zobel], *Lasting of the Mohegans*, 8–12, and *Medicine Trail: The Life and Lessons of Gladys Tantaquidgeon* (Tucson: University of Arizona Press, 2000), 25–27; Eric S. Johnson, "Uncas and the Politics of Contact," in Grumet, *Northeastern Indian Lives*, 30–32; Oberg, *Uncas*, 18–19, 50–51. According to Melissa Tantaquidgeon Zobel, the name *Mohegan* refers to the Delaware wolf clan, from which the Pequots and Mohegans originated. According to oral tradition, the Mohegans migrated from the Taconic mountains, in what is now New York, in response "to rumors of fine hunting and shellfish along the Connecticut coast." On the Delawares and their relations, see chapter 3. On the historical relationship between Pequots and Mohegans, see also Dena F. Dincauze, "A Capsule History of Southern New England," in Hauptman and Wherry, *The Pequots*; Carroll Alton Means, "Mohegan–Pequot Relationships, as Indicated by the Events Leading to the Pequot Massacre of 1637 and Sub-

sequent Claims in the Mohegan Land Controversy," *Bulletin of the Archaeological Society of Connecticut* 21 (1947): 26–33; Amy Den Ouden, *Beyond Conquest: Native Peoples and the Struggle for History in New England* (Lincoln: University of Nebraska Press, 2005); Starna, "Pequots," 33; Laurie Weinstein, "Land Politics and Power: The Mohegan Indians in the Seventeenth and Eighteenth Centuries," *Man in the Northeast* 42 (1991): 9–16.

13. "Petition of Mahomet to the King 1736," in "Land Disputes between the Colony of Connecticut and the Mohegan Indians, 1736–1739," Ayer Ms. 559, Edward Ayer Collection, Newberry Library, Chicago, reprinted in "Talcott Papers," *Collections of the Connecticut Historical Society* 4: 368–72; Fawcett, *Lasting of the Mohegans,* 13; Johnson, "Uncas and the Politics of Contact," 32–33.

14. Fawcett, *Lasting of the Mohegans,* 13. Narragansetts quoted in Gary B. Nash, *Red, White, and Black: The Peoples of Early North America* (Englewood Cliffs, N.J.: Prentice-Hall, 1992), 84; Robinson, "Lost Opportunities," 22–23. On the Pequot massacre, see Alfred A. Cave, *The Pequot War* (Amherst: University of Massachusetts Press, 1996); Den Ouden, *Beyond Conquest,* 11–15, 40, 217; Hauptman, "The Pequot War"; Johnson, "Uncas and the Politics of Contact," 33–37; Oberg, *Uncas,* 63–72; and Salisbury, *Manitou and Providence,* 211–25. Den Ouden rightly observes, "The colonial story of the 'Pequot War' is not really a story about Pequots; nor is it solely a story about colonial 'bravery' in the face of 'evil,' or of 'civilization' over 'savagery': it is, perhaps most importantly, a story that is meant to render the colonizers a natural presence in the landscape. It is Pequots who are cast as aliens, and their 'hostile' presence is swept from the terrain by the will of the English god. But this myth was contested in the eighteenth century not just by Pequots but by other Native people who dared to assert their land rights and to question colonial justice" (40).

15. Johnson, "Uncas and the Politics of Contact," 36–46; Oberg, *Uncas,* 75–109; Robinson, "Lost Opportunities," 23–28; Salisbury, *Manitou and Providence,* 225–35, and "Indians and Colonists," 87; Melissa Tantaquidgeon Zobel, personal communication, April 14, 2007. *Wliwni* to Melissa for sharing this insight.

16. Salisbury, "Indians and Colonists," 87; Daniel Richter, *The Ordeal of the Longhouse* (Chapel Hill: University of North Carolina Press, 1992), 24. Richter is speaking of the Haudenosaunee, but his point applies equally to northeastern Algonquians. Johnson, "Uncas and the Politics of Contact," 23–24.

17. Salisbury, *Manitou and Providence,* 231, and "Indians and Colonists," 87–89; Oberg, *Uncas,* 95–98; Robinson, "Lost Opportunities," 26–28.

18. Lion Gardiner, "Lieut. Lion Gardener, His Relation of the Pequot War," *Collections of the Massachusetts Historical Society,* 3rd ser., 3: 154. Gardiner arrived in Connecticut ca. 1633 and built a fort at the mouth of Kwinitekw; he wrote this account in 1660 from his papers, for friends. Colonial reports

274 NOTES TO CHAPTER 2

suggest that Miantonomo's alliance involved Indians from the Wabanaki coast to the Mohawk River. See Oberg, *Uncas*, 96–97. On Miantonomo's speech, see Salisbury, *Manitou and Providence*, 13–14, 231–32.

19. Salisbury, *Manitou and Providence*, 232.

20. William Bradford, *Of Plymouth Plantation, 1620–1647* (New York: Random House, 1981), 329; Gardiner, "Relation of the Pequot War," 162; Robinson, "Lost Opportunities," 22; Salisbury, *Manitou and Providence*, 231.

21. Gardiner, "Relation of the Pequot War," 162; Johnson, "Uncas and the Politics of Contact," 37, 40; Oberg, *Uncas*, 81, 89; Salisbury, *Manitou and Providence*, 226; Kevin McBride, "The Legacy of Robin Cassacinamon: Mashantucket Pequot Leadership in the Historic Period," in Grumet, *Northeastern Indian Lives*, 75–78. On the roles of Pequot women, see Den Ouden, *Beyond Conquest*.

22. Johnson, "Uncas and the Politics of Contact," 36–37, Oberg, *Uncas*, 83–84, 90–99. As Melissa Tantaquidgeon Zobel pointed out to me, suspicion of poison could have been Uncas's motivation for declining the offer of the dish, as poisoning was a common way to take down an enemy. Sharing the same pot, like sharing the same space, also involved assessing levels of risk and trust. Melissa Tantaquidgeon Zobel, personal communication, April 14, 2007.

23. Fawcett, *Lasting of the Mohegans*, 14, and *Medicine Trail*, 18, 27; Oberg, *Uncas*, 102–5; Salisbury, *Manitou and Providence*, 232–33.

24. Samson Occom, "An Account of the Montauk Indians, on Long Island" (1761), *Collections of the Massachusetts Historical Society*, 1st ser., 10: 107; Johnson, "Uncas and the Politics of Contact," 44.

25. Fawcett, *Lasting of the Mohegans*, 14, and *Medicine Trail*, 27; Oberg, *Uncas*, 103–5; Salisbury, *Manitou and Providence*, 233. According to Oberg, the United Colonies formed "directly in response to the Mohegan–Narragansett conflict."

26. Johnson, "Uncas and the Politics of Contact," 45–46; Fawcett, *Medicine Trail*, 146; David W. Conroy, "The Defense of Indian Land Rights: William Bolan and the Mohegan Case in 1743," *Proceedings of the American Antiquarian Society* 103 (1993): 402.

27. Although it is impossible to provide a full account of the war here, I hope to explore this confederation more extensively in a future project. See Jill Lepore, *The Name of War: King Philip's War and the Origins of American Identity* (New York: Knopf, 1998); Russell Bourne, *The Red King's Rebellion* (New York: Atheneum, 1990); Douglas Edward Leach, *Flintlock and Tomahawk: New England in King Philip's War* (New York: Macmillan, 1958); Eric B. Schultz and Michael J. Tougias, *King Philip's War: The History and Legacy of America's Forgotten Conflict* (Woodstock, Vt.: Countryman, 1999).

28. Nathaniel Saltonstall, *The Present State of New England with Respect to the Indian War* (London: Dorman Newman, 1675), 13.

29. See Lepore, *The Name of War*, 173–75; Cotton Mather, *Magnalia Christi Americana* (Hartford, Conn.: Silas Andrus and Son, 1853), 2: 516.

30. "The Complaint and Prayer of Owaneco and Ben Uncas, 1700," in "Land Disputes between the Colony of Connecticut and the Mohegan Indians, 1736–1739," Ayer Ms. 459, Edward Ayer Manuscript Collection; "Petition of Mahomet, 1736," 1–2; "Case of the Appellants," in Governor and Company of Connecticut and Moheagan Indians by Their Guardians, *Certified Copy of the Book of Proceedings before the Commissioner of Review* (London: W. and J. Richardson, 1769), 4; Den Ouden, *Beyond Conquest*, 4, 24, 92, 98–100; J. H. Trumbull, ed., *Public Records of the Colony of Connecticut* (Hartford: Case, Lockwood, and Brainard, 1850–1890), 3: 56–57.

31. Guardians, *Book of Proceedings*, 58. Here Papaquanaitt referred to the third "Anglo–Abenaki War" or Queen Anne's War.

32. This framework is inspired by Ngũgĩ wa Thiong'o's powerful three-part talk titled "Remembering Africa: Burial and Resurrection of African Memory," delivered at Harvard University on April 14, 15, and 16, 2006, and sponsored by the Dubois Institute.

33. Ngũgĩ, "Remembering Africa"; Gordon M. Day, *Western Abenaki Dictionary* (Hull, Quebec: Canadian Museum of Civilization, 1994), 1: 318; Joseph Aubery and Stephen Laurent, *Father Aubery's French Abenaki Dictionary* (Portland: Chisholm Brothers, 1995), 356. On the Mohegan land case, see Conroy, "Defense of Indian Land Rights"; John W. De Forest, *History of the Indians of Connecticut from the Earliest Known Period to 1850* (Hartford, Conn.: W. J. Hamersley, 1851), 324–41 and 451–70; Joseph Johnson, *To Do Good to My Indian Brethren: The Writings of Joseph Johnson, 1751–1776*, ed. Laura J. Murray (Amherst: University of Massachusetts Press, 1998), 30–40; William DeLoss Love, *Samson Occom and the Christian Indians of New England* (Syracuse, N.Y.: Syracuse University Press, 2000), 117–29; Means, "Mohegan–Pequot Relationships"; Den Ouden, *Beyond Conquest*, esp. chap. 4; Bernd Peyer, *The Tutor'd Mind: Indian Missionary-Writers in Antebellum America* (Amherst: University of Massachusetts Press, 1997), 62–63 and 72–74; Mark D. Walters, "*Mohegan Indians v. Connecticut* (1705–1773) and the Legal Status of Aboriginal Customary Laws and Government in British North America," *Osgoode Hall Law Journal* 33 (1995): 786–829; and Weinstein, "Land Politics and Power."

34. As Amy Den Ouden has demonstrated, the Mohegans were not alone in this endeavor, but were engaged, along with the Pequots and Niantics, in a "shared struggle to protect lands," which nearly always involved writing (Den Ouden, *Beyond Conquest*, 155).

35. Cronon, *Changes in the Land*, 58, 60–62, 68.

36. Ibid., 59–64. As Cronon indicates, because land usage was always relational, to attempt to make clear "distinctions" between these types of land tenure is to engage in a "somewhat artificial" process of delineation. On the

Mohegan case, land tenure, and "aboriginal customary law" under the British legal system, see Walters, "*Mohegan Indians v. Connecticut.*"

37. Cronon, *Changes in the Land*, 58, 61 (emphasis in original).

38. "Case of the Appellants," 4.

39. Weinstein, "Land Politics and Power," 10–11. The terms *amity, alliance,* and *friendship* connoted, in both colonial law and Native diplomacy, political equality. Even under British law, this provided the legal grounds for British preemptive rights, but did not imply "rights of sovereignty over Native peoples" or relinquishment of Native rights unless "friends" formally ceded land or became "enemies" whose lands could be gained by "conquest." See Walters, "*Mohegan Indians v. Connecticut,*" 793–95, 804, and 813. Note that a dubious land "agreement" from 1640 also played a role in the case; however, it is not mentioned in the Mohegan narratives, which I have chosen to privilege here. See Conroy, "Defense of Indian Land Rights," 397 and 400; Den Ouden, *Beyond Conquest,* 99 and 109–111; "Case of the Appellants," 15–16; Love, *Samson Occom,* 120; Margaret Wickens Pearce, "Native Mapping in Southern New England Indian Deeds," in *Cartographic Encounters: Perspectives on Native American Mapmaking and Map Use,* ed. G. Malcolm Lewis (Chicago: University of Chicago Press, 1998); Peyer, *Tutor'd Mind,* 62–63; Joseph Henry Smith, *Appeals to the Privy Court* (New York: Columbia University Press, 1950), 423; and Weinstein, "Land Politics and Power," 11–12.

40. "Petition of Mahomet, 1736," 1–2. Den Ouden notes that "in 1687 the Connecticut government began to grant parcels of Mohegans' reserved lands to Connecticut towns." At the same time, they encouraged the practice of "making pitches" on lands perceived to be unoccupied (Den Ouden, *Beyond Conquest,* 100, 66).

41. In 1646, New London was established as the "Pequot Plantation" by John Winthrop Jr. in the territory of Nameag, with Pequot consent. Winthrop had viewed the settlement as a "curb" on Mohegan power. In 1703, the town sought an expansion. The 1704 New London patent clearly recognized the Mohegans' "right and property," but did not indicate the bounds of those reserved lands. The "Pequot Plantation" had originally been in competition with the Mason settlement "at Mohegan," which later became Norwich. Den Ouden, *Beyond Conquest,* 104–6; D. Hamilton Hurd, *History of New London County, Connecticut* (Philadelphia: J. B. Lippincott, 1882), 137–43; McBride, "Legacy of Robin Cassacinamon," 85–86.

42. Guardians, *Book of Proceedings,* 28–29, 58.

43. Ibid., 28–29, 56–58; Den Ouden, *Beyond Conquest,* 103–7. According to Den Ouden, "Massapeague, which means 'great water land' or 'land upon the great cove' in Mohegan–Pequot language, refers to 'a fine tract of land on the [Thames] river, within the bounds of Mohegan proper.'" See Den Ouden, *Beyond Conquest,* 104, quoting J. Hammond Trumbull, *Indian Names of Places,*

etc. in and on the Borders of Connecticut (Hartford: Brown and Gross, 1881), 24; and Frances M. Caulkins, *History of New London, Connecticut* (New London: H. D. Utley, 1895), 122–23.

44. Guardians, *Book of Proceedings*, 28–29, 58. Serving as scouts for the English, a party of Mohegans tracked into unfamiliar northern territory following the 1704 Deerfield raid one year after they delivered this statement. Traveling up Kwinitekw into Koesek, they killed an extended family and prevented a large contingent of Abenakis from returning to Koesek to cultivate their planting fields. Haefeli and Sweeney, *Captors and Captives*, 140–41.

45. Guardians, *Book of Proceedings*, 6–7; Smith, *Appeals to the Privy Court*, 424; Ouden, *Beyond Conquest*, 100–3.

46. De Forest, *History of the Indians of Connecticut*, 290, 308–13; "Case of the Appellants," 5–6; "Mahomet's Petition, 1736," 2. Conroy, "Defense of Indian Land Rights," 403–4; Love, *Samson Occom*, 121; Peyer, *Tutor'd Mind*, 62–63; Den Ouden, *Beyond Conquest*, 100–3.

47. Guardians, *Book of Proceedings*, 6–7; Smith, *Appeals to the Privy Court*, 424; Den Ouden, *Beyond Conquest*, 100–3. The relationship between the Masons and the Mohegans was founded in Uncas's policy of alliance with the English. Uncas assisted Major John Mason during the Pequot War, and Mason aided the Mohegans during their conflicts with the Narragansetts. The two men maintained an alliance throughout their lives, with Mason often serving as an "intermediary" between the Mohegans and the English. Mason's land claims rested on Uncas's grants, and Uncas made Mason a trustee for the Mohegan lands to protect the community against fraudulent land sales. Although social ties waned in subsequent generations, the Mohegans and Masons remained political allies in pursuit of the land case. In fact, the Masons were known as "Native rights men" for their participation in the controversy. The Masons, of course, had their own interests in mind, but their land rights were irrevocably intertwined with the Mohegans'. See Conroy, "Defense of Indian Land Rights"; De Forest, *History of the Indians of Connecticut*, 324–41 and 451–70; Den Ouden, *Beyond Conquest*, 94; Wendy St. Jean, "Inventing Guardianship: The Mohegan and Their 'Protectors,'" *New England Quarterly* 72, no. 3 (September 1999): 362–87; Johnson, *To Do Good*, 30–40; Means, "Mohegan-Pequot Relationships"; Weinstein, "Land Politics and Power"; and Peyer, *Tutor'd Mind*, 62–63 and 72–74.

48. Guardians, *Book of Proceedings*, 6.

49. Ibid. Note also that colonial politics played a strong role in the case: the Masons were "bitterly estranged from Winthrop family" (Conroy, "Defense of Indian Land Rights," 403). See also St. Jean, "Inventing Guardianship," 376.

50. "Complaint of Owaneco, 1700." Owaneco, Ben, and Mahomet I presented a similar petition to the Connecticut General Assembly in 1703,

278 NOTES TO CHAPTER 2

reminding the colonial governors of their long-standing relationship and formal agreements and protesting against the colonists who had "settled upon our Land without our consent" (Den Ouden, *Beyond Conquest,* 67–68, 103–4).

51. Guardians, *Book of Proceedings,* 26–29. See also Walters, "*Mohegan Indians v. Connecticut,*" 812, and Johnson, *To Do Good,* 34.

52. "Petition of Mahomet, 1736," 2.

53. Gordon Saltonstall succeeded his friend and business partner Fitz-John Winthrop. See "Case of the Appellants," 11–12; *Public Records of the Colony of Connecticut,* 6: 31–32, 77–78, 148–49, and 199–205; Den Ouden, *Beyond Conquest,* 83–88 and 112–18; and De Forest, *History of the Indians of Connecticut,* 315 (emphasis in original).

54. The 1721 decision allowed that when "the stock of said Indian are extinct . . . the said eastern part, which is now settled upon the Indians, shall for ever belong to the town of New London" (Guardians, *Book of Proceedings,* 194; Den Ouden, *Beyond Conquest,* 117).

55. "Mahomet's Petition, 1736," 2; De Forest, *History of the Indians of Connecticut,* 323; "Case of the Appellants," 13; Johnson, *To Do Good,* 26–27, 34; Den Ouden, *Beyond Conquest,* 126. Captain John Mason was brother to Samuel and grandson to Uncas's contemporary. Thanks to Faith Davidson for clarifying Mason's genealogy.

56. "Mahomet's Petition, 1736," 1–4; Den Ouden, *Beyond Conquest,* 93–95.

57. "Mahomet's Petition, 1736," 1–4; Haefeli and Sweeney, *Captors and Captives,* 265.

58. "Case of the Appellants," 13, 16; De Forest, *History of the Indians of Connecticut,* 324–34; Conroy, "Defense of Indian Land Rights"; Walters, "*Mohegan Indians v. Connecticut,*" 28. The entire record of this hearing was published in 1769 as a *Book of Proceedings* that included attorneys' arguments, witness testimony, and Native proclamations.

59. "Case of the Appellants," 1–4.

60. Conroy, "Defense of Indian Land Rights," 407–9; Guardians, *Book of Proceedings,* 138–58; Smith, *Appeals to the Privy Court,* 440.

61. "Complaint of Owaneco, 1700"; Cronon, *Changes in the Land,* 56–57; Roger Williams, *A Key into the Language of America* (Boston: George Dexter, 1643), preface.

62. "Case of the Appellants," 1–4, 7–9. For legal analysis of Mohegan sovereignty and the land case in the context of international law, see Walters, "*Mohegan Indians v. Connecticut.*"

63. "Complaint of Owaneco, 1700"; "Mahomet's Petition, 1736"; Guardians, *Book of Proceedings,* 58.

64. With Greylock's War brewing in the north, the Connecticut colony not only called on the Mohegans as scouts but enforced restrictions on their movements. The colony enacted a series of laws, including "An Act for Better Securing our Frontiers against the Skulking Parties of Indians" (1724), which

severely limited the areas in which Indians were allowed to hunt, fish, or travel and authorized the killing and scalping of any Indians found outside the boundaries set by law. It was in this climate of "surveillance" and fear that the sachemship was usurped. See Den Ouden, *Beyond Conquest,* 78–82. See also Calloway, *Western Abenakis of Vermont,* 113–31, and Haefeli and Sweeney, *Captors and Captives,* 265.

65. De Forest, *History of the Indians of Connecticut,* 308–18; Johnson, *To Do Good,* 36; Oberg, *Uncas,* 174, 210; Den Ouden, *Beyond Conquest,* 121–22.

66. "Case of the Appellants," 13.

67. Colonial representatives told the Mohegans that the Abenakis were "coming upon" them just as settlers were pushing northward on Kwinitekw. The Mohegans, as long-standing English allies, felt equally threatened by the possibility of raids. Ironically, the colony used its alliance with the Mohegans to secure compliance with their dispossession. See Guardians, *Book of Proceedings,* 196–98 and 218, and "Case of the Appellants," 14–16.

68. John was likely the son of Uncas's son John/Kittateash (Fawcett, *Lasting of the Mohegans,* 18; Guardians, *Book of Proceedings,* 229; Faith Davidson, personal communication).

69. Guardians, *Book of Proceedings,* 218.

70. Den Ouden, *Beyond Conquest,* 137. However, as Den Ouden points out, Governor Talcott (who followed Saltonstall) used the participation of the Niantics and Pequots to challenge whether the statements were the production of "proper Moheags" or "imposters."

71. The issue of the sachemship and the conceptualization of Native governance systems were critical to the hearing. As Walters relates, "The two New York council members dissented, stating to the Board of Trade, 'it came out that by the constitution of the tribe the sachemship was hereditary and that John Uncas was the *sachem de jure,*' and although Ben Uncas has been '*sachem de facto*' he had been 'deposed by the tribe.' Suspecting bias on the part of the Rhode Island members of the court, the New York commissioners withdrew from the proceedings." As Walters points out, this discussion demonstrated the ways in which colonial officials were obligated to honor "aboriginal customary law" and even to absorb it into their own sense of "common law." Only because internal Native customs regarding governance were commonly accepted as lawful did Connecticut officials feel obliged to manipulate the institution of the sachemship in order to legitimize their claim. See Walters, "*Mohegan Indians v. Connecticut,*" 816–18.

72. "Address of Ben Uncas, 1739," in "Land Disputes between the Colony of Connecticut and the Mohegan Indians, 1736–1739," Ayer Ms. 559, Edward Ayer Collection, Newberry Library, Chicago; Murray, *Indian Giving,* 55, 60–61.

73. Guardians, *Book of Proceedings,* 12–4, 223, 229; "Case of the Appellants," 18.

74. Guardians, *Book of Proceedings,* 229.

75. Ibid., 223, 229.

76. Ibid., 110–15. Samson Occom was taking over this role from his father, who died during that year. See Joanna Brooks, "'This Indian World': An Introduction to the Writings of Samson Occom," in *The Collected Writings of Samson Occom, Mohegan: Literature and Leadership in Eighteenth-Century Native America* (New York: Oxford University Press, 2007), 12–14.

77. Guardians, *Book of Proceedings*, 12–14. These towns were only a half mile apart.

78. De Forest, *History of the Indians of Connecticut*, 322–23, 333–34; Guardians, *Book of Proceedings*, 95; Joseph Tracy to William Johnson, July 11, 1764, in *The Papers of Sir William Johnson*, ed. James Sullivan (Albany: 1921–65), 4: 459; "Ben Uncas, Zachary Johnson, Simon Choychoy to Gov. Fitch, May 18, 1765," William Samuel Johnson Papers, Connecticut Historical Society, Hartford, Connecticut; "Memorial of Ben Uncas to the General Assembly, May 20, 1765," Indian Papers 2: 103–5, Connecticut State Library, Hartford, Connecticut.

79. Guardians, *Book of Proceedings*, 14, 95.

80. Ibid., 91–92. See also Conroy, "Defense of Indian Land Rights," 412.

81. St. Jean, "Inventing Guardianship," 377; "To Augh Quant Johnson Otherwise Cato, of the Mohegan Tribe of Indians, a Young Man Who Came Over to England with Mr. Mason in the Beginning of the Year 1736," William Samuel Johnson Papers, Connecticut Historical Society, Hartford, Connecticut; Love, *Samson Occom*, 74–75; Johnson, *To Do Good*, 25–26; Guardians, *Book of Proceedings*, 4–15, 229.

82. Samson Occom, "A Short Narrative of My Life," in *The Norton Anthology of American Literature*, ed. Nina Baym et al., 5th ed. (New York: W. W. Norton, 1998), 1: 614–15. As Dana D. Nelson keenly observes, although Occom's conversion to Christianity was certainly sincere, "we should not overlook how the spiritual and political converge in his actions. His Christian conversion could have been as much a politically strategic choice as a private decision . . . made as part of a complex and calculated response to dwindling Mohegan populations, political power, and land entitlements." See Dana D. Nelson, "'I Speak Like a Fool but I Am Constrained': Samson Occom's Short Narrative and Economies of the Racial Self," in *Early Native American Writing: New Critical Essays*, ed. Helen Jaskoski (New York: Cambridge University Press, 1996), 45. Occom's Christianity has been the subject of much of the scholarship about his writing. See Love, *Samson Occom*; Peyer, *Tutor'd Mind*, 54–105; Michael Elliott, "'This Indian Bait': Samson Occom and the Voice of Liminality," *Early American Literature* 29, no. 3 (1994): 233–53; Eileen Razzari Elrod, "'I Did Not Make Myself So . . .': Samson Occom and American Religious Autobiography," in *Christian Encounters with the Other*, ed. John C. Hawley (New York, N.Y.: New York University Press, 1998); Arnold Krupat, *The Voice in the Margin: Native American Literature and the Canon* (Berkeley:

University of California Press, 1989); David Murray, *Forked Tongues: Speech, Writing, and Representation in North American Indian Texts* (Bloomington: Indiana University Press, 1991), 44–56; A. Lavonne Brown Ruoff, "Introduction: Samson Occom's *Sermon Preached . . . at the Execution of Moses Paul,*" *Studies in American Indian Literatures* 4 (1992): 75–105; Margaret Szasz, *Between Indian and White Worlds: The Cultural Broker* (Norman: University of Oklahoma Press, 1994); Jace Weaver, *That the People Might Live: Native American Literatures and Native American Community* (New York: Oxford University Press, 1997), 46–53; Laurie Weinstein, "Samson Occom: A Charismatic Eighteenth-Century Mohegan Leader," in *Enduring Traditions*; Hilary E. Wyss, *Writing Indians: Literacy, Christianity, and Native Community in Early America* (Amherst: University of Massachusetts Press, 2000),123–53.

83. Samson Occom, "Short Narrative," 615–18, "Journal," Eleazar Wheelock Papers, Special Collections, Baker Library, Dartmouth College, "An Account of the Montauk Indians on Long Island" (1761), *Collections of the Massachusetts Historical Society,* 1st ser., 10: 106–111, and "Petition of the Montauk Indians to the Governor of New York, drafted by Samson Occom," Folder 13: "Correspondence before 1792," Samson Occom Papers, Connecticut Historical Society, Hartford, Connecticut; Love, *Samson Occom,* 34–55; Peyer, *Tutor'd Mind,* 64–69; John A. Strong, *The Montaukett Indians of Eastern Long Island* (Syracuse, N.Y.: Syracuse University Press, 2001), 68–71.

84. Love, *Samson Occom,* 56–81; Peyer, *Tutor'd Mind,* 65–82; James Dow McCallum, *The Letters of Eleazar Wheelock's Indians* (Hanover, N.H.: Dartmouth College, 1932); Margaret Szasz, *Indian Education in the American Colonies, 1607–1783* (Albuquerque: University of New Mexico Press, 1988); Eleazar Wheelock, *A Plain and Faithful Narrative of the Original Design, Rise, Progress and Present State of the Indian Charity School at Lebanon, Connecticut* (Boston: Richard and Samuel Draper, 1763), 29. Chenango was a multinational village in Haudenosaunee territory, at the junction of the Susquehanna and Chenango Rivers, which included a strong contingent of Nanticokes who had moved from Maryland, accepted Iroquois protection, and pledged "to guard the southern door of the Confederacy." See R. S. Grumet and J. Q. Hays, *Journey on the Forbidden Path* (Philadelphia: American Philosophical Society, 1999); Frank W. Porter III, "Strategies for Survival: The Nanticoke Indians in a Hostile World," *Ethnohistory* 26, no. 4 (1979): 325–45; and Paul A. W. Wallace, "They Knew the Indian: The Men Who Wrote the Moravian Records," *Proceedings of the American Philosophical Society* 95, no. 3 (1951): 290–95.

85. Peyer notes, "In fact, [Occom] and David Fowler paved the way for the Reverend Samuel Kirkland, who is generally credited with having pioneered the Oneida mission" (Peyer, *Tutor'd Mind,* 71). See McCallum, *Letters of Wheelock's Indians,* 85–113, and Walter Pilkington, ed., *The Journal of Samuel Kirkland* (Clinton, N.Y.: Hamilton, 1980). See also Love, *Samson Occom,* 105–18; William Kellaway, *The New England Company* (New York: Barnes and

Noble, 1962), 258–60; Johnson, *To Do Good,* 50–167; and Szasz, *Indian Education,* 233–50.

86. De Forest, *History of the Indians of Connecticut,* 450–53; Love, *Samson Occom,* 82–87; Peyer, *Tutor'd Mind,* 67–71; Sullivan, "Meetings of the Mohegan Indians," *William Johnson Papers,* 2: 836–37; *Collections of the Connecticut Historical Society* 17: 338–39; "Treaty with the Mohawks and Stockbridge Indians, April 12, 1763," Indian Papers 2: 98, Connecticut Archives; Johnson, *To Do Good,* 26. For Johnson's letter, see chapter 6.

87. Occom Journal, Wheelock Papers; "William Johnson to Correspondents of the Society for Promoting Christian Knowledge, Dec. 9, 1761," French and Indian War Collection, American Antiquarian Society, Worcester, Massachusetts. See also Love, *Samson Occom,* 87–95. For more on Molly Brant and William Johnson, see chapter 3.

88. Colin G. Calloway, *The American Revolution in Indian Country: Crisis and Diversity in Native American Communities* (New York: Cambridge University Press, 1995), 120–21; Alan Taylor, *William Cooper's Town: Power and Persuasion on the Frontier of the Early American Republic* (New York: Alfred A. Knopf, 1995), 36; Love, *Samson Occom,* 76–77, 97–98; McCallum, *Letters of Wheelock's Indians,* 32–45, 275; Wheelock Papers, Mss. 761601, 762227, 763465.3, 763519.3, 763520. To foreground the request for Ashpo's services as a teacher is not to elide the colonial context through which Indians indoctrinated other Indians. I only mean to emphasize that Native people had their own reasons for desiring "instruction" and made their own choices about how they would practice education and religion and through whom they would receive it.

89. McCallum, *Letters of Wheelock's Indians;* Johnson, *To Do Good,* 26; Occom Journal, Wheelock Papers; Peyer, *Tutor'd Mind,* 71; William Stone, *Life of Joseph Brant, Thayendanegea* (New York: George Dearborn, 1838).18; Eleazar Wheelock, *Narrative, A Continuation of the Narrative of the State, &c. of the Indian Charity School at Lebanon, in Connecticut; from Nov. 27th, 1762 to Sept. 3d, 1765* (Boston: Richard and Samuel Draper, 1765), and *A Continuation of the Narrative of the State, &c. of the Indian Charity School at Lebanon, in Connecticut... 1769* (London: J. and W. Oliver, 1769). On Joseph Brant, see chapter 3. On Joseph Johnson, see Johnson, *To Do Good,* and chapter 6.

90. Occom Journal, Wheelock Papers; Love, *Samson Occom,* 93; McCallum, *Letters of Wheelock's Indians,* 35–36.

91. Guardians, *Book of Proceedings,* 13; Love, *Samson Occom,* 75; Peyer, *Tutor'd Mind,* 70–71; Wheelock Papers, Mss. 762312, 763521.2, 763658, 764121, 764174, 764158, 764230. On the overseers, see St. Jean, "Inventing Guardianship," 362–63 and 383–87.

92. Sullivan, "Meetings of the Mohegan Indians," 4: 375–76; Wheelock Papers, Ms. 764121; De Forest, *History of the Indians of Connecticut,* 459; Guardians, *Book of Proceedings,* 94; "Case of the Appellants," 17; Love, *Samson Occom,* 28–31, 122–23.

93. Women played an important role in the reconstruction of the networks of relations and the reclamation of land in southern New England. See Den Ouden, *Beyond Conquest.*

94. Sullivan, "Meetings of the Mohegan Indians," 4: 375–76.

95. Ibid., 4: 375-6.

96. Occom and Ashpo's familiarity with Haudenosaunee protocol may have led them to use the rhetoric of "one mind" and "one body" in their own councils. They may have been drawing on the Great Law as a means to clear tension and build unity between hostile factions. See chapter 3.

97. Even Ben Uncas had demonstrated concern over the problem of division, although he did not comprehend its colonial underpinnings. In his memorial to the General Assembly, he expressed great concern "for our broken divided miserable case" and complained that "these Indians . . . wont unite with us." Writing to the Connecticut Governor, he related, "I am really afraid murder will be committed here soon" and admitted that "Samson is as uneasy as ourselves." See "Ben Uncas to Governor Fitch, May 24, 1765," Indian Papers 2: 258, Connecticut Archives.

98. "Letter draft," Folder 2: "Correspondence, 1761–5," Occom Papers. Note that this is not merely language that appeals to colonial paternalism, although that context should not be disregarded. In Algonquian and Haudenosaunee circles, the language of kinship was part of diplomacy. Occom's appeal was made within the context of the alliance between the Mohawks, Mohicans, Mohegans, and the English, a network within which Johnson acted as a mediating force and in which he wielded considerable power. For an examination of pleas for pity within the context of Native diplomacy, see Murray, *Indian Giving,* 27–29, and chapter 6.

99. "Letter draft."

100. "Cipher," *Oxford English Dictionary,* http://dictionary.oed.com (accessed January 14, 2003). Used by agreement with Cornell University.

101. "Letter draft." Here Occom was asserting the legitimacy of "aboriginal customary law." Walters notes that the Mohegan case is significant because it "confirm[s] that British law recognized that such nations were, in certain circumstances at least, governed internally by systems of Aboriginal customary law and government which were independent from the local legal systems of the colonies in which they were located" (Walters, "*Mohegan Indians v. Connecticut,*" 788, 794).

102. The royal proclamation was published in October 1763 in *Gentleman's Magazine,* which would have been available to Occom in New England. See *By the King, a Proclamation* (London: Mark Baskett, 1763).

103. As DeVorsey has observed, historians have sometimes interpreted the proclamation to apply only to Indian nations west of the Appalachians, but a close reading of the document confirms that it could be applied to any lands within the colonies that had not yet been "ceded" by the Native inhabitants.

Louis DeVorsey, *Indian Boundary in the Southern Colonies, 1763–1775* (Chapel Hill: University of North Carolina Press, 1961), 36–38; Guardians, *Book of Proceedings*, "Appellants Case, 23; and Smith, *Appeals to the Privy Court*, 437.

104. "Ben Uncas [et al.] to Gov. Fitch, May 18, 1765," "Statement of Charles Bill," and "Statement of Zachary Johnston, March 1765," William Samuel Johnson Papers, Connecticut Historical Society; "Memorial of Ben Uncas to the General Assembly, May 20, 1765," Indian Papers 2: 103–5, Connecticut Archives; "Robert Clelland to Thomas Fitch, New London, December 26, 1764," *Collections of the Connecticut Historical Society* 18: 313–15; "Henry Babcock to [Gov.] William Pitkin, Stonington, January 18, 1769," *Collections of the Connecticut Historical Society* 19: 160–61; "Thomas Fitch to Richard Jackson, Norwalk, February 23, 1765," *Collections of the Connecticut Historical Society* 19: 275; Steven F. Johnson, *Ninnuock: The Algonquian People of New England* (Marlborough, Mass.: Bliss Publishing, 1995), 231; Peyer, *Tutor'd Mind*, 72; Wheelock Papers, Mss. 764290, 764307.1, 764318.1, 764461, 764472.1, 764526.2, 764560.2.

105. Robert Clelland to Thomas Fitch, New London, December 26, 1764, *Collections of the Connecticut Historical Society* 18: 313–15. Note that Clelland was concerned about his own position as schoolmaster. Mohegans were protesting against him, Occom was drawing away his students, and his funding was dwindling. Wheelock Papers, Mss. 764526.2, 764461; "Mohegan, April 26, 1764," Samson Occom Papers, Folder 2: "Correspondence, 1761–5," Connecticut Historical Society, Hartford; Love, *Samson Occom*, 123–29; Peyer, *Tutor'd Mind*, 72–73; Faith Davidson, personal communication.

106. Wheelock Papers, Mss. 764560.2, 765304, 765129.1, 765202.1, 765169.2; Love, *Samson Occom*, 123–29; Peyer, *Tutor'd Mind*, 72–73. Nathaniel Whitaker told Wheelock that Occom "looks on Mr. Jewett as having injured the Indians and improved some their land," remarking that "he is, I fear, too credulous of Indian stories" (Wheelock Papers, Ms. 764461).

107. Wheelock Papers, Mss. 765129.1, 765169.2, 765202.1, 765212.7, 765304; Johnson, *To Do Good*, 26–27; "Statement of Zachary Johnston, March 1765," and "Statement of Sarah Mohomet, 1765," William Samuel Johnson Papers, Connecticut Historical Society, Hartford.

108. "Minutes of the Connecticut Correspondents, March 12, 1765," quoted in Love, *Samson Occom*, 127. See also Peyer, *Tutor'd Mind*, 72–74. Manuscript draft in Wheelock Papers, Ms. 765212.10.

109. "Ben Uncas [et al.] to Gov. Fitch, May 18, 1765."

110. On "the motif of the 'poor Indian'" in Occom's writing, see Weaver, *That the People Might Live*, 51–53.

111. "Ben Uncas [et al.] to Gov. Fitch, May 18, 1765"; Sullivan, "Meetings of the Mohegan Indians," 4: 727; "Memorial of Ben Uncas to the General Assembly," and "Ben Uncas to Governor Fitch, May 24, 1765," Indian Papers 2: 103–5, 258, Connecticut Archives.

112. Sullivan, "Meetings of the Mohegan Indians," 4: 727–28.

113. Memorial of Ben Uncas to the General Assembly, Indian Papers 2: 103–5; Wheelock Papers, Mss. 764457, 764503, 764508.3, 764475.2, 764526.2, 765304, 765310, 765429.1.

114. McCallum, *Letters of Wheelock's Indians*, 79.

115. Quoted in Love, *Samson Occom*, 123; Peyer, *Tutor'd Mind*, 74.

116. Occom Papers, Folder 16: "Records of the Mohegan Tribe," Connecticut Historical Society, Hartford. The council's proclamation that they would consider all Mohegans of "one family" was particularly significant because Zachary Johnson, even after Ben Uncas's death and the formal dissolution of the sachemship, continued to oppose Occom and other leaders, fomenting division by characterizing some inhabitants as "strangers" who would ostensibly have fewer rights in the community. See "Zachary Johnson to Richard Law, May 30, 1781," Ayer Ms. 459, Edward Ayer Collection, Newberry Library, Chicago; De Forest, *History of the Indians of Connecticut*, 472–76; and Peyer, *Tutor'd Mind*, 82.

117. Wheelock Papers, Ms. 785340. Cuish and the Poquiantups were Niantic leaders. Note also that Occom had previously worked at Niantic as a minister, bolstering the ties between the two groups.

118. Fawcett, *Lasting of the Mohegans*, 18–19, and *Medicine Trail*, 135–36; Johnson, *To Do Good*, esp. 200–233; William DeLoss Love, "The Founding of Brothertown," *Utica Morning Herald*, February 4, 1894; Love, *Samson Occom*, 167, 188–367; Peyer, *Tutor'd Mind*, 82–85; Strong, *The Montaukett Indians*, 75–81; Wyss, *Writing Indians*, 123–53.

119. As Amy Den Ouden has noted, such privatization of land is also reflective of the adoption of patriarchal power structures at Mohegan, which was common in the region during this period. See Den Ouden, *Beyond Conquest*, 83.

120. Lucy was married to John Tantaquidgeon, a Mohegan counselor descended from the runner who captured Miantonomo. See Fawcett, *Medicine Trail*, 12, 17–19, 24, 35–40, 47–54, 120, 131, 143–47, 170–71; Frank Speck, "The Modern Pequots and Their Language," *American Anthropologist* 5, no. 2 (1903): 195–96. Thanks to Amy Den Ouden for pointing out the timing of the "black dance." See Den Ouden, *Beyond Conquest*, 134.

121. For the Mohegan Tribe, federal recognition in 1994 was a major triumph. As part of the agreement, Fort Shantok and the state park that surrounded it were returned to the tribe.

122. Fawcett, *Medicine Trail*, 26–27.

3. Two Paths to Peace

1. Timothy Pickering Papers, Massachusetts Historical Society (TPP), 60: 103. Pickering noted that Young Peter "is the son of Good Peter, the great

speaker of the Oneida Nation" (TPP, 60: 70). Newtown was a new American settlement located on the Chemung River, on the site of the former village of Chuknut. According to Isabel Kelsay, some thousand people attended this council. See Isabel Thompson Kelsay, *Joseph Brant, 1743–1807: Man of Two Worlds* (Syracuse, N.Y.: Syracuse University Press, 1984), 453–54.

2. Several key sources have been instrumental to this chapter, including Richard White, *The Middle Ground: Indians, Empires, and Republics in the Great Lakes Region, 1650–1815* (New York: Cambridge University Press, 1991); Kelsay, *Joseph Brant*; Alan Taylor, "Captain Hendrick Aupaumut: The Dilemmas of an Intercultural Broker," *Ethnohistory* 43, no. 3 (1996): 431–57; James P. Ronda, "'As They Were Faithful': Chief Hendrick Aupaumut and the Struggle for Stockbridge Survival, 1757–1830," *American Indian Culture and Research Journal* 3, no. 3 (1979): 43–56. Thanks to the American Antiquarian Society for research support and to the Massachusetts Historical Society for access to the Timothy Pickering Papers. Special thanks to Alyssa Mt. Pleasant for sharing her research on Buffalo Creek and for insightful suggestions on an early adraft. See Alyssa Mt. Pleasant, "After the Whirlwind: Maintaining a Haudenosaunee Place at Buffalo Creek, 1780–1825," Ph.D. diss., Cornell University, Ithaca, N.Y., 2007.

3. Note that a previous assault by the Army on the Western Indians' central council fire, in 1790, gave the Haudenosaunee ample grounds for suspicion. See Kelsay, *Joseph Brant*, 444–45, 456; Mt. Pleasant, "After the Whirlwind"; TPP, 60: 106; United States Congress, *American State Papers: Indian Affairs* (ASP), 2 vols. (Washington: Gales and Seaton, 1832–61), 1: 139–40; and White, *Middle Ground*, 448–54.

4. The Six Nations included the Mohawks, Oneidas, Onondagas, Cayugas, and Senecas, along with the Tuscaroras, who were formally adopted into the Haudenosaunee Confederacy in the early 1700s.

5. Both Aupaumut's Mohicans and some Tuscaroras were living in villages at Oneida.

6. TPP, 61: 222, 60: 70, 94.

7. TPP, 59: 8A, 10A. Aupaumut's numerous reports include a June 1791 speech: TPP, 60: 70–73; an October 1791 report: TPP, 59: 8–13; a February 1792 "narrative": TPP, 59: 18–21; a December 1792 report: TPP, 59: 26–27; February 1793 "queries": TPP, 59: 38–43; and Hendrick Aupaumut, "A Narrative of an Embassy to the Western Indians, from the Original Manuscript of Hendrick Aupaumut," *Collections of the Massachusetts Historical Society*, 1st ser., 9: 61–131.

8. John Norton, Carl Frederick Klinck, and James John Talman, *The Journal of Major John Norton, 1816* (Toronto: Champlain Society, 1970), 88. Norton was a Scotch Cherokee and adopted Mohawk, raised in Scotland by a Cherokee captive and a Scottish mother. He entered the Ohio Valley as a British soldier, but quickly embedded himself in the network of relations, redistributing his pay among Native families. Brant befriended Norton, then adopted

him as his nephew. Norton married a Mohawk woman and raised Mohawk children, serving as a scribe and war chief for the Six Nations at Grand River.

9. Norton, Klinck, and Talman, *Journal of Major John Norton*, 88–89. Skyholder is also known as "New Tree" or "Sapling." The literal translation of Skyholder's action, in Oneida, is "he was born, for one to be born human," echoing the Abenaki association of human "being" with birth. See Demus Elm, Harvey Antone, Floyd Glenn Lounsbury, and Bryan Gick, *The Oneida Creation Story* (Lincoln: University of Nebraska Press, 2000), 76. See also John Mohawk, "A View from Turtle Island: Chapters in Iroquois Mythology, History, and Culture," Ph.D. diss., State University of New York, Buffalo, 1993; John Mohawk, *Iroquois Creation Story: John Arthur Gibson and J. N. B. Hewitt's Myth of the Earth Grasper* (Buffalo, N.Y.: Mohawk Publications, 2005), and Joanne Shenandoah and Douglas M. George, *Skywoman: Legends of the Iroquois* (Santa Fe: Clear Light, 1998), 22.

10. Norton, Klinck, and Talman, *Journal of Major John Norton*, 88–89.

11. Kevin A. Connelly, "The Textual Function of Onondaga Aspect, Mood, and Tense: A Journey into Onondaga Conceptual Space," Ph.D. diss., Cornell University, Ithaca, N.Y., 1999, 75. Connelly's dissertation focuses on the analysis of aspect in Onondaga stories, revealing the centrality of space and human participation in Haudenosaunee language and cosmology. Special thanks to Kevin for many insightful conversations and for sharing his work.

12. Elm et al., *Oneida Creation Story*, 77–79.

13. Cusick's was the first published version to use the terms "Good Mind" and "Bad Mind." David Cusick, *Sketches of Ancient History of the Six Nations (1825)* (Lockport, N.Y.: Niagara Country Historical Society, 1961), 19.

14. This participatory mode is evident in the earlier part of the story as well: the water animals worked together to provide a place for Sky Woman to land, unaware that they were actually involved in a much larger project — the creation of the earth.

15. See Elm et al., *Oneida Creation Story*, 19, 159.

16. Love suggests that Hendrick Aupaumut may have even been "a descendant" of Hendrick, although I have not yet found substantiation for this claim. See William DeLoss Love, *Samson Occom and the Christian Indians of New England* (Syracuse, N.Y.: Syracuse University Press, 2000), 239.

17. White, *Middle Ground*, 186–88; Kelsay, *Joseph Brant*, chaps. 1–4; William Stone, *Life of Joseph Brant, Thayendanegea* (New York: George Dearborn, 1838), 1: 1–18; Lois M. Huey and Bonnie Pulis, *Molly Brant: A Legacy of Her Own* (Youngstown, N.Y.: Old Fort Niagara Association), 13–21. On the Covenant Chain, see Francis Jennings, *The Ambiguous Iroquois Empire: The Covenant Chain Confederation of Indian Tribes with English Colonies from Its Beginnings to the Lancaster Treaty of 1744* (New York: Norton, 1984).

18. Barbara Graymont, "Koñwatsiãtsiaéñni," in *Dictionary of Candian Biography* (Toronto: University of Toronto/Université Laval, 2000), http://

www.biographi.ca/EN/ShowBio.asp?BioId=36113&query=
molly%20AND%20brant (accessed August 7, 2006); Lois M. Feister and Bonnie Pulis, "Molly Brant: Her Domestic and Political Roles in Eighteenth-
Century New York," in *Northeastern Indian Lives, 1632–1816*, ed. Robert Steven
Grumet (Amherst: University of Massachusetts Press, 1996), 295–320; Gretchen
Green, "Molly Brant, Catharine Brant, and Their Daughters: A Study in Colonial Acculturation," *Ontario History* 81, no. 3 (September 1989): 235–50.

19. Stone, *Life of Joseph Brant*, 3, 18.

20. Stone notes that a company of Stockbridge Mohicans traveled to
Mohawk country to console them on the loss of Hendrick (Stone, *Life of Joseph
Brant*, 18).

21. Colin G. Calloway, *The American Revolution in Indian Country: Crisis
and Diversity in Native American Communities* (New York: Cambridge University Press, 1995), 88–89; Patrick Frazier, *The Mohicans of Stockbridge* (Lincoln:
University of Nebraska Press, 1992). For the location of the Wappingers, refer
to Map 6 in chapter 2.

22. "Speech Delivered by Captain Solomon Uhhaunauwaunmut, the Chief
Sachem of the Moheakunnuk Tribe of Indians Residing in Stockbridge, on
the 11th Day of April, 1775," *American Archives*, 4th ser., 2: 315. Uhhau-
nauwaunmut was a key leader at Stockbridge and had traveled with Daniel
Nimham to London to bring their land claims to the king (Frazier, *Mohicans
of Stockbridge*, 160–64). On Mohican participation in the Revolution, see Ted
Brasser, *Riding on the Frontier's Crest: Mahican Indian Culture and Change*
(Ottawa: National Museums of Canada, 1974); Calloway, *The American Revolution in Indian Country*; Frazier, *Mohicans of Stockbridge*; and Ronda, "As They
Were." The works of Colin Calloway and Barbara Graymont, cited throughout, were instrumental to my understanding of the Revolution. I also wish
to acknowledge the insight I gained from consulting Darren Bonaparte's
Web site, "The Wampum Chronicles," www.wampumchronicles.com, which
clarified my understanding of the breakdown of the clan mother's power
and the rise of young men like Brant. Thanks also to Maurice Kenny for the
poems in *Tekonwatonti: Molly Brant* (Buffalo: White Pine Press, 2002), the first
source I consulted to understand Molly's role.

23. "Provincial Congress to the Moheakuunuck Tribe of Indians, Living
in and about Stockbridge, June 8, 1775," *American Archives*, 4th Ser. 2, 937.

24. Calloway, *The American Revolution in Indian Country*, 93–94; Barbara
Graymont, *The Iroquois in the American Revolution* (Syracuse, N.Y.: Syracuse
University Press, 1972), 72.

25. Graymont, *The Iroquois in the American Revolution*, 81, 104–5; Kelsay,
Joseph Brant; Stone, *Life of Joseph Brant*.

26. Occom, quoted in Bernd Peyer, *The Tutor'd Mind: Indian Missionary-
Writers in Antebellum America* (Amherst: University of Massachusetts Press,
1997), 85–86; "Oneidas' Declaration of Neutrality... to the Four New England

Colonies," *American Archives*, 4th ser., 2: 1116–17; Calloway, *The American Revolution in Indian Country*; Graymont, *The Iroquois in the American Revolution*.

27. Calloway, *The American Revolution in Indian Country*, 122–23; Graymont, The *Iroquois in the American Revolution*, 52–55, 66–107, 110.

28. Calloway, *The American Revolution in Indian Country*, 123; Graymont, *The Iroquois in the American Revolution*, 21–23, 86–128; Barbara Mann, *Iroquois Women: The Gantowisas* (New York: Peter Lang, 2004), 117, 132, 135, 179–80.

29. Calloway, *The American Revolution in Indian Country*, 47, 51, 99; Graymont, *The Iroquois in the American Revolution*, 196–220; Mann, *Iroquois Women*, 43–46.

30. Kelsay, *Joseph Brant*, 453–54; Calloway, *The American Revolution in Indian Country*, 51, 99; Ronda, "As They Were," 47; Graymont, *The Iroquois in the American Revolution*, 129–56. "Chuknut" would be renamed "Newtown." Note that Oneidas and Tuscaroras also served the Americans in Sullivan's campaign, acting as necessary guides through Iroquoia. The Oneidas requested that the Cayugas be spared from the assault, but Sullivan rejected their plea. Graymont, *The Iroquois in the American Revolution*, 197, 207, 218.

31. Graymont, *The Iroquois in the American Revolution*, 218–20.

32. Calloway, *The American Revolution in Indian Country*, 129, 134–36, and chapter 5 generally; Graymont, *The Iroquois in the American Revolution*, 13, 47, 157–161; Graymont, "Koñwatsiátsiaéñni"; Feister and Pulis, "Molly Brant," 306–13; Green, "Molly Brant," 240–41; Huey and Pulis, *Molly Brant*, 49, 53, 107; Mann, *Iroquois Women*, 160–61.

33. Calloway, *The American Revolution in Indian Country*, 132; Graymont, *The Iroquois in the American Revolution*, 5; Mann, *Iroquois Women*, 126–46; Shenandoah and George, *Skywoman*, 99. Special thanks to Alyssa Mt. Pleasant, who first introduced Jigonsaseh to me and shared her own important research, including an unpublished essay, "Searching for Her Rightful Place: Jigonsaseh's Legacy amongst the Haudenosaunee."

34. Mann, *Iroquois Women*, 149–51; "Ganondagan State Historic Site," http://www.ganondagan.org/sitehist.html (accessed August 8, 2006); Mt. Pleasant, "Searching for Her Rightful Place," 1). The Marquis de Denonville was then the Governor of New France.

35. Huey and Pulis, *Molly Brant*, 41, 53–55, 59; Feister and Pulis, "Molly Brant," 306–7; Graymont, *The Iroquois in the American Revolution*, 64–70; Graymont, "Koñwatsiátsiaéñni." John Norton related in his *Journal* that Joseph and Molly were "descended from Wyandot prisoners adopted by the Mohawks both on the father and the mother's side." Norton, Klinck, and Talman, *Journal of Major John Norton*, 105.

36. Huey and Pulis, *Molly Brant*, 43–44; Green, "Molly Brant," 239–41. The protection of the Johnson family was at the forefront of the Mohawks' demands as early as the Albany Treaty. As Little Abraham told the Albany representatives, "You all know that during Sir William Johnson's lifetime,

and since, we have been peaceably disposed; but we were greatly alarmed at the report of a design against Col. [John] Johnson; for he is our property, and we shall not part with him.... Besides his being our Superintendent, the love we have for the memory of Sir William, and the obligations the whole Six Nations are under to him, must make us regard and protect every branch of his family" (*American Archives,* 4th ser., 2: 843).

37. Mann, *Iroquois Women,* 98; Graymont, *The Iroquois in the American Revolution,* 79; Huey and Pulis, *Molly Brant,* 41.

38. TPP, 59: 9.

39. Note that after the majority of Oneida warriors had joined the American side in the Revolution, they had a marginally more secure hold on their land, which benefited the New Stockbridge and Brothertown communities.

40. There has been some debate among historians over Brant's claim that "King" Hendrick was his grandfather. See, for instance, Stone, *Life of Joseph Brant,* 2–3. Some have interpreted this comment as a braggart's claim, mistakenly projecting European structures of kinship onto Brant's words. The comment makes a great deal of sense within Haudenosaunee conceptualizations of kinship. As the primary leader of Brant's clan in the village they both inhabited, Hendrick played a strong role as "grandfather" to the younger Mohawk, perhaps even acting as a stronger influence than his biological grandfathers.

41. ASP, 1: 8; Stone, *Life of Joseph Brant,* 280.

42. ASP, 1: 8.

43. Ibid., 1: 9.

44. State Historical Society of Wisconsin, Draper Manuscript Collection, Joseph Brant Ms. 11F204–5 (microfilm copy at Dartmouth College). Aupaumut noted, "Colonel McKee is half Shawanny, and the other British," and said that he was an "exceeding good instrument for the British." See Aupaumut, "Narrative of an Embassy to the Western Indians," 105. On McKee and other traders in the network of relations, see White, *Middle Ground,* 324, 456. The moon of wampum sealed the agreement between nations and was a center on which the four paths converged.

45. Kelsay, *Joseph Brant,* 346. According to Calloway, "Anthony Wayne described this as 'the grand emporium of the hostile Indians of the West,' and claimed he had never seen 'such immense fields of corn, in any part of America, from Canada to Florida'" (Calloway, *The American Revolution in Indian Country,* 289). White has observed that the "greatest political accomplishment" of the confederation was the "acceptance" among all "that the land belonged equally to all Indians of the *pays d'en haute,* could not be ceded without the consent of the entire confederation, and would be defended by all" (White, *Middle Ground,* 435). Lytwyn notes, "The words *dish with one spoon* and other similar terms have been used since time immemorial by aboriginal people in the Great Lakes and St. Lawrence valley.... The dish symbolizes a common hunting ground, while the spoon denotes that people are

free to hunt within it and to eat the game and fish together." See Victor P.
Lytwyn, "A Dish with One Spoon: The Shared Hunting Grounds Agreement
in the Great Lakes and St. Lawrence Valley Region," in *Papers of the Twenty-
Eighth Algonquian Conference* (Ottawa: Carleton University, 1994), 210. See
Draper Ms. 11F23; White, *Middle Ground*, 413–68; Kelsay, *Joseph Brant*, 344–47,
399–405, 410, and chap. 20; Stone, *Life of Joseph Brant*, 248–54, 264–72; Paul
Williams, "Treaty Making: The Legal Record," in *Treaty of Canadaigua 1794*, ed.
G. Peter Jemison and Anna M. Schein (Santa Fe: Clear Light Publishing, 2000),
38–39. See also Kelsay, *Joseph Brant*, 410–457, and White, *Middle Ground*, 441.

   46. ASP, 1: 9.

   47. Draper Ms. 23U31. On the Fort Stanwix and Great Miami Treaties, see
Kelsay, *Joseph Brant*, 354–61, 367, 396–97; John C. Mohawk, "The Canandaigua
Treaty in Historical Perspective," in Jemison and Schein, *Treaty of Canadaigua*,
48–49; Stone, *Life of Joseph Brant*, 243–44; Anthony F. C. Wallace, *The Death and
Rebirth of the Seneca* (New York: Vintage Books, 1972), 151–55; White, *Middle
Ground*, 417, 435–39; Williams, "Treaty Making," 39.

   48. Seneca leader Cornplanter told General Anthony Wayne that the Western Indians "wish it to be considered that they were the first people the Great
Spirit seated on this island, for which reason we look on the Americans as
children, to call them our younger brethren" (ASP, 1: 337).

   49. ASP, 1: 9.

   50. Ibid.

   51. Ibid. Colonial leaders were especially concerned about Brant. While
he was en route to Fort Stanwix in 1784, New York Governor George Clinton
instructed interpreter Peter Ryckman, "If you find . . . any Jealousy of, or envy
to[wards] Brant, you will try to discover who are most jealous or envious of
him and promote it as much as you prudently can." See "Clinton to Ryckman, August 14, 1784," in *Proceedings of the Commissioners of Indian Affairs,
Appointed by the Law for the Extinguishment of Indian Titles in the State of NY*,
ed. Franklin B. Hough (Albany, N.Y.: Joel Munsell, 1861), 1: 25.

   52. E. A. Cruikshank, ed., *The Correspondence of Lieutenant Governor John
Graves Simcoe*, 5 vols. (Toronto: The Society, 1923–31), 5: 3. According to Kelsay, Lieutenant Governor Simcoe of Canada said of Brant that the union was
"the first wish of his heart" (Kelsay, *Joseph Brant*, 492). American "divide-
and-conquer" policy continued in parallel to Brant's unifying effort. Knox
wrote to Governor Clinton in May, 1791 that "Brandt's exertions . . . to form a
grand confederation of all the Indians northwest of the Ohio . . . could not be
for the interest of the US: for, although justice, policy, and humanity, dictate a
liberal treatment of the Indians, it cannot be for the public interest to consoli-
date them in one body, which would be liable to a single impulse" (ASP, 1:
168). Brant and Kirkland had both been students at Wheelock's school, and it
was Brant who had first taught Kirkland the Mohawk language. Kirkland
was a missionary at Oneida for many years. See James Dow McCallum, *The*

Letters of Eleazar Wheelock's Indians (Hanover, N.H.: Dartmouth College, 1932), 293–94; Walter Pilkington, ed., *The Journal of Samuel Kirkland* (Clinton, N.Y.: Hamilton, 1980), xvi–xviii.

53. Aupaumut, "Narrative of an Embassy to the Western Indians," 76.

54. TPP, 59: 8.

55. Aupaumut, "Narrative of an Embassy to the Western Indians," 76, 101.

56. TPP, 60: 71.

57. Ibid.; Taylor, "Captain Hendrick Aupaumut," 442.

58. TPP, 59: 9. Aupaumut noted that he had been "invited last spring" by his Western relations to visit and council with them. On Aupaumut's motivations, see Taylor, "Captain Hendrick Aupaumut."

59. TPP, 60: 71.

60. On Aupaumut's role in renewing the Mohican position as "the front door," see Taylor, "Captain Hendrick Aupaumut," 432–57. See also Ronda, "As They Were," 47. The Mohawks are positioned at the eastern door of the Haudenosaunee Confederacy.

61. Kelsay, *Joseph Brant,* 340–50; William N. Fenton, "Structure, Continuity, and Change in the Process of Iroquois Treaty Making," in *The History and Culture of Iroquois Diplomacy,* ed. Francis Jennings and William N. Fenton (Syracuse: Syracuse University Press, 1985), 13; Doug George-Kanentiio, "The Mohawk Nation and the 1794 Treaty of Canadaigua," in Jemison and Schein, *Treaty of Canadaigua,* 124–26; Mt. Pleasant, "After the Whirlwind"; Robert J. Surtees, "The Iroquois in Canada," in Jennings and Fenton, *History and Culture,* 73–78; Wallace, *Death and Rebirth,* 149–83.

62. Aupaumut, "Narrative of an Embassy to the Western Indians," 78.

63. Aupaumut's relationship with Washington was forged during the Revolutionary War, when the general appointed Aupaumut captain of his Mohican company at the age of 23 (Calloway, *The American Revolution in Indian Country,* 99).

64. TPP, 59: 8. Although most of the Western Indians referred to Americans generally as "big knifes," Aupaumut took pains to distinguish between the American leadership and the back-country settlers, referring most often to the latter as "big knifes." However, in this case he was relaying the Western perspective, so he used the term to refer to the commissioners. See TPP, 60: 72 and White, *Middle Ground,* 429–31.

65. Aupaumut concluded his report with a further explication of this injustice: "The Western Indians (and my Cousin) gave me this account of the treaty at Fort McIntosh. That the Commissioners repeatedly urged them to sell their lands, which they constantly refused. At length the Commissioners caused all their soldiers to be drawn up under arms. That they intimidated the Chiefs: Captain Pipe in particular, could hardly hold his pipe to his mouth. Then the Chiefs agreed to whatever the Commissioners were pleased to dic-

tate." See TPP, 59: 13. See also Kelsay, *Joseph Brant*, 367–68, and White, *Middle Ground*, 417 and 435–39.

66. TPP, 59: 12.

67. On the Muskingum Compromise and the Fort Harmar councils, see Kelsay, *Joseph Brant*, 418–25; White, *Middle Ground*, 443–47; Wallace, *Death and Rebirth*, 156–59.

68. On the original Fort Stanwix Treaty, see White, *Middle Ground*, 351–54.

69. Stone, *Life of Joseph Brant*, 278.

70. Draper Ms. 23U66–9.

71. TPP, 59: 12.

72. Cruikshank, *Correspondence of Simcoe*, 2: 14–15.

73. ASP, 10. See also White, *Middle Ground*, 446.

74. TPP, 59: 12A.

75. ASP, 1: 481.

76. TPP, 59: 8A, 9; Cruikshank, *Correspondence of Simcoe*, 5: 34.

77. For instance, Knox described the Confederated Indians as "the tribes of Indians within the limits of the United States" (ASP, 9).

78. TPP, 59: 54. See Map 12 for these the territories to which Aupaumut referred. At the time of his visit, the Shawnees and Delawares were living near the rapids and the forks.

79. Pohquonnopeet lived at Big Cat's village on the AuGlaize River. He was probably related to Peter Poquanopeet, a leader at New Stockbridge who attended Dartmouth and was friendly with both Aupaumut and Samson Occom. See Aupaumut, "Narrative of an Embassy to the Western Indians," 87, 97–8; Calloway, *The American Revolution in Indian Country*, 100; Electa F. Jones, *Stockbridge, Past and Present; or, Records of an Old Mission Station* (Springfield, Mass.: S. Bowles, 1854), 75; and Love, *Samson Occom*, 238–39, 251, and 254. On Mohican movement to the Western country, see Taylor, "Captain Hendrick Aupaumut," 436–39, and Frazier, *Mohicans of Stockbridge*.

80. Hendrick Aupaumut, "Extract from an Indian History," *Collections of the Massachusetts Historical Society* 1, no. 9 (1804), 101. For Aupaumut's motivations regarding New Stockbridge, see Taylor, "Captain Hendrick Aupaumut," 443. For Northeastern Algonquian identity, see Colin G. Calloway, *After King Philip's War: Presence and Persistence in Indian New England* (Hanover, N.H.: University Press of New England, 1997), and *The Western Abenakis of Vermont, 1600–1800: War, Migration, and the Survival of an Indian People* (Norman: University of Oklahoma Press, 1990); Evan Haefeli and Kevin Sweeney, Haefeli and Sweeney, "Wattanummon's World: Personal and Tribal Identity in the Algonquian Diaspora, c. 1660–1712," in *Papers of the 25th Algonquian Conference* (Ottawa: Carleton University, 1994); William A. Haviland and Marjory W. Power, *The Original Vermonters: Native Inhabitants, Past and Present* (Hanover, N.H.: University Press of New England, 1994); Daniel R. Mandell,

Behind the Frontier: Indians in Eighteenth-Century Eastern Massachusetts (Lincoln: University of Nebraska Press, 1996); Kenneth M. Morrison, *The Embattled Northeast: The Elusive Ideal of Alliance in Abenaki–Euramerican Relations* (Berkeley: University of California Press, 1984); Amy Den Ouden, *Beyond Conquest: Native Peoples and the Struggle for History in New England* (Lincoln: University of Nebraska Press, 2005); Neal Salisbury, *Manitou and Providence: Indians, Europeans, and the Making of New England, 1500–1643* (New York: Oxford University Press, 1982). On similar organizational principles among Western Algonquians, see White, *Middle Ground,* 389, 413.

81. The relationship between Haudenosaunee identity and maternity is illustrated by the example of Brant. Because his mother was a Mohawk, although Brant had ancestral ties to the Wyandots and had been born in the Ohio Valley, he never mentioned these ties in his communications with the Western Indians. He identified exclusively as a Mohawk and a member of the Six Nations. This contrasts markedly with Aupaumut's emphasis on his connections with relatives who had relocated to the Ohio Valley. See Norton, Klinck, and Talman, *Journal of Major John Norton,* 105; Kelsay, *Joseph Brant,* 343; and Stone, *Life of Joseph Brant,* 2–3.

82. For instance, because of the status of Joseph's maternal family within the Confederacy, he could be, and was, assigned the role of "Pine Tree chief," or war chief, but not of clan chief. Kelsay, *Joseph Brant,* 32–33, 123.

83. On Haudenosaunee identity, see Akwesasne Notes, ed., *Basic Call to Consciousness* (Summertown, Tenn.: Book Publishing Co., 1991); Taiaiake Alfred, *Peace, Power, Righteousness: An Indigenous Manifesto* (New York: Oxford, 1999); Fenton, "Structure, Continuity, and Change"; Michael K. Foster, Jack Campisi, and Marianne Mithun, *Extending the Rafters: Interdisciplinary Approaches to Iroquoian Studies* (Albany: State University of New York Press, 1984); Oren Lyons, ed., *Exiled in the Land of the Free: Democracy, Indian Nations, and the U.S. Constitution* (Santa Fe: Clear Light Publishers, 1992); Jennings, *Ambiguous Iroquois Empire;* Mann, *Iroquois Women;* Arthur Caswell Parker, "The Constitution of the Five Nations," in *Parker on the Iroquois,* ed. William Fenton (Syracuse: Syracuse University Press, 1968), 42; Daniel Richter, *The Ordeal of the Longhouse* (Chapel Hill: University of North Carolina Press, 1992); Robert W. Venables, "Some Observations on the Treaty of Canadaigua," in Jemison and Schein, *Treaty of Canadaigua;* and Paul Wallace, *Death and Rebirth* and *White Roots of Peace* (Santa Fe: Clear Light Publishers, 1994).

84. Aupaumut, "Narrative of an Embassy to the Western Indians," 78.

85. Aupaumut, "Extract from an Indian History"; Jones, *Stockbridge,* 20.

86. TPP, 59: 43, 52. This "young man" was likely the grandson of John Waumwaumpequunaunt, one of the first Mohicans to acquire literacy. The elder John left his village of Kaunaumeek — near present-day New Lebanon, New York — at 12 or 13 to attend Timothy Woodbridge's school at Stock-

bridge (apparently "crying" to his parents to let him go), and later he taught David Brainerd and Jonathan Edwards the Mohican language and served as clerk for a Stockbridge company during the French and Indian War. John Sargeant described Waumwaumpequunaunt as having "superior abilities," while Edwards remarked on his formidable skills in reading, writing, interpreting, and exegesis, describing him as "an extraordinary man." See Frazier, *Mohicans of Stockbridge*, 45, 94, 120. See also Jones, *Stockbridge*, and Brasser, *Riding on the Frontier's Crest*.

87. Arthur Caswell Parker, "Constitution of the Five Nations," 17, and Seneca *Myths and Folk Tales* (Lincoln: University of Nebraska Press, 1989), 404. See also Akwesasne Notes, *Basic Call to Consciousness*; Alfred, *Peace, Power, Righteousness*; Jose Barriero, ed., *Indian Roots of American Democracy* (Ithaca, N.Y.: Akwekon Press of Cornell University, 1992); Fenton, "Structure, Continuity, and Change," 12–25; Lyons, *Exiled in the Land of the Free*; Irving Powless Jr., "Treaty Making," in Jemison and Schein, *Treaty of Canadaigua*; Venables, "Observations on the Treaty of Canadaigua," 95–98; and Wallace, *Death and Rebirth*, 39–42, and *White Roots*.

88. Parker, "Constitution of the Five Nations," 25, 29; Parker, *Seneca Myths and Folk Tales*, 405. The rhetoric of union appears frequently in Haudenosaunee speeches preceding the American Revolution. See, for instance, Cadwallader Colden, *The History of the Five Indian Nations* (Ithaca, N.Y.: Cornell University Press, 1994), and Carl Van Doren and Julian P. Boyd, eds., *Indian Treaties Printed by B. Franklin, 1736–62* (Philadelphia, 1938).

89. Parker, "Constitution of the Five Nations," 37, 45.

90. Such phrases as "United Nations," and "United Indian Nations" were commonly used by the Haudenosaunee to refer to themselves and the nations "united" under them during the French and Indian War, but in the Ohio Valley after the Revolution the phrase was used to invoke a union of equal nations, all invested in maintaining a bounded geographic and political space. On Haudenosaunee force and diplomacy in the Ohio Valley prior to the Revolution, see George Hunt, *The Wars of the Iroquois* (Madison: University of Wisconsin Press, 1940); Jennings, *Ambiguous Iroquois Empire*; Richter, *Ordeal of the Longhouse*; Wallace, *Death and Rebirth*; and White, *Middle Ground*.

91. TPP, 59: 19, 62: 10 (emphasis in original).

92. ASP, 168–69. See Knox correspondence with Clinton, Pickering, and Kirkland, ASP, 1: 165–68, 226–31, and 236, as well as Kelsay, *Joseph Brant*, 431–32, 438, 443, and 454. The principles of the dish, as articulated by Brant and other Haudenosaunee leaders, were instrumental to the passage of the 1790 Trade and Intercourse Act, which prohibited states from buying and selling Indian lands and vested the authority for land transactions with the federal government and Native nations. See Jemison and Schein, *Treaty of Canandaigua*, 4 and 50. Washington described "the Five Nations of Indians"

as "the Senecas, Oneidas, and Stockbridge Indians, incorporated with them the Tuscaroras, Cayugas, and Onondogas." See ASP, 1: 231–32.

93. TPP, 59: 49.

94. ASP, 1: 244.

95. TPP, 59: 19.

96. ASP, 1: 231, 245; Kelsay, *Joseph Brant*, 461–73; Stone, *Life of Joseph Brant*, 328–29; Cruikshank, *Correspondence of Simcoe*, 1: 224, 242.

97. TPP, 59: 41.

98. Aupaumut, "Narrative of an Embassy to the Western Indians," 92; Calloway, *The American Revolution in Indian Country*, 104. In fact, because of Aupaumut's status as a mediator, he secured a larger piece of the pot than did the Oneidas, causing some resentment among their Haudenosaunee hosts (Calloway, *The American Revolution in Indian Country*, 105). In recording the annuities article Washington noted, regarding the Five Nations, that the United States had thus "provided for you as for a part of themselves," suggesting that the "Five Nations" were contained within American space. See ASP, 1: 231–32. Brant's Mohawks were increasingly "excepted" from treaties between the Six Nations and the United States, largely due to their geographic and political attachment to the British.

99. Aupaumut, "Narrative of an Embassy to the Western Indians," 83–91.

100. Ibid., 86–113.

101. *Wenuhtkowuk* and *Kuhnauwautheew* are Mohican names for the Unalachtigo and Unami, brothers to the Mohicans, and clans of the Delaware. "Monthees" are Munsees. Also note that the term *Wauponnuhk* is linguistically similar to *Wabanaki(k)*, *Wampanoag*, and even *Wappinger*, all of which translate to "people of the dawnland," or "easterners." See Aupaumut, "Narrative of an Embassy to the Western Indians," 114–15. On the 1792 councils, see Kelsay, *Joseph Brant*, 477–82, and White, *Middle Ground*, 456–64. On Aupaumut's "Narrative of an Embassy to the Western Indians," see Ronda, "As They Were," 47–49, and Taylor, "Captain Hendrick Aupaumut," 444–47.

102. Aupaumut, "Narrative of an Embassy to the Western Indians," 113.

103. Ibid. See also Draper Ms. 11F116.

104. Aupaumut, "Narrative of an Embassy to the Western Indians," 113.

105. Ibid., 129. Note that Aupaumut even used the old Algonquian word for Mohawks, *Maqua*, which means "flesh-eater."

106. Aupaumut, "Narrative of an Embassy to the Western Indians," 115.

107. Ibid., 116. Aupaumut's account of this confrontation is supported by the council record in Cruikshank, *Correspondence of Simcoe*, 1: 220. Note that Aupaumut's image of a tightly woven Algonquian confederation was diffused by his need to placate the American readers of his report, relating in an aside, "I privately advised my friend Red Jacket, to tell these nations that they ought to speak to the Big knifes for peace." Also, although Aupaumut

wrote Brant into his dualistic Algonquian-Haudenosaunee narrative, Brant was not so much a target of these admonitions as Red Jacket's Senecas. When he arrived at the council, Brant joined the Western Indians in questioning the Senecas' loyalty. Cruikshank, *Correspondence of Simcoe,* 1: 224, 242.

108. See Taylor "Captain Hendrick Aupaumut," 444–5.

109. TPP, 59: 41.

110. TPP, 59: 42.

111. Cruikshank, *Correspondence of Simcoe,* 1: 221, 225–26.

112. Ibid., 1: 225, 242.

113. TPP, 59: 43.

114. Aupaumut, "Narrative of an Embassy to the Western Indians," 128.

115. Taylor, "Captain Hendrick Aupaumut," 448; TPP, 62: 45–48. In his letter to Pickering, Kirkland remarked, "There is not an Indian in the compass of my knowledge (Capt. Brant only excepted) who has more inveterate prejudices against white people than Mr. Occum, although his education and professional calling in most cases restrains them."

116. Cruikshank, *Correspondence of Simcoe,* 1: 242. Aupaumut did report that he received invitations from the Mohawk and Delaware villages at Grand River, as well as from the Western Indians, for the Mohicans to come live with them, but he presented this as evidence of their good standing as relations. He revealed only that he planned to take their messages home. See TPP, 59: 19.

117. ASP, 1: 346–47, 336–37. The Six Nations told the Americans to "send forward agents, who are men of honesty, not proud land-jobbers, but men who love and desire peace." They received a compromise appointment: the commission included Pickering, a man trusted by most of the Haudenosaunee leadership, but also Benjamin Lincoln of Massachusetts, who had little experience in Indian Affairs and believed quite firmly in Manifest Destiny. Beverley Rudolph of Virginia was the third member. See White, *Middle Ground,* 469–70. On the military expeditions, see White, *Middle Ground,* 454.

118. ASP, 1: 341. Washington was prepared to offer the Western Indians $50,000 "in goods," as well as $10,000 "in goods" annually (ASP, 1: 341).

119. ASP, 1: 346; TPP, 59: 203.

120. Cruikshank, *Correspondence of Simcoe,* 2: 6.

121. TPP, 59: 203.

122. Cruikshank, *Correspondence of Simcoe,* 2: 5–7. On the 1793 councils, see Kelsay, *Joseph Brant,* 491, and White, *Middle Ground,* 464–68.

123. Cruikshank, *Correspondence of Simcoe,* 2: 7, 5: 37; White, *Middle Ground,* 495–6.

124. Note that the Delawares suspected that the Wyandots and Shawnees were being stirred to war by the British; they remarked that the trader Simon Girty was "creep[ing] about like a serpent to le[a]d poor Indians astray,

by giving bad advise, and oppose the chiefs, and overthrow good things." Aupaumut reported to Pickering, "I find many well disposed who sincerely wished to have peace. But the Shawanese & Wyandots & Miamis are very willful." Furthermore, he wrote, "My younger brothers, the Shawanese, are much stupefied since the last war, they are become very foolish and obstinate, and are very high for war." He said that some of "the back nations" had even threatened to "boil the Shawanese" in their "kittles," a very different use of the metaphor of the pot, suggesting that the only way to rid the "pot" of dangerous people is to "boil" them in their own anger. See Aupaumut, "Narrative of an Embassy to the Western Indians," 111 and 106. See also Kelsay, *Joseph Brant*, 421.

125. Cruikshank, *Correspondence of Simcoe*, 2: 9–10.

126. Ibid., 2: 10–12 (emphasis in original).

127. Ibid., 2: 12.

128. Ibid., 2: 12–13. Both Brant and Aupaumut would later point to this "alarming voice" as a factor in the failure of their peacemaking missions (Cruikshank, *Correspondence of Simcoe*, 2: 103; Aupaumut, "Narrative of an Embassy to the Western Indians," 98).

129. Cruikshank, *Correspondence of Simcoe*, 2: 13; White, *Middle Ground*, 448.

130. Cruikshank, *Correspondence of Simcoe*, 2: 14–15.

131. Ibid., 2: 16. The Seven Nations of Canada were generally led by Mohawks and consisted of Haudenosaunee, Abenakis, Hurons, and Nipissings who lived in mission villages along the St. Lawrence River and had been previously allied with the French.

132. TPP, 59: 203.

133. Cruikshank, *Correspondence of Simcoe*, 2: 16, 102, 193, 3: 314. See also Kelsay, *Joseph Brant*, 498 and 505.

134. See Cruikshank, *Correspondence of Simcoe*, 1: 208, 308, 5: 317; Kelsay, *Joseph Brant*, 441, 483–91; Stone, *Life of Joseph Brant*, 270; and Wallace, *Death and Rebirth*, 156.

135. Cruikshank, *Correspondence of Simcoe*, 1: 309.

136. Ibid., 2: 17.

137. TPP, 59: 209.

138. "Le Capitaine Hiroquois ayant receu ces presens se leue & regardant le Soleil & puis toute l'assemblée, Onontio, dit-it, tu as dissipé tous les nuages, l'air est serain, le Ciel paroist à descouuert, le Soleil est brillant, ie ne vois plus de trouble, la paix a tout mis dans le Calme, mon Coeur est en repos, ie m'en vais bien content." Barthelemy Vimont and Jerome Lalemant, *Relation de la Nouvelle France és Anées 1644 & 1645* (Paris: Crovoisy, 1646), 122. My translation.

139. Peyer, *Tutor'd Mind*, 19.

140. Aupaumut's own narrative suggests that he was not complicit. When Brant accused him of being an agent of division, he insisted, "I had come with no such intention." Perhaps, Aupaumut reflected in his report,

Brant referred to the division between those who wanted peace and those who wanted war and this was the "division" he was accused of fomenting. Still, Aupaumut seems to have become increasingly aware of the possibility that he was being manipulated, and he frequently used the words of Brant and his relations to raise questions about U.S. duplicity. As Aupaumut reported to Pickering, Brant's message warned: "I have seen the great men of the US — they speak good words to the Muhheconnuck, but they did not speak so well to the Five Nations, and they speak contrary to the Big knifes, that the Big knifes may prepare for war." Aupaumut was especially anxious because he was risking his own position in the network. If he could not persuade his relations that the new colonial government was sincere, he risked not only the failure of his peacemaking mission but the loss of the Mohicans' newly secured place in Native space. See TPP, 59: 41, and Aupaumut, "Narrative of an Embassy to the Western Indians," 124.

141. The metaphor of "brush and briars" is common to Haudenosaunee speeches and the Sky Woman story. See Augustine Lan Van Pham, "English Colonial Treaties with American Indians: Observations on a Neglected Genre," Ph.D. diss., Fordham University, New York, 1977, 82–84, and Parker, *Seneca Myths and Folk Tales*, 65. The metaphor is also present in Aupaumut's journal (Aupaumut, "Narrative of an Embassy to the Western Indians," 87).

142. TPP, 60: 72A, 59: 56; Stone, *Life of Joseph Brant*, 278. While waiting at Niagara in 1791, the Mohican leader expressed great disappointment when he heard that the "army tis gone across the Indian Country, for which I was very sorry" (TPP, 59: 10–10A). In 1793, he told Pickering, "The Operations of the army was great obstacle" (TPP, 59: 203).

143. Cruikshank, *Correspondence of Simcoe*, 2: 6. In describing a previous United Indian Nations council, Brant related, "We went through our ancient custom of condoling with them, by giving about 10,000 wampum as we could not proceed with our public business till such time as that ceremony was over" (Brant to J. Johnson, August 28, 1788, quoted in Stone, *Life of Joseph Brant*, 276).

144. Aupaumut, "Narrative of an Embassy to the Western Indians," 81–84.

145. Ibid., 83, 85, 87.

146. Ibid., 88.

147. Ibid., 91.

148. Mann, *Iroquois Women*, 81. On the battle of Fallen Timbers, see Kelsay, *Joseph Brant*, 510–11; White, *Middle Ground*, 466–68; and Gregory Evans Dowd, *A Spirited Resistance: The North American Struggle for Unity, 1745–1815* (Baltimore: Johns Hopkins University Press, 1992), 113–14.

149. Taylor, "Captain Hendrick Aupaumut," 451.

150. Cruikshank, *Correspondence of Simcoe*, 2: 217. On Canandaigua, see Schein, *Treaty of Canandaigua*. Pickering was an instrumental force in negotiating the agreement, also known as the Timothy Pickering Treaty. Brant was

not present at the treaty council, although he was a key participant in the councils that led up to it.

151. Jones, *Stockbridge*, 95.

152. In many ways, Skyholder becomes synonymous with the "Great Spirit" and even with the Christian "God." See, for instance, Elm et al., *Oneida Creation Story*, 162.

153. Draper Ms. 12F78–9.

154. Mann, *Iroquois Women*, 135.

4. Regenerating the Village Dish

1. On Apess's life and writings, see William Apess and Barry O'Connell, eds., *On Our Own Ground: The Complete Writings of William Apess, a Pequot* (Amherst: University of Massachusetts Press, 1992). See also Bernd Peyer, *The Tutor'd Mind: Indian Missionary-Writers in Antebellum America* (Amherst: University of Massachusetts Press, 1997), chap. 4. I offer great thanks to Apess, O'Connell, and Peyer for their vital research and good advice. For a good discussion of the initial critical conversation about Apess, see Jace Weaver, *That the People Might Live: Native American Literatures and Native American Community* (New York: Oxford University Press, 1997). On the Mashpee Revolt, see Donald M. Nielsen, "The Mashpee Indian Revolt of 1833," *New England Quarterly* 58 (1985): 400–420; Jack Campisi, *The Mashpee Indians: Tribe on Trial* (Syracuse, N.Y.: Syracuse University Press, 1991); and Daniel R. Mandell, *Behind the Frontier: Indians in Eighteenth-Century Eastern Massachusetts* (Lincoln: University of Nebraska Press, 1996). See also James Clifford, *The Predicament of Culture: Twentieth-Century Ethnography, Literature, and Art* (Cambridge, Mass.: Harvard University Press, 1988), 277–346. On *Indian Nullification*, see Theresa Strouth Gaul, "Dialogue and Public Discourse in William Apess' Indian Nullification," *American Transcendental Quarterly* 15, no. 4 (2001): 275–92.

2. Apess and O'Connell, *On Our Own Ground*, 169–70.

3. Ibid., 170.

4. See Brian W. Dippie, *The Vanishing American* (Lawrence: University Press of Kansas, 1982); Robert F. Berkhofer, *The White Man's Indian: The History of an Idea from Columbus to the Present* (New York: Knopf, 1978); and Roy Harvey Pearce, *Savagism and Civilization: A Study of the Indian and the American Mind* (Baltimore: Johns Hopkins University Press, 1967). See also Peyer, *Tutor'd Mind*, 119–22; Barry O'Connell, "'Once More Let Us Consider': William Apess in the Writing of New England Native American History," in *After King Philip's War: Presence and Persistence in Indian New England*, ed. Colin G. Calloway (Hanover, N.H.: University Press of New England, 1997), 164–69; and Maureen Konkle, "Indian Literacy, U.S. Colonialism, and Literary Criticism," *American Literature* 69, no. 3 (1997): 464–66.

5. Theresa Gaul has observed, "In this passage, Apess plays with the contemporary fascination with skin color as the marker of race. Pretending uncertainty as to the racial identity of the congregation, something contemporary racial theories held could be ascertained visually through inspection of the body, Apess equates whiteness with death, rebutting centuries of positive associations with the color. Indeed, the living occupants of the meetinghouse appear to be deader than the Indians buried in the nearby graveyard, imbued as it is with natural imagery, a contrast that obliquely emphasizes the legacy of genocide borne by Euroamericans." Gaul, "Dialogue and Public Discourse in Indian Nullification," 281.

6. Apess and O'Connell, *On Our Own Ground*, 171 (emphasis in original).

7. See Philip Deloria, *Playing Indian* (New Haven: Yale University Press, 1998), and Gaul, "Dialogue and Public Discourse in Nullification," 282. See also Helen Carr, *Inventing the American Primitive: Politics, Gender, and the Representation of Native American Literary Traditions, 1789–1936* (Cork, Ireland: Cork University Press, 1996), esp. 143–45, and Susan Scheckel, *The Insistence of the Indian: Race and Nationalism in Nineteenth-Century American Culture* (Princeton, N.J.: Princeton University Press, 1998), esp. 19–25.

8. Apess and O'Connell, *On Our Own Ground*, 171. Apess is using the Bible to take Christians to task, one of his most common strategies for exposing the hypocrisy of injustice that is masked by religion. Many critics have already explored Apess's Christianity and his strategic use of Christian doctrine, so I have chosen not to focus on it here. See, for instance, Apess and O'Connell, *On Our Own Ground*, xxi–xxiii, xxxi–xxxiv, lv–lxi, and lxix–lxxii; Barry O'Connell, "William Apess and the Survival of the Pequot People," in *Algonkians of New England: Past and Present; The Dublin Seminary for New England Folklife Annual Proceedings*, ed. Peter Benes and Jane Montague Benes (Boston: Boston University Press, 1991); David Murray, *Forkedd Tongues: Speech, Writing, and Representation in North American Indian Texts* (Bloomington: Indiana University Press, 1991), 57–64; Sandra Gustafson, "Nations of Israelites: Prophecy and Cultural Autonomy in the Writings of William Apess," *Religion and Literature* 26, no. 1 (1994): 31–53; Carolyn Haynes, "'A Mark for Them All to...Hiss At': The Formation of Methodist and Pequot Identity in the Conversion Narrative of William Apess," *Early American Literature* 31, no. 1 (1996): 25–44; Karim Tiro, "Denominated 'Savage': Methodism, Writing, and Identity in the Works of William Apess, a Pequot," *American Quarterly* 48, no. 4 (1996): 653–79; and Hilary Wyss, *Writing Indians: Literacy, Christianity, and Native Community in Early America* (Amherst: University of Massachusetts Press, 2000), 154–67.

9. Apess and O'Connell, *On Our Own Ground*, 171; Mandell, *Behind the Frontier*, 53, 69, 74, 108–9; 176–80; Campisi, *Mashpee Indians*, 80–81.

10. Gaul astutely observes, "The meetinghouse became the physical space on the Mashpee plantation from which white control emanated. To the

Mashpee, reclaiming the space of the meetinghouse from the whites became an important symbolic maneuver in their effort to gain the right of self-governance." Gaul, "Dialogue and Public Discourse in Indian Nullification," 281. See Mandell, *Behind the Frontier*, 53, 69, 74, 108–9; and 176–80, and Campisi, *Mashpee Indians*, 80–81. On New England Indians and Christianity, see Mandell, *Behind the Frontier*; Peyer, *Tutor'd Mind*; William DeLoss Love, *Samson Occom and the Christian Indians of New England* (Syracuse, N.Y.: Syracuse University Press, 2000); O'Connell, "Introduction" to *On Our Own Ground*; O'Connell, "William Apess"; Neal Salisbury, "Red Puritans: The 'Praying Indians' of Massachusetts Bay and John Eliot," *William and Mary Quarterly* 31 (1974): 27–54; William Scranton Simmons, "The Great Awakening and Indian Conversion in Southern New England," in *Papers of the Tenth Algonquian Conference*, ed. William Cowan (Ottawa: Carleton University Press, 1979), and "Red Yankees: Narragansett Conversion in the Great Awakening," *American Ethnologist* 10 (1983): 253–71; and Wyss, *Writing Indians*.

11. Apess and O'Connell, *On Our Own Ground*, 172, 269, 169.

12. Campisi, *Mashpee Indians*, 76–80, 91; Mandell, *Behind the Frontier*, 149–69, 117–25, 176–79; Benjamin F. Hallett, *Argument of Benjamin F. Hallett, Counsel for the Memorialists of the Marshpee Tribe, before the Joint Committee of the Legislature of Massachusetts* (Boston: J. Howe, 1834), 2; Apess and O'Connell, *On Our Own Ground*, 238. See also Jean M. O'Brien, *Dispossession by Degrees: Indian Land and Identity in Natick, Massachusetts, 1650–1790* (Cambridge: Cambridge University Press, 1997). Hallett's *Argument* was published at the "request of Isaac Coombs, Daniel Amos, and William Apess, the Marshpee Delegation."

13. Campisi, *Mashpee Indians*, 86; Timothy Dwight, *Travels in New England and New York*, ed. Barbara Miller Solomon, 4 vols. (Cambridge, Mass.: Harvard University Press, 1969), 4: 38–40; William Cronon, *Changes in the Land: Indians, Colonists, and the Ecology of New England* (New York: Hill and Wang, 1983), 13, 28–29, 47–51, 90–91, 118–19; William A. Patterson III and Andrew E. Backman, "Fire and Disease History of Forests," in *Vegetation History*, ed. B. Huntley and T. Webb III (Boston: Kluwer Academic, 1988); William A. Patterson III and Kenneth E. Sassaman, "Indian Fires in the Prehistory of New England," in *Holocene Human Ecology in Northeastern North America*, ed. George P. Nicholas (New York: Plenum, 1988); Tom Wessels, *Reading the Forested Landscape: A Natural History of New England* (Woodstock, Vt.: Countryman Press, 1997), 31–38; USDA Forest Service, "Fire Ecology: Pinus Rigida," in *Fire Effects Information* (FEIS), http://www.fs.fed.us/database/feis/plants/tree/pinrig/fire_ecology.html (accessed June 28, 2003). Special thanks to Bill Patterson, who has been working for over twenty-five years on recovering the process of controlled burns, for taking the time to talk with me about how fire operates in New England forests and for inviting me to participate in learning from the forest firsthand.

14. FEIS; Cronon, *Changes in the Land,* 29; Wessels, *Reading the Forested Landscape,* 31.

15. Mandell, *Behind the Frontier,* 81–91; Campisi, *Mashpee Indians,* 86–92; Petition of the Proprietors of Marshpee (1788), quoted in Hallett, *Argument,* 20.

16. For a full analysis of this phenomenon, see Cronon, *Changes in the Land,* 114–26. The title of this section is taken from chapter 6 of *Changes in the Land* (108), in which Cronon fully explores the ideology, process, and effects of colonial deforestation.

17. Mandell, *Behind the Frontier,* 137.

18. Dona Brown, *Inventing New England: Regional Tourism in the Nineteenth Century* (Washington: Smithsonian Institution Press, 1995), 212; Cronon, *Changes in the Land,* 120–21; Dwight, *Travels in New England and New York,* 4: 151, 332. This Timothy Dwight, the president of Yale College, was a direct descendant of the Timothy Dwight who had commanded Fort Dummer during Greylock's War, lending special irony to his use of the phrase "our forests." Barbara Miller Solomon, "Introduction" to Dwight, *Travels in New England and New York,* 1: xi.

19. Dwight, *Travels in New England and New York,* 3: 56; Henry David Thoreau, *Cape Cod* (New York: Thomas Y. Crowell, 1961), 25, 296–97; Campisi, *Mashpee Indians,* 88–91; Mandell, *Behind the Frontier,* 176–205.

20. Ibid., 74–76, 90–91, 110, 125–26; Campisi, *Mashpee Indians,* 82.

21. Campisi, *Mashpee Indians,* 89.

22. Mandell, *Behind the Frontier,* 147.

23. Ibid., 141, 147, 152.

24. Hallett, *Argument,* 18; Mandell, *Behind the Frontier,* 147, 138–39, 156.

25. Cognehew's participation in the Mashpee case, like Apess's sixty years later, reflects the extensive social networks of Native New England. See Mandell, *Behind the Frontier,* 125–26 and 181, and Amy Den Ouden, *Beyond Conquest: Native Peoples and the Struggle for History in New England* (Lincoln: University of Nebraska Press, 2005), 154–55.

26. "Petition of Reuben Cognehew," *Massachusetts Archives* 33: 144–48; Hallett, *Argument,* 19; Campisi, *Mashpee Indians,* 84–85; Mandell, *Behind the Frontier,* 156–58.

27. Hallett, *Argument,* 9, 19–21; Campisi, *Mashpee Indians,* 84–85; Mandell, *Behind the Frontier,* 156–58.

28. Apess and O'Connell, *On Our Own Ground,* 4–7; Dwight, *Travels in New England and New York,* 1: 125; Ouden, *Beyond Conquest,* 155, 166, 175. On Apess's title, see Apess and O'Connell, *On Our Own Ground,* l–liii. See also Weaver, *That the People Might Live,* 55–56; Robert Warrior, *The People and the Word* (Minneapolis: University of Minnesota Press, 2005), 1–47. On Pequot history, see Ouden, *Beyond Conquest,* chaps. 1, 2, 3, and 5.

29. Apess and O'Connell, *On Our Own Ground,* 32–33.

30. Peyer, *Tutor'd Mind,* 135; Apess and O'Connell, *On Our Own Ground,* lx–lxi, 40, 148–51; O'Connell, "'Once More,'" 173; Peyer, *Tutor'd Mind,* 135–36.

31. Roger Williams, preface to *A Key into the Language of America* (Boston: George Dexter, 1643). See also Vine Deloria Jr., *God Is Red* (Golden, Colo.: Fulcrum, 1992), 77.

32. "Conference with Polin &c Indians of Presumpscot, August 10, 1739," in *Baxter Manuscripts: Documentary History of the State of Maine,* ed. James P. Baxter, 24 vols. (Portland: Maine Historical Society, 1869–1916), 23: 257; "Observations on the Western Territory and the Indian War," Thomas Wallcut Papers, American Antiquarian Society, 66. Note that the Wabanaki creation story describes human beings' creation from the ash tree. See Joseph Bruchac, *The Faithful Hunter: Abenaki Stories* (Greenfield Center, N.Y.: Greenfield Review Press, 1988), 9–10.

33. Dwight, *Travels in New England and New York,* 1: 75, 3: 16; Barbara Miller Solomon, "Introduction" to Dwight, *Travels in New England and New York,* 1: xi; Crevecoeur quote in Mandell, *Behind the Frontier,* 182; Jedidiah Morse, *A Report to the Secretary of War of United States, on Indian Affairs* (New Haven, Conn.: S. Converse, 1822), 75; "Editorial," *Oregonian* 1, no. 2. (November 1838), 54.

34. See Apess and O'Connell, *On Our Own Ground,* 200, 212, and 172. In contrast with Apess, Dwight suggested that the cause of Indian "degradation" was the loss of the hunting life and a consequent lack of "motive" for laboring, which might ultimately be replaced with "the love of [individual] property." Dwight, *Travels in New England and New York,* 3: 17–18.

35. Dwight, *Travels in New England and New York,* 3: 14, 17.

36. Apess and O'Connell, *On Our Own Ground,* 172, 179. Thanks to Barry O'Connell for confirming my suspicion about the connection between Apess's pamphlet and the "Eulogy." On the "Eulogy," see Apess and O'Connell, *On Our Own Ground,* 275–310, chap. 5.

37. Apess and O'Connell, *On Our Own Ground,* 172.

38. Ibid., 172–73.

39. Ibid., 174.

40. Apess may have been invoking the memory of King Philip's distribution of wampum. In the "Eulogy," Apess observed that in "an act that outweighs all the princes and emperors of the world," King Philip cut his coat of wampum in "pieces and distributed it among all his chiefs and warriors.... It cheered their hearts still to persevere to maintain their rights and expel their enemies." Apess and O'Connell, *On Our Own Ground,* 297.

41. Apess and O'Connell, *On Our Own Ground,* 173.

42. Steve Pike and Michael Keith, *Geographies of Resistance* (London: Routledge, 1997), 23.

43. Apess and O'Connell, *On Our Own Ground,* 166, 174.

44. "Documents Relative to the Marshpee Indians," Senate doc. no. 14, 3–7, *Documents Printed by Order of the Senate of the Commonwealth of Massachusetts* (Boston: Dutton and Wentworth, 1834). This petition is mentioned, but not quoted in full, in *Indian Nullification.* Apess and O'Connell, *On Our Own Ground,* 174.

45. "Documents Relative to the Marshpee Indians."

46. Ibid.

47. Ibid.

48. Ibid.

49. Ibid.

50. Senate doc. no. 14, 7; Apess and O'Connell, *On Our Own Ground,* 175.

51. In *Indian Nullification,* Apess included an article from the *Boston Daily Advocate,* probably written by Hallett, reporting that "one-fifth" of the volunteers from "the whole county of Barnstable" were Mashpees. The article noted, "No white town in the County furnished anything like this proportion of the 149 volunteers." It also noted that "most of the women in Marshpee had lost their husbands in the war," and only one Mashpee veteran survived. Apess and O'Connell, *On Our Own Ground,* 240.

52. Apess and O'Connell, *On Our Own Ground,* 239.

53. Ibid., 176.

54. Ibid., 175–77.

55. Ibid., 178–79; "Statement of Solomon Attaquin," Hearing before the Committee on Indians, February 9, 1869, manuscript on file at the Massachusetts Archives, Boston, Mass., 86 (emphasis in original). Solomon Attaquin was an entrepreneur and leader at Mashpee in the 1860s.

56. Apess and O'Connell, *On Our Own Ground,* 180.

57. Ibid., 181.

58. Ibid.

59. Ibid., 182–84. See Gaul, "Dialogue and Public Discourse in Indian Nullification," 279–80.

60. Apess and O'Connell, *On Our Own Ground,* 183. See also Senate doc. no. 14, 9–34. Hallett argued that the Mashpees were "not a domestic nation, as the Cherokees are declared by the Supreme Court of the United States" (Hallett, *Argument,* 9). For more on the legal concept of "domestic dependent nation," see Michael Paul Rogin, *Fathers and Children: Andrew Jackson and the Subjugation of the American Indian* (New York: Vintage Books, 1976), and David E. Wilkins, *American Indian Sovereignty and the U.S. Supreme Court* (Austin: University of Texas Press, 1997). See also Konkle, "Indian Literacy"; Peyer, *Tutor'd Mind,* 119–22; Anne Marie Dannenberg, "'Where, Then, Shall We Place the Hero of the Wilderness': William Apess' Eulogy on King Philip and Doctrines of Racial Destiny," in *Early Native American Writing: New Critical Essays,* ed. Helen Jaskoski (New York: Cambridge University Press, 1996), 66–82.

61. Apess and O'Connell, *On Our Own Ground*, 191–92. On Manifest Destiny, see Reginald Horsman, *Race and Manifest Destiny: The Origins of Racial Anglo-Saxonism* (Cambridge, Mass.: Harvard University Press, 1981). See also Carr, *Inventing the American Primitive*, 9.

62. Note that many Mashpees had acquired literacy long before Apess arrived, including Daniel Amos, Ezra Attaquin, and Isaac Coombs. Apess and O'Connell, *On Our Own Ground*, 219; Peyer, *Tutor'd Mind*, 146.

63. Apess and O'Connell, *On Our Own Ground*, 186, 190, 198.

64. Ibid., 195.

65. Ibid., 205.

66. Ibid., 176.

67. Ibid., 212.

68. Ibid., 198, 205.

69. "Memorial of the Marshpee Indians," House Document no. 11, *Massachusetts House Documents* (Boston: Dutton and Wentworth, 1834), 1; Apess and O'Connell, *On Our Own Ground*, 206–8, 219.

70. Apess and O'Connell, *On Our Own Ground*, 219–221, 226.

71. Ibid., 225, 219; "Memorial of Phineas Fish" and "Remonstrance of Nathan Pocknet, etc.," House Document no. 18, *Massachusetts House Documents* (Boston: Dutton and Wentworth, 1834), 2–5.

72. Apess and O'Connell, *On Our Own Ground*, 218.

73. Ibid.

74. According to Hallett, this petition was composed in council and boasted 287 signatures; the opposition petition bore only 50 signatures, a number of them signatures of members of one family, and only ten of them signatures of actual "proprietors" (Apess and O'Connell, *On Our Own Ground*, 231). The document itself was signed by "78 males and 92 females on the Plantation; and in behalf of 79 males and 37 females who are absent, and will not return to live under the present laws — in all 287" (House Document no. 11, 13).

75. House doc. no. 11, 2. In referring to those who were manipulated through drink, the Mashpee leadership was certainly referring to Nathan Pocknet, the first signer of the remonstrance. Pocknet testified in court that they "had liberty enough." Addressing his testimony, Apess observed: "It was a notable piece of policy on the part of the overseers to make a few friends among the Indians, in order to use them for their own purposes. Thus do pigeon trappers use to set up a decoy. When the bird flutters, the flock settles round him, the net is sprung, and they are in fast hands." In later years, Pocknet would describe the revolt as a great moment of success, speaking as if he had participated on the same side as Apess, Amos, and the majority of Mashpees. Nielsen, "Mashpee Revolt," 417; Apess and O'Connell, *On Our Own Ground*, 229; Hearing before the Committee on Indians, February 9, 1869, 61–66. See also Ann Marie and Gregory Button Plane, "The Massachu-

setts Indian Enfranchisement Act: Ethnic Conflict in the Historical Context, 1849–1869," *Ethnohistory* 40, no. 4 (1993): 587–618.

76. Apess and O'Connell, *On Our Own Ground*, 239–40, 222–24.

77. House doc. 11, 2. Although Apess references the petition, he does not quote it in full, noting that the Mashpees wrote it "by themselves, without assistance." Apess and O'Connell, *On Our Own Ground*, 206, 231–32.

78. See Dannenberg, "'Where Then,'" 75; O'Connell, *On Our Own Ground*, lxx.

79. House doc. 11, 2.

80. House doc. 11, 3.

81. Ibid., 6.

82. Ibid., 6–8. The Mashpees reported that the overseers were selling, on average, "not less than twelve hundred cords per year of cord wood, besides other wood that is sold for fires around about us; and if we want any, we have to pay one dollar per cord for pine wood, and one dollar fifty cents for oak, out of our commons, and then sell it to just such men as the Overseers say, and to no others; and we think that such a tax is erroneous, to pay for our own wood."

83. House doc. 11, 8, 11; Apess and O'Connell, *On Our Own Ground*, 212.

84. House doc. 11, 12–13 (emphasis in original).

85. Apess and O'Connell, *On Our Own Ground*, 241, 264; Campisi, *Mashpee Indians*, 105.

86. Apess and O'Connell, *On Our Own Ground*, 170. The Mashpees' title to their meetinghouse was recognized in 1840, but Massachusetts passed a law the same year that required allotment of the Mashpee reserve, dividing the common lands against the will of the majority of the members of the tribe. Campisi, *Mashpee Indians*, 107; Plane, "Indian Enfranchisement," Hearing before the Committee on Indians, February 9, 1869.

87. O'Connell, "Introduction," xxxviii.

5. Envisioning New England as Native Space

1. On the *Eulogy*, see Barry O'Connell, "Introduction" to Apess and O'Connel, *On Our Own Ground*, lxix–lxxv; Barry O'Connell, "'Once More Let Us Consider': William Apess in the Writing of New England Native American History," in *After King Philip's War: Presence and Persistence in Indian New England*, ed. Colin G. Calloway (Hanover, N.H.: University Press of New England, 1997); Bernd Peyer, *The Tutor'd Mind: Indian Missionary-Writers in Antebellum America* (Amherst: University of Massachusetts Press, 1997), 159–65; Anne Marie Dannenberg, "'Where, Then, Shall We Place the Hero of the Wilderness': William Apess' *Eulogy on King Philip* and Doctrines of Racial Destiny," in *Early Native American Writing: New Critical Essays*, ed. Helen Jaskoski (New York: Cambridge University Press, 1996); Maureen Konkle,

"Indian Literacy, U.S. Colonialism, and Literary Criticism," *American Literature* 69, no. 3 (1997): 457–86; Sandra Gustafson, "Nations of Israelites: Prophecy and Cultural Autonomy in the Writings of William Apess," *Religion and Literature* 26, no. 1 (1994): 31–53.

2. See Russell Bourne, *The Red King's Rebellion* (New York: Atheneum, 1990); Douglas Edward Leach, *Flintlock and Tomahawk: New England in King Philip's War* (New York: Macmillan, 1958); Jill Lepore, *The Name of War: King Philip's War and the Origins of American Identity* (New York: Knopf, 1998); Russell Bourne, *The Red King's Rebellion* (New York: Atheneum, 1990); Eric B. Schultz and Michael J. Tougias, *King Philip's War: The History and Legacy of America's Forgotten Conflict* (Woodstock, Vt.: Countryman, 1999); Richard Slotkin and James K. Folsom, *So Dreadful a Judgment: Puritan Responses to King Philip's War, 1676–1677* (Middletown, Conn.: Wesleyan University Press, 1978).

3. Apess and O'Connell, *On Our Own Ground,* 218; Lepore, *Name of War,* 191–226. Lepore notes that *Metamora* had a long run at the Tremont Theatre, where the Mashpee delegation gave one of its rousing speeches either during the play's run or just after it closed. She also observes that the Odeon was "just a few blocks away from the Tremont." The Odeon had recently been converted into a lecture hall, replacing the Boston/Federal Street Theatre, one of the most famous theaters in the nation. See Proprietors of the Boston Athenaeum, "Brief Histories of Boston Theaters," 2001, http://www.bostonathenaeum.org/bostontheaterhistoriesa.html (accessed April 12, 2004).

4. Apess and O'Connell, *On Our Own Ground,* 277.

5. Ibid., 286.

6. Ibid., 276. See also Konkle, "Indian Literacy," 466.

7. Konkle, "Indian Literacy," 467.

8. As Konkle notes, Apess's assertion that "Indian government precedes European civilization or society in America . . . is no minor point in the nineteenth century, when the common conception was that Indians, as savages in a state of nature, were incapable of forming stable political associations" (Konkle, "Indian Literacy," 467). See also Dannenberg, "'Where Shall We Place the Hero,'" 71.

9. Apess and O'Connell, *On Our Own Ground,* 280, 294.

10. O'Connell observes that although Apess "never says whether he speaks Pequot," his close relationships with Sally George, who spoke "little English," and other Pequot speakers suggests "that he had some fluency in his first language." O'Connell also proposes that although Apess was an indentured servant for much of his childhood, his Pequot relations remained close by: "He may even have seen some of his relatives daily" and maintained "regular contact . . . with members of his family and other Pequots." This would have enabled him to maintain conversational fluency, which

would have aided his communications with other Algonquian peoples, including Abenakis at Lake Champlain and Mississaugas at the Bay of Quinte. O'Connell, "'Once More,'" 173.

11. Currently, *ndakinna* is used most frequently, with a conscious sense of the power relations of colonialism. See, for instance, Joseph Bruchac, *Ndakinna: New and Selected Poems* (Albuquerque: West End, 2003), and Cheryl Savageau, "Like the Trails of Ndakinna" in Savageau, *Dirt Road Home* (Willimantic, Conn.: Curbstone, 1995). *Wliwni* to John Moody for explaining the difference between *kdakinna* and *ndakinna*. For examples in Abenaki and Mohegan–Pequot, see Joseph Laurent, *New Familiar Abenaki and English Dialogues* (Quebec: L. Brousseau, 1884), 58–59, and Frank Speck, "Native Tribes and Dialects of Connecticut: A Mohegan–Pequot Diary," *Annual Report of the Bureau of American Ethnology, 1925–6* 43 (1928), 282–83.

12. Apess and O'Connell, *On Our Own Ground*, 278.

13. Ibid.

14. Ibid., 277.

15. Ibid., 279.

16. Ibid.

17. Helen Carr has noted that by the mid-nineteenth century, Indians were commonly regarded as "failures in the evolutionary process" which "must disappear along with the buffalo and the forests from whom they could scarcely be distinguished." See Helen Carr, *Inventing the American Primitive: Politics, Gender, and the Representation of Native American Literary Traditions, 1789–1936* (Cork, Ireland: Cork University Press, 1996), 67. See also Susan Scheckel, *The Insistence of the Indian: Race and Nationalism in Nineteenth-Century American Culture* (Princeton, N.J.: Princeton University Press, 1998), 5, and Dannenberg, "'Where Shall We Place the Hero,'" 72–73.

18. Dannenberg observes, "Throughout, Apess' *Eulogy* argues that our reading of the past determines our understanding of the present" (Dannenberg, "'Where Shall We Place the Hero,'" 67). See also O'Connell, "Once More," 165–66, 172; Konkle, "Indian Literacy," 460, 473.

19. Apess and O'Connell, *On Our Own Ground*, 280; Dannenberg, "'Where Shall We Place the Hero,'" 72.

20. Apess and O'Connell, *On Our Own Ground*, 281–82.

21. Konkle, "Indian Literacy," 466, 470–71; Dannenberg, "'Where Shall We Place the Hero,'" 67; Peyer, *Tutor'd Mind*, 119; Jace Weaver, *That the People Might Live: Native American Literatures and Native American Community* (New York: Oxford University Press, 1997), 56.

22. Apess and O'Connell, *On Our Own Ground*, 284.

23. Ibid., 285.

24. See Dannenberg, "'Where Shall We Place the Hero,'" 72, and Lepore, *Name of War*, 191–226.

25. Apess and O'Connell, *On Our Own Ground,* 286. In citing December 22, Apess is mimicking local celebrations of the mythological Plymouth landing, most notably Daniel Webster's speeches on December 22, 1820, and July 4, 1826. O'Connell notes, "Apess is, very consciously, I think, echoing and disputing Webster's reverential reading."

26. Apess and O'Connell, *On Our Own Ground,* 286.

27. Ibid., 287. See also Dannenberg, "'Where Shall We Place the Hero,'" 72.

28. Apess and O'Connell, *On Our Own Ground,* 287.

29. Ibid.

30. Ibid., 288.

31. Ibid., 291.

32. O'Connell, "Once More," 163–65, 172; Konkle, "Indian Literacy," 469–71.

33. Apess and O'Connell, *On Our Own Ground,* 297.

34. Ibid., 299.

35. Ibid., 300–301.

36. Ibid., 306. Note that Apess's "canker" is an older word for "cancer." "Canker," "Cancer," *Oxford English Dictionary,* http://dictionary.oed.com (accessed August 10, 2003). Used by agreement with Cornell University.

37. Apess and O'Connell, *On Our Own Ground,* 307.

38. Ibid., 306.

39. Dannenberg, "'Where Shall We Place the Hero,'" 79. See also Lucy Maddox, *Removals: Nineteenth-Century American Literature and the Politics of Indian Affairs* (New York: Oxford University Press, 1991), 6.

40. Konkle confirms that Apess is arguing for the "*coexistence* of the U.S. and Indian nations, a goal that would be achieved when Indian citizens could reside unmolested in Indian nations" (Konkle, "Indian Literacy," 469).

41. Apess and O'Connell, *On Our Own Ground,* 288, 308.

42. Ibid., 309.

43. Ibid., 10.

44. Ibid., 310.

6. Awikhigawôgan

1. These interpretations arose from my contemplation and study of Native-language texts.

2. Gordon M. Day, *Western Abenaki Dictionary* (Hull, Quebec: Canadian Museum of Civilization, 1994), 1: 50, 2: 44, 457. Note that the same is true for Eastern Abenaki. A contemporary Passamaquoddy dictionary defines *wikhikon* as "book, letter, any written material" and *wikhike* as "he writes, paints, draws, takes a picture, etc." Robert M. Leavitt and David A. Francis, eds., *Kolusuwakonol: Peskotomuhkati–wolastoqewi naka Ikolisomani latuwewakon — Philip S. LeSourd's English and Passamaquoddy–Maliseet Dictionary* (Perry, Me.: Passamaquoddy–Maliseet Bilingual Program, ESEA Title VII, 1986), 105–6.

3. Bill Ashcroft, *On Post-Colonial Futures* (New York: Continuum, 2001), 19.

4. Joseph Johnson, *To Do Good to My Indian Brethren: The Writings of Joseph Johnson, 1751–1776*, ed. Laura J. Murray (Amherst: University of Massachusetts Press, 1998), 26.

5. Ibid.

6. Ibid., 192.

7. Ibid., 183, 186.

8. Sarah Wyacks to Samson Occom, Mohegan, August 2, 1763, Folder 2: Correspondence, 1761-5, Samson Occom Papers, Connecticut Historical Society, Hartford, Connecticut; Jacob Fowler to Samson Occom, Groton, December 17, 1772, Folder 6: Correspondence, 1771-2, Samson Occom Papers (emphasis in original).

9. Walter Pilkington, ed., *The Journal of Samuel Kirkland* (Clinton, N.Y.: Hamilton, 1980), 4; "Letter draft," Folder 2: "Correspondence, 1761-5," Samson Occom Papers.

10. Hendrick Aupaumut, "A Narrative of an Embassy to the Western Indians, from the Original Manuscript of Hendrick Aupaumut," *Collections of the Massachusetts Historical Society*, 1st ser., 9: 81, 110; E. A. Cruikshank, ed., *The Correspondence of Lieutenant Governor John Graves Simcoe*, 5 vols. (Toronto: The Society, 1923–31), 2: 17; Timothy Pickering Papers, Massachusetts Historical Society (TPP), 59: 43.

11. TPP, 60: 96, 105; State Historical Society of Wisconsin, Draper Manuscript Collection, Ms. 23U33.

12. Aupaumut, "Narrative of an Embassy to the Western Indians," 106; TPP, 59: 9. On continuing use of wampum, see Aupaumut, "Narrative of an Embassy to the Western Indians," 81–95, 100–104, and 130, and Cruikshank, *Correspondence of John Simcoe*, 2: 5, 7, and 10–16.

13. Samson Occom, *A Sermon, Preached at the Execution of Moses Paul* (New Haven, Conn: T & S Green, 1772); John Norton, Carl Frederick Klinck, and James John Talman, *The Journal of Major John Norton, 1816* (Toronto: Champlain Society, 1970), 9; David Murray, *Indian Giving: Economies of Power in Indian–White Exchanges* (Amherst: University of Massachusetts Press, 2000), 28–29; Richard White, *The Middle Ground: Indians, Empires, and Republics in the Great Lakes Region, 1650–1815* (New York: Cambridge University Press, 1991), 129. Thanks to Kate Shanley, who first got me thinking about the meaning of prayers for pity in her course at Cornell.

14. Bernd Peyer, *The Tutor'd Mind: Indian Missionary-Writers in Antebellum America* (Amherst: University of Massachusetts Press, 1997), 155, 163; Jace Weaver, *That the People Might Live: Native American Literatures and Native American Community* (New York: Oxford University Press, 1997), 51–53; Laura J. Murray, "'Pray Sir, Consider a Little': Rituals of Subordination and Strategies of Resistance in the Letters of Hezekiah Calvin and David Fowler to Eleazar Wheelock, 1764–1768," *Studies in American Indian Literatures* 4,

nos. 2–3 (1992): 48–81. On "Indian humor," see Vine Deloria, *Custer Died for Your Sins* (New York: Avon Books, 1969), 148–68, and Joseph Bruchac, *Roots of Survival* (Golden, Colo.: Fulcrum, 1996), 153–62. On "survivance," see Gerald Vizenor, *Manifest Manners* (Hanover, N.H.: University Press of New England, 1994).

15. Note that Aupaumut and Brant also wrote petitions on behalf of their communities at New Stockbridge and Grand River.

16. Samson Occom, Journal 1: December 6, 1743–November 29, 1748, Eleazar Wheelock Papers, Dartmouth College Special Collections, Hanover, N.H. Joseph Johnson used the same phrase in speaking of Mohegan to the Oneidas. See William DeLoss Love, *Samson Occom and the Christian Indians of New England* (Syracuse, N.Y.: Syracuse University Press, 2000), 216. Vine Deloria has described this "deep emotional sense of knowing" that one "belongs" to the land of one's home place as the very foundation of American Indian religious experience. See Vine Deloria Jr., *God Is Red* (New York: Putnum, 1973).

17. Samson Occom, Journal 2: June 21, 1750–February 9, 1751, and Journal 3: June 28, 1757–September 25, 1760, Dartmouth College Special Collections; Love, *Samson Occom*, 252.

18. Johnson, *To Do Good*, 160–61. The "truer friend" is Jesus.

19. On Apess's "circular plot," see Peyer, *Tutor'd Mind*, 151. Laura Murray observes that "Johnson's arrival 'once more on Mohegan land'" is one of the strongest "moments of resolution in his diary." She notes, "In contrast to the narrative emphasis placed on homecoming . . . Johnson's depiction in the diary of his conversion to Christ is initially unresounding." For Johnson, like Apess, Christian "conversion was . . . a consequence of his return to Mohegan." Johnson, *To Do Good*, 85–86. Occom's own return home from Iroquoia was likewise a critical moment. Similar narratives of a young hero's journey are common in traditional Algonquian oral literature. For a fictional recreation based on these stories, see Joseph Bruchac, *Dawn Land* (Golden, Colo.: Fulcrum, 1993).

20. Aupaumut, "Narrative of an Embassy to the Western Indians," 76–77, 84–85, 87–89, 97–99.

21. Samson Occom, Journal, May 30–July 7, 1761; Journal September 1761–October 22, 1761, Dartmouth College Special Collections; Peyer, *Tutor'd Mind*, 88.

22. William N. Fenton, "Structure, Continuity, and Change in the Process of Iroquois Treaty Making," in *The History and Culture of Iroquois Diplomacy*, ed. Francis Jennings and William N. Fenton (Syracuse: Syracuse University Press, 1985), 5. On treaty literature, see Augustine Lan Van Pham, "English Colonial Treaties with American Indians: Observations on a Neglected Genre," Ph.D. diss., Fordham University, New York, 1977; Lawrence Wroth, "The Indian Treaty as Literature," *Yale Review* (1928): 749–66; Carl Van Doren, "Intro-

duction," in *Indian Treaties Printed by B. Franklin, 1736–62,* ed. Carl Van Doren and Julian P. Boyd (Philadelphia, 1938); Maureen Konkle, *Writing Indian Nations: Native Intellectuals and the Politics of Historiography* (Durham: University of North Carolina Press, 2004), 3–18; and Peyer, *Tutor'd Mind,* 106, 112–13.

23. Wroth, "Indian Treaty," 749–51; Pham, "English Colonial Treaties with American Indians," 3, 16–20, 93–94, 100–105, 141; Van Doren, "Introduction," xviii; Fenton, "Structure, Continuity, and Change," 5–7. Pham roots the European fascination with treaties in the 1710 publication of the speeches of the Four Indian Kings, a delegation of Mohawk and Mohican leaders to London, including the young Hendrick (134). "The Four Indian Kings Speech to Her Majesty, London, April 20, 1710" (broadside document); John G. Garratt, *The Four Indian Kings* (Ottawa: Public Archives, 1985).

24. Pham, "English Colonial Treaties with American Indians," 3, 41, 49–51, 68–69, 134, 149; Van Doren, "Introduction," xvii–ix, xiii; Fenton, "Structure, Continuity, and Change," 6–7.

25. Konkle, *Writing Indians,* 5.

26. Eleazar Wheelock, *A Plain and Faithful Narrative of the Original Design, Rise, Progress and Present State of the Indian Charity School at Lebanon, Connecticut* (Boston: Richard and Samuel Draper, 1763), 30. On the "dying Indian," see for instance, Robert F. Berkhofer, *The White Man's Indian* (New York: Knopf, 1978), 29, 88, 101, and 144–45.

27. Van Doren and Boyd, *Franklin Treaties,* 150, 207; Herbert C. Kraft, *The Lenape: Archeaology, History, and Ethnography* (Newark: New Jersey Historical Society, 1986), 229–32; James H. Merrell, *Into the American Woods: Negotiators on the Pennsylvania Frontier* (New York: W.W. Norton, 1999), 88–89, 104, 238, 273, 288, 297–98; Samuel Smith, *The History of the Colony of Nova-Caesaria, or New Jersey* (Burlington: James Parker, 1765), 440–55; C. A. Weslager, *The Delaware Indians* (New Brunswick: Rutgers University Press, 1972), 260–71.

28. Pham, "English Colonial Treaties with American Indians," 20; Van Doren and Boyd, *Franklin Treaties,* 199; Francis Jennings, *Empire of Fortune: Crowns, Colonies, and Tribes in the Seven Years War in America* (New York: W. W. Norton, 1988), 253–81, 341–48, 369–404; Kraft, *The Lenape,* 229–30; Merrell, *Into the American Woods,* 225–301. Alexander McKee's father, Thomas, served as interpreter for the British during the making of these treaties, while Conrad Weiser, who had ties to the Haudenosaunee, was interpreter for the Colony of Pennsylvania. Note that there is a complicated history behind the Easton Treaties, particularly concerning the convoluted political relationships between the Haudenosaunee, Delaware, and Pennsylvania colonists, which I do not delve into here because it would require a great deal of background explanation.

29. Van Doren and Boyd, *Franklin Treaties,* 157. On Walking Purchase, see Francis Jennings, *Empire of Fortune,* 25–28 and 278–80, and *The Ambiguous Iroquois Empire* (New York: Norton, 1884), 325–50, and "The Scandalous Indian

Policy of William Penn's Sons: Deeds and Documents of the Walking Pur-
chase," *Pennsylvania History* 37 (1970): 19–39; Kraft, *The Lenape,* 225–28; and
Mark Warhus, *Another America: Native American Maps and the History of Our
Land* (New York: St. Martin's Griffin, 1997), 82–89.

30. Charles Thomson, *Enquiry into the Causes of the Alienation of the Delaware and Shawanese Indians from the British Interest (1759)* (Philadelphia: John
Campbell, 1867), 101; Jennings, *Empire of Fortune,* 279.

31. Thomson, *Enquiry into the Causes of Alienation,* 110–17; Van Doren and
Boyd, *Franklin Treaties,* 191.

32. Van Doren and Boyd, *Franklin Treaties,* 200–201.

33. Ibid., 196, 201, 206; Wheelock, *Narrative of the Indian Charity School,* 30.

34. Van Doren and Boyd, *Franklin Treaties,* 197–98; Jennings, *Empire of Fortune,* 346; Thomson, *Enquiry into the Causes of the Alienation,* 115; Warhus, *Another America,* 82–83.

35. *A Treaty, Held at the Town of Lancaster, in Pennsylvania, by the Honourable
the Commissioners for the Provinces of Virginia and Maryland, with the Indians of
the Six Nations, in June, 1744* (Philadelphia: Benjamin Franklin, 1744); Fenton,
"Structure, Continuity, and Change," 29; Edmund O'Callaghan, ed., *Documents Relative to the Colonial History of New York,* 15 vols. (Albany: Weed, Parsons, 1855–61) (NYCD), 9: 966–67, reprinted in Colin G. Calloway, *Dawnland
Encounters: Indians and Europeans in Northern New England* (Hanover, N.H.:
University Press of New England, 1991), 111–18. Loron appeared to be serv-
ing as speaker for the combined Wabanaki nations, as well as providing testi-
mony as a witness to the proceedings. Greylock and the Missisquoi Abenakis
refused to participate in the conference. See Colin G. Calloway, *The Western
Abenakis of Vermont, 1600–1800: War, Migration, and the Survival of an Indian
People* (Norman: University of Oklahoma Press, 1990); David L. Ghere,
"Abenaki Factionalism, Emigration, and Social Continuity: Indian Society in
Northern New England, 1725 to 1765," Ph.D. diss., University of Maine,
Orono, 1988; Kenneth M. Morrison, *The Embattled Northeast: The Elusive Ideal
of Alliance in Abenaki–Euramerican Relations* (Berkeley: University of California
Press, 1984).

36. Calloway, *Dawnland Encounters,* 116–17.

37. Ibid., 117–18.

38. William Apess, *On Our Own Ground: The Complete Writings of William
Apess, a Pequot,* ed. Barry O'Connell (Amherst: University of Massachusetts
Press, 1992), 186.

39. Reflecting on his experiences under servitude, Apess wrote, "I had a
sister who was slavishly used and half starved; and I have not forgotten, nor
can I ever forget the abuse I received myself." Apess wrote about alcohol
as one of the means traders and colonial leaders used most effectively "to
steal away [Natives'] brains, knowing their lands would follow." Apess and
O'Connell, *On Our Own,* 186–88, 250; Barry O'Connell, "'Once More Let Us

Consider': William Apess in the Writing of New England Native American History," in *After King Philip's War: Presence and Persistence in Indian New England,* ed. Colin G. Calloway (Hanover, N.H.: University Press of New England, 1997), 162.

40. Apess and O'Connell, *On Our Own Ground,* 188.

41. Ibid., 212.

42. Peyer, *Tutor'd Mind,* 157; Theresa Strouth Gaul, "Dialogue and Public Discourse in William Apess' Indian Nullification," *American Transcendental Quarterly* 15, no. 4 (2001): 275–94, quotes on 275–77.

43. Ibid., 196; Peyer, *Tutor'd Mind,* 159; Gaul, "Dialogue and Public Discourse," 275–77, 288; Pham, "English Colonial Treaties with American Indians," 3, 41, 49; Van Doren, "Introduction," xvii. The consensus that Apess strove to build was not only with his Native "brethren" but with other people of "integrity," such as Benjamin Hallet. Therefore, in *Nullification,* as Gaul has observed, Apess put the "sons of the Pilgrims" in debate with each other, creating "counter-dialogue." Apess also fosters this discursive space in the *Eulogy on King Philip,* in which, as Peyer has observed, "Apess' polyphonic literary voice seems to have reached its maximum force of expression." See also Arnold Krupat, *Ethnocriticism: Ethnography, History, Literature* (Berkeley: University of California Press, 1992). On Apess's use of the documentary record, see O'Connell, "Once More Let Us Consider." On Apess and treaty literature, see Maureen Konkle, "Indian Literacy, U.S. Colonialism, and Literary Criticism," *American Literature* 69, no. 3 (1997): 457–86.

44. Aupaumut, "Narrative of an Embassy to the Western Indians," 94–95; Pham, "English Colonial Treaties with American Indians," 41.

45. See Eleazar Wheelock, *Narrative of the Indian Charity School,* and *A Continuation of the Narrative of the State, &c. of the Indian Charity School at Lebanon, in Connecticut . . . 1769* (London: J. and W. Oliver, 1769); James Dow McCallum, *The Letters of Eleazar Wheelock's Indians* (Hanover, N.H.: Dartmouth College, 1932); Johnson, *To Do Good;* and Margaret Szasz, *Indian Education in the American Colonies, 1607–1783* (Albuquerque: University of New Mexico Press, 1988).

46. Records of the Mohegan Tribe, Samson Occom Papers; Johnson, *To Do Good,* 206–22; Stockbridge Indian Papers, Huntington Free Library, San Marino, California; Draper Manuscript Collection, State Historical Society of Wisconsin, Joseph Brant Manuscript; John Norton Letterbook, Ayer Ms. 654, John Norton Papers, 1804–1816, Edward E. Ayer Manuscript Collection, Newberry Library, Chicago, 101, 118; Peyer, *Tutor'd Mind,* 106, 112.

47. Electa F. Jones, *Stockbridge, Past and Present, or Records of an Old Mission Station* (Springfield, Mass.: S. Bowles, 1854),14.

48. John W. Quinney, "Celebration of the Fourth of July, 1854, at Reidsville, New York: Interesting Speech of John W. Quinney, Chief of the Stockbridge Tribe of Indians," *Wisconsin Historical Collections* 4 (1859): 315.

49. A. Holmes, "Memoir of the Moheagans," *Collections of the Massachusetts Historical Society* 1, no. 9 (1804): 98–99; Hendrick Aupaumut, "Extract from an Indian History," *Collections of the Massachusetts Historical Society* 1, no. 9 (1804); John W. Quinney, "Memorial of John W. Quinney," *Wisconsin Historical Collections* 4 (1859): 313 –15; Ted Brasser, *Riding on the Frontier's Crest: Mahican Indian Culture and Change* (Ottawa: National Museums of Canada, 1974), 41–43. Brasser notes that Aupaumut composed the "Extract" "about 1791, [when] he wrote down the traditional history of the Mohican Nation, parts of which have been preserved by early publication. The original manuscript, however, has disappeared." Electa Jones mistakenly assumed that Timothy Dwight had "access to a perfect copy" when writing his *Travels*. However, he was only quoting from the Massachusetts Historical Society version. Ironically, although Dwight refers to Aupaumut several times in his *Travels*, he does not acknowledge Aupaumut's authorship of the *History* except to say that the text is from "an Indian historian" or "a writer of their own." See Timothy Dwight, *Travels in New England and New York*, ed. Barbara Miller Solomon, 4 vols. (Cambridge, Mass.: Harvard University Press, 1969), 1: 77, 79, 88. Aupaumut's history was later reprinted in a missionary tract and in Jones's *Stockbridge Past and Present*. Hendrick Aupaumut, "History of the Muhheakunnuk Indians," *First Annual Report of the American Society for Promoting the Civilization and General Improvement to the Indian Tribes of the United States* (New Haven, Conn., 1824); Jones, *Stockbridge Past and Present*, 15–23.

50. Quinney, "Memorial of John W. Quinney," 313–15; Jones, *Stockbridge Past and Present*, 75; Love, *Samson Occom*, 238–40, 321; Brasser, *Riding on the Frontier's Crest*, 41–43. Dartmouth was founded as an expansion of Wheelock's Indian Charity School. Occom raised a large amount of funds to establish the college for the education of Indians, and he was angered at Wheelock for turning the school to the training of white missionaries rather than Occom's Indian "brethren" and for moving the school to "the woods of Coos," in Abenaki territory (Love, *Samson Occom*, 158–59).

51. Aupaumut, "Extract from an Indian History," 100; Quinney, "Celebration of the Fourth of July," 316–17.

52. The publication of Norton's *Journal* was postponed by various circumstances until historians Carl Klinck and James Talman received permission (in 1966) to publish the manuscript, which had been held in a Scottish duke's castle for generations. The text contains a circular journey journal of Norton's travels from his "home" of Grand River to his father's relations in Cherokee country and back; a section in the travelogue that relates the traditional narratives of Haudenosaunee history and the relationship between the Haudenosaunee and the Cherokee; and an addendum with an alternate historical narrative, written in a linear, chronological manner and centered on military history, which would have appealed to his intended European audience. Norton, Klinck, and Talman, *Journal of John Norton*.

53. Norton, Klinck, and Talman, *Journal of John Norton;* David Cusick, *Sketches of Ancient History of the Six Nations (1825)* (Lockport, N.Y.: Niagara Country Historical Society, 1961); Arthur Caswell Parker, "The Constitution of the Five Nations," in *Parker on the Iroquois,* ed. William Fenton (Syracuse: Syracuse University Press, 1968), and Seneca *Myths and Folk Tales* (Lincoln: University of Nebraska Press, 1989); Fenton, "Structure, Continuity, and Change," 15.

54. Demus Elm, Harvey Antone, Floyd Glenn Lounsbury, and Bryan Gick, *The Oneida Creation Story* (Lincoln: University of Nebraska Press, 2000), 8–10; Norton, Klinck, and Talman, *Journal of John Norton,* xiv, 47, 88–105, 109, 198, 208; Cruikshank, *Correspondence of John Simcoe,* 5: 3; William Stone, *Life of Joseph Brant, Thayendanegea* (New York: George Dearborn, 1838), 287–88; Douglas W. Boyce, "A Glimpse of Iroquois Culture through the Eyes of Joseph Brant and John Norton," *Proceedings of the American Philosophical Society* 117, no. 4 (1973): 286–94; Cusick, *Sketches of Ancient History,* 3–4; William Martin Beauchamp, *The Iroquois Trail: Footprints of the Six Nations* (Fayetteville, N.Y.: H. C. Beauchamp, 1892), 42, 66–67; William Fenton, "Introduction," *Parker on the Iroquois* (Syracuse, N.Y.: Syracuse University Press, 1968), 38–41; Fenton, "Structure, Continuity, and Change," 15; "Henry Aaron Hill," "John Norton," *Dictionary of Canadian Biography* (Toronto: University of Toronto Press, 1965), 6: 373, 552. Henry Aaron Hill was the son of David Hill and a Harvard-trained scholar. He collaborated with Norton on the publication of several biblical translations.

55. Cusick, *Sketches of Ancient History,* 29; Beauchamp, *Iroquois Trail,* 67, 73.

7. Concluding Thoughts from Wabanaki Space

1. James Fenimore Cooper, *The Last of the Mohicans* (Philadelphia: H. C. Carey and I. Lea–Chesnut-Street, 1826), 29.

2. On the orality/literacy debate, see Ruth Finnegan, *Literacy and Orality: Studies in the Technology of Communication* (New York: Basil Blackwell, 1988); Maureen Konkle, *Writing Indian Nations: Native Intellectuals and the Politics of Historiography* (Durham: University of North Carolina Press, 2004), esp. 28–29; Larry Evers and Barre Toelken, *Native American Oral Traditions* (Logan: Utah State University Press, 2001); Arnold Krupat, *The Voice in the Margin: Native American Literature and the Canon* (Berkeley: University of California Press, 1989); Henri LeFebvre, *The Production of Space,* trans. Donald Nicholson-Smith (Oxford: Blackwell, 1991); Jill Lepore, *The Name of War: King Philip's War and the Origins of American Identity* (New York: Knopf, 1998); Walter Ong, *Orality and Literacy: The Technologizing of the Word* (New York: Methuen, 1982); Bernd Peyer, *The Tutor'd Mind: Indian Missionary-Writers in Antebellum America* (Amherst: University of Massachusetts Press, 1997), 9–10; Jace Weaver, *That the People Might Live: Native American Literatures and Native American*

Community (New York: Oxford University Press, 1997), 21–26, 40–42; Craig S. Womack, *Red on Red: Native American Literary Separatism* (Minneapolis: University of Minnesota Press, 1999), 12–16.

3. Henry David Thoreau, *The Maine Woods* (New York: Penguin Books, 1988), 189.

4. Linda Frost, "'The Red Face of Man,' the Penobscot Indian, and a Conflict of Interest in Thoreau's *Maine Woods*," *ESQ* 39, no.1 (1993): 33; Thoreau, *Maine Woods*, 190. Aitteon was from a prominent leadership family at Old Town and had served as governor. Swasen was a well-known Abenaki family name that was also present at Penobscot. Fannie Hardy Eckstrom, *Old John Neptune* (Orono: University of Maine, 1980), 123; Gordon M. Day, *The Identity of the Saint Francis Indians* (Ottawa: National Museums of Canada, 1981), 95; Colin G. Calloway, *The Western Abenakis of Vermont, 1600–1800: War, Migration, and the Survival of an Indian People* (Norman: University of Oklahoma Press, 1990), 208, 215.

5. Thoreau, *Maine Woods*, 274; Eckstrom, *Old John Neptune*, 153, 168–69, 179, 185–87; Frost, "'Red Face of Man'"; Robert F. Sayre, *Thoreau and the American Indians* (Princeton, N.J.: Princeton University Press, 1977).

6. Thoreau, *Maine Woods*, 401–3; Eckstrom, *Old John Neptune*, 164; Frost, "'Red Face of Man,'" 38–41; Day, *Identity of the Saint Francis Indians*, 88–90. Thanks to Darren Ranco for providing an overview of the complexities of Penobscot political history.

7. Joseph Nicolar, *The Life and Traditions of the Red Man* (Bangor, Maine: C. H. Glass, 1893). Nicolar was the grandson of Governor John Neptune. He wrote articles for Bangor newspapers and the short-lived *Oldtown Herald*. Masta was a nephew of Peter Paul Wzokhilain. Laurent's name traces back to the Penobscot speaker Loron, although variations of Loron (Lolo, Lola, Laurent) became such common family names in Wabanaki communities that direct descent cannot be assumed. Both men served as chiefs at Odanak. Eckstrom, *Old John Neptune*, 31–38, 179; Gordon M. Day, *Identity of the Saint Francis Indians*, 81–83, 85, 88–90, and *Western Abenaki Dictionary* (Hull, Quebec: Canadian Museum of Civilization, 1994), 1: iii, xviii; Charles C. Leland, *Algonquin Legends* (New York: Dover, 1992); Henry Lorne Masta, *Abenaki Indian Legends, Grammar and Place Names* (Victoriaville, Quebec: La Voix des Bois-Francs, 1932); Peter Paul Wzokhilain, *Kagakimzouiasis Ueji Uo'Banakiak Adali Kimo'Gik Aliuitzo'Ki Za Plasua* (Québec: Fréchette et cie., 1832), *Wawasi Lagidamwoganek Mdala Chowagidamwoganal Tabtagil, Onkawodokodozwal Wji Pobatami Kidwogan* (Boston: Crocker and Brewster, 1830), and *Wobanaki Kimzowi Awighigan* (Boston: Crocker and Brewster, 1830).

8. The word *Odanak* itself literally means "at the village or town." See Joseph Laurent, *New Familiar Abenaki and English Dialogues* (Quebec: L. Brousseau, 1884), 54; Day, *Western Abenaki Dictionary*, 1: 394.

9. For example, see Joseph Bruchac, *Bowman's Store: A Journey to Myself* (New York: Dial, 1997); William A. Haviland and Marjory W. Power, *The Original Vermonters: Native Inhabitants, Past and Present* (Hanover, N.H.: University Press of New England, 1994); John W. Johnson, *Life of John W. Johnson* (Biddeford, Me., 1861); Cheryl Savageau, *Mother/land* (Cambridge, England: Salt, 2006); and Frederick Matthew Wiseman, *The Voice of the Dawn: An Autohistory of the Abenaki Nation* (Hanover, N.H.: University Press of New England, 2001).

10. Laurent, *Abenaki and English Dialogues*, 51–54; Day, *Identity of the Saint Francis Indians*, 60–61.

11. Laurent, *Abenaki and English Dialogues*, 53–54, 58–59. See also Joseph Bruchac, *No Borders* (Duluth, Minn.: Holy Cow! Press, 1999), and *Hidden Roots* (New York: Scholastic Press, 2004), esp. 19–31 and 179–94, and Cheryl Savageau, *Dirt Road Home* (Willimantic, Conn.: Curbstone, 1995).

12. Joseph Bruchac has noted that the word for "nation" in the Abenaki language is "*negewetkamigwezo,* which means 'families gathered together'" (Bruchac, *Hidden Roots,* 30).

13. Savageau, personal communication, September 29, 2003.

14. Arthur Caswell Parker, *Seneca Myths and Folk Tales* (Lincoln: University of Nebraska Press, 1989), 64.

15. Nicolar, *Life and Traditions of the Red Man,* 18, 57–64. See also Natalie Curtis, *The Indians' Book* (New York: Grammercy Books, 1994), 4–5, and Paula Gunn Allen, *The Sacred Hoop* (Boston: Beacon Press, 1992), 26. Thanks also to Marilou Awiakta for sharing the Cherokee Corn Mother story and its significance. See Marilou Awiakta, *Selu: Seeking the Corn Mother's Wisdom* (Golden, Colo.: Fulcrum, 1993).

16. Nicolar, *Life and Traditions of the Red Man,* 57–60.

17. Ibid., 59–64.

18. Laurent, *Abenaki and English Dialogues,* 20; Nicolar, *Life and Traditions of the Red Man,* 18. The Sky Woman and First Mother stories play an important role in contemporary Haudenosaunee and Abenaki literature. See, for instance, Peter Blue Cloud, "Turtle," in *Harper's Anthology of Twentieth-Century Native American Poetry,* ed. Duane Niatum (New York: Harper Perennial, 1988), 83–85; Beth Brant, "Ride the Turtle's Back" and "Native Origin," in *Songs from This Earth on Turtle's Back,* ed. Joseph Bruchac (Greenfield Center, N.Y.: Greenfield Review Press, 1983), 30–33; Joseph Bruchac, *Iroquois Stories* (Trumansburg, N.Y.: Crossing Press, 1985); Dawnland Singers, *Alnobak,* CD (Good Mind Records, 1994); Savageau, *Dirt Road Home,* 19–20, 71–72, 92; and Joanne Shenandoah and Douglas M. George, *Sky Woman: Legends of the Iroquois* (Santa Fe: Clear Light, 1998).

Index

Aaron (cousin of Hendrick Aupaumut), 138, 143
Abenaki language: memory in, 66;
place names in, 249–50; pronoun
"we" in, 202; revitalization project
for, 251–52, 262n28; writing in,
xxi, xxii
Abenakis: alliance with Mohawks,
28; captives of, 37–38; ceremonial
councils of, 4; conceptualization
of land, 251; at Deerfield Conference, 28, 33; Kwinitekw Valley
rights of, 35; literacy among, 247–
48; Missisquoi, 314n35; network
of relations, xliv, 28; raids on
English, 40, 41, 42; relationship
with Schaghticokes, 264n42; resistance by, 43, 45–46, 49; Thoreau
on, 247; threat from Mohegans,
279n67; tribal office of, xliv; use
of formal writing, 49; visit to
Phineas Stevens, 269n84; in
wampum trade, 272n10; Western
and Eastern, 259n1. *See also* petition to the General Assembly (1747)
abolition: rhetoric of, 180, 187–88
Abraham (brother of Hendrick
Aupaumut), 44, 48, 49, 111
Acquumeh people: use of foreign
rituals, xxvii
"Act for Better Regulating the
Indians" (Massachusetts, 1746),
170–71

Adams, Solomon, 227
Adlum, John, 159
Africa: colonial project in, 65
Aitteon, Joe, 247, 318n4
Albany conference (1745), 40, 41
Albany Treaty (1775), 114, 120, 289n36
Alfred, Taiaiake, xxxii, 255n7
Algonquian language: Apess's °
uency in, 308n10; personal
pronouns in, 202; Wabanaki as
speakers of, 259n1
Algonquian literature: heroes'
journeys in, 312n19
Algonquians: during beaver wars,
32; *besoins* of, 225; Brant and, 147;
concept of Native space, 138, 218;
concept of nativity, 1–3; Eastern
and Western, 131, 294n80; in fur
trade, 23; land tenure system of,
35, 67–68, 69; missionary-teachers
among, 88, 90; Mohican position
within, 149; peacemaking protocols of, 139; relationship with
United States, 160; resistance by,
90; resource sharing among, 5;
restoration of network, 128, 131,
143–49; suspicion of Haudenosaunee, 146; in United Indian
Nations, 124, 140
Allen, Chad, xxxviii
alliance: in colonial law, 276n39
alnôbawôgan (becoming human),
1–3, 243

321

Jigonsaseh (women leaders): Molly
Brant and role of, 119–20; and
Great Law, 119, 140, 162; peace-
making by, 159, 161; Seneca, 161–62
Johnny, Captain, 153, 154
Johnson, Amy, 87
Johnson, Augh Quant, 74; literacy
of, 84
Johnson, Guy, 115, 120
Johnson, James, 268n68; captivity of,
37–38
Johnson, Joseph, 89, 312n6; at Fort
William, 88; letter to wife, 220–21;
tracking skills of, 221; writings of,
xxxi, 84
Johnson, Joseph, Jr., 87, 89–90;
Christianity of, 312n19; education
of, 239; journey journals of, 227–
28; letters to Occom, 221–22;
recording of spoken word, 240
Johnson, Susannah, 37–38
Johnson, William, Sir, 88–89; mar-
riage to Molly Brant, 112; in
Mohegan land case, 97, 98;
Occam's correspondence with,
93–94, 95, 172, 190, 222, 283n98,
283n101; relations with Mohawks,
289n36; and rent rioters, 113; role
in native alliances, 283n98
Johnson, Zachary, 96, 285n116
Jones, Electa, 316n49; Stockbridge
Past and Present, 241
"Journal of the Proceedings at the
General Council Held at the Foot
of the Rapids of the Miamis"
(Brant), 141, 151–55, 238–39
journey journals, 226–29; in Native
space, 229; in network of relations, 226
journey maps, 226
Justice, Daniel, xxvii

Kalifornsky, Peter, xxv, xxvi
kdakinna (our land), 202, 251

Keewauhoose (Chee Hoose),
264n42; at Deerfield Conference,
35; literacy of, 47; name of, 27
Kellogg, Joanna, 30
Kellogg, Joseph, 32; in Covenant of
Peace and Unity, 36–37; at Deerfield Conference, 30, 37; during
Greylock's War, 51; scouting by,
30–31; service as interpreter, 39,
270n93; ties to Kahnawake,
268n64; trading mission of,
33, 34
Kellogg, Martin, 31, 270n93; as
interpreter, 265n48
Kellogg, Rebecca, 30, 265n48
Kelsey, Penelope: Tribal Theory
in Native American Literature,
xxx
Kespek (Mi'kmaq village):
writing at, 8
kettle of peace, 265n45; at Deerfield Conference, 28; in Native
space, 24–37
King, Young (Seneca), 107
King Philip's War, xxxiii, 264n38,
274n27; destruction during, 201;
Mohawks in, 31; Mohegans in, 64;
refugees from, 26, 27; writing
during, 46. See also Anglo-Abenaki
wars; Eulogy on King Philip; Philip,
King
King William's War, 264n38
kinship, xxxv; formalization of,
265n45; Haudenosaunee concept
of, 290n40; in Indian identity, xxxii;
role in diplomacy, 283n98. See also
network of relations
Kirkland, Samuel, 127, 281n85; on
Aupaumut, 148, 297n115; correspondence with Brant, 141–42;
embassy to Senecas, 222; at
Wheelock's school, 291n52
knowledge, indigenous: exchange
of, 99; recovery of, xxxix

Wheelock, xli, 84, 85, 96, 316n50; writing ability of, 226; writings of, xxx, xxxi. Works: *Sermon on Moses Paul,* 225; "Short Narrative of My Life," 84–85

O'Connell, Barry, xxx, 175, 308n10

Odanak: village of, 249, 318n8

Odeon lecture hall, 308n3; Apess's address at, 198, 199, 200–217

Odyoughwanoron, 48, 49. *See also* Old Town (Mohawk)

Ohio River: as western boundary, 152, 153, 154, 155

Ohio Valley: American settlement in, 152; Aupaumut's travels in, 145, 228; boundary negotiations for, 151–55; false treaties concerning, 133; Haudenosaunee in, 295n90; multiethnic villages of, 111; narratives of common pot in, 140–55; Native sovereignty in, 122–23, 124, 129; U.S. Army in, 156–57, 299n142

Ojibwe birchbark records, xx

ôjmowôgan (history), 245

Old Town: oral narratives from, 249; Penobscot community at, 248

Old Town (Mohawk), 42, 111; literacy of, 47–48; at Stockbridge council, 44–45

Oneidas: alliance with English, 88; in American Revolution, 116, 119, 290n29; Brothertown and, 103; at Buffalo Creek council, 107–8; Mohican relocation among, 121, 242, 286n5; Occom as teacher among, 88–90; in Sullivan's campaign, 289n30; support for American Revolution, 116

Onkwehonwe languages, 255n7

Onondagas: centrality of space for, 287n11; disease among, 116; petition to Great Spirit, 225; relations with French, 44

oral tradition: common pot and, 260n3; writing and, xx, xxi, xxii, xxiii, xl, xliv, 246, 317n2

orators, Native, 189–90, 230

Oriskany, battle of, 116

Ortiz, Simon, xxvii, xxxi; on resistance, 256n18

Overseers, Mashpee, 169; appointment of, 167, 171; Mashpee opposition to, 191–92, 194, 195–96, 307n82

Owaneco, 65; alcoholism of, 71; death of, 78; petition to Queen Anne (1700), 66, 72, 76, 78, 84

Papaquanaitt (Mohegan), 65

Parker, Arthur, 9–10, 139–40, 252; *Constitution of the Five Nations,* 243, 244; *Seneca Myths and Folk Tales,* 243

Pastonkiak people, 251

Peacemaker (Dakanawida), 119, 140, 159

peacemaking: Algonquian protocols for, 139; ceremony of condolence in, 144, 157; failure of, 298n128; Haudenosaunee protocols for, 139–40; Mohican protocols for, 139; in Native space, 159; obstacles to, 158–59; paths to, 106–8; process of, 156–62; role of clan mothers in, 159, 161; wampum in, 139, 152, 153, 157, 158. *See also* boundaries, western

Penacooks, 17; land loss by, 23; refugees with, 46; and writing, 46

Penn, William: sons of, 232

Penobscots, 17, 248; political history of, 318n6; and Thoreau, 247–248

Pequots: alliance with Dutch, 56, 57–58, 272n10; distributive role of, 59; division of, 58; effect of colonization on, 61; English attack on, 263n34; during Greylock's War, 51;

Sargeant, John, 295n86
Sarris, Greg, xxv, xxvi
satire: Native use of, 226
Savageau, Cheryl, xxx, xxxiv, 252;
"At Sugarloaf, 1996," 20–21
Schaghticokes: at Deerfield Conference, 28, 34–35, 267n61; kinship
networks of, 28; Kwinitekw Valley rights of, 34, 35, 36; literacy of,
46, 47; migrations of, 27; refugee
village of, 25–26; relationship
with Abenakis, 264n42; and
Wawanowalet, 39
scholars, indigenous:
histories by, xxvii; literary traditions
of, xxix; oral histories of, xxxiv
scholarship, tribally specific, xxx
scrolls, birchbark, xx, 229; Montagnais, 11; Passamaquoddy, 10
Senecas: American assault on, 117;
in American Revolution, 116, 118;
Kirkland's embassy to, 222; in
Ohio Valley, 146–47; relations
with French, 44
Senier, Siobhan, xxx
Sergeant, John, 5–6, 47, 242
Seven Nations of Canada, 154,
298n131
Shantock Rock: Uncas at, 105
Shawnees: advocacy of war, 142,
157, 297n124; association with
British, 155; in boundary negotiations of 1793, 152–53; Brant
and, 151; in Ohio Valley, 293n78;
on treaties with United States, 125
Sheldon, George, 267n61
Silko, Leslie Marmon, xxxii, 255n14;
Almanac of the Dead, xx–xxii
Simcoe, John, 155, 291n52
sisters, three (corn, beans, squash),
253, 254
Six Nations: on boundary commissioners, 297n117; in boundary
negotiations of 1793, 152, 153, 154,
155; at Buffalo Creek council, 107,

131; communal histories of, 243;
in Covenant Chain, 116; in Lancaster treaty, 234; members of,
286n4; reconstruction of, 160;
treaties with United States, 296n98;
written communications of, 223.
See also Haudenosaunee
skin color, as racial marker, 301n5
Skyholder (Teharonghyawago), 109,
110, 130; as Great Spirit, 300n152
Sky Woman, 2–3, 111, 243, 252,
319n18; grandsons of, 109–10
slaves, African American, 194
Smilbert, Nathaniel: portrait of
Samson Occom, 85
Society for the Propagation of the
Gospel, 48
Sokokis, 14–15; alliances of, 22, 33,
27–28. See also Sokwakik
Sokwakik: in Kwinitekw Valley, 17,
25, 267n61
Son of the Forest, A (Apess), 173–74
spatiality: of awikhigawôgan, xxii; in
creation stories, xxiii; nonlinguis-
tic communication of, 12, 13. See
also Native space
Speck, Frank, 249
"Speech of the United Indian
Nations, The" (Brant), 122–23,
124–25, 126
St. Clair, Arthur, 107, 135; on Muskingum Compromise, 136; and
United Indian Nations, 126–27
Stevens, Phineas, 38, 269n79; Abenaki
visit to, 269n84; at Montreal Conference, 45; and Pinewans, 42, 44
St. Georges: trading post at, 236
Stockbridge: in American Revolution, 113; cooperative living project at, 33, 37, 113; councils at, 44–
45, 48; Mohicans of, 46–47, 288n20;
network of relations in, 138; settlers' domination of, 121; western
relations of, 131. See also New
Stockbridge

Stoddard, John, 32; at Albany
conference, 41; in Covenant of
Peace and Unity, 36–37; in Grey-
lock's War, 30–31
Stone, William, 112–13, 288n20
Stuart, Gilbert: portrait of Joseph
Brant, 123
Sullivan, John, 117
Sullivan's campaign, 116–18, 128;
Oneidas in, 289n30
Swasen, Tahmunt, 247, 250, 318n4
Sweeney, Kevin, 26; on Deerfield,
28; on trading posts, 267n58

Talcott, Joseph, 80, 279n70
Talman, James, 316n52
Tantaquidgeon (Mohegan), 62
Tantaquidgeon, Lucy Occom,
103, 104
Teedyuscung (Delaware leader): at
Easton councils, 232–33, 234; map
of, 234, 235; narrative of land
fraud, 233
Temple, Josiah, 267n61
text-maps, interactive, xxv–xxvi
Theyanoguin. See Hendrick, Chief
Thomson, Charles, 232, 233
Thoreau, Henry David, xliii; The
Maine Woods, 247–48, 250; and
Polis, 248
Titigar, Francis, 264n40
Trade and Intercourse Act (1791),
295n92
trading posts: location of, 267n58
transformation: and birth, 3, 243;
communal histories of, 243; and
Manitou, 8; and Native space,
10, 13, 23, 108, 176, 241, 254;
poetics of, 220
treaties: Brant on, 127, 132–33,
238, 239; broken, 213; condolence ceremonies in, 230; false,
131–36, 145, 234, 239; with individual nations, 125; published,
229–30, 231, 233, 238–39;

symbolic language in, 239;
written, 47
treaty literature, 229–34, 236–41,
312n22; Apess's knowledge of,
238; Aupaumut's, 231; Brant's,
231; in Native space, 229, 230;
non-Native recording of, 231
Treaty of Canandaigua, 160;
Pickering's role in, 299n150
Treaty of Casco Bay (1725–27),
234, 236
Treaty of Paris, 106–7
trickster stories, 43
Tuhiwai-Smith, Linda, xxxvi; Decolonizing Methodologies, xxvi–
xxvii, xliv
Tuscaroras: at Oneida, 286n5; in
Sullivan's campaign, 289n30

Uhhaunauwaunmut, Solomon, 113–
14, 288n22
Uncas (Mohegan chief), 58; alliance
with English, 59, 61, 65, 69–70, 74;
coalitions of, 61–62; fear of
poison, 274n22; land agreements
by, 69; League of Alliance and
Amity, 66, 69–70, 74, 75, 80; and
John Mason, 277n47; and Miantonomo, 62–63; in Mohegan land
case, 71; Narragansett threat to,
62; role in colonial politics, 63–64;
at Shantock Rock, 105; wives of,
61, 62
Uncas, Ben, I, 65; petition to Queen
Anne (1700), 66, 72, 76, 78, 84;
sachemship of, 78, 279n64
Uncas, Ben, II, 73; address to Crown,
81, 82–83; disavowal of land
rights, 78, 80–83; on Mohegan
factions, 283n97; Mohegans'
deposition of, 79, 80, 81–82, 104,
279n71; Occom's relationship to,
83, 91, 280n76; payments from
Connecticut colony, 83; sachemship of, 78, 79, 81–82

White, Richard, 225
whiteness and death, 301n5
wikhikon (book), 310n2
Willard, Josiah, 39, 268n68
Willard, Samuel, 268n68
Williams, Eunice, 29, 40
Williams, Israel, 37
Williams, John, 29
Williams, Roger, 62; on hunting
grounds, 210; *A Key into the
Language of America*, 77; on the
Narragansetts, 5, 7–8, 175–76; on
Native rights, 76–77
Williams, Stephen, 29, 33
Wilson, Waziyatawin Angela, xxiii,
xxiv; on Dakota culture, xxv
Winthrop, Fitz-John, 71, 72, 278n53
Winthrop, John, 76; on colonial
ownership, 103
Winthrop, John, Jr., 276n41
wlôgan (dish), 3, 4
wôlhanak (river intervales), 4; of
Kwinitekw Valley, 17, 20; of
Wabanaki, 18–19
Womack, Craig, xxxii; *Red on Red*,
xxi, xxviii–xxix
women, Native: descent of property
through, 25, 34, 138; in network of
relations, 283n93; sustainment of
village dish, 103–4. *See also* clan
mothers; Jigonsaseh
Woodbridge, Timothy, 269n84,
294n86
Woyboy, Samson, 87
writing: as adaptive tool, xxviii;
agency for construction, xxviii; in
awikhigan system, 13; birchbark,
xix–xx, xliii, 11, 10, 229;
communication of community,
222; counteracting of colonization,
239; historical, xxiii; and purity,
246; instrumental activity of, xxii,

219–20; of journey journals, 226–
29; in Kwinitekw Valley, 46–50;
literary, xxiii; as map, xxviii;
marriage proposals in, 221–22; in
Mashpee Woodland Revolt, 196–
97; in Mohegan land case, 80;
Mohican use of, 241; Narragansetts on, 7–8; Native esteem for,
236–37; in Native space, xli, 8,
47, 197, 220, 241; in network of
relations, 222; and oral tradition,
xx, xxi, xxii, xxiii, xl, xliv, 246;
317n2; re-memberment through,
78–83, 197; spatialized, 226; travel
along waterways, 8; Wabanaki
use of, 8–9; and wampum, 12, 47,
222–23, 240–41, 245. *See also
awikhiganak*
writing, indigenous: Abenaki, xxi,
xxii; entry in to Native space, xli;
genres of, xl, 13, 219–245; Mayan,
xix–xxi; and oral tradition, xxi,
xxii, xxiii, xliv; place in common
pot, xliii; spatial tradition of, xl;
wampum as, 9, 12
Wroth, Lawrence, 230
Wyandots: advocacy of war, 297n124;
in American Revolution, 119
Wyomings: map of territory,
234, 235
Wyss, Hillary, xxxi
Wzokhilain, Peter Paul, 2, 175, 248;
on *alnôbawôgan*, 243; *Wobanaki
Komzowi Awikhigan*, 249

Young Peter, 106, 107, 108, 156;
father of, 285n1

Zobel, Melissa Tantaquidgeon,
xxxiv, 52, 105; on Mohegans,
272n12; on Mohegan women, 104;
on Uncas, 59

Lisa Brooks (Abenaki) is assistant professor of history and literature and of folklore and mythology at Harvard University.

Made in the USA
Monee, IL
19 January 2022